A POLITICAL HISTORY OF CHINA

Volume 1

From the Early Dynasties to the Fall of the Qing
c.2000 BCE – 1912 CE

Jean Kuo Aitchison

Edited by Ian J. R. Aitchison
with the assistance of Ying Cheng and Hilary Tan

Published in the United States by Ian J. R . Aitchison

ISBN 979-8-218-98423-6

Book Design & Layout:
Kristen Lohnes Johnson
Graffik Dezine
graffikdezine@comcast.net

Printed by Copy Factory
www.copyfactory.com

Palo Alto, California USA

Photograph on front cover:
The Song emperor receives a candidate during the palace examination
(Wikipedia: retrieved on 26 November 2023 from
https://en.wikipedia.org/wiki/Imperial_examination)

*For
Katherine and Elizabeth,
Danny and Ben*

Contents

Preface

As a bilingual Chinese American comfortable in both cultures, I have developed a life-long interest in China and in interpreting events in China to my Western friends. My desire to deepen my knowledge of that country led me to complete a Ph.D. in Chinese history at London University's School of Oriental and African studies during a career gap. Although such a degree normally suggests an academic career, an opportunity for starting a niche business in import and export of scientific materials from China appeared in the early 1980s. This was soon after 1978, the year when Deng Xiaoping, China's paramount leader, introduced a historic 'reform and opening up' policy, with the aim of modernizing China through opening its door to commercial and other exchanges with the economically developed and technologically advanced Western countries, and Japan. Prior to that date, the Communist Party that governed China since 1949 had isolated the country from trading and contact with the capitalist economies. The business opportunity enabled me to foster my interest in China though frequent visits to that country. My network of contacts, and experience of dealing with people in business there, gave me valuable insight into how the society operated.

China was a very poor country around the time of its 'opening.' Its people had suffered seemingly endless rounds of foreign invasions, civil wars, and revolutionary upheavals for nearly 140 years, after Great Britain forcibly opened Qing dynasty China in 1842 for trade with Western nations on their terms, at the time of the Opium Wars. Since that time, many generations of Chinese people had dreamed of their country regaining its wealth and strength. It was heartening for them, and for those who wished them well, that they were finally able to embark on their country's modernization, without which they would have remained poor, and their country weak. It was an incredibly interesting time for me to witness China's remarkable transformation.

At first, China's opening to global trade and investments was well received by the West. Since China desired a peaceful and stable international environment for its development, it strove to minimize friction and to ensure friendly relationships with its Western trading partners. In a little over two decades after China's opening, its astonishingly rapid economic growth enabled it to gain notable geopolitical power and influence. Although China endeavored to keep a low profile in the international arena, its rise has been perceived by the West, especially the United States - the dominant Western nation - as a challenge, if not also a threat, to its position (after the dissolution of the Soviet Union) as the world's sole superpower. There is even persistent talk about the eventual likelihood of war between the U.S. and China.

As an American of ethnic Chinese background, the thought that the two countries, to both of which I am deeply attached, were falling into an adversarial position against one another troubled me deeply. I saw the need for the West, especially the U.S., to accommodate a rising China through peaceful co-existence at the very least, and more positively through a relationship of mutual respect and cooperation. I believed that these goals could be more easily achieved if Western readers, instead of being exposed only to Western-oriented sources, were given a more balanced picture of the developments in China since Deng Xiaoping's reform and opening-up policy in 1978. Furthermore, since the Chinese remain a people highly conscious of their history, who believe in using the past to serve the present (*gu wei jin yong*), a broader knowledge of Chinese history is of vital importance for Westerners to gain insight into contemporary China, and its international relations. So, returning to my training in Chinese history, and with the perspective of a Chinese American who is sympathetic to both traditions, I began to entertain the idea of writing a history of China to inform Western readers how, from its ancient beginnings, China became the country it is today.

Today, notions of Great Power superiority and dominance are dangerous. For their part, the leaders of China have repeatedly stressed that U.S.-China cooperation is indispensable for peace and stability of the Asia-Pacific, and for coping with the many urgent challenges of the 21st century, such as climate change, poverty reduction, mass migrations, terrorism, nuclear proliferation, epidemic diseases, the militarization of space, and cybersecurity. They have expressed a determination to avoid the kind of Great Power confrontation that has occurred throughout history. They believe that China can cultivate a state-to-state relationship with the U.S. that will enable the two countries to transcend their differences and work together to build a new type of major country relationship, one that aims at peaceful co-existence under new historical conditions. It is reasonable to hope that the economies of both countries, and indeed the world economy, will benefit from a deepening of U.S.-China engagement - and to fear that the consequences of enmity between the two countries will be devastating for the entire world.

There is, in short, a great need for the peoples of America and China, having evolved from different civilizations, to build bridges of understanding to help them not only to co-exist in peace, but also to cooperate in meeting new challenges in this nuclear-armed and globalized world. My hope is that this book will advance the much-needed mutual understanding between East and West.

Jean Kuo Aitchison

Editor's Preface

As she wrote in her own Preface to this book, my late wife Jean Kuo Aitchison (1936 - 2021) was passionately concerned that the United States and China – the two nations to which she was deeply attached – should not become adversaries, let alone enemies. She conceived the idea of writing a history of China, primarily for Western readers, which she hoped would contribute to advancing mutual understanding between the people of these two great nations. Jean continued to work on the project until a few months before she died. A year or two earlier, she had completed the first draft of her history, from the beginnings of historical records (about 1000 BCE) to the modern era (up to 2013). But she had then become fascinated by the archaeological work going on in China, which is revealing traces of the very earliest Chinese civilizations; she was also intensely interested in contemporary developments. These preoccupations so much absorbed her that she did not return, before her death, to the extensive earlier material to prepare it for publication. It seemed obvious that this material, so close to her heart and the product of many years of work, should not be allowed to remain unpublished, and it was natural for me to undertake the task of editing it for publication.

Unfortunately, Chinese history is very far from my own field, which is theoretical physics. The task would, indeed, have been beyond me if I had not had the essential help of two assistant editors, Ying Cheng and Hilary Tan. Between them they read the entire manuscript with meticulous care, focusing especially on consistency in Pinyin spellings, and on historical accuracy. Without their expert help, it would not have been realistic to seek publication. However, I take responsibility for any errors or omissions which remain, and I would be most grateful to have them brought to my attention at the address ijraitchison1@gmail.com. An Errata sheet can be posted on Jean's website, which is usachinaperspectives.com.

My contribution has been to assume the remaining responsibilities of a copy editor. In planning the overall format, I decided not to include anything on the archaeology of the pre-history period, on which Jean had left only rough notes. Much the same applied to the contemporary China of Xi Jinping. I then organized the draft text into two volumes, the dynastic era until 1911, and the modern era until 2013. Within these volumes, I am responsible for most of the layout, including the division into chapters and sections. I also allowed myself a little diversion by choosing the illustrations. In volume 2, I supplied a short summary at the beginning of each chapter, and in some cases a list of the principal actors and their positions in the government. Apart from some re-ordering of the text in a few places, the only changes to Jean's writing that have been made are the usual minor ones, involving punctuation, grammar, and readability issues.

A word needs to be said about citations. We cannot know now exactly what final form Jean intended her book to take, but I think it is most likely that she aimed to offer a broad two-volume review of the sweep of Chinese history, rather than an academic treatise. Her work drew on many well-known and authoritative histories by Western authors, such as Jacques Genet, Ezra Vogel, Jonathan Spence, and John Fairbank, for example. She included very few citations in her draft, and I have only been able to suggest relevant general references, to authors such as those just mentioned, at the end of each chapter. I must apologize to any authors who feel that their work has not been properly cited here, and I invite them to write to me so that I may post a suitable citation on the website.

Ian J R Aitchison

A note on Romanization and pronunciation of Chinese words

Chinese is written in non-alphabetic characters, which are transcribed into Latin letters (as used in English) by a system called Romanization. Most Western books on China published since the mid-1979s use the Pinyin system (sometimes called Hanyu Pinyin), as will be the case here. Although the letters used are Latin letters, the way that some of them are pronounced differs from the standard English pronunciation. The following guide covers most of the occurrences which an English reader is likely to need.

Consonants
'x' = English 'sh' as in sheep
'q' = English 'ch' as in cheap
'zh' = English 'j' as in jet
'c' before a vowel = English 'ts' as in cats
'z' before a vowel = English 'dz' or 'ds' as in cads

Vowels
'ou' = English 'o' as in snow
'u' = English long 'oo' as in boon
'ong' = English short 'oo' as in book + ng
'ui' = English 'ay' as in sway
'ai' = English 'eye'
'ao' = English 'ow' as in howl
'a' after y, i or u = English 'e' as in yet
'a' elsewhere = English 'ah' as in father
'e' after y = English 'e' as in get
'e' elsewhere = English 'uh' as in uh huh
'i' after s, c or z is much like English 'uh'

Examples
The Song (*Soong*) Dynasty   The Zhou (*Joe*) Dynasty   The Qin (*Cheen*) Dynasty
The philosopher Laozi (*Laudzuh*)   The Empress Cixi (*Tsuhshee*)
Premier Zhou Enlai (*Joe Enleye*)   Premier Zhao Ziyang (*Jow Dzuhyang*)
Chairman Mao Zedong (*Mow Dzedoong*)   Tiananmen (*Tienahnmuhn*) Square

Spoken Mandarin uses four intonations ('tones') which distinguish Chinese syllables. There is a notation for the tones, but it is rarely used in Romanized English texts, and is not used here. Speaking a Pinyin word without tone markings will therefore generally not produce the correct Chinese vocalization. Also, note that some Chinese names are so well established that the old usage is commonly retained – for example, Chiang Kai-shek rather than the Pinyin Jiang Jieshi.

The information in this guide is mostly taken from the website https://pages.ucsd.edu/~dkjordan/resources/PronouncingMandarin.html (accessed 1/31/24) which contains much more detail.

Chapter 1

The Early Dynasties

From the Ancient Three Dynasties to the Qin Dynasty (c. 2070 – 206 BCE)

The ancient Three Dynasties

The history of the Chinese civilization traditionally begins with the ancient Three Dynasties, the Xia (c. 2070 – c. 1600 BCE), the Shang (c. 1600 – c. 1046 BCE) and the Zhou (c. 1046 – 221 BCE). A major project commissioned by the Chinese government in 1996 placed the Xia between approximately 2070 BCE and 1600 BCE. However, the earliest written mention of Xia is from the Western Zhou period (c. 1046 – 771 BCE). There is no reference to Xia in the earliest Chinese written sources, which include the inscriptions on oracle bones dating from the later Shang period (thirteenth to twelfth centuries BCE). The historicity of the Xia therefore remains a matter for debate. Archaeologists in China continue to search for signs of the Xia capital city, with little success so far. Some Chinese scholars suggest that the Xia may be identified with the Bronze Age Erlitou Culture, which is determined to have existed in the Yellow River valley during the eighteenth to the sixteenth centuries BCE.

Although there were also no written records of the Shang dynasty until the Western Zhou period, archaeological evidence firmly supports its existence. Excavations near pres-

Inscriptions on an oracle bone (turtle shell) from the late Shang period. (*Museum of the Institute of History and Philology, Taipei, Taiwan (ROC)*: retrieved on 30 November 2023 from https://museum.sinica.edu.tw/en/exhibitions/21/?lang=en&item=21

ent-day Anyang allow the site to be identified with the ruins of Yin, the capital city of the Shang. This site yielded a large collection of oracle bones, which provide important information about this early stage in the Chinese civilization.

The Zhou dynasty, which followed the Shang, lasted for nearly 800 years, the longest of any Chinese dynasty. The Zhou is noted for its remarkable bronzeware, for being the cradle of three major Chinese philosophies (Confucianism, Taoism, and Legalism), and for the evolution of the Chinese written script.

We shall now describe, in broad outline, some essential features of the early Chinese polity represented in these dynasties, which we shall see repeated many times in the later dynasties.

Characteristic features of the early Chinese polity

During the two millennia when these dynasties waxed and waned, until 221 BCE when the Qin unified China under its rule, many of the basic and long-lasting features of Chinese civilization were already in evidence. The power of the state was vested in the person of the head of the state, the emperor or king, who ruled, in theory, absolutely. Those who assisted him would form a part of the ruling elite. The society was patriarchal as well as hierarchical, with fine distinctions of status and position. Even within families, the fundamental building blocks of society, there was a clear ordering. A father was considered superior to his son, just as a man was to his wife and an elder brother to his younger brother. Those in the inferior positions were obliged not only to respect their superiors but also to obey them. Relatives on the paternal side took precedence over those on the maternal side. One of the most significant forms of social division was that between the ruling elite and the ruled. The ancient philosopher Mencius (372 – 289 BCE) summarized the situation succinctly with the statement that those who work with their minds rule over those who work with their hands. The ruling elite was spared the arduous physical toil of the primary producers, the fruits of whose labour sustained this upper social and political stratum and their high living standard.

What were the sources of the ruler's power or authority? Like heads of state in other civilizations, Chinese rulers relied on physical force, on their ability to muster, organize, control, and deploy armed personnel, for maintaining internal security and resisting external foes. The founder of a Chinese dynasty often achieved his goal of controlling a larger area by conquering and annexing the territory of his neighbours. However, force alone was not sufficient for him to govern the country. For this he also depended on the assistance of civilian administrators, who ruled on his behalf. Another important source of his authority was spiritual in its origin, and this was derived from the cult of ancestor worship. The Chinese believed that the spirits of the ancestors in the world of the afterlife when appealed to, served, and propitiated, would protect their descendants and help them to thrive in this world. Those who prospered must have mighty ancestral spirits who blessed and supported their earthly enterprises. The Chinese head of state was believed to be crucial in the performance of the rite of ancestor worship. This awe-inspiring role would confer upon him a spiritual authority that was further reinforced by the idea that he was the Son of Heaven (*Tianzi*), a god or god's representative on earth. He had the Mandate of Heaven (*Tianming*), meaning a divinely ordained right to rule over All under Heaven (*Tianxia*), a term customarily taken to mean China, before the Chinese became aware of a much larger world outside their polity. Heaven, *Tian*, stood for a spiritual realm possessing supernatural power over our mundane world, though without a supreme deity.

In any given dynasty, succession normally went to the male heirs of the founder in succeeding generations. After many generations, a time would come when a Son of Heaven

Map of the approximate boundaries of the Three Dynasties (*World History Encyclopedia*: retrieved on 8 April 2024 from
https://www.worldhistory.org/image/16231/shang-dynasty-of-china-c-1100-bce/)

appeared to have lost his grip on his patrimony. Chaos would ensue. There would be a period of dynastic interregnum, and after power struggles and military contests among ambitious would-be Sons of Heaven, a new dynasty would be founded by the head of another powerful family or lineage group. Such a phenomenon has been described by Chinese historians as the dynastic cycle. To Chinese observers, a dynasty seemed to have a life cycle: it underwent birth, maturity, and decay, like a living organism. Although the length of dynasties varied, they inevitably came to an end, which was widely understood by the populace as the judgment of heaven. The consequent withdrawal of the Mandate of Heaven from the ruling dynasty was a result of the ruler's lack of virtue.

The above conclusion was in line with the ancient Chinese ideology as expressed by the Confucian school, a major philosophical school of thought based on the teachings of Confucius, who lived from 551 BCE to 479 BCE. These thinkers saw the universe as a moral entity, and human society, being a part of this cosmos, must obey the same universal moral code. Apart from being a legitimate successor to his forebears, an emperor's right to rule rested on another, very different, test: his moral character. In a well-ordered society, the emperor was like a benevolent patriarch of a state-wide family. A good emperor, who demonstrated exemplary propriety in his conduct, would inspire his ministers to govern the country well. He would be successful in his role as an intercessor for his people with the powers in heaven. His prayers would be heard, and heaven would rain blessings on his land. Were he to fail this test, the opposite would result. The end of a dynasty was often accompanied by natural disasters, such as widespread floods or droughts, and by man-made troubles such as internal rebellions and foreign invasions. These negative events would have been viewed more as signs that the ruler had lost his mandate to rule because of his moral shortcomings rather than any actual mistakes or wrong decisions made while governing his realm. Historians of another time or from a different culture might offer other explanations for the rise and fall of Chinese dynasties, but in traditional China the foregoing was the commonly accepted account. The rise of a new dynasty in China did not mean wholesale innovation in the Chinese political, economic, or cultural sphere. Changes and refinements were continually being made, but they mostly took place within the framework of a cultural tradition that had already developed a cer-

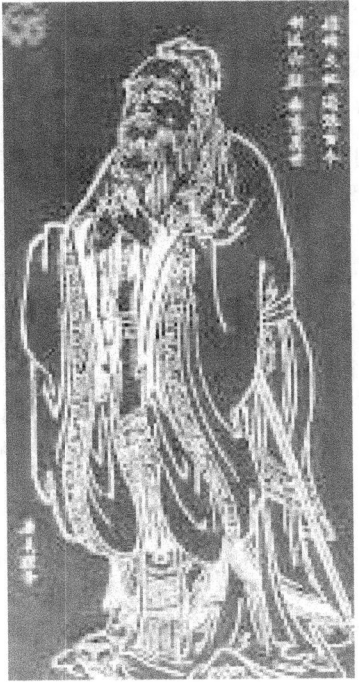

Portrait of Confucius by the Tang dynasty painter Wu Daozi (*Mesosyn*: retrieved on 30 November 2023 from http://mesosyn.com/cp2.html)

tain established pattern.

Confucianism was only one among many schools of thought that vied with one another for popular following and princely sponsorship before the grand unification of China by the Qin Dynasty (221 – 206 BCE). Besides being a philosophy of individual ethics like other competing schools, it was also deeply concerned with the morality of government. However, the ancient Chinese thinkers who were most narrowly focused on governance and statecraft were the Legalists (c. 400 - 300 BCE). Proponents of this school had no use for the Confucian ideal of a benevolent monarch governing his country by moral leadership and putting his people and their needs before himself and his own interests. The Legalists, on the contrary, held that social and political order could only be ensured through strong state control and absolute obedience to authority. The ruler was viewed as a means to achieving this aim. All the machinery of the state, together with its people, were to be used to serve the ruler's interests and objectives, first and foremost among which was the preservation of his own position and power, in order to secure social and political stability.

The establishment of the Qin

The Legalists were masters on the subject of power and its exercise, in theory as well as in practice. Not surprisingly, the rulers of the Qin found the teachings of this school so attractive that two outstanding Legalists were, as Qin prime ministers, given the opportunity to put their ideas into practice. Around the middle of the fourth century BCE, Shang Yang, a talented exponent of Legalism, helped Duke Xiao, the head of the Qin, to concentrate power into his own hands at the expense of the old aristocracy. The government was systematically reorganized and staffed by bureaucrats, who became a new elite group to rival the old aristocrats. The bureaucrats were government appointees, chosen irrespective of birth or privileged social connection. These people owed their position, authority, status, and income to the ruler alone, and so they became the ruler's dependants. At the local level, the authority of the feudal lords in their fiefdoms was replaced by that of the centrally appointed county magistrates, who reported directly to the court and were subject to recall. In addition to losing political authority, the nobles lost their privileged position in the eyes of the law. Traditionally they were exempt from criminal punishment, a practice sanctioned by the conservative Confucianists. When the Qin government adopted a Legalist measure that treated all people as being equal under the law, the nobles (in theory) no longer enjoyed this immunity.

Chinese civilization would not have developed without agricultural surpluses sufficiently large to support an upper stratum of the ruling elite and their servants, as well as other functionally specialized members of the society, such as artisans and merchants, who did not work on the land. Ancient Chinese rulers including the Qin recognized the importance of agriculture and saw it as the economic mainstay of their states. The foundation of the wealth of the feudal lords also lay in their hereditary right in connection with the land in their fiefdoms. The Qin court, as guided by Shang Yang, effected a revolutionary change on the millennia-old ancient Chinese system of land tenure, by giving the tillers the right to own the land they cultivated. Land was no longer an inalienable part of the feudal domain of the aristocrats; it became a commodity that could be bought and sold. This reform, in addition to the curtailment of the power and privileges of the aristocracy as described above, brought about the terminal decline of feudalism in the kingdom of Qin.

Since the livelihoods of the bulk of the people and the income of the state came from land cultivation, increasing land yield was a preoccupation of not only the agriculture producers; the Chinese ruling elite also took an interest and at times played a significant role, especially in connection with organizing large-scale irrigation and water control works. The state of Qin strengthened itself economically by providing leadership in irrigation projects and canal building. The change in the system of land tenure also stimulated the economy and increased state revenue.

Following Shang Yang's reform, the Qin became a dominant player among the seven major states of the Warring States Period (475 – 221 BCE). These kingdoms conquered or absorbed their weaker neighbours through diplomacy or war, after the Zhou Dynasty gradually but irreversibly lost authority and control over the multitudes of fiefdoms within its empire. As the name of this period suggested, the states that remained intact were rivals, continually at war with each other. During several hundred years of military contests, warfare grew more ruthless, and the technology of war became more efficient. Harder iron weaponry was introduced, and that of bronze; massive infantry forces armed with crossbows were deployed, and chariots were replaced by the more mobile cavalry.

About a century later, another Legalist statesman, Li Si, as the Qin prime minister (246-206 BCE) under King Ying Zheng (later known as Qin Shi Huang), reinforced the Legalist style of government. Having subjugated the nobles and with greater control of the economic resources, the autocratic Qin king commanded the obedience of the people to his will through a regime of harsh laws and severe punishments. But for those who served him well, there were rewards. The Legalists advocated the use of rewards and punishments as the 'two handles' by which the ruler could dominate and subdue his people. With power so effectively centralized, the Qin king was able to mobilize the population massively for war, or for other purposes according to his wishes. By 221 BCE Ying Zheng was able to conquer all the other major kingdoms of the Warring States to establish the Qin dynasty (221– 207 BCE), and crown himself as Qin Shi Huang, the first emperor of the Qin empire. This was one of the climactic moments in Chinese history.

The Qin might appear superficially to be just another dynasty replacing the Zhou, though with a much larger domain. But there were significant differences. While the king of Zhou presided as a suzerain over feudal vassals, who were the real hereditary powerholders of the fiefdoms, the emperor of Qin exerted control of his far-flung empire through his own bureaucratic appointees, whose income and career depended on him, and who exercised power on his behalf. The first emperor ruled at the capital, where he held court, and where he was assisted by the officials of the central government heading various specialized departments. Civil governors and military commanders governed the thirty-six (later increased to forty-eight) commanderies at the next level, and magistrates administered the hundreds of counties at the base. His regional and local government officials implemented his policy, reported to the court in writing, and were subject to central supervision and recall. The aristocratic families of the vanquished kingdoms were moved to the capital, away from their former power base to prevent their resurgence. The feudal or *fengjian* institutions of China's classical age thus came to an end, and were replaced by a centrally controlled bureaucratic system, which prevailed in China for over two millennia thereafter. The Qin unification therefore marked the beginning of China's existence as a centralized bureaucratic state, occupying a significantly increased area as compared with the ancient Three Dynasties.

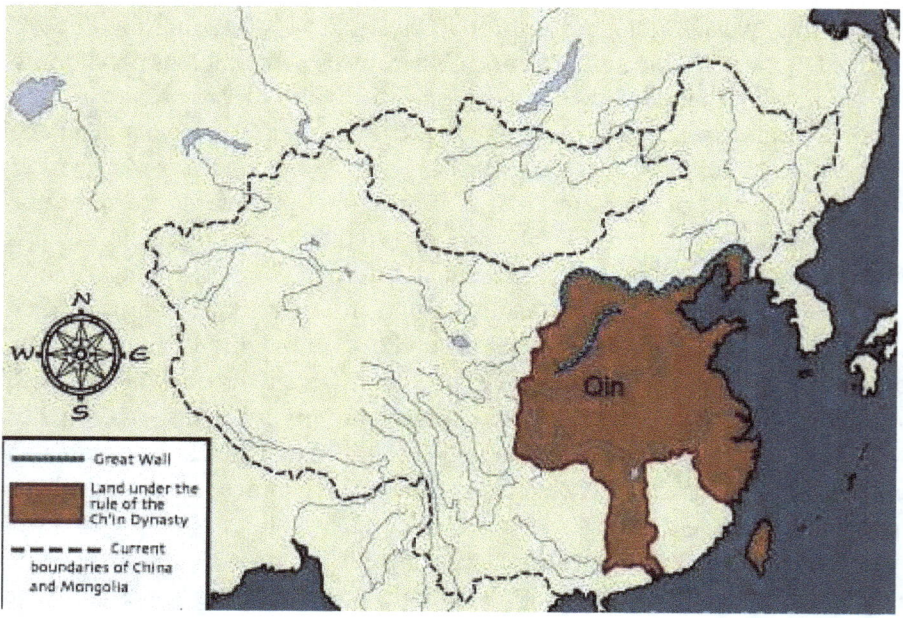

Map of the territory of the Qin dynasty (*China Education Center*: retrieved on 30 November 2023 from https://www.chinaeducenter.com/en/whychina/qin.php)

In addition to setting up the administrative structure and promulgating a code of law for the entire conquered area, certain measures were taken by the Qin court to enable it to govern the extensive territory more effectively. Standardized weights and measures, and currency, were adopted throughout the empire. To facilitate transport and communications, major road building and canal construction programmes were undertaken. A government postal system was established. Communication in writing was facilitated by the standardization of the styles of written characters, whereby one formal and one cursive style became the norm.

The imposition of uniformity on the Chinese script was possible because the language was not based on a phonetic alphabet, although the pictographic-representational characters sometimes incorporated a phonetic element in their composition. The earliest writing in the development of the Chinese civilization consisted of inscriptions on the shoulder blades of slaughtered domestic animals, or on turtle shells - 'oracle bones'- apparently used in connection with divination. Such writing evolved into a powerful and versatile tool for the ruling elite in government administration, its function being by no means limited to communicating with the world of ancestral spirits. Laws and edicts were promulgated in writing. Population censuses and taxation business were carried out in writing, with records also kept in writing. Compared with oral tradition, written records had far greater reliability and permanence. Before the invention of paper during the Han Dynasty (206 - 220 CE), ancient Chinese writing on bamboo or silk remained available for future generations. The usefulness of writing was not limited to transmitting information from one period to another, however; it was also a vitally important medium for official communications between the central government and the regional and local officials, and among the officials themselves. (Of the many large historical empires, only the Inca managed the functions of government without a written language.) The first emperor of Qin, with the help of his officials, was able to control his large empire, with people speaking a variety of dialects and tongues, largely because the business of government was conducted in the common system of writing. The imposition of uniformity on the written characters lessened the chances of mistakes and misunderstandings in the information transmitted. A unified written language gave China a common linguistic thread. It was a vital factor contributing to the longevity of China's civilization, and to the repeated reassertion of a unified empire under other major dynasties during the two thousand years following the Qin, even after long periods of disunion.

Having extended his government and consolidated his rule of the conquered areas, the first Qin emperor set about strengthening the defence of his realm. Military governors were placed in all the commanderies alongside their civilian colleagues. A system of collective responsibility tailored towards controlling the population was set up, which obliged groups of households to curb or report to the government unlawful activities among family members or neighbours, or suffer the penalties for not doing so. With a little variation in the details, this divisive means of maintaining internal security was used by many subsequent regimes down to the modern era. However, the most intractable security problem was external, posed by the warlike nomads on the northern and the north-western frontier of the Qin empire.

The challenge of maintaining the security of the northern border

North of a band where rainfall became variable or scarce, conditions of grassland, steppe, and semi-desert or desert prevailed. This kind of environment could not fully support the intensive arable farming of the North China Plain, where the Chinese Three Dynasties had carved out their domains. A vast area unsuitable for farming was instead only able to support migratory pastoral herders of livestock, who laid down tents where they could find food and water for their domesticated animals. These animals provided for their basic material needs such as food, materials for clothing, bedding and shelter, as well as acting as their beasts of burden. Other needs they could endeavour to satisfy by trade or by raid.

To the sedentary Chinese agriculturalists in the south, the nomadic Northerners appeared lacking in both material civilization and high culture. Without adherence to the kind of manners, morals, and the regulated social relationships commonly practised by the Chinese, they were perceived as rough and uncouth, and even labelled as barbarians. Through successful intensive agriculture in a settled region, the Chinese were able to produce the surplus wealth to support politicians, scholars, artisans, and a host of other specialists, to produce an abundance of material things, and to build a rich and varied civilization. In contrast, pastoralists faced significant challenges in meeting even their basic needs, often lacking sufficient resources for themselves and their animals. Given their desire for Chinese goods, and their mobility on horseback, some of the tribal peoples were easily tempted to raid and loot weakly defended Chinese farming communities in their vicinity. When bands of nomads of similar ethnic origin joined together under a strong and ambitious leader, they could and often did pose serious military challenges to many Chinese dynasties.

The difference in economic and societal organization had a bearing on the disposition towards combat between the nomadic tribes and the Chinese. Physical contests, trials of strength, and military skirmishes were a way of life among the tribal peoples living on the otherwise unprotected grassland or open steppe. When armed with crossbows and other weapons, they were formidable as mounted warriors, well versed in military manoeuvres. Every nomad was a potential soldier. They constituted, in effect, a standing army, always ready to be called upon to fight. The Chinese, on the other hand, were not so warlike. Apart from the generals and the high-ranking officers who were professionally involved in military service, the Chinese fighting forces were made up mostly of farmers, who were mobilized to serve as soldiers in times of need.

How did the Chinese deal with this constant frontier threat in the north? Over the next two thousand years, the rulers of China would use several strategies. Under a militarily strong regime, the Chinese could and often did choose to fight. If the nomads did not want to fight, they would flee and retreat to a point where the Chinese army in pursuit would find themselves in an untenable position of being far from their base with an over-extended supply line. The first emperor of Qin, being a strong and aggressive ruler, wanted to stabilize this borderland. He sent an army of reportedly 300,000 to drive out the Xiongnu, a powerful Turkic tribal people, from the northern and north-western frontier. An imperial highway was built straight into the semi-desert Ordos region, and in 211 BCE roughly 30,000 Chinese families were moved to settle in this area previously controlled by the Xiongnu. Walls were erected in the north to protect this settlement.

Chinese civilization was, in fact, closely identified with fortified walled cities. Before China was unified under the Qin, walls were also built by various states along their borders to defend themselves against both Chinese and nomad enemies. After the unification, the Qin emperor connected those walls of the Warring States which could serve as defensive walls against nomad incursion. Together with the wall north of Ordos, this extremely long wall was extended westward to Ningxia. Although even such a fortified wall could not fully keep nomad invaders out of China, it remained a key long-term defensive strategy against invasion from various pastoral tribal peoples along the northern border of the Chinese empire, stretching from the northwest to the northeast.

The conquest under the first emperor of Qin represented a major expansion of the Chinese state and civilization. The Qin readily consolidated its rule over the territory of the other former Warring States as these areas were already largely Chinese in culture. The Chinese hold on Ordos to the north, an area more suitable for the pastoral economy, was shakier. To the south, the Qin's hold on the conquered Yue (today's Guangdong and Guangxi provinces) and northern Annam (Vietnam) was also tenuous, because these areas were already settled by people ethnically and culturally distinct from the Chinese.

The first emperor's harsh rule and his massive mobilization of the people for war, wall construction, road, and canal building, not to mention his stupendous tomb[1], proved to be too much for the long-suffering peasants of China. Not long after his death in 210 BCE, peasant rebellions broke out and spread rapidly. A powerful force under Xiang Yu, a scion of the former kingdom of Chu, gave the Qin dynasty the fatal blow, ending the dream of a dynasty that was supposed to last forever, and the life of an emperor who fervently sought immortality.

After several years of general chaos and civil war, an astute rebel leader of peasant origin called Liu Bang emerged as the winner. He became the new Son of Heaven and founded the Han dynasty in 202 BCE, with its capital at Chang'an (now Xi'an).

---

[1] In present-day Xi'an, now known to millions for the army of terracotta warriors, guarding the mausoleum.

The terra cotta army at the tomb of the first emperor, Qin Shi Huang, in Xi'an (c. 210 BCE) (*Archaeology Wiki:* retrieved on 30 November 2023 from https://www.archaeology.wiki/blog/2022/03/31/the-terracotta-army-the-clay-army-with-the-greek-signature/)

The Han Dynasty (206 BCE – 9 CE, 25 – 220 CE)

After peace was once more restored, the Han dynasty succeeded in taking control of what had been the Qin empire. Although not from an aristocratic lineage himself, the Han founder, Liu Bang, divided his empire roughly down the middle, and gave the territory in the eastern part to his royal relatives as their fiefdoms. The remaining territory in the western part was administered as commanderies and counties under the direct control of the imperial government and its delegates, who became the regional and local bureaucrats, as had been the case under the Qin.

In 206 BCE Liu Bang assumed the dynastic title of Han Gaozu, the first emperor of the Han dynasty. The dynasty was relatively long-lived: it lasted over four hundred years, from 206 BCE to 220 CE, apart from a brief interruption and a change of capital. The longevity and prestige of this dynasty made such an impact on China that an overwhelming majority of people in modern mainland China identify themselves as ethnically Han, which is also an official designation distinguishing them from the ethnic minorities in the People's Republic of China.

The Han's adoption of Confucianism

The Han emperors, especially the Martial Emperor (Emperor Wu) who reigned from 141 to 87 BCE, sought to solidify the dynasty's political power by putting it on a strong cultural or ideological foundation. The Han avoided the harshness of the Legalist philosophy as practised by the Qin, and instead embraced as the state orthodoxy a large body of ideas of Confucian origin. Emperor Wu established an Imperial Academy in the capital to train students and promote scholarly study of the state-authorized Confucianism. Graduates from this establishment would constitute a body of literate, well-educated young people, providing a pool of talents to draw upon for governmental service. This became a regular new channel for civil service recruitment, in addition to the established practice of recommendation by other officeholders. Its most distinguished scholars could be called upon to advise the emperor on subjects ranging from public policy to ritual observances. Proper performance of rites devoted to the imperial ancestors and to heaven was a very serious matter, which required the emperor personally to take an active part. To perform this important duty properly, the emperor needed the assistance of consummate interpreters of Confucianism, who functioned as the guardians of these rites.

In general, any stable political regime cannot govern by force alone. It needs at least the acquiescence of the people, if not also their acceptance and active cooperation. Legalism had relied on imposing the will of the government on the people by using rewards and punishments. While not wholly abandoning this 'carrot and stick' approach, the Han endeavoured to secure the people's acceptance and cooperation by placing more emphasis on the spiritual foundation of its legitimacy. This was pursued through the active promotion of Confucian traditions, including the worship of heaven and reverence for imperial ancestors. By strengthening the popular belief that the dynasty had the Mandate of Heaven, and was protected by powerful ancestral spirits, this Confucian-inspired policy likely contributed to social stability.

The selection of government officials from among those who had received an education based on the Confucian classics had several implications. The officials so selected could be expected to have achieved a certain standard of literacy and cultural attainments, and to have a solid grounding in the morality and ethics central to the teachings of Confucius and Mencius. They formed a new elite, commonly known as *shi dafu* (scholar-officials), sharing a common worldview and code of morality. In time, the language and moral precepts in communications between the court and its officials, and among the officials themselves, were couched in the Confucian cultural framework.

Confucian philosophy presupposed an orderly universe or world, where the universal order would be preserved if everyone behaved according to the ethics governing his or her station or position in life. It taught the way of the golden mean, which valued harmony, modesty, and moderation, while opposing assertiveness, competitiveness, strife, and extremism in personal behaviour and social conduct. Despite the religious elements in connection with the role of the emperor and the legitimacy of the dynastic rule, Confucianism as a political ideology was notable in the pre-modern world for its secular and this-worldly orientation.

Transgression in this moral universe, particularly if committed by the ruler, was likely to result in disorder. While an emperor stood above the law, which was made by him or in his name, the universal morality applied to the whole society, the emperor included. A wise emperor would exercise his power within the Confucian moral framework in order not to invite a 'lecture' from his bolder ministers, or risk heaven's disapproval and witness the dynasty losing the Mandate of Heaven. This moral framework provided some restraint on autocratic excesses of an emperor.

While law and punishment were mechanisms of external control on a person, internalized morality could predispose a person to exercise self-control. A person might evade law without suffering punishment; immoral behaviour, however, might lead to self-reproach and a feeling of shame. The Confucian philosophy was orientated more towards collective wellbeing than the rights of an individual. It stressed obligations rather than rights. The cardinal Confucian virtues such as benevolence, loyalty, filial piety, righteousness, trustworthiness, and good faith were the commonly held values of the educated class. Although government officials in traditional China were often recognized for their human foibles rather than for being embodiments of virtue, they had at least a body of ethical standards and moral criteria to uphold, by which the conduct of themselves and others would be judged. Confucianism provided an ethical framework for the governing elite, and a moral foundation for the formulation and application of government regulations. This approach in governing a society in effect gave morality rather than law the primal position.

The Han promotion of Confucianism as the official philosophy of the state and society was a visionary as well as a practical stroke of immense significance, with far-reaching consequences for the dynasty itself and for China. It was a kind of Chinese Renaissance. Like the Western Europeans harnessing and building upon the knowledge of ancient Greece and Rome to achieve their cultural Renaissance, the Han dynasty Chinese reached back to draw upon the valuable cultural heritage of a not so distant past and used it to satisfy the political and administrative needs of the time, as well as to provide long-term social stability in a sustainable social order with a strong cultural underpinning. When the Han dynasty eventually declined and disintegrated, Confucianism was eclipsed to some extent until its great resurgence, in a reinterpreted form, about one thousand years later in the Song Dynasty (960-1279 CE). Subsequently, apart from a brief spell under the Mongol Yuan Dynasty (1271-1368 CE), Confucianism grew from strength to strength until near the end of the Qing Dynasty (1644-1911 CE). It was disseminated by a myriad of schools, private as well as government-run, which catered to the education of the candidates for the greatly expanded state-sponsored examination system for the selection of officials. During this long period, Confucianism was not only the prevailing culture of the ruling elite; it came close to being a traditional Chinese mass culture. Although this philosophy served the Chinese state and society in some ways, such as promoting social harmony, it did have important drawbacks. One was the low position of women, who were relegated to second-class citizenship. Another was the conservatism that glorified the past and past achievements, rather than embracing the future and its potential for innovative changes.

Internal and external challenges to the Han state

Chinese statesmen were aware that the stability of a state depended on many elements which included, in addition to the political and administrative aspects, also economic and military security. Some of the more benevolent Han rulers paid attention to the peoples' livelihood by lowering taxes, supporting irrigation works, and by encouraging agriculture and the rural handicraft industry. Since peasant rebellions were often fomented by people who were desperately poor, these positive measures that enabled the people to enjoy economic wellbeing, or at least to have means for subsistence, were no doubt helpful towards maintaining a peaceful society. When challenged by force internally, or threatened by an invading army from the outside, military strength came to the fore in ensuring the security and continuity of the dynasty. For over four hundred years, the Han dynasty - both the Western Han (202 BCE - 8 CE) and the Eastern Han (25 - 230 CE) - were sufficiently strong militarily to defeat enemies from within and beyond the empire's frontiers.

Notwithstanding such stabilizing factors, there were internal structural weaknesses and external forces that threatened the security of the Han empire. One major weakness was connected to the founder's policy of awarding large tracts of land to his relatives as their fiefdoms. The ten kingdoms thus created had the wealth and the manpower to raise armies and challenge the authority of the court. One such major challenge, known as the Seven Kingdoms Rebellion, took place early in Emperor Jing's reign (157-141 BCE). Although the rebellion was promptly put down, it exposed a weakness in the system that remained a problem for the central authority.

Another structural weakness was related to the emperor's own household establishment. There were two groups of people close to the emperor, the centre of power. One group was the empress together with her relatives. A powerful empress could dominate a weak emperor and rule the country with her relatives placed in key posts. An emperor in his minority was especially vulnerable to being controlled by an ambitious dowager empress. Near the beginning of the Han dynasty, the founder's consort, Empress Lu, was such an example. Later, in 9 CE, an empress' nephew, Wang Mang, usurped the throne and set up a short-lived Xin dynasty (9-23 CE).

A second group that could potentially threaten the central power were the eunuchs, the castrated male servants of the emperor and his wives, who lived in their private quarters inside the palace. They were mostly from lower social classes without a Confucian-style education. Those who won the emperor's trust, or became his favourites, could use their positions in the inner court to gain enormous power and wealth through manipulation and intrigue. Some of them even became high officials. They tended to represent a corrupting influence. When a strong empress or her relatives, or a powerful eunuch, interfered too much in the affairs of the state, the dynasty could become weakened or be set on the path of decline. From the point of view of Confucian scholars, these were perennial problems of the Chinese dynastic rule, and likely contributory factors in the later stages of the dynastic cycle.

The Han ability to impose peace along its extended border survived many trials of strength during the dynasty's existence. There were challenges from two different directions at the empire's frontier: Chaoxian (or Gaoli) and Nanyue. The former was situated in today's Korean peninsula, and the latter occupied today's Guangdong and Guangxi provinces in southern China. The rulers of these regions were vassals to the Han and some of its predecessors. Should they rebel or refuse to acknowledge Chinese suzerainty, strong Chinese rulers would send punitive expeditions against them. During Emperor Wu's long reign (141-87 BCE), the Han suppressed rebellions from these regions by force and governed them as commanderies, because the two regions were ethnically non-Han. The people there were not nomadic, being sedentary farmers like Han Chinese. While Guangdong and Guangxi eventually became a part of China, Chaoxian did not. A strong central authority in China could retain Chaoxian's allegiance as a subordinate state, but it would break away when China became weak or disunited. Its people had a different ethnic identity and language from the Han Chinese. Instead of being absorbed by China, the people of Chaoxian eventually became modern Koreans.

The Han empire was particularly threatened by a Turkic tribal alliance, called the Xiongnu, who frequently raided and invaded Han territory on its north-western frontier. Several Han emperors despatched punitive military expeditions to subdue the Xiongnu with only temporary and partial success. Sometimes, the Xiongnu were able to muster a large force of several hundred thousand men, strong enough to match or outnumber the Han army gathered to fight them. With their martial habits and skilful horsemanship, they were able to score some victories against the Han. Against such a formidable foe, some Han emperors resorted to a conciliatory policy called *heqin*, 'peace and kinship'. Accordingly, Han princesses would be given in marriage to Xiongnu tribal chieftains with a dowry, lavish gifts, and concessions in trade, to secure peace with these troublesome neighbours. This approach bought peace now and again for some periods of time, but it provided no lasting solution against nomadic encroachment.

Emperor Wu, one of the most vigorous of the Han emperors, was determined to find a long-term winning strategy against the Xiongnu by combining war with diplomacy. Near the beginning of his reign, he despatched an envoy, Zhang Qian, to the western region to seek allies against the Xiongnu. During his first trip, Zhang was captured and detained by the Xiongnu for ten years, and he returned to the court having failed to find any tribal group who would join the Han to fight the Xiongnu. Undeterred, Wu sent him west for the second time. He traversed again the ancient Silk Road, this time reaching as far as Persia. From his two journeys, the information he brought back about the different lands and peoples of Central Asia enabled the Han empire to expand westward with an army across the Pamir Plateau to occupy Ferghana, where exceptional horses were bred. In parallel with the diplomatic efforts, Wu sent large armies of up to 300,000 men at a time, led by his best generals, who waged a series of victorious campaigns to remove the Xiongnu from around the Gobi Desert region. Wu's efforts curbed the Xiongnu's aggressive activities for several decades. Later, renewed Xiongnu incursions prompted other Han emperors to station troops, with military settlements, to support a Protector General to keep peace in Xiyu, or Western Territory. This region corresponds to today's Xinjiang Uyghur Autonomous Region (XUAR).

The Han dynasty saw a further expansion of China's territory beyond what it had inherited from the Qin. The process was seldom easy. The Han might conquer and occupy neighbouring regions by force or even rule them as commanderies, but the people there were liable to rise up to throw off the Han yoke as soon as the Han court showed signs of weakness. For example, when Wang Mang usurped the Eastern Han throne to set up his own Xin Dynasty (9-23 CE), the Han Protectorate in Xiyu was lost for a time until the Western Han rulers re-conquered the territory. Neighbouring areas that favoured lasting Chinese rule were those that could sustain a sedentary agricultural economy or absorb a significant number of Chinese migrants amid a local population susceptible to Sinicization. At its greatest expanse, Han territory extended westward to Ferghana, and eastward and southward to present-day Korea and Vietnam. These latter areas remained non-Chinese in the long run, while parts of Xiyu and Nanyue are within contemporary China.

After having ruled China for over four hundred years, the Han dynasty suffered a terminal decline and came to an end in 220 CE. In its final decades, the elements of instability inherent in the system came to the fore. One of these was the appearance of a separatist tendency from powerful regional authorities against a discredited centre. The court was enfeebled by factional fighting, power struggles, and intrigues among empresses, eunuchs, and their relatives and supporters amid a rapid succession of emperors too young or too weak to keep the palace in order, all compounded by insubordinate regional competitors for power.

There are parallels to be found between the Han and the Roman empires, which were comparable in size and overlapped to some extent in time. Both empires declined and disintegrated with 'barbarian' invasions and successor states occupying parts of the old empires. In the case of Rome, the barbarians established themselves in the western parts,

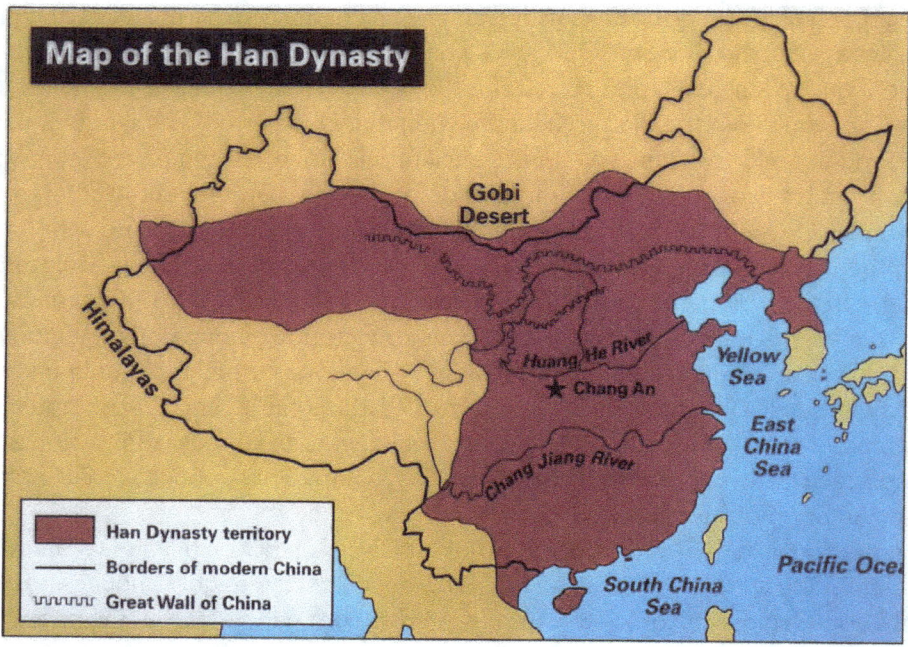

Map of the territory of the Han dynasty (*China Mike:* retrieved on
30 November 2023 from https://www.china-mike.com/chinese-history-timeline/part-4-
han-dynasty

while Roman rule continued in the east. In the Han case, barbarian states controlled
northern China, while ethnic Han regimes ruled southern China. From the fourth century,
religions of foreign origin spread like wildfire in the lands once governed by Rome and
by the Han capital. Christianity from the Middle East took firm hold in the barbarian successor states of Western Europe and in the Eastern Roman Empire. Meanwhile, Buddhism
from India made enormous headway among people of all social classes in China, both in
the barbarian-ruled north and in the Han-controlled south. The similarities must have
been coincidences, since these empires had no direct contact or influence over one
another, apart from the fact that Chinese silk found its way into Roman markets through
intermediaries over the Silk Road. One difference worthy of note was that Rome's fragmentation in the west gave rise to many different nation states in Europe, whereas the
barbarian dynasties in northern China voluntarily Sinicized themselves and became incorporated later into a unified Chinese state.

The Northern Wei was not the only nomad regime that willingly adopted the Chinese
manner of government. For example, the Western Wei (535-557 CE) and the Northern

Zhou (557-581 CE) used the Han *fubing* system of dividing the country into cantons, each populated by farmers-cum-soldiers, who were exempt from taxes but obligated to fight for the state when needed. One might ask: why did they follow the Chinese way so willingly? The nomad rulers must have realized that they were called upon to govern a region with a sedentary agricultural economy different from their own, and that they had little experience in so doing. On the contrary, the Chinese in northern China had, over the centuries, developed a demonstrably successful model for ruling such a land. The nomads therefore adopted the Chinese model and employed Chinese officials to help them create Confucian governments. Although the Chinese did not espouse a martial way of life, many Chinese people in the north were seasoned enough at warfare, due to frequent military combats, to have earned the respect of the more militaristic steppe people. Perhaps the prestige associated with the material and cultural attainments of the Chinese was sufficiently strong to attract these border people to join with the Chinese, rather than retain their separate identity. Intermarriage between the nomad and Chinese aristocratic families led to a situation where the ruling houses of three important dynasties, the Sui, the Tang, and the Song, which later controlled the whole or a major part of China, came from a mixed nomad-Chinese background.

At this point one might ask: why was it that the disintegrated Han empire did not remain in a permanent state of fragmentation like that of the Roman empire after its breakup in the West? Rome started its expansionist career through military conquest as a city-state with the characteristic limits in territory and population of such a city-state, and within a few hundred years it came to rule a vast empire of alien lands and large groups of heterogeneous peoples. Unlike Rome, the Chinese expanded from a much larger and more populous core area, the North China plain, Zhongyuan, which had a history dating back to antiquity. By the time of the Qin-Han unifications, the Chinese had had two thousand years of accumulated experience in developing relatively sophisticated political institutions and infrastructures to govern distant regions from their ancient power base, where they also developed the art of war. During this long period, the people of the Chinese empire had much time to assimilate the culture of the ruling elites, and to become more homogeneous. The Qin-Han unifications demonstrated the potential for China to exist as a single stable political entity covering a far greater area than its ancient heartland, over an extended period of time. After the Han, a unified China, *tongyi*, was generally regarded as the norm, although periodically the unity could not be sustained. During a period of disunion, a state of war would normally prevail in China, because tension and military conflicts usually arose among the warlords or successor states that followed the dismemberment of the empire. Towards the end of such struggles, a winner would emerge, who would have defeated all his competitors for power and would claim to be the new Son of Heaven, at the head of a new dynasty with the Mandate of Heaven to rule the whole of China.

Short-lived Dynasties and the Great Disunion (220 - 589 CE)

After losing its mandate, the Han dynasty was succeeded by three regional powers: the kingdoms of Wei, Shu, and Wu (220 – 280 CE). The head of the Wei, Cao Cao, was portrayed in the Chinese classic, *Romance of the Three Kingdoms*, as someone who practised Machiavellian statecraft. He had a eunuch connection at the Han court, and from the position of prime minister, he dominated and controlled the last Han emperor, Xian (r. 189-220 CE). The Wei dynasty proclaimed by Cao Cao's heirs effectively took over from the Han the old Eastern Han capital of Luoyang, and its surrounding areas in North China along the Yellow River. The Kingdom of Shu in southwestern China (today's Sichuan) was created by Liu Bei, who possessed an aura of legitimacy through being a descendant, though a fairly distant one, of the founder of the Western Han. The Wu was led by Sun Quan, an aristocratic general, who controlled the lower Yangtze region in southeastern China. For sixty years, these kingdoms were incessantly at war with each other until the demise of the Shu in 263 CE, the Wei in 265 CE and the Wu in 280 CE. The Jin dynasty founded in 265 CE by Sima Yan, a Wei General who usurped the Wei throne, ruled over a once more united China, but not for long.

Early in the Jin dynasty, there was already much evidence of a serious power struggle and intrigue inside the palace, an element of instability that had undermined the Han dynasty. In 316 CE, the Xiongnu overran the Jin capital of Luoyang and the court fled to Jiankang (present-day Nanjing) in southeast China, where an Eastern Jin dynasty with its capital at Jiankang was established in 317 CE. Its predecessor from Luoyang came to be known as the Western Jin dynasty in Chinese historical chronicles. The Eastern Jin ruled southern China for over one hundred years from 317 CE to 420 CE.

Meanwhile, northern China fell into the hands of various nomadic tribal invaders with the Xiongnu as only one such among other major tribal and ethnic groups. These included the Xianbei, (proto-Mongol), the Qiang (proto-Tibetan), the Jurchen (proto-Manchu), the Liao and the Di (Mongol), and the Tuoba (Turks). When they settled and ruled northern China, they became rapidly Sinicized. Leaders of these tribes established a succession of Chinese-style dynasties with reign titles. They adopted Chinese political institutions and governed with the support of Chinese ministers. These regimes were relatively unstable: many of them did not last more than three decades and did not rule northern China entirely. This period, from 304 to 439 CE, was known as the Sixteen Kingdoms in northern China, while the Eastern Jin ruled southern China.

In 420 CE, the Liu Song dynasty took over from the Eastern Jin dynasty in the south. From then on for 169 years, southern China, ruled by ethnic Chinese, was also characterized by political instability. Three different dynasties succeeded the Song, each lasting only a few decades.

When south China was troubled by the conflicts accompanying the rapid turnover of ruling houses, the political situation in north China became more settled with the ascendancy of the Tuoba Turks, who brought the whole of north China under their sway by military conquest. The Northern Wei dynasty (386-534 CE), which they created, chose to submerge their own language and customs, and embrace the Chinese way of life instead. They encouraged inter-marriage with the Chinese, and the use of Chinese language, even to the extent of adopting Chinese names. They provided leadership in managing the country's agriculture-based economy. To stimulate farm production and increase revenue from taxes, a Northern Wei emperor, Xiaowen (r. 471-499 CE), carried out a programme of land redistribution that was modelled on the 'equal field' system used in late Western Han. Remarkably, the Northern Wei dynasty survived for 148 years during this age of turmoil.

Political chaos and internecine wars lasted for more than three centuries (220-589 CE), a time characterized by Chinese historians as the Period of Great Disunion. We will witness China breaking down into warring regional political entities again, but not for quite as long. The political cohesion of the country depended not just on the state, but also on the society. There were regional differences between different parts of China in the culture, history, and ethnic origin of the people and in the physical environment, leading to differences in the economy. A united China with a high degree of cohesion, particularly as the territory controlled by the dynasties in China expanded, was a developing process that took a long time in the making. Factors contributing to this process included the Sinicization of non-Chinese peoples, the Qin-Han policy of settling Chinese in military colonies on the frontiers, and the institutions devised by various dynastic central authorities, refined over the centuries, to govern and control the far-flung regions. The frequent invasion of the nomadic tribes after the collapse of the Han dynasty led to significant population movement of Han Chinese from north China to the south. As mentioned previously, the court of the Jin dynasty fled south when the Xiongnu took Luoyang and re-established itself in a new capital at Jiankang. Many northern Chinese aristocratic families also moved south, inserting themselves into south China as an upper-class ruling elite.

For nearly two hundred years during the Great Disunion, there was a clear political division between north and south China with the Huai River as the line of demarcation. This was the time of the Northern and Southern dynasties. The Northern dynasties, with rulers of nomadic tribal origin, occupied the Yellow River basin region that contained the North China plain, the core area of the ancient Three Dynasties which had achieved cultural and political dominance. The Southern dynasties, which began with the migrant Eastern Jin, controlled the Yangtze River basin, a more sparsely settled area with the local population made up of various semi-Sinicized tribal groups with their own language and customs. The agricultural economy of the warm and watery south was based on rice, whereas millet and wheat were the northern staples. The regional differences tended to undermine political unity, unless a strong regime ruling from north China managed to keep a firm grip on the south. For decades during the time of disunion, the more militaristic Northern dynasties were too devastated to conquer the prosperous and politically more tranquil south. In 383 CE when the Northern Qian Qin emperor, Fu Jian, attempted to invade Eastern Jin with a massive cavalry force, he was resoundingly defeated by the far smaller force of his southern adversaries, who were fighting for survival. This won the Southern dynasties a respite from Northern aggression until 581 CE, when the Sui dynasty, starting from the north, united China once more.

The Sui Dynasty (581 – 618 CE)

The post-Han armed struggle for ascendancy lasted well over three centuries. The length of this interregnum may be attributed to the fact that north China sustained much economic damage and population loss from the unprecedented waves of invasion of different nomadic tribes, in addition to natural disasters and civil wars among the Chinese themselves. The population loss was not simply due to mortality caused by those events; they also triggered large-scale internal migrations of the Han Chinese who fled *en masse* from north China to areas south of the Yangtze River. Many great northern aristocratic families, *men di*, together with other bearers of the Han Chinese culture, also uprooted themselves and went south. These movements contributed to the increase in agricultural production south of the Yangtze and helped to Sinicize non-Han ethnic groups in southern China.

The relative peace and prosperity enjoyed by the southern dynasties did not incline them to invade north China, from where the winners of contests for supreme power in China appeared to have originated so far. Surrounded by warlike nomadic tribes to the north, northeast and northwest, Chinese rulers with their capitals situated traditionally in this region were obliged to develop strong military forces and be prepared to defend their territory against frequent tribal incursions. The north China plain had been the scene of much large-scale warfare. During the period of the Great Disunion, Chinese rule in the north succumbed to the more militaristic nomadic tribal leaders, many of whom, as we have seen, chose to adopt Han Chinese culture and style of government. This marriage of nomad military vigour with Chinese statecraft bore fruit.

The unification of China that ended the absence of central authority did indeed come from north China. After this region had sufficiently recovered from the ill effects of the wars and disorder, all that was needed was the emergence of a capable and ambitious leader from a powerful northern dynasty, who was able to mobilize massively the economic and human resources of this region to embark on a war of conquest of rival regimes, both north and south. Yang Jian, the product of the successful union of a Chinese aristocratic family from the ancient Chinese heartland and a leading nomad clan, was such a leader. As a senior military commander of Northern Zhou, the last of the northern dynasties, he led victorious military campaigns that destroyed Northern Zhou's competitors in the north before he usurped the throne and founded the Sui dynasty in 581 CE, as Emperor Wen. In 589 CE, his army brought about the demise of the Chen, the last of the southern dynasties. The Sui dynasty (581-618 CE) brought an end to the relatively long period of strife that characterized the Great Disunion, and restored peace to a once more unified empire, encompassing the large territories of what were the northern and southern dynasties.

Wen's ambition to rule the united empire was matched by a capacity for the role. In the areas of government administration, he pursued an innovative approach while seeking

Map of the territory of the Sui Dynasty (*Wikipedia*: retrieved on 8 April 2024 from https://en.wikipedia.org/wiki/Sui_dynasty#/media/File:Cheui_Dynasty_581_CE.png)

inspiration from the past. He re-invigorated the use of the examination system for official recruitment. His methodically structured central government with separate ministries and well-defined functions has a modern ring. This system stood the test of time as it was adopted by later dynasties, many of which also continued to use the preventive measures against corruption that Wen introduced. In consideration of the people's livelihood and government revenue, he fostered agriculture and re-instated the 'equal field' system of land tenure that had been used in the more distant past. Having the resources of the entire country at his command, he embarked on many major public works, among which were the rebuilding of both the capitals at Chang'an and Luoyang. Between these great cities, huge granaries were constructed. To keep the nomad raiders out, the Great Wall was further extended. Despite funding such a major public works programme and absorbing the expenses of a strong military stance against insubordinate frontier states, he managed to reduce taxes, and his reign left a legacy of economic prosperity and full granaries to his successor.

Emperor Yang (r. 604-618 CE), who ascended to the throne following a succession dispute, pursued public works with even more enthusiasm. He was faulted by future generations for lavishing enormous expense on building luxurious palaces and enormous parks for his personal pleasure, and for his megalomaniacal display of power and grandeur. Yang was compared with the first emperor of Qin for making excessive demands on the resources of the country for gigantic construction schemes and military campaigns. As the Qin emperor was remembered for connecting and extending the ancient Great Wall, Yang's monument was the Grand Canal, a premodern feat of water engineering. The Sui Grand Canal was approximately 1,750 kilometres long and 40 metres wide, with an imperial road running parallel to it. There were also imperial resting places and relay-post stations liberally dotted along it. It started at Hangzhou in southeast China, traversing in a northeast direction and crossing the Yangtze River to reach the prosperous city of Yangzhou. From there it headed north to Kaifeng and the region of Luoyang, Sui's eastern capital. Then it continued on to Chang'an, the western capital, before eventually turning northeast to end at Beijing.

Constructing such a canal was only conceivable in a unified China. A principal driving force behind this project was to enable the politically dominant north to exploit the rich economic resources of the south, grain in particular, to support the large population in the region of the two capitals and beyond. Between these populous cities, huge granaries were located, with a capacity for storing 33 million bushels of grain. While north China was suitable for farming cereals, such as wheat, millet, and barley on dry fields, south China's warm climate and water-rich environment lent itself to wet rice farming. During the three centuries preceding the Sui unification, the economy of the region of the Yangtze estuary and plain had developed rapidly, largely as a result of the mass movement of people from north China into this area. Many had been displaced by wars and included families of the vanquished ruling elite. The Grand Canal was of vital importance for the shipment of grain from the abundant rice-producing regions in south China to support the capitals and the troops at the frontiers. In addition to rice, much silk, salt, and tea was produced in south China, and these too were transported along the Grand Canal to the north and from there via the Silk Road to foreign countries in the west. This man-made waterway, together with the lakes and rivers it incorporated on its way, formed a vital economic artery between northern and southern China.

The re-establishment of a strong central authority in China usually signalled a re-adjustment of its relationships with the neighbouring countries. The states that had been willing to pay homage to the Son of Heaven in this East Asian 'Universal Empire', or accept the status of being his vassals, tended to break away from the Chinese orbit when the empire became weakened or fell apart. Faced with the challenge of re-asserting Chinese control of the once submissive frontier regions, the two Sui emperors forced the tribal regimes in the northwest and in the extreme south to return to the Chinese fold. Emperor Yang, for example, despatched troops to Liuqiu to subdue this island. Neither of them succeeded in imposing Sui suzerainty over Gaoli (Korea), however, though military forces as large as a million men were massed for this purpose.

Like the first emperor of the Qin, Emperor Yang's overambitious construction projects and military campaigns, particularly the failed military efforts to subdue Gaoli, severely strained the human resources of the country, and consequently peasant uprisings and aristocratic rebellions spread rapidly, leading to the rapid decline of his reign, and with it the Sui dynasty. Among the rebels was a commander of Yang's army, Li Yuan, who marched into the capital Chang'an and forced Yang to abdicate in 618 CE. In that year, Li Yuan installed himself as the head of a new dynasty, the Tang.

The Tang Dynasty (618 - 907 CE)

Like the Sui rulers, Li Yuan and his successor, Li Shimin, were descended from a similar north China mixed lineage of Chinese aristocratic and nomad clans, and were well equipped to fight and to govern. Unlike the long hiatus in central authority between the Han and the Sui, the transition between Sui and Tang was brief, more like a succession within the same ruling house than a transfer of power from one to another. At its beginning, the newly proclaimed Tang dynasty did not remain unchallenged by other contenders for supreme power, but within seven years, Li Shimin defeated all his rivals and consolidated Tang power in a once more united empire.

The Tang dynasty started with many advantages: two magnificent refurbished capitals, the Grand Canal, and a unified empire – all its predecessor's achievements. Capping this promising beginning, Li Shimin, the second Tang emperor with the reign title of Taizong

(r. 626-649), turned out to be a strong ruler. As regards government institutions, he had already inherited a relatively mature and finely tuned instrument for central and regional government. With the help of a group of distinguished advisors, he modified and re-organized both the central and regional governments to tailor them into even more effective instruments for his purposes, and for the needs of his time. Schools and academies of different levels were set up in provincial cities and at the capital, to train potential civil servants in the Confucian classics for entering government service. A comprehensive code of law laying down the penalties covering various types of offences was compiled and twice revised during his reign. On the economic front, he adopted a system of equal distribution of plots of land (*juntian*) to peasants, with life-tenure, to enable them to support themselves and to pay taxes and render labour services to the state. On military matters, he enlarged the *fubing* system of militias used in the Northern Zhou (557-581 CE) to include not just professional military families but also peasant recruits. Those who served in the militia enjoyed tax exemption, but they had to provide their own food and military equipment. Since horses played a vital part in any military conflict with the people of the steppes, the Tang set aside large pastures for stud-farms, and went into horse breeding in a serious way, raising as many as 700,000 horses in the middle of the seventh century, before nomad incursions made it very difficult for the Chinese to continue to do so.

With the empire internally at peace and well-ordered, the early Tang rulers, Taizong and his successor Gaozong (r. 649-683 CE), had the economic strength, political power, and military preparedness to take a strong position towards the border states, particularly the different nomadic tribal powers formed in the north, northeast, and northwest of the empire, where incursions often occurred. The Turks, who founded empires of the steppes in northwest China and Central Asia during the middle of the sixth century, were especially menacing to the Tang around this time. Between 629 and 630 CE, the Tang forces defeated the Eastern Turks, and other nomadic tribal armies that threatened the Tang's security or that of its allies or protectorates. The Chinese drive secured the trade and communication of oasis towns and cities along the Silk Road, and it had such a momentum that the Tang military and political presence was felt on the far side of the Pamirs in Central Asia, all the way to Persia. When the powerful kingdom of Tibet sent a force to invade a Chinese-pacified nomad area, the Tang stopped its advance. Good neighbourly relationships were restored when Taizong accepted the marriage proposal of the Tibetan king to a Tang princess in 641 CE. The marriage of King Songtsen Gampo and Princess Wencheng was a success, since it brought peace between the two empires for a while, and it facilitated the transfer of Chinese knowledge and technology to Tibet. Tang miliary prowess brought Manchuria, the Korean peninsula, and northern Vietnam under Chinese control. This vast territory conquered by force was organized into six military protectorates, *Duhu Fu*. These were Anxi (in modern-day Kansu), Annam (northern Vietnam), Andong (northeastern China and Korea), Anbei (in northwestern Ordos), Beiting (Urumqi) and

Shanyu (northeastern Ordos). The extensive military thrusts supported by administrative organization and diplomatic activities during the seventh and the first half of the eighth century made Tang China the greatest power in Asia, meeting and halting the eastward Arab advance during that time.

Map of the territory of the Tang dynasty (*Wikipedia*: retrieved on 8 April 2024 from https://en.m.wikipedia.org/wiki/File:Map_of_the_Tang_Empire_and_its_Protectorates_circa_660_CE.png)

The Tang expansion into Central Asia secured the commercial and communication links between East Asia and this region, facilitating the two-way exchange of goods and cultural influences between east and west. The seventh century Tang capital at Chang'an was a grand cosmopolitan city without peer. Among its two million inhabitants, half of whom lived outside the city wall, there were foreigners from Central Asia and many other lands, including Persians, Sogdians, Indians, Arabs, Jews, Nestorian Christians, and Japanese, bringing with them foreign produce, arts, and religions.

Buddhism in early China

The foreign import that had the greatest impact on China was Buddhism from India. Its introduction to China around the beginning of the Christian era was closely linked with foreign mercantile activities. Foreign merchants brought Buddhism to China through two types of trade routes. One was the Central Asian oasis overland route, and the other the Indo-Iranian Sea route from the Indian Ocean around Southeast Asia to China. According to Chinese records, by 65 CE a Buddhist community existed in northern Jiangsu. Two centuries later, the influence of Buddhism in China was still hardly noticeable. During the third and fourth centuries, Buddhist texts translated by bilingual monks of Central Asian origin caught the attention of some Chinese upper-class circles in the Southern Dynasties, as they found certain philosophical ideas in Buddhism corresponded with their own Taoist world view. In northern China, several rulers of nomad origin became believers and offered patronage to Buddhist monks. Some Taoists became interested in Buddhism because of its practice of meditation and yoga. After a slow start and a longish period of

Figure of the Maitreya Buddha, Dunhuang caves (c. 400 CE)
(*Vision Times*: retrieved on 30 November 2023 from
https://www.visiontimes.com/2022/11/13/dunhuang-caves-earthly-glimpse-other-worldly-realms.html)

gestation, during which better and fuller translations and interpretations of Buddhist texts became available, Buddhism began to take China by storm during the fifth century. From then onwards until the middle of the ninth century, it grew into the dominant religious force in Chinese life, at times over-shadowing Confucianism.

Around the middle of the fifth century, Buddhism became virtually a state religion in the Northern Wei dynasty through its rulers' enthusiastic support. Court patronage led to a situation where Buddhist institutions, such as monasteries, temples, schools, great shrines carved into rocks, and lay communities, flourished near the capital, which was first at Datong and later at Luoyang. In southern China, it grew at first through the leadership of scholarly monks and the support of aristocratic converts. As a result, the centres of Buddhist activities were not concentrated at the sites of one or two capital cities but were more scattered. Because of the largesse of rich and powerful patrons, Buddhist monasteries and lay communities became owners of large estates that were governed by their own rules and were exempt from the taxes, labour, and military services normally imposed by the state. Their autonomy extended to being free from the application of the State's penal code. During the high tide of Buddhist religious fervour, there were many pilgrimages by Chinese monks, who undertook the arduous journey through the Central Asian oases to Kashmir and India (though some took the sea route), to learn from Indian masters and to obtain Buddhist scriptural texts. 'New Translations', *xinyi*, made in the Tang dynasty, were carried out as teamwork with division of labour and careful checking to exacting standards, and these were accompanied by voluminous bibliographical catalogues.

The appeal of Buddhism was not limited to the rulers and the elite of the society. As a religion of universal salvation, it had mass appeal. The Buddhism that had taken hold in China had already undergone a process of adaptation to, and assimilation of, Chinese traditional ideas, morality, and ways of worship. The translation of the texts itself unavoidably gave rise to a certain amount of Sinicization. Its attraction to the Chinese was not that it was foreign, but that it contained elements that resonated with and echoed what was already familiar and understood by the Chinese. The foreign elements that succeeded in inserting themselves into Chinese Buddhism were accepted as sources of enrichment, rather than as upsetting or unsettling influences. For example, the worship of ancestors and the Earth God could easily accommodate the worship of the Buddhist pantheon of the Bodhisattvas and Buddhas. There was no need for them to be mutually exclusive. The Buddhism that conquered China was an amalgam of Chinese and foreign religious ideas and practices, a syncretistic product also containing elements of Taoism and Confucianism. As a result, Buddhism existed, on the whole, peacefully in China, alongside local religions like Taoism and philosophical schools like Confucianism.

The enormous success of Buddhism during the height of its popularity in China probably contributed to its undoing. Apart from suppression by the government of peasant rebellions marching under the banners of religious cults, traditional China was relatively free from wars over religious differences[2]. There had not been any war between the adherents of Taoism and Buddhism, but rivalry between these two groups existed. Taoist jealousy of the wealth, power, and privileges of the Buddhist church, led to two instances of persecution of the Buddhists by certain monarchs in northern China. In any case, the expansion of the autonomous Buddhist religious community that deprived the state of taxation and jurisdiction was bound to come into conflict with the interest of the state. Under the Tang dynasty, the revived imperial bureaucracy, whose education was cast in the Confucian mould, moved to bring the Buddhist church under firm state control through administrative regulations. For example, the government took over the function of the issue of ordination certificates. For a monk to be ordained, he would need to be educated well enough to pass examinations not only on Buddhist canons but also on Confucian classics. During the ninth century, particularly around the time of the well-remembered persecution in 842-845 CE, the Tang authorities made attempts to reduce and restrict the amount of property held by Buddhist churches, as well as the number of monks, some of whom were forced to return to the laity. Buddhism's foreign origin did not help its cause when society's mood that had earlier been receptive to foreign influences instead turned antipathetic. In general, without a centralized state-wide organization (or large regional ones), supported by an active and politicized lay congregation, neither the Buddhist nor the Taoist churches could mount a substantial challenge to the authority of the state. Not surprisingly, the kind of struggle for power between Church and State known in Western Christendom did not occur in China. Buddhist and Taoist temples and priesthoods existed as local religious expressions in China, and they depended on the support of the local communities; they lacked the capacity to challenge the authority of the ruling government.

The persecutions, particularly the 842-845 CE proscription under the Tang, undermined the autonomy of the Buddhist religious institutions and its free expansion in China. From the middle of the ninth century onwards, the Buddhist fervour subsided in China, but that was not entirely or even largely due to the temporary expression of official hostility. The political, social, and economic situation that favoured the reception, adoption, and expansion of this religion of foreign origin in Chinese life from the fifth to the ninth centuries, had changed so much that the social fabric which had helped Buddhism spread had become weakened. However, it was not going to vanish from the Chinese scene. The Buddhism that had undergone transformation in China had also transformed China itself permanently and was there to stay. This religion had important effects on many aspects of Chinese life: social, political, economic, and cultural. The Chinese landscape had been changed by the presence of Buddhist temples, pagodas, and statues, large and small, carved out of rocks, and by religious wall paintings in rocky grottoes or shrines. It was a source of enrichment that exercised a profound influence on Chinese literature, art, and artistic sen-

---

[2] The nineteenth century Taiping Rebellion based on a Christian cult might be considered an exception, though the rebellion was not entirely motivated by religion.

sibility, as well as on the Chinese worldview as embodied in a new kind of Confucianism developed in a later period. Its religious ideas and practices inspired the development of the Taoist churches and the pantheon of Taoist deities. It promoted charitable activities of a more public and universalistic kind outside the close family network. Its beliefs and moral precepts modified peoples' behaviour and even their dietary habits: for example, some people practised fasting, or avoided eating animal products at certain periods, or became entirely vegetarians.

At a time when the Buddhist influence was still strong during the Tang dynasty, Empress Wu Zetian, the wife of the third Tang emperor Gaozong (r. 649-683 CE), made herself the sovereign ruler of a new dynasty called the Zhou, a few years after her husband's death. In a male dominated society such as China, a strong empress had been known to exercise power through her husband or her son, as dowager empress. Empress Zetian's reign (690-705 CE) was unprecedented, and no woman ever ruled as emperor in China again. She was a devout Buddhist and a great benefactress of the Buddhist church. Besides her extraordinary political skill, her cause must have been helped by the Buddhist prediction that she was a reincarnation of the Bodhisattva Maitreya and was destined to be emperor. Zetian's claim of divine origin is reminiscent of Hatshepsut (r. 1478/9 – 1458 BCE), ancient Egypt's only female pharaoh, who also claimed divine ancestry to support her right to rule. During Empress Zetian's reign, and even before she assumed formal control, she endeavoured to destroy the power of the north-western aristocracy, which together with the royal Li clan had managed the affairs of the Tang empire from its beginning; many of them were executed under her orders. She gave more opportunity for the elite families of the old North China plain to participate in government, and she revitalized and reorganized the examination system for entry into government service.

The later Tang, An Lushan Rebellion, and the fall of the Tang

After Empress Zetian's death, the Tang dynasty was restored in 705 by her son Zhongzong (r.705-710 CE), who was soon murdered by his consort, Empress Wei. Fortunately for the Tang, Emperor Xuanzong (r.712-756 CE), who killed Empress Wei and took over the throne from his father, was an able monarch. He energetically and effectively put the affairs of the government in good order, and was popularly acclaimed as the Brilliant Emperor, Ming Huang[3]. For nearly half a century he presided cover the 'golden age' of the Tang dynasty. Tang China's prestige and influence in Asia reached its peak. It was a period of relative peace and prosperity. The highly accomplished Tang works in scholarship, art, and literature, poetry in particular, greatly enriched the Chinese culture.

During Xuanzong's long reign, serious societal changes had taken place, and a re-organization of the military system became necessary. The military aristocracy and the con-

---

[3] The Chinese character Ming, as in the Ming dynasty, can also be translated as 'enlightened'.

Tang dynasty glazed earthenware camel. Courtesy of the Asian Art Museum, The Avery Brundage Collection. (*Khan Academy*: retrieved on 8 April 2024 from https://www.khanacademy.org/humanities/art-asia/imperial-china/tang-dynasty/a/an-introduction-to-the-tang-dynasty-618906)

scripted *fubing* militia had combined successfully to enable the Tang dynasty to become a formidable military power and carve out the greatest empire in Asia during the seventh century. But the aristocracy had settled into a long-term decline and the *fubing* militia could no longer be relied upon to defend the realm. To remedy the situation, the frontiers were divided into military regions guarded by military governors or generals, each commanding a professional fighting force of mercenary soldiers. This system was not without shortcomings, partly because of its high cost, but more importantly because of the enormous power of the generals, who could act independently of, or even become a threat to, the central government.

By the middle of the eighth century, the emperor in his twilight years fell in love with a beautiful young imperial concubine Yang Guifei, and became engrossed in amorous activities with her rather than attending to state affairs. There was a disastrous competition for the prime ministership between Yang Guozhong, a powerful cousin of Yang Guifei, and the ambitious Sogdian general, An Lushan, a favourite of the emperor and of Yang Guifei. An Lushan was made the military governor of three frontier regions, with a large army under his control. When Yang Guozhong became the prime minister, An Lushan marched with 150,000 troops to capture Chang'an, causing the emperor and his court to flee from the capital. The rebellion started by An Lushan in 755 CE devastated the country before it finally ended in 763 CE. The Tang dynasty never fully recovered from this severe blow.

Even before the rebellion, troubles on the frontiers were already brewing. In 751 CE, defeat by the advancing Arabs forced the Tang to relinquish control of the Pamirs and territory further to the west. During the second half of the eighth century, the kingdom of Silla in Korea in the northeast declared itself independent of the Tang, and in the southwest, the kingdom of Nanchao in present-day Yunnan extracted territorial concessions and the control of communication lines to Vietnam from China. Meanwhile, the Tibetans were advancing into the western part of the empire, and periodically their forces threatened Chang'an. With the growing powers of the semi-nomadic Uyghur Turks in the northwest, and with the Arabs controlling the Kashgar region, the territories west of the Yumen Pass were lost to the Tang. The high tide of Tang Chinese expansion that began in 630 CE receded by the middle of the eighth century, and the empire was rolled back from its outlying regions.

The Tang dynasty limped on after these setbacks and continued to provide the political superstructure over a Chinese society that was undergoing momentous changes underneath it. One of these changes was the shift of the economic centre of gravity from the dry farming (wheat, millet, and barley) of the north China plain to the wet rice farming of the Yangtze basin. The waves of southward migration that had started during the period of the Great Disunion contributed to this change and produced by late Tang a shift in the centre of gravity of the population to south China. The equal-field system used in early Tang to provide the farmers with land and the government with taxes became increasing untenable, particularly in the rice growing regions. In recognition of this reality, in 780 CE the Tang government overhauled its policy on taxation from taxing the person (as was used in all the preceding dynasties) to taxing the land. Subsequent dynasties also adopted this fiscal approach.

Another significant change was the decline of the endogamous aristocracy, which constituted the ruling elite, meaning the people of a particular social stratum who served as government officials under a given dynasty. In imperial China power, wealth, and high social standing were normally associated with being in the service of the government. Although members of this group were mostly not hereditary nobles as under the pre-Qin feudalism, a way had been found to perpetuate their privileged position in society that lasted several hundred years, going back to the Northern and Southern dynasties in the fourth century, and through to the Sui-Tang unification and beyond. These dynasties kept lists of great families or lineages, nomad clans included, from whose ranks government officials were chosen. These lineages made marriage alliances within their own narrow circles and networked with one another politically. The Tang founders remade the lists in favour of the mixed nomad-Chinese aristocracy of the northwest, like themselves. Among these illustrious lineages, the imperial Li clan stood out as *primus inter pares*. Empress Wu decimated the aristocratic clans of the northwest and advanced the interests of the old Chinese families of the northeast. She also strengthened the system of official selection through examination. Although the examination provided some opportunities for ambitious outsiders to rise socially, most of the officials came nevertheless from the long-established office-holding lineages. Because of the Chinese practice of partible inheritance (division of an estate among all the male heirs, as opposed to primogeniture) members of these families needed to enter and re-enter government service without long generation gaps if they were to maintain their high social and economic positions.

After An Lushan's rebellion, from the middle of the eighth century, certain events and developments militated against the interest of this upper-class society, making it very difficult for them to keep their social and economic ascendancy. One was the division of the country into many military regions, not just at the frontier, but also into the interior. This was the policy adopted by the weakened court for the sake of maintaining order and security, but a high price had to be paid for it. These regional military governors, who controlled their own troops and revenue from taxes, became increasingly independent of the centre. Although the succession of the Tang emperors in Chang'an took place as usual for another one hundred and fifty years, the court could only control a small sector of the country, which, in addition to the region around the capital, fortunately included the rich rice-producing lower Yangtze and Huai River basins. As time went on the country became more militarized and regionalized. The military governors were likely to have been self-made militarists (rather than central appointees), who rose to the top because they had proved themselves in the arena of war and had the loyalty and support of their troops. They ruled their regions with a high degree of autonomy, organized their own civilian administration, and used local staff. This development greatly reduced the career opportunities of the aristocratic lineages, whose declining fortunes reflected the dwindling power of the court. Furthermore, these once powerful and wealthy clans were not spared the effects of the devastating civil disorder caused by a savage itinerant rebellion led by a bandit chief named Huang Chao. From 875 to 884 CE, his horde of outlaws raged up and down the empire, plundering, pillaging, and wreaking havoc in their wake. The trail of destruction covered the areas in and around the two capitals, Chang'an and Luoyang, where many of the estates of the aristocratic families were located. Finally, in 907 CE, a military governor, who was a former rebel himself, ended the Tang Dynasty officially by setting himself up as the emperor of the Later Liang, with its capital at Kaifeng, in the province of Henan. The fall of the Tang brought the Chinese aristocratic era to a close.

References

A General History of China (in Chinese), by Bai Shouyi (Shanghai People's Publishing House, Shanghai, 1999).

A History of Chinese Civilization by Jacques Gernet (English Edition, Cambridge University Press, Cambridge, second edition 1996), chapters 1-13.

China: A History Volume 1 From Neolithic Cultures through the Great Qing Empire 10,000 BCE – 1799 CE by Harold M. Tanner (Hackett Publishing Company, Inc., Indianapolis/Cambridge, 2010), chapters 1-6.

Chapter 2

The Song Dynasty (960-1279)

The Song and the Nomadic Empires

The Song, the Liao, and the Western Xia (Xixia)

In 907[4] the Liang dynasty ushered in the break-up of the Tang, leading to the following periods known as the Five Dynasties and the Ten Kingdoms in the Chinese historical chronicles. This period of disunion was similar to the one at the end of the Han: the once unified empire broke down into a number of separate political entities, each of which claimed sovereignty within its own domain. But unlike the time of the Great Disunion after the Han, which lasted some three hundred years, this period of absence of central authority lasted less than eighty years. The Five Dynasties regimes ruled northern and central China sequentially during a period of fifty-three years, the last dynasty being the Later Zhou. Between 907 and 960, the Ten Kingdoms emerged, mainly in southern China, and sometimes overlapped with one another in time. Many of these corresponded with a natural regional boundary. They were all relatively unstable regimes, each lasting only a few decades, due to the incessant wars of conquest and annexation they waged against one another, and their vulnerability to the internal usurpation of supreme power by ambitious generals. A number of these kingdoms rose out of the Tang military regions, where some military governors, who were already the *de facto* rulers, simply proclaimed

---

[4] All dates will be assumed to be CE unless explicitly indicated otherwise.

regional sovereignty on the Tang's demise.

During this period of short-lived dynasties competing militarily for ascendancy, and especially for the prize of reuniting China, Zhao Kuangyin, an exceptionally capable military commander and an astute politician of the Later Zhou (951-960) dynasty, usurped the Zhou throne and in 960 set himself up at Kaifeng as the emperor (r. 960-976) under a new dynasty called the Song. The Later Zhou, already the dominant power in northern China, had been poised to annex other kingdoms, after putting in place a series of measures to promote economic reconstruction. Zhao Kuangyin and his successor completed what the Later Zhou had begun, after another two decades of fighting that culminated in the conquest of the Northern Han in 979. Unlike the Sui-Tang reunification of China, the Song empire did not incorporate territory in modern-day Korea, Mongolia, Manchuria, and central Asia. In 981, the Song expedition to regain Dai Co Viet (today's Vietnam) in the south was repelled. The kingdom of Dali, a successor state of Nan Zhao, prevented any Song expansion to the southwest.

While the Song dynasty had a territory about seven times that of modern France at the time when it unified China, its authority did not even extend to all of northern China. Unfortunately for the Song, during the tenth to the fourteenth centuries powerful empires

Map showing the territory of the Song and neighbouring dynasties, c. 1000
(*nationsonline.org*: retrieved on 26 November 2023 from
https://www.nationsonline.org/oneworld/map/Chinese_dynasties/Song_Dynasty_Map)

of nomadic or semi-nomadic peoples emerged to the north, northwest, and northeast of the Chinese domain. Among these was the empire of the Qidan, called Liao (916-1125). The Qidan were a semi-nomadic Mongolian people, whose territory ranged between Manchuria and Inner Mongolia. The Liao emperor presided over a state the southern part of which included the Sixteen Prefectures of Yanyun, which comprised parts of present-day Beijing, Tianjin, Hebei, and Shanxi. A Chinese-style civil bureaucracy governed this area. While the south had an agricultural economy, the much larger northern part had a pastoral economy of the steppe, and men on horseback ruled it. This area provided some 600,000 cavalry troops, organized into mobile units called ordos (which gave rise to 'horde' in English). Trials by strength on the battlefield between the warlike Qidan mounted archers and the Song forces convinced the latter that it was preferable to buy peace, rather than have a continual state of war with the Liao. In 1004 the Liao, also exhausted by war, accepted peaceful co-existence, but at a price. A treaty was concluded between the two states. The Song agreed to pay annually 200,000 rolls of silk and 100,000 ounces of silver to the Liao, so that a friendly treaty was concluded between the two 'brotherly' states, with the Song emperor Zhenzong being the older brother (meaning a more respected senior status, in Confucian terms). Both sides kept to the terms of the treaty for over four decades. In 1042, the Song's military weakness was once more exposed by their being defeated by another neighbouring state, the Western Xia (Xixia). The Liao took the opportunity to extract from the Song an additional annual 'tribute' of 100,000 rolls of silk and 100,000 ounces of silver, as the price of keeping the peace between them.

Towards the last decades of the tenth century when the newly founded Song dynasty was endeavouring to unite the Chinese lands, Li Jiqian (963-1004), the scion of a leading clan of a formerly nomadic people called the Tangut, nursed an ambition to carve out a kingdom independent of the Song in northwestern China. This region had been settled by the Tangut, and it also had other tribal populations, such as Tibetans, Mongols, and Turks, with Chinese scattered among them. Through decades of inter-tribal politics, wars, and alliances, and years of persistent military campaigns against the Song, Li Jiqian and his son Li Deming (981-1032) succeeded in establishing the kingdom of Western Xia in a territory that was situated at the southwest of the Liao and northwest of the Song empires. Sandwiched between the two larger neighbours, the rulers of the Western Xia learned to play one against the other. Since they were often at war with the Song, they accepted the position of being subordinate in terms of diplomatic formalities while not actually under the control of the emperor of the Liao, to gain recognition and to keep peace with this northern regime. To build an even closer relationship, they formed marriage alliances with the Liao royal family, marrying Liao princesses. Although there were occasional disputes between the Liao and the Western Xia that led to military combat, on the whole peace was maintained.

Both these states to the north of the Song desired the latter's wealth in agricultural and other resources and tried to overwhelm their southern neighbour by force of arms. The Song doggedly resisted these aggressors to keep its territory intact, winning a military victory now and again amid many setbacks. In 1006, the Song changed its hard stance against the Western Xia and offered to conclude a peace treaty with this upstart power on generous terms, though not from a position of weakness. The Song bestowed official and kingly titles on Li Deming, with gifts of silver, silk, and teas, as well as other symbolic and material gifts valued by people of this region. At the Western Xia's request, the Song also agreed to maintain markets at certain border posts for commercial exchanges between their subjects. In the treaty, the word *feng* was used as the bestowal of official titles and the word *ci* as the giving of gifts. These were expressions normally used by an emperor to his subjects. Acceptance of Song official titles and gifts in such terms rendered the Western Xia subordinate to the Song as a state. Like the relationship between Western Xia and the Liao, the subordination was in form but not in substance. The Western Xia functioned as an entirely independent sovereign state. The treaty did secure peace for over three decades between these two neighbours.

In 1032, Li Deming's son, Li Yuanhao, an ambitious empire builder, ascended the throne of the Western Xia. He enlarged the territory of the Western Xia by annexing independent tribal areas in his vicinity through military force. After he had brought under his control the entire region called the corridor west of the Yellow River (*Hexi Zoulang*), which covered the modern Gansu province, he set up a capital and various military and civilian institutions for governance. Then in 1038 he made himself the emperor of the Great Xia - an empire as distinct from a mere kingdom – with much pomp and pageantry. He also exhibited a remarkable ethnic consciousness in seeking to lessen the cultural influences of the Tang and Song dynasties, by adopting and promoting a Western Xia writing script for official and general use in his empire. Documents transmitted between the Western Xia and the neighbouring Song and Liao empires would be written in both Chinese and Western Xia languages. He abolished the Chinese surnames of Li and Zhao given by Chinese emperors of the Tang and Song dynasties to the Tangut royals and adopted traditional tribal names instead. He also purged music, customs, and ceremonial usage of excessive Chinese influence. His decrees even included how his subjects should attire themselves: the emperor and his officials of different grades were dressed each in their regulated clothing styles, while the commoners were only allowed to wear dark green clothes. With the emperor in the lead, Tangut men were ordered to shave their heads. Despite his effort to diminish Chinese cultural influences, he still saw the need to adopt Song administrative institutions in governing his empire. His descendants in the twelfth century had no such ethnic scruples, and some were enthusiastic about embracing the Confucian culture and institutions of the Song.

Having made these changes, Li Yuanhao requested the Song to grant him formal recognition. The Song court not only refused to grant his request; it stripped him of his official titles and, as an insult, posted warrants for his arrest along the border between the two countries, with high rewards to those who captured him. Subsequently, the warlike emperor of Western Xia, who did not seem to have a high opinion of the Song's military prowess, was preparing to fight the Song. From 1040 to 1042, the Western Xia attacked the Song many times and won three major victories. With the outbreak of hostilities, the Song closed the border markets, ceased to purchase salt produced in Western Xia, and stopped the annual gifts of money, silk, and tea to that country. Even if the Song economic sanctions did not ruin the Western Xia economy, high price inflation and severe shortages of goods, including daily necessities, appeared as the wars proceeded. The economic hardship and the mounting toll of people suffering death or injury produced a war weariness in the people of Western Xia, making it difficult for its ruler to continue his policy of aggression, despite military triumphs.

In 1043, the emperor of the Western Xia made an overture to the Song court for peace. The other important party of the triangular relationship, namely the state of Liao, had not remained entirely quiescent during the military conflict between the Western Xia and the Song. As we have seen, the emperor of Liao demanded, with the threat of force, cessation of land (without success), and an increase of the annual tribute (successfully) from

The iron pagoda at Kaifeng (built in 1049)
(*visitourchina.com*: retrieved on 26 November 2023 from
https://www.visitourchina.com/kaifeng/attraction/iron-pagoda.html)

the Song. The Liao attempt to sabotage peace between their two neighbouring states failed. After over a year of negotiations, in 1044 a peace treaty was concluded, whereby the Song agreed to pay the Western Xia annually 72,000 ounces of silver, and more rolls of silk and catties of tea, but refused to cede any territory. Trade was restored between them at the border markets as well as at the Song capital. Li Yuanhao would remain subordinate to the Song emperor as the ruler of the Western Xia, but to avoid kneeling and other gestures of obeisance, he would not receive the Song emissaries at his capital. These representatives of the Song emperor were instead directed to another appointed city.

Until the first decades of the twelfth century, an uneasy balance of power existed amongst these three states, with shifting alliances of one with another against the third. On the whole, peace prevailed between the Song and the Liao. Occasionally fighting broke out between the Western Xia and the Liao, without creating major political or territorial changes. Some Western Xia rulers after Li Yuanhao, particularly Xia empress dowager Liang, for internal political reasons waged war on the Song more than fifty times during the years from 1085 to 1099. In addition to military resistance, the Song would respond by stopping the annual gifts and by closing the trading posts. Without being able to make much headway on occupying Song territory, and facing the loss of the Song annual gifts, on the death of the empress dowager in 1099, the sixteen-year-old Western Xia emperor Chongzong put himself under the tutelage of the Liao emperor, ceased the invasions and border raids, and communicated to the Song his desire for peace, with the restoration of the annual gifts. The Song emperor at first rebuffed the Western Xia approach, but later accepted peace with the gifts to Western Xia, after the intervention of the Liao and further conciliatory gestures from the Western Xia.

Chongzong was a great admirer of the Confucian culture of the Chinese. He settled the century-old dispute within the Western Xia polity on whether to adhere to the indigenous culture of the northwest or that of the Chinese to the south, in favour of the latter. The ruling elites of the Western Xia were aware of the examples of other and earlier semi-nomadic empires, such as the Northern Wei (386-535), which had flourished in northern China with the wholesale adoption of the Han Chinese culture. Under Chongzong's reign peace prevailed for over a decade between the Western Xia and the Song until, starting in 1104, a new Song emperor Huizong, with a new prime minister Cai Jing, pursued a policy of territorial expansion against the Western Xia with limited success. For two decades thereafter, the two sides were intermittently at war or conducted negotiations for peace, until the attention of the leaders of both countries was drawn to a startling new development, which was the sudden and stunning rise of yet another semi-nomadic pastoral people, the Nuzhen (or Jurchen), in northeast China.

During the early years of the eleventh century, a dominant clan among the Nuzhen tribes called Wanyan took the lead in organizing their fellows, who were scattered in the territory of the Liao in northern Manchuria, into a tribal alliance. A well organized and regulated tribal alliance, with a governing council under a strong leadership, and with executive and coercive powers backed by military force, had often been the first step towards building a state or an empire by nomadic or semi-nomadic peoples of the Asian steppes. The head of a powerful tribal alliance would normally expect to be recognized by the neighbouring states or empires, which might confer official titles on him and conduct diplomatic relations with him with exchange of gifts, either on the basis of equality, or between superiors and inferiors depending on his relative status vis-à-vis the heads of the neighbouring countries. Such recognition would enhance the prestige and strengthen the position of the (normally hereditary) heads of the clan that led the tribal alliance. After one, two, or more generations of consolidation of power and expansion within the tribal areas, or further afield, the tribal alliance might be transformed into an empire, on the emergence of an exceptionally ambitious and capable leader, particularly in military matters. Wanyan Aguda (1068-1123), the founder of the Jin dynasty, a man noted for his prodigious physical strength and extraordinary accuracy in archery, was such a leader of the Nuzhen. When, at the age of forty-three, he succeeded his brother in 1113 as the leader of the Nuzhen tribal alliance, he had already proved himself as a seasoned warrior and a victorious military commander. In addition to being a gifted general, he was also a sound strategic planner, skilled in politics and diplomatic gamesmanship.

Enter the Jin

At this point, after nearly two centuries of ruling the vast expanse of the north-eastern corner of Asia, the Liao dynasty had declined in vigour. The Nuzhen tribes grew restive with the increasing exactions from their politically corrupt Liao overlords. When Wanyan Aguda decided to lead the Nuzhen tribes to revolt against the Liao, he took care to legitimize this move with ritual and ceremony, claiming it a righteous act against the exploitation and oppression under the rule of the Liao emperor, who had lost the Way (Dao). His emissaries also succeeded in persuading many other surrounding tribal groups to make common cause with the Nuzhen, so that he would not need to fight on many sides with many different enemies. Late in 1114, he led a modest army of a few thousand men against far larger numbers opposing him from the Liao side, and he won such resounding victories that at the beginning of 1115 the Nuzhen hailed him as their emperor. Thus began the Jin dynasty, with Wanyan Aguda reigning as Jin Taizu. As the war against the Liao continued to progress in the Jin's favour, with an expansion of territory and an increase in the number of troops, there was a need for Jin Taizu to consolidate his rule. This he did through restructuring the Nuzhen tribal organization under a military aristocracy, dominated by members of his own clan with slaves at its base. Under Jin Taizu and his successor, Jin Taizong, the Nuzhen tradition of slavery became institutionalized, but it was regulated in such a way as to offer opportunities for freedom, and to prevent people from being made slaves by force during chaotic times of military conflict or other crises. Excessive enslavement benefited the owners of slaves rather than the ruling dynasty, whose interest lay in having more farmers with smallholdings to cultivate the fields and to provide taxes. The reformed Nuzhen institutions were at first imposed on the conquered Liao territory, but with the conquest progressing apace, the Jin ruler soon decided to continue to use the Liao system of governance.

By 1120, the nature of the war against the Liao had changed from one of fighting against oppression to that of overthrowing the dynasty to form a united empire under the Jin. At this point it seemed to make strategic sense to Jin Taizu to conclude a treaty with the Song, promising to give the latter certain Liao territory if the Song would become allied with the Jin, and fight against the Liao. The Song agreed, but it would be a short-lived alliance. While the Liao remained at peace with the Song provided the latter paid the annual 'tribute' to it, the Jin turned out to be a much more aggressive adversary and one far more difficult to appease. In 1121, the Jin emperor focused his efforts on destroying the Liao and keeping the Song on his side. Despatching a major force against the Liao, the politician and propagandist in Jin Taizu announced to the commanding general that he was sent to wage a war of unification, and to strike down a dynasty that had been abandoned both by the gods and men because of its misrule. With their morale thus strengthened, within just one year in 1122, the Jin forces captured the three remaining capitals of the Liao, sending their once arrogant overlord on the run. As regards the people in the territory once controlled by the Liao, Jin Taizu ordered them to come forward to surrender themselves to the Jin rule: slaves surrendering before their masters would be freed, and those who led groups to surrender would be given official posts. Displaced persons were encouraged to return to their home villages, and agriculture was to be promoted. Many surrendered without a fight. The Jin turned over to the Song certain cities seized from the Liao in accordance with the above-mentioned treaty between them, but that was only after the Jin had carried away all the treasures, the wealthy clans, the artisans, and even the ordinary people from these places. In August 1123, Jin Taizu died before he had completed the conquest of the Liao.

Jin Taizong, who succeeded the Jin founder in 1123, sent troops in hot pursuit of the fleeing Liao emperor, in case he became a rallying point for Liao loyalists, or sought shelter in the Western Xia, whose ruler had taken a Liao princess as his concubine and had been friendly and supportive of the Liao emperor during this conflict. To induce the Western Xia to change sides, the Jin offered to cede to the Western Xia certain former Liao territory if the latter would maintain the same friendly subordinate state relationship with the Jin as it did with the Liao. An additional stipulation was that the Western Xia would hand over the Liao emperor to the Jin, should he flee to that country. This territorial inducement was difficult for the leader of the Western Xia to refuse; and in 1124 the Western Xia accepted the Jin terms and was able to extend its territory at the Liao's expense. In 1125, the Jin forces captured the Liao emperor and put an end to the Qidan dynasty that had ruled a large tract of territory in northern and northeastern China for over two hundred years since 916. Some Qidan aristocrats moved westward to parts of present-day Kazakhstan and Kyrgyzstan, where they set up the Western Liao empire.

In just ten years the leaders of a relatively obscure Nuzhen tribal alliance had led their people to overthrow the Liao dynasty and replace it with their own Jin dynasty. Since the Nuzhen tribal organization was not adequate to the task of administering all the territory now under Jin control, particularly the predominantly agricultural areas, the Jin rulers continued to use the Liao system of governance, with the participation of former Liao and Han Chinese officials. The Nuzhen were the forerunners of the Manchus who, several centuries later in 1644, began their conquest of the whole of China when the Ming dynasty went into terminal decline.

After taking over considerable lands of the Liao empire – except for a few limited former Liao areas which the Jin allowed Western Xia to take – the Jin rulers did not rest content with their gains. Before 1125 ended, the Jin leaders were already focusing their attention on the militarily weak but materially rich Song empire as the next target to subjugate by force. Early in 1126, Jin forces threatened Kaifeng, the Song capital, and emperor Song Huizong abdicated and fled the city. His successor, Song Qinzong, tried to appease the Jin by ceding territory, increasing the annual payment, and honouring the Jin emperor as 'uncle' in official exchanges. This brought the Song only a few months of respite before the Jin resumed the attack later in the year. Near the end of 1126, Song Qinzong surrendered after Kaifeng came under siege. A few months later, the Jin also captured Song Huizong and took the two Song emperors with their wives and retinues north.

At this point, unlike the Liao, the Song dynasty that had begun in 960 did not come to a complete end, even with the seizure of its capital and emperors. 1126 only marked the end of the Northern Song dynasty. In 1127 Zhao Gou, a son of the emperor Huizong, became emperor and reigned as Song Gaozong of the Southern Song. After a decade of escaping from the pursuing Jin forces, moving from city to city in southeast China, in 1138 Song Gaozong was finally able to set up his capital at the city of Lin'an (present-day Hangzhou) in southeastern China. Although Song Gaozong provided a rallying point for the people of China to rise and fight for their country, the credit for the survival of the Song dynasty at this point was largely due to the stout resistance of the regular military forces led by able generals and supported by armed bands.

In these desperate times, people in both northern and southern China had been swept up, by a certain patriotic fervour, into organizing themselves spontaneously as *yi jun*, righteous or loyalist armies, to fight the Jin invaders; bandits and displaced persons also joined the ranks. Under continuous Jin aggression, the more pugnacious among the Southern Song commanders had become toughened by frequent engagements against Jin forces, which earlier on had inspired such fear amongst Song army officers that they had tended to retreat or escape rather than fight. In less than a decade, a crop of Southern Song generals had won fame fighting the Jin. Many of these joined the Song military through enlistment as militiamen or common soldiers and rose from the ranks on merit. They were able not only to stand up to Jin military assaults: some of them were eager to turn the tables on the Jin by advancing into the territory controlled by their adversary. Yue Fei was an outstanding example. In 1140, during a two-months drive north, Yue Fei's troops time and again defeated the most powerful Jin forces amassed against them, and recovered many important cities in northern China, among which were Zhengzhou and Loyang, the western capital of Northern Song. Just as Yue Fei was poised to recover Kaifeng, the Northern Song capital, he had to pull back reluctantly on the strict orders of the Song prime minister, Qin Hui, who adamantly pursued a policy of appeasement towards the Jin. Equally strong for the opposite policy stood Yue Fei, who was among the most ardent of the Southern Song generals and officials wishing to recover the Northern Song lands, and to reject any humiliating Jin terms for peace.

After destroying the Northern Song and installing a Jin puppet regime in its place, the Jin were bent on the conquest of the entire Chinese lands. At the beginning of the reign of Song Gaozong, a Southern Song prime minister and other officials conceived a plan for *zhong xing*, meaning the recovery of the old Song capital and northern China by fighting the Jin. But being the successor of the two Northern Song emperors who had been taken captive by the Jin, Gaozong did not really desire their return in case his own position was jeopardized. Although he had to appear to welcome the idea of *zhong xing*, he rejected proposals for taking a strong and active military stance against the Jin. The officials who took such a line were demoted, removed from power, or even put to death, while those who supported a negotiated peace with the Jin were given important posts. He chose flight instead of fight, and for many years he used Qin Hui, a ruthless politician with special links to the Jin, as prime minister to facilitate and promote a policy of appeasement, on which Qin Hui had built his official career. The Jin rulers tempted the Song with the prospect of peace, but they were not serious about it until the Song generals demonstrated their ability to defend their country. Several Southern Song commanders of large forces placed themselves strategically, and together they formed a strongly defended line south of the Huai River, halting further Jin advances. In any event, the Jin military found itself at a disadvantage operating in the unfamiliar terrain of the watery southern region of China. Between 1133 and 1136, a series of military offensives against the Southern Song by the Jin and its puppet Chinese regime met with nothing but setbacks. Concluding that waging war against the Song was past the point of diminishing returns, the Jin were ready, in 1137, to negotiate in earnest a treaty of peace with the Song court.

In its terms for peace the Jin, like the Liao before it, demanded a large annual subsidy of 250,000 taels of silver and 250,000 rolls of silk from the Song. Such payment was burdensome, but war could arguably have been worse. There was an additional condition that required the Song emperor to become a subject or vassal of the Jin. This condition was deeply humiliating to the Song, and it amounted to a surrender of sovereignty at a time when the Song military was fighting the Jin forces to a standstill. To sweeten the pill, the Jin emperor offered an inducement, which was to turn over to the Southern Song some of the territory of its puppet state in the north, considering that the Song emperor was himself about to accept the position of a puppet of the Jin. When the news broke, there was a huge outcry from Song officials, military leaders, and the public against signing such a demeaning treaty. Despite fierce opposition, the Song emperor and his prime minister, Qin Hui, did sign the peace treaty with the Jin in 1138. Just over a year later, in 1140, the Jin abrogated the treaty, and sent a large army to invade the Southern Song. The Song emperor quickly deployed his most able commanders to defend his realm, and defence was all that they were strictly meant to do. Because he and Qin Hui were still set on the course of making the peace treaty with the Jin work, he soon sent orders to the front, requesting the Song commanders, who were successfully beating back the Jin forces, not to pursue the enemies to the north but to retreat to a defensive line. All the Song generals retreated from the front, except for Yue Fei, whose troops had already marched northward, and in a brief span of about three months they won many victories and recovered many important former Northern Song cities. In the end, Yue Fei too was forced to pull back on urgent orders from Qin Hui.

Not being able to achieve its goal of destroying the Southern Song through military means, the Jin court responded positively to overtures from Qin Hui, who had once again been begging for peace. Yue Fei's military advance in North China constituted a threat to Qin Hui's appeasement policy. To show that he was serious about peace with the Jin, Qin Hui not only ordered the victorious Song generals, including Yue Fei, to draw back from the front but also relieved them of their military commands. The peace treaty concluded in 1141 between the two countries included the same burdensome and dishonourable terms as the earlier one, but with one difference. It obliged the Song to return to the Jin some of the territory which the Jin had granted to the Song in the earlier treaty. As mentioned, the territory in question had once belonged to Jin's former puppet state in northern China. The triumphs and fighting spirit demonstrated by the Song military counted for little in the treaty negotiations. The weak-kneed Song emperor and Qin Hui, his prime minister, each had personal reasons to make peace with the Jin, however high the price, and however strong the internal opposition. In Qin Hui's mind, there was no room for Yue Fei in this scheme of things, and he had to be eliminated to satisfy the Jin commander, Wanyan Zonghi, and as a warning to others. Yue Fei, his son, and an aide were all executed on Qin Hui's orders, on a false charge of treason.

From that time onwards, there were leaders on the Jin side with renewed appetite for conquering the Southern Song, or on the Song side for seeking to recover the lost lands of the Northern Song, but neither side made significant headway militarily against the other. In 1208, their treaty-based state relationship took a worse turn for the Song, shortly after a Song commander surrendered to the Jin during a renewed 'Northern Expedition' against the Jin. Another Song prime minister with dictatorial powers killed the Song official leading the war against the Jin, as Qin Hui had done before him, and accepted peace with the Jin on exceedingly onerous terms. The treaty that was reached in 1208 increased the annual Song subsidy to the Jin from 200,000 taels of silver to 300,000 taels. In addition, the Jin exacted a huge and unprecedented bounty of three million taels of silver for their victorious army. There was also a clause that lowered the position of the Song vis-à-vis the Jin.

Not surprisingly the Mongols, a rapidly rising military power from the steppes of East Asia early in the thirteenth century, were able to exploit the bitter animosity between the Song and the Jin to persuade the former to join them as allies in their war against the Jin. From a strategic point of view, this turned out to be a mistake similar to the one the Northern Song had made a century earlier, when it allied itself with the upstart Jin to eliminate the Liao. The Mongol war machine had already put an end to the Western Xia in 1227, and in 1234 it destroyed the Jin. After the fall of the Jin, there was nothing that stood between the mighty Mongol hordes, driven by a lust for conquest, and the riches of the Southern Song. How the Mongols took over China under the Song will be treated in chapter 3.

The Military Weakness and the Cultural Strength of Song China

Military weakness

China during the Song exhibited extraordinary economic vitality, political dynamism, and cultural achievements, as we will shortly discuss, but its fatal military weakness cast a long shadow over the land. There appeared to be several reasons for the incapacity of the Song military. The founder of the Song dynasty, Zhao Kuangyin (emperor Taizu), was a military commander, who usurped the throne of the Later Zhou, whose ruler had himself usurped the throne of the Later Han. Usurpation, as well as military competition for ascendancy, provided the mechanisms behind the multiplicity and the rapid turnover of many kingdoms and dynasties that followed, after the Later Liang replaced the Tang Dynasty in 907. Given this historical background, the Song emperors tended to be wary and mistrustful of their military commanders, particularly the more capable and successful ones. They devised measures to prevent the regional military leaders from becoming too powerful or independent of the court. For example, Zhao Kuangyin relieved even his sworn brothers of their military commands and gave them civilian posts instead, after he consolidated power as the emperor of the new dynasty. This practice of taking away the generals' troops was still followed even during the time of Song Gaozong's reign, when the Song dynasty was in danger of being annihilated by the Jin. During the entire Song dynasty, the military officials were firmly under civilian control, both by the emperor and by the prime minister. The court's policy and practice of holding tight reins on the military commanders hindered the development of a strong Song military force.

There were other factors that contributed to the Song's military weakness. The Chinese dynasties that demonstrated periods of great military strength and extended their frontiers, such as the Han, the Sui, and the Tang before An Lushan's rebellion, based their fighting force on peasant militia or farmer-soldiers. The Song inherited the practice of using mercenaries, who could be ex-bandits, pardoned criminals, homeless migrants, or those with no means of subsistence, from the lower ranks of society. Not surprisingly, professional soldiers had very low social esteem, as attested by the familiar Chinese saying that good men do not become soldiers, any more than good iron would be made into nails. These soldiers tended to have poor discipline and fighting spirit, so despite being costly to maintain, they constituted an ineffective fighting force.

The semi-nomadic peoples who invaded the Song from the north were skilled at hunting, livestock breeding, and cavalry warfare. Fighting the mounted warriors from the steppes, the Han had found it necessary to buy horses from the Central Asia. The Tang, in addition to purchasing horses, also developed stud farms for breeding horses. In case of need, the Tang would resort to hiring foreign cavalry troops to augment their own. The rise of the Western Xia as an antagonist, controlling areas from where the Tang had once bred and sourced horses and hired foreign auxiliary troops, prevented the Song from doing likewise. The shortage of horses put the Song at a serious disadvantage in cavalry warfare, in which the people of the steppes excelled. These shortcomings made the Song vulnerable to military aggression from the semi-nomadic empires along its northern frontiers, stretching from Tibet to the sea.

Political reforms

The military weakness of the Song contrasted markedly with the strength of its developments in other areas. The Song dynasty (both Northern and Southern) presided over an age remarkable for innovative and creative activities in China. These encompassed the political, economic, social, and cultural fields. There was significant population expansion and growth in the economy, in commerce, and in wealth. It was a period of high cultural and intellectual achievements, helped by the promotion and the spread of education. During the three centuries when the Song held sway politically, the society underneath the polity underwent profound changes. Buddhism, which dominated the Chinese scene from the fifth century, had waned during the ninth century. The faith-based menagerie of gods and demons and the cycle of reincarnation had receded into the background, bringing to the fore a more secular landscape, apprehensible by reason. During the Song, China transformed itself from the outmoded world dominated by aristocratic lineages which had characterised the Tang into a new world, 'whose basic characteristics are already those of the China of the modern times'[5].

Rulers in imperial China and their scholar-officials were traditionalists, who kept historical records assiduously and made it their business to learn from past experiences to guide the present. They would try to avoid past mistakes, and reform any defects in the institutions that they were going to adopt. Having taken steps to rein in the power of the military, the Song court set to work perfecting the civilian government. In traditional China, all political power in theory emanated from the emperor. In practice, the power had always been shared between the emperor and the officials who served him, the central as well as the regional, through delegation. The emperor's personal circle, the empress, her relatives, and the eunuchs, who constituted an inner court, had opportunities to exercise power because of their closeness to the emperor. The Song was unusual in setting up a system in which the sharing of power between the emperor and the highest officials at the court, such as the prime ministers, was tilted in favour of the latter. This regime made it difficult for an emperor to exercise power arbitrarily. It also kept the empresses and the eunuchs from interfering in state affairs, as they had done so notoriously during the Tang dynasty.

The State Council, the highest organ of the government, was a collective decision-making body of five to nine high officials who, along with the emperor, ruled the country. The formulation of government policy by the State Council was made by first gathering necessary information; then undertaking a thorough discussion and debate, where opinions of different sides were heard; and finally, the resulting policy statement was voted on by the members. The emperor was normally expected to ratify a decision so arrived at, or he might have the casting vote. In no other dynasty were the scholar-officials as powerful as those in the Song. Furthermore, in no other dynasty were people from different walks of life allowed to submit plans and proposals to offices of the government. Although the Song system of government was initially modelled on the Tang, it was transformed by the Song in the course of time, according to the exigencies and ethos of its era. Not having to share power with the military aristocracy, as had been the case under the Tang, the Song government was able to achieve much greater centralization of power. Despite this concentration of power, the government made itself more in touch with its own civil ser-

---

[5] *A History of Chinese Civilization*, by Jacques Gernet (Cambridge University Press, New York, NY, second edition 1996) p 300.

vants and the public, by having three independent services hearing their opinions, suggestions, and complaints.

Politics under the Song was lively and full of passion with the leading figures, and their
followers, divided into opposing groups which behaved in some ways like members of
modern political parties, having different socio-economic agendas, philosophical outlooks,
and concrete policies. They lobbied the emperors and even empresses, networked with
like-minded colleagues, energetically promoted their own views and proposals, and denounced vehemently those of their opponents. The struggle between the reformers, as
represented by Wang Anshi, and the conservatives led by Sima Guang, fully exemplified
this situation during the eleventh century.

The ideology of the two sides reflected the social situation and the cultural climate of
the time. Some of the radical measures of the reforms were tailored to remedy the Song's
perpetual military weakness, as well as to meet the increasing financial burden of the military establishment, and of wars and tribute payments. The crisis provoked by the emergence of a militarily aggressive Western Xia around the middle of the eleventh century
added impetus to the reform movement.

Wang Anshi was well aware that the burden of taxes on land and labour services imposed by the government fell mainly on the shoulders of the small farmers or peasants,
while the landowners and merchants with large estates often found ways to pay little or
no taxes. The peasants, who lived on the edge of solvency, often needed to borrow money
during planting and growing, and loans from private moneylenders were obtainable
mostly on exorbitant rates of interest. They were thus vulnerable to losing their land. It
was a classic situation of the rich becoming richer and the poor poorer. Wang Anshi's reforms included the offering of state loans to the farmers at a reasonable rate of interest,
payable after harvest. He rationalized the process of tax collection by converting labour
services – a kind of capitation tax levied again mostly on smallholders – to a tax in the
form of money, while at the same time significantly reducing their total tax obligation. By
keeping the small farmers in business, and by supporting agricultural production through
better irrigation and other forms of improvement on land use, he hoped to increase the
total amount of taxes collected on land, despite halving the land tax. In fact, taxes from
commerce and industry, and new sources of revenue from the government monopoly on
certain commodities, such as salt and liquor, in addition to the land tax, did enable the
state to increase its income.

Wang Anshi's intervention to lighten the load on the small farmers was in tune with
the sense of equity and social justice current in eleventh and twelve century China. An
even more practical consideration related to the security of the state. By giving these
people a stake in the society, he hoped that they might not foment rebellion – the Song,
like many other dynasties, had not been spared many instances of peasant rebellions –
and that they might cooperate more willingly with their rulers in resisting the military ag-

gression of the nomadic empires. He organized and trained peasant militia, instead of relying solely on an army of mercenary soldiers, whose effectiveness as a fighting force continued to decline, while their number kept on increasing. Using peasant militia and
replacing the soldiers' role in keeping internal order by re-vitalizing the traditional mutual
responsibility (*bao jia*) system in the countryside, he managed to reduce the swollen regular
army and thus cut down the escalating military cost.

Another fiscal reform concerned government intervention in price stabilization, by pre-
venting large monopoly merchants from manipulating prices by stockpiling, and then selling the commodities, such as cereals, at high prices. Instead, the government would
purchase the goods when the market price was low, and sell them to small traders on
credit, for resale. This benefited the retailers by keeping them from being squeezed by
rich merchants, and also the public by keeping goods in circulation at stable prices. He
evidently believed that by securing the livelihood and liberating the economic power of
the multitude of small players, the production and circulation of wealth of the entire country would improve, which would benefit both the state and the people.

Wang Anshi's reform programme was wide ranging. In addition to the fiscal, economic,
and military matters, it established many public charities such as hospitals, hospices, dispensaries, and orphanages. It set up regional public schools to widen educational opportunities. It changed the content of the civil service examination to include more practical
subjects like law, economics, and geography. In the interest of justice, the teaching of law
in the schools, and examinations on law, were particularly emphasized so that judgment
and sentencing of offenders would be based on and bound by the written code, rather
than allowing the prevailing practice of relying on the personal discretion of the relevant
officials to continue. Many of Wang Anshi's reform measures were strongly opposed by
the conservative ruling elite, and his attempt to limit the amount of landholding and private
property was the most damaging to their interest.

Wang Anshi was a radical thinker, who believed that he was reviving the true teachings
of Confucius and Mencius, and he used these as a guide for setting up a perfect social
order using the power of a benevolent state. He thought that large private landholdings
effectively reduced the power of the state and its revenue, and that restricting private
wealth and power would promote a more equitable society. Wang Anshi believed that
using the criteria of rationality and objectivity to run a government efficiently, and apply
the written law strictly, would lead to a situation where the polity was just and the society
harmonious, and the two would merge into one. His ideal could be represented by a ubiq-
uitously displayed eight-character couplet still seen on scrolls and public building today:
tian xia wei gong, shi jie da tong, meaning the world is in harmony when it is for the
benefit of the public. This expression embodies a perpetual Chinese longing for a world
of equity and peace. On the other side, the reality of the Chinese society had always been
one where powerful lineages carved out disproportionate shares of the society's wealth

for themselves and their descendants.

People in our modern society might find Wang Anshi's position on private property and state power repellent and suggestive of totalitarianism. Despite his efforts at centralization, imperial China did not have the means to control its people as effectively as, for example, Nazi Germany, Stalinist Russia, or Maoist China. However, rulers in China had never been shy of state power: allowing society space to grow and to develop independent institutions outside the government's control had not been a part of either the theory or the practice of their tradition of governance. The idea that a government should be separated into legislative and executive branches, which balanced each other's power and exercised checks on each other, did not emerge in a significant way from China's experience of governance, and there was never an independent judiciary. After all, in the Chinese patrimonial state, the emperor represented an idealized father figure, who had authority by right and, in the Chinese Confucian universe, would exercise his authority in a virtuous and benevolent way. Should an emperor be lacking in virtue, heaven would supposedly call him to account.

Wang Anshi was able to push through his reforms in the teeth of fierce opposition because he had the support of the emperor. Facing an empty treasury and social unrest, Song Shengzong (r.1067-1085) subscribed strongly to Wang Anshi's reform programme, believing that it would make the troubled empire wealthy and powerful and, in particular, militarily strong. From 1069 to 1075, he gave Wang full authority to implement various planks of the programme. But as the reform progressed, the attack from the rich and powerful, among whom were many conservative officials, was so overwhelming that the emperor softened his stance, and let Wang Anshi resign from the post of prime minister and the overseeing of the reform. In 1085, when Shenzong died, the conservatives dominated the court, and dismantled most of the measures put in place by Wang Anshi and his fellow reformers. Wang Anshi's reform had highlighted some deep-rooted long-term problems in the Chinese society, and its failure showed the difficulty of making radical changes or administering correctives to the existing social structure.

The reform that the Song dynasty did succeed in making, and that had lasting impact on China, was in connection with education and the civil service examination. As mentioned earlier, Wu Ti of the Western Han had used examination on the Confucian classics as one channel for the recruitment of officials. After the chaotic times of the Great Disunion, when this institution fell into a state of neglect, the Sui (581-618) and Tang (618-90) dynasties revived it for the same purpose. The Song dynasty reunited China after a century under regional military rule. It elevated the recruitment examination for the civil service into a major structure because it laid great store by a well-managed civilian government that functioned efficiently and was effectively controlled from the centre. It is important to note that, unlike civil servants in modern democratic countries, who are the servants of their elected political masters, their Song counterparts were themselves also holders of political offices, because there was no distinction between the functions and roles of civil servants and civil politicians in Song times. That is still the case in contemporary China.

Rationality and objectivity were principles well understood and applied by those who built and managed the well-ordered Song civil service. For example, the powers and the areas of competence of the various government offices were separate and clearly defined. To reduce the temptation of corrupt practices, such as milking the public by charging irregular fees, the Song officials were well paid. The Song dynasty increased the number of officials recruited through the civil service examination to about 30%, as against 15% during the Tang. It included in the examination practical subject matters in connection with government administration, in addition to the Confucian classics. The examiners endeavoured to prevent cheating by assigning numbers to the candidates and having their scripts copied to obscure their identities and calligraphy. They systematized the selection by a three-tiered competition and broadened the base of participation by starting the initial round at the prefectural level. Those who qualified would progress to the next level of examination at the capital, supervised by the Imperial Secretariat. The winners from there would take part in the final round of selection, competing in the palace in the presence of the emperor, who would award to those whose performance was outstanding the most coveted scholarly title, *jinshi*. Although not all successful candidates would be

The Song emperor receives a candidate during the palace examination
(*Wikipedia*: retrieved on 26 November 2023 from https://en.wikipedia.org/wiki/Imperial_examination)

awarded official positions, they effectively joined a pool of well-educated talents, from which officials could be drawn when needed. By presiding over the imperial examinations and rewarding the best educated with titles or honours, the emperor might benefit from the strengthening of his authority, through the bond of personal loyalty which this process was likely to instil in the successful candidates.

Did the Song state examination system create a meritocracy? It must have inspired hope among countless families with young boys, causing them to steer the cleverest of their sons starting from six or seven years old to devote a decade or, for some, a lifetime to poring over Confucian classics and other worthy books, in pursuit of an elusive distinction, for the glory and enrichment of the family. This situation was encapsulated by the well-known myth of a poor lonely scholar, struggling in a chilly room in front of a window without any visitors, who would one day win worldwide fame through examination success. However, it was extremely difficult for those without a family background of wealth and learning to become degree-holders through sheer effort and determination. Upward social mobility through this channel was probably only a trickle rather than a flood. In an empire governed by around 20,000 officials, the greater part (about 70 percent) of this ruling elite began their official life through the *yin* (i.e. hereditary) privilege granted to the offspring of high officials, or through recommendation by serving officials. Even the 30 percent who were chosen on merit through scholarly competitions were not doing so on a level field. Some well-connected people were allowed to take special or restricted examinations that were easier to pass than the regular ones. For these reasons, even though the Song made great efforts towards perfecting the system of examination, and relied more on it for official recruitment, it did not lead to the empire becoming a true meritocracy.

The gentry

The Song official examination did contribute towards the emergence of a Chinese 'gentry' society. The Chinese gentry were a special breed, distinguished more by superior education rather than by land ownership. The resurgence of the institution of the imperial examination under the Song produced a great impetus for education. The growth of state and private schools produced from ten to several hundred thousand students, many of whom would become candidates for the examinations. Over time, the pass rate decreased: for example, 5 out of 10 passed in 1023, 1 out of 10 in 1093, and 1 out of 200 in 1275. Not all successful candidates for the imperial examinations would get official posts. Those who passed the examinations would gain honours from the degrees, even without the additional benefit of having official posts. Those who did not pass would probably still have social esteem as being part of the educated elite, with opportunities for employment, such as teaching, which would not be available to an uneducated person.

In the narrowest sense a member of the Chinese gentry in the Song is thought to be a degree-holder, but this would be an over-simplification of the situation. Although a few exceedingly bright boys from poor families, through application, determination, and luck, might manage to educate themselves to a high enough level to pass the examinations, most of the successful candidates came from prosperous families with a tradition of learning, access to books, and ample funding for education, and with degree-holders or government officials among their own members or networks of relatives and other associates. In the broader sense, the Chinese gentry were the local elite, the socioeconomic upper stratum of Chinese families or lineages - rather than just individuals - that provided the seedbed from which the scholar-officials sprung. Mere wealth, without educated members in the family, would render a rich household vulnerable to official exaction, or other forms of victimization. The reformed Song civil service examination aroused high hopes and stimulated popular education and enthusiastic participation in this enormously stressful mental competition, but it did not lead to a huge increase in the number of officials recruited through this channel. Its more significant consequence was the increase in the ranks of the educated, with or without the degrees, among the well-to-do or wealthy people in the empire. These people, embedded largely in the gentry families, served to strengthen the influence and consolidate the wealth and social position of the local elite.

The Chinese gentry or local elite served many necessary public functions. They formed the buffer between the government officials above and the peasant society below, from the Song dynasty onwards to the end of the Qing in 1911, with the exception of the Yuan dynasty under Mongol rule. They took part in the allocation and collection of taxes in the countryside, supervised the periodic markets, organized public works (such as the building of dikes against floods), mediated disputes, acted as advisors in lawsuits, and set up local militia or other security forces, in addition to playing major roles in the local educational, charitable, and cultural activities. The gentry assumed the role of the unofficial arm of the government, because the government in late imperial China was content to limit itself to providing a superstructure staffed by a relatively small number of officials, who were to govern an increasingly large number of people as the population grew.

The number of Song official posts in twelfth century China was listed as 20,000, and the same number was listed in the Qing during the nineteenth century, while during the intervening centuries the population in China grew from 110 million in 1190 to over 400 million in 1850. During the same period, the number of counties (*xian*), the most basic territorial administrative units, grew by only a little over 10 percent. The official arm of the government extended to the county level, which was normally governed by the county magistrate, a central government appointee. The average number of people governed by a single county magistrate grew from about 90,000 to 300,000 between the Song and the Qing late dynasties. The county magistrate was normally not a native of the district he governed, because of the 'rule of avoidance'. This rule, which prohibited local officials from serving in their native districts, was used to minimize the temptation for corruption and favouritism. Since the Sui, most of the subsequent dynasties had adopted this practice. Although a county magistrate normally had his own paid assistants, such as secretaries, and several low status employees, like messengers and jailers, they were few in number. For the country magistrates to fulfil their open-ended responsibility for governing their districts, the help and support of the local gentry was indispensable. Although the gentry were normally not a part of the paid staff of the county magistrate, income from commissions or fees was derivable from many of their multifarious functions. The gentry functioned as the intermediary between the local population and central government appointees, who would be unfamiliar with the local situation. They administered local populations numbering in the tens to hundreds of thousands, and territories that could be as large as Rhode Island. Without the help of the local gentry, the government of imperial China during the last thousand years would not have been able to manage the empire smoothly, if at all. (But we should note that the century of Mongol rule from 1279 to 1368 formed an exception, to be covered chapter 3.)

Neo-Confucianism

The gentry were closely connected with the revival of Confucianism stimulated by the Song policy of strengthening the civil service recruitment examination. For several centuries, roughly from the fifth to the ninth, Confucianism had been overshadowed by Buddhism in both the popular and elite culture. During the Song intellectual ferment, Confucianism underwent a 'renaissance'. From a large body of classical texts accumulated during the Sui-Tang era, Zhu Xi (1130-1200), the chief proponent of the Song Confucianism, selected four classical texts as the embodiment of the truth of the teaching of the ancient masters: the Analects (*Lunyu*) of Confucius; the Mencius, a work of Confucius' chief disciple; the Doctrine of the Mean (*Zhongyong*); and the Great Learning (*Daxue*). Zhu Xi's interpretation of Confucian texts, as provided by his commentary, represented a synthesis of the Song intellectual currents and a new philosophy. Neo-Confucianism, the name given to it by the Jesuits, united rational, moral, and metaphysical elements into a philosophical worldview, which integrated the human sphere with the cosmic order.

Neo-Confucianists assumed that the universe was governed by a moral force, apprehensible by an individual's mind and reason. This moral universe, not buttressed by divine sanction, was eminently rational and humane. Confucius and Mencius, in the chosen texts as reinterpreted by Zhu Xi, provided the key to open the door of this universe. They had shown the Way (*Dao*) for the moral improvement of an individual, whose character could be formed or transformed by the *Dao* through disciplined self-cultivation. Having subdued the self through a rigorous process of education, a scholar's ultimate goal was not just to improve himself, but to improve the whole society. His mission in life would begin with self-cultivation (*xiu shen*), then it would progress to giving order to his family (*qi jia*); after that he would be ready to govern the country (*zhi guo*), and finally he would provide peace or harmony to the world (*ping tian xia*). What he sought, therefore, was not a Buddhist Nirvana, nor salvation of his own soul in an afterlife. He did not seek to escape from the world or hold himself aloof from or above the world's fray, like a Daoist. His final objective was social, orientated towards this world, for involvement in the public service as a morally autonomous being, an individual with a conscience of his own.

Neo-Confucianism, propagated in the schools, and legitimized by the official examinations, became the orthodox philosophy of governance during the Song. Through the activities of the scholar-gentry, such as teaching in schools, and 'preaching' in Community Compacts (*xiangyue*), which were a kind of local residents' meetings, it filtered downward and permeated into the whole society. As a result, it did not remain the culture of the elite; it also coloured deeply the culture of the masses. The Yuan dynasty (1279-1368) of the Mongols, who ruled China after the Song with the help of non-Chinese, was ambivalent towards the Chinese culture and did not use the civil service recruitment examination until 1315. Nevertheless, Neo-Confucianism survived the Yuan. Under the Ming (1368-1644), the Chinese dynasty which overthrew the Yuan, it became again the state orthodoxy. Wang Yangming, the outstanding Ming exponent of Neo-Confucianism, advocated, in addition to the rational approach, the use of meditation as a means to gain intuitive knowledge. When the semi-nomadic Manchus conquered Ming China and set up the Qing dynasty (1644-1911), these foreign rulers endeavoured to rule as legitimate emperors of China sanctioned by Confucianism. They endorsed Neo-Confucianism as the official ideology of the state, supported the Confucian social order, and performed the rites and rituals established by that tradition. They capitalized on the civil service recruitment examination system, sponsored literary publications and cultural projects, and issued many sacred edicts based on Confucian precepts for the edification of their subjects. With political support from above and deep roots in the society below, the Confucianism propagated by the Song and Ming thinkers prevailed as the dominant worldview in China, until the second decade of the twentieth century.

Printing, firearms, and ships

Many factors converged to contribute to the dynamism of the Song intellectual and cultural scene. An exceptionally important one related to the development of printing on paper. Paper produced with plant fibre was invented during the Han. Woodblock printing of Buddhist pictures and texts on paper began during the Tang dynasty near the end of the eighth century. During the Song, the technique became popularized and was widely used. From the tenth century onward, printing proliferated with accurate reproduction of illustrations and texts on a wide variety of subjects and for different purposes, including promissory notes and government decrees, not to mention books on the classics. During the mid-eleventh century, movable type was invented, but woodblock engraving remained in use because it was easy and cheap to produce and well suited to a language like Chinese, which has an enormous number of different characters. Song China, being the first country in the world to produce printed books, generated tens of thousands of volumes of books to satisfy the demands of private collectors and government libraries, as well as the literate public. The availability of cheaply and speedily produced printed works made education more accessible and provided opportunities for more people to participate in the cultural and intellectual life of the country. Printing contributed to the growth in education and of the gentry class, as well as the cultural 'renaissance' of that era.

Song China took over another Tang invention - firearms - that was later transmitted to Europe with enormous repercussions to the world. Gunpowder had been used by the Tang military in incendiary projectiles, after being discovered by experimenting Daoist alchemists. The Song, struggling desperately against aggressive nomadic neighbours, developed several weapons that made use of the incendiary, smoke-producing, and explosive properties of gunpowder, between the eleventh and the thirteenth centuries. The Song forces used gunpowder packed in incendiary or explosive grenades, thrown by catapults into their enemy's

Movable type from the Song dynasty period (*coursedesignmatters*: retrieved on 26 November from https://coursedesignmatters.wordpress.com/2016/09/28/china-what-do-they-have-to-do-with-type/)

ranks. They also deployed rockets propelled by gunpowder in bamboo or wooden tubes to deliver incendiary arrows. In the thirteenth century, the Mongols, who were quick to adopt new armaments in warfare, hit their enemies with the 'thunderbolts that shake the sky', which were exploding projectiles cased in metal. The global consequences of the development of muskets, cannons, and a host of powerfully destructive weapons in the modernizing Europe after the Tang-Song invention of firearms are still being played out. As regards China, only the state had the authority to undertake or authorize its subjects to undertake projects on firearms, and the succeeding dynasties did not pursue the development of firearms in the manner of some of the warring and colonizing states of Europe, until late Qing times. Towards the middle of the nineteenth century when the British attacked Chinese coastal cities using modern cannons from gunboats, the defending forces of the Qing with their outmoded weapons could offer little resistance. It was after many such lessons that the Qing government tried grudgingly to modernize its armaments and fleets through importing products, technology, and know-how from the West.

In nautical technology, as in the knowledge and use of firearms, Song China led the world by several centuries. Partly because the overland trade along the Silk Road between the Song and Central Asia was blocked by the rise of the semi-nomadic empires, the Chinese turned more to overseas trade, using the well-traversed sea routes that linked the Chinese coast with the regions of south-east Asia to the Persian Gulf. Although the Arabs had dominated this trade since the Tang, the Chinese were able to participate in this maritime commercial activity by tapping into their centuries-old experiences in shipbuilding, navigating along their great inland rivers and canals and out into the high seas. During that time, seaworthy Chinese sailing ships were the most advanced in the world. A large ship would have up to four decks and large watertight compartments. It could be equipped with four to six masts, a dozen canvas or rigid-matting sails, pivoted oars, stern-post rudders, and mariners' charts, maps, and compass, and be capable of carrying 500 men. During the two centuries from the beginning of the Song dynasty, the collection of maritime customs duties increased from half a million strings of copper cash[6] to 65 million strings. This increase in the tax receipts surely reflected the growth in maritime trade during this period.

Song dynasty 'cash' coinage (*Wikipedia*: retrieved on 26 November 2023 from https://en.wikipedia.org/wiki/Southern_Song_dynasty_coinage)

Economic growth

The expansion in foreign trade was only a part of the story. It was a subplot of the

---

[6] One string represented a unit of 1000 round copper coins, each with a square hole in the middle, held together by the string threaded through the holes.

great economic expansion and growth in domestic commerce in Song China. The Song dynasty benefited from the southward shift of the population and the economic centre of gravity that was already apparent during Tang times. The development of rice cultivation in the water-rich lands south of the Yangtze River played a crucial role in the Song economic upsurge. Technical improvements like the double cropping of early ripening varieties of rice led to increased yields of a cereal crop which already had the highest yield per acre. The resulting surplus enabled the population to grow and provided the basis of accumulation for investments in other economic activities, such as manufacturing, trade, and services.

The economic growth was accompanied by societal changes that altered the relationship between the social classes, a development that was already well underway from the late Tang. In place of the Tang military aristocracy, with their self-sufficient domains, maintaining an essentially patriarchal patron-client relationship between themselves and those who served them, there appeared a new class of landlords, who tended to settle in the growing townships and cities, enjoying the richness and amenities of life in an urban setting, on income derived from land ownership, while leaving the management of their estates to their stewards. The relationship between the landlords and tenants was simply a matter of economics, involving the payment and collection of land rents and debts, rather than one of personal subjection or dependency.

Rich landlords were often closely connected with, if not actual members of, the gentry-official class, and as such had ways to avoid tax payment or to pay very little of it. As a result, an estimated 70% of the cultivated acreage was not liable to tax. The land tax burden fell almost entirely on the 30% of the cultivated areas left to the independent tillers of small plots. The poorer ones among them eked out such a precarious living that they were left with very few resources to tide them over a poor harvest, price fluctuations, or other contingencies. They often needed to borrow because of the time gap between sowing and harvesting. They lived under a constant threat of losing their land if they could not pay back the loans, often obtained on usurious rates of interest. Default on debt payments would lead to the loss of their land to the rich landlords or merchants who provided the loans. Consequently, the rich would become richer, and the poor would join the ranks of the landless peasants, while the government would collect less taxes. Wang Anshi's reforms of 1068-1085 ameliorated this situation for a period until the forces favouring the interests of the rich and powerful landlords struck back during the reign of Song Huizong (1082-1135), who did not share his predecessor's enthusiasm for the reforms.

Where could the landless peasants go, if they could not make a living, as tenants or labourers in the countryside? They could join the floating population in the burgeoning cities or towns and find employment opportunities or some niches for survival. The Song economic growth was accompanied by an enormous urban expansion. The burgeoning cities and towns during the Song had a different character from those of the Tang. Large cities under the Tang, being centres of government administration with residences of the families of the officials and separate quarters for commerce and crafts, were aristocratic in character. Within the outer ramparts, inner walls divided the different districts of these cities. Commerce and markets were strictly regulated and controlled by government officials, and there was a curfew at night. In Song times, the bursting urban population spilled over to outside the city boundary, and the ring of a city wall could no longer contain the spread of their economic activities. The inner walls had also lost their ability to confine the different occupational groups into separate districts. Shops, workshops, factories, taverns, inns, teahouses, market stalls, and places for entertainments of various kinds sprang up on streets that had acquired names of their own. These were grass-roots developments, arising from popular needs and demands, rather than government planning. Curfews as well as many other official regulations and controls had been abandoned because of the difficulty of enforcement. The inhabitants were free to move about, frequenting establishments for business or amusement that remained open throughout the night. The Song cities as well as the growing towns were therefore commercial in character, bustling with economic activities, providing different kinds of employment for the expanding population.

Settled in these urban sprawls were merchants, large and small, as well as the rich landlords. These 'urban bourgeoisie' were a vital component of the Song economic expansion. While cottage industries and small-scale craft enterprises or workshops could be set up by those with modest means for large scale manufacturing and trade, particularly interregional or foreign trade whether overland or by sea, the rich landlords and merchants were the main sources of the seed capital. One area of the Song economic growth involved commercialization of crops with high market demand. These included tea, hemp, cotton, sugar cane, lacquer-producing trees, and mulberry trees for silkworms. The rich landlords and merchants were well positioned to invest in the cultivation of these plants, the processing of the raw materials derived from them and the making of the end products, as well as in product distribution. The availability of capital, coupled with improved technology and rising demand, propelled Song China to become a major producer of metals, particularly iron (for agricultural implements, cookware, and weapons) and copper (for coins). The newly discovered explosives were used to open up the mines. In 1078, the production of cast iron reached over 114,000 tonnes, while over seven hundred years later in 1788, England, the leading European industrial power, was producing only 68,000 tonnes[7]. Intense empire-wide commercial activities involved not just those mentioned, but a host of other craft products, such as ceramics, silks, ornaments, furniture, papers, and printed books. Inter-regional trade was facilitated by the more than 50,000 kilometres of navigable waterways formed by the Yangtze River and its tributaries and the canals connecting them. Some of the products such as ceramics, silks, and tea were produced not

---

[7] *A Dictionary, Practical, Theoretical, and Historical, of Commerce and Commercial Navigation*, by J. R. McCulloch (Longman, Orme, Brown, Green and Longman, London, 1839).

just for the domestic market, but also for large overseas demands, distributed via both overland and sea routes.

The contribution of the rich landlords and merchants during the Song to the growth in economic production and trade was due not only to their capacity for investment, but also to the market demand created by them. Because of the large number of wealthy land-owners and merchants during the Song, they had a great impact on the economy as consumers. The demand from their lifestyle and tastes stimulated not only domestic production, but also the importation of foreign luxury goods, such as furs, incense, rare stones, ivory, coral, and spices. The Song paid for their foreign trade not only by selling Chinese products, but also in copper cash. This trade was considerable and widespread. The copper cash minted by the Song could be found in the empires of the nomads to the north, the lands of South-East Asia and Indian Ocean, and in Japan, where it was used as a local currency because of its abundance.

In addition to the private enterprises, the Song government became directly involved in the business of raising funds to cover the heavy military expenditure that was not met by ordinary taxation. There were large state-owned shops, factories, and mines managed by civil servants. Products like tea, alcohol, salt, and perfume were state monopolies. Because of the enormous Song commercial expansion, income from the state-owned enterprises as well as the taxes on manufactured and traded goods, in addition to the customs duties on trade, both internal and foreign, formed an increasingly more important part of the state revenue, as compared with the taxes levied on the agricultural community. During the eleventh to the early twelfth centuries, revenue from the agricultural sector, which comprised taxes on land and labour services, was about equal to that raised from commerce and industry. Later in the twelfth and thirteenth centuries, income from the latter far exceeded that from the former. Song China revealed an economic trend, which showed up also in late Ming and Qing times, that the empire's wealth was largely derived from the economic activities of trade and craft production. This fact remained largely unrecognized, because China's Confucian rulers could only imagine wealth in terms of land ownership and agricultural production.

Money

The unprecedented economic expansion and high military expenditure obliged the government mint to cast more and more copper coins. Around the turn of the eleventh century, the annual issue of copper coins (strung together in units of 1000 coins per string) grew from a few hundred thousand strings to over a million. Seven to eight decades later, annual production reached around six million strings. The Northern Song (960-1126) was estimated to have issued 200 million strings of copper coins, but even such a volume of the metal coinage was insufficient to meet the currency needs of the time. To supplement the shortfall, silver (not minted) also went into circulation also. A more drastic remedy came in the form of paper money printed by the state during the first decade of the eleventh century. This monetary innovation evolved from the use of the certificates of deposit, issued by government agents in favour of merchants or among the merchants themselves during the ninth century. Between the eleventh and the thirteenth centuries, the use of paper currency became widely adopted in Song China and spread to the neighbouring Liao and Jin empires. In addition to the paper currency, the Song mercantile world also introduced other modern monetary devices, such as promissory notes, bills of exchange, and the cheque. Paper money, made possible by the invention of printing, greatly assisted the Song economic expansion by reducing the pressure on the government mint to provide increasingly large numbers of copper coins, thus removing this monetary impediment to growth. The issue of paper money reached an equivalent of 400 million strings of copper coins during the Southern Song (1126-1279). The Yuan dynasty (1279-1368) which succeeded the Song embraced the use of paper currency. While the Song limited the validity of the issues to certain areas and periods of time, the Mongols in 1260, already in control of North China and Sichuan, issued a paper currency to be circulated as the only valid form of money, which would not expire, in their Chinese territory. The value of this form of money declined when its conversion into gold or silver was prohibited. The power to print money and to fix the exchange rate between the paper issues and the precious metals, or the power to prohibit such exchanges, could easily be misused or abused by the authorities concerned. The Chinese society suffered the ill consequences of monetary mismanagement at the end of both the Song and the Yuan dynasties.

Intellectual life

The monetary economy was one of the signs of an emergent modern society during Song dynasty China from the eleventh to the thirteenth century, before its appearance in Europe. Indications of a similar trend included: the rapid economic and population expansion; the changes that took place in the socioeconomic relationships in the country side; the burgeoning urban centres that broke down official restrictions so as to enable many newfound freedoms; the increasing population mobility, particularly the movement of people from the countryside into the growing towns and cities; the spread of private schools and of education; and the rise of a new printing industry producing a large volume of printed works, including encyclopaedias and the growth of library collections. Among the important characteristics of the modern world that arose out of the European experience were rationalism and secularism. The Song society was manifestly secular, and its 'renaissance' gentlemen typically cultivated a rational, or even scientific, approach to the acquisition of knowledge. Their intellectual curiosity covered a wide variety of subjects on which they left written records in the form of treatises, monographs, or books. These included the worlds of nature, mathematics, astronomy, geography, cartography, history, archaeology, epigraphy, technology, and medicine. A book published in 1092 (the *Kaogu Tu*) demonstrated one of the first scientific attempts to classify and date the ancient Chinese bronzes. Song scholars' approach to the study of history was notable for their concern to exhaustively seek the sources, which they examined with a critical rationality worthy of their modern counterparts. Their interest in mathematics contributed to the development of algebra. Their scientific aptitude led them to use experiments to test and examine their knowledge critically. Some of their ideas on art would appeal to our contemporary sensibility. Shen Kua, a Song physicist and astronomer who also commented on art, looked upon paintings as pictorial representations that did not need to bear a close visual resemblance to the subjects being painted. In his view, the value of a work of art lay in the revelation of the mind, culture, and human quality of its creator.

During the eleventh to the thirteenth centuries, Song China led the world in the volume of trade, level of technology, political organization, scientific knowledge, and in arts and letters. Its population of around one hundred million was larger than that of the whole of Europe during that time. The technology or inventions of the Song (and those of older dynasties) that were transferred to Europe contributed significantly to the rise of modern Europe. Among these were the compass and sternpost rudder (for navigation), the wheelbarrow, the spinning wheel, the application of watermills to looms, printing and paper, gunpowder, the counterweight trap that revolutionized warfare, and iron casting. Despite the cultural brilliance and economic expansion of the Song, it lacked sufficient military strength to check the irresistible advance of the conquering Mongols, who overcame the last stand of the Song loyalists in 1279.

References

A General History of China (in Chinese) by Bai Shouyi (Shanghai Peoples' Publishing House, Shanghai, 1999).

A History of Chinese Civilization by Jacques Gernet (English Edition, Cambridge University Press, Cambridge, second edition 1996), chapters 14-15.

China: A History Volume 1 From Neolithic Cultures through the Great Qing Empire 10,000 BCE – 1799 CE by Harold M. Tanner (Hackett Publishing Company, Inc., Indianapolis/Cambridge, 2010), chapter 7.

China: A New History by John King Fairbank (Belknap Press, Cambridge , 2nd revised and enlarged edition, 2006), chapter 4.

Chapter 3

The Mongols and the Yuan Dynasty of China (1271-1368)

The Mongols

In 1206 a momentous event took place on the grassland of northern Asia: the proclamation of a Mongol chieftain, Chinggis, to be the Great Khan of all Mongols. Within seven decades, his armies and those of his sons and grandsons would conquer a vast stretch of land. It stretched from the seacoasts of China and Korea through Central Asia and across Iran and Iraq; then further west to European Russia, also including Ukraine and parts of eastern Europe, north of the Black Sea. The conquered territories were formed into four Khanates, ruled by his sons and grandsons and their descendants. Song China and its neighbours, the Western Xia and Jin empires, were incorporated into the empire of the Great Khan, the foremost of the four Khanates.

How did a relatively small population, from a group of obscure tribes, scattered in a particularly inhospitable environment, succeed in overpowering the armies of much richer and more populous countries? For thousands of years, nomadic herders like the Mongols inhabited the enormous expanses of the steppe, stretching from northeast Asia to eastern Eurasia, where the winter was bitterly cold. Because of the scarcity of water, the land in this region was more suitable for growing grass than cultivated crops. Perhaps the extreme harshness of the homeland of the Mongols, and the competition amongst them for scarce resources, helped them to develop into an extraordinarily hardy and warlike people. They depended on their livestock for most of their basic needs: food (meat, milk, and blood), clothing (leather, felt, furs, and wool), shelter (tenting materials and carpets), transportation (beasts of burden), and fuel (dried animal dung for cooking). They therefore had to move

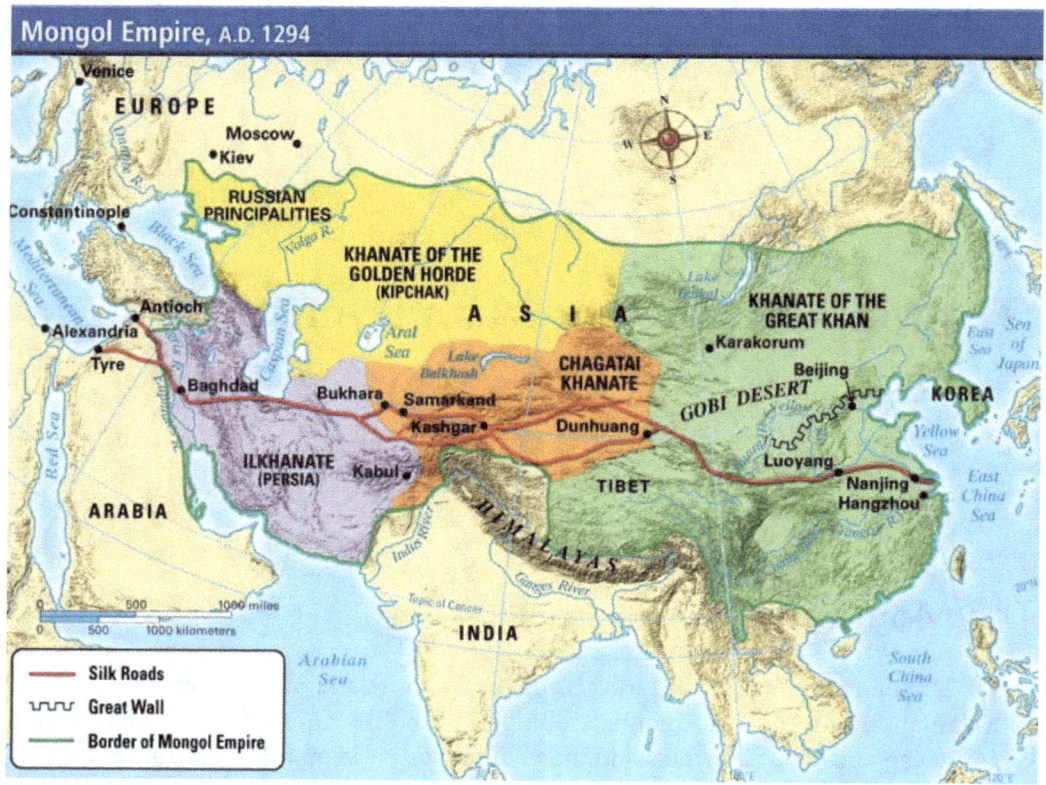

Map showing the four Khanates (*Weebly*: retrieved on 26 November 20233 from
https://mongolempirewhap.weebly.com/decline-and-fall.html)

in response to seasonal climatic changes and set up their yurts (tents supported by wooden posts) to where grass was plentiful for their animals to graze. Having to travel with their necessities on draft animals or animal-drawn carts, they did not burden themselves with surplus possessions. The storage of grain for food as practised by the sedentary farmers was not a practical option for them. They hunted wild animals, but these were not a reliable source of food supply. Such a challenging habitat and lifestyle rendered them very vulnerable to inclement weather, or sickness of their herds.

There was intense competition for the meagre resources among rival groups or clans on the grassland, which led to violence among them. Raids for capturing animals and people, and vendettas over past injuries, were commonplace occurrences. Besides fighting, they were also accustomed to conducting diplomatic negotiations or marriage alliances to establish a pecking order, or to achieve a position of dominance in each territory. Warfare, to the Mongols, was a way of life.

Having ridden from an early age and being frequently exposed to armed combat, the Mongols were superb cavalrymen and mounted archers. The short and stocky Mongolian horses, a true match for the hardiness of their riders, were great assets in any military campaign. These pony-like horses could survive long journeys in bitterly cold winters, being able to forage even under the snow. They were very agile in battle, capable of turning quickly in different directions during military manoeuvres.

Marco Polo, who served as an administrative official in China under Mongol rule, bore witness to what the Mongol soldiers and their horses could endure:

They are capable of supporting every kind of privation, and when there is a necessity for it, can live for a month on the milk of their mares, and upon such wild animals as they may chance to catch. The men are habituated to remain on horseback during two days and two nights, without dismounting, sleeping in that situation whilst their horses graze. No people on earth can surpass them in fortitude under difficulties, nor show greater patience under wants of every kind.

He also described the Mongol soldiers as "brave in battle, almost to desperation, setting little value upon their lives, and exposing themselves without hesitation to all manner of danger".[8]

The invention of the stirrup enabled the Mongol horsemen to shoot even when retreating (*arstechnica*: retrieved on 26 November 2023 from https://arstechnica.com/science/2017/05/the-mongols-built-an-empire-with-one-technological-breakthrough/}

---

[8] *Ibid.*

The transformation of the Mongol tribes

These hardy and warlike nomadic Mongol tribes, spread out north of the Gobi Desert, would not have become a serious threat to their well-armed neighbours, namely the empires of the Liao, the Western Xia, the Jin, and the Song, until they had gone through a process of social and political transition, like lone grasshoppers gathering into swarms. The process often involved the change from several simpler clan-based units of roughly equal status, related to one another through kinship and sharing communally owned property, into a more complex society of different social classes based on less egalitarian sharing of power and wealth. This development was likely to have occurred because of population growth that intensified the competition for the limited resources in the Mongol tribal homeland. Stronger and well-armed clans would raid others to occupy their lands, take their livestock, and capture their people to enslave them. They would become richer and more powerful. As the competition continued, some tribes might be weakened by vendettas while others might gain greater wealth and power. As regards the weaker clans, they had the option of submitting themselves voluntarily as vassals to the powerful ones, exchanging freedom for the security umbrella, or taking the risk of being captured and forced into slavery. This development opened up a great socio-economic gap between the ordinary nomadic herders and the wealthy military aristocracy, which became the ruling class, wielding political power and specializing in warfare. Below these were the slaves, often captured like booty after military action. They became the owners' chattels, like goods and animals that could be passed down to future generations, unless they had a lucky break to gain their freedom. The military struggles might eventually lead to the unification of all tribes, or to a balance of power among the leading clans in each region. In case of the latter, the leading clans might join together to form a tribal alliance and put their forces under a unified command to defend themselves against a common enemy, or to invade other tribes or states. Such a development would increase the power of the whole organized tribal alliance and the efficiency of its armed forces. However, serious military setbacks could lead to the breakdown of the alliance and the scattering of its members.

For a tribal alliance to become even more cohesive and militarily powerful, there was another threshold to cross. The next step required the emergence of an ambitious empire builder, a 'strong' man, who would most likely, but not necessarily, have come from the leading clan. A typical profile would describe him as being highly gifted in military leadership, power politics, and organization skills. He would begin his career by dominating the tribal alliance, crushing all internal opposition, and concentrating power, both military and political, in his own hands. Then he would embark on military campaigns, defeating powerful enemies and expanding into their lands. To consolidate his hold over the conquered territories and peoples, he would need to proceed politically, to establish a government with laws, institutions, and an officialdom to support his rule. At some point during his triumphal ascent, he would perpetuate his own power and position, as well as those of his heirs, by setting himself up with due pomp, pageantry, and ceremony, as the official head of a new dynasty.

There were many examples of such transformations having taken place among powerful nomadic tribes of the East Asian steppe grassland, starting with the tribal alliance of the Xiongnu before and after the reign of Modu Chanyu between 209 and 174 BCE at the beginning of the Han Dynasty, and continuing to the empires of the Tanguts, Qidans, and the Nuzhen, which existed contemporaneously with the Mongols, as discussed in chapter 2. After having gained ascendancy over their neighbouring nomadic tribes, the most ambitious nomadic empire builders would carry the fight to the rich Han Chinese empire, if they had the capacity to amass a considerable number of elite troops, upwards of one hundred thousand, to fight pitched battles against the normally larger forces of the populous Chinese. The rulers of the nomadic peoples, who extended their territories by incorporating more agricultural lands, farmers, market towns and cities into their realms, naturally enjoyed greater wealth, but they had to pay a price. The character of their state was altered. In the case of the Liao and the Jin, both countries became semi-nomadic, developing a mixed economy and a dual system of governance – one for the nomadic herders and another for the settled crop growers. Their very success contained the seeds of their own destruction. The hereditary dynasties of the Liao and the Jin, like their Chinese counterparts, experienced dynastic decline and shared similar weaknesses. In the course of time, their military edge also became blunted.

The transformation described above, particularly the initial stages, was taking place among the Mongols from the late eleventh century to the early years of the twelfth century. During the tenth to most of the eleventh century under Liao rule, the relatively weak and obscure Mongol tribes scattered in the Mongolian plateau traded and co-existed peacefully with the Qidans. As time went on, as a result of economic development and population growth, together with the impact of the Liao, the Mongol tribal society consolidated itself through internal fighting and alliance-making, whereby the rich and powerful clans with larger grazing land, herds, and manpower, became even more dominant. The position and power of some of the leading clans became greatly reinforced after having received official titles from the Liao rulers. The poorer and less powerful ones would become degraded into being their subjects or serving them as their vassals.

The heads of the prominent or aristocratic clans of the Mongols, commonly called Khans, commanded armed forces of clansmen, vassals, and slaves, and together became a military aristocracy. Before the end of the eleventh century, 1089 to be exact, a powerful chief of the Kereit Mongols led the troops of a confederation of Mongol tribes to challenge the Liao. During the first half of the twelfth century, the Mongol military aristocracy had already achieved a Grand Alliance of all Mongols under a paramount chief. One such leader, Hulegu Khan, led as many as several hundred thousand troops fighting against the Jin, which had by then replaced the Liao dynasty as the dominant power of the East Asian steppe. The Grand Alliance did not develop into a lasting empire, and the Mongol aristocratic clans were still fighting each other until the emergence of their own empire builder to unite them under his iron rule.

Chinggis Khan (1162 - 1227)

The greatest empire builder of the Mongols, Temujin, better known as Chinggis Khan, was born in 1162 - an auspicious time, because by then the weak and scattered Mongol tribal society had already been compacted into larger units of clans dominated by military aristocrats, who could be further amalgamated into a force to challenge the great empires of that region. Chinggis Khan was himself the scion of a Mongol military aristocrat of the Qiyan clan, whose death by poisoning led his troops to disperse, leaving Chinggis, still a minor, his younger brothers, and widowed mother in a vulnerable situation. Chinggis sought the protection of his father's brotherly ally, Toghrul Khan, who was the chief of the Kereit Mongols, and he became the latter's subject. As he grew older, he began to gather his father's old followers and troops, but he could not prevent the forced abduction of his wife and other family members by the Merkit Mongols. He asked Toghrul Khan and another ally to join him to fight the Merkits. His side won a resounding victory. In addition to retrieving his wife and family members, the winners took away quantities of loot and many slaves. Chinggis, then around twenty years of age, had thus successfully launched his career as a military leader.

As the number of his followers grew following the military victory, Chinggis decided to move away from his mentor and ally and set up his own camp. Many Qiyan relatives and notable members from his father and mother's clan came to join him, and together they recreated a tribal alliance of Qiyan clan members. In 1189, the aristocratic members of the tribal alliance met to elect the twenty-seven-year-old Chinggis as their leader. At this point Chinggis demonstrated his considerable ability for systematic organization, by appointing officers to take charge of various functions and roles vital to the operation and maintenance of his army. The appointees were all people with whom he had a special personal bond. They, and the newly established corps of personal guards, were his most trusted and loyal servants. These measures, calculated to strengthen the effectiveness of his military organization, also enhanced his own power.

As the reformed Qiyan tribal alliance under Chinggis' leadership grew strong, rival Mongol tribes or even former allies felt threatened. During the next seventeen years, Chinggis was occupied with military contests among the Mongols. He appears to have been focused on eliminating potential or actual rivals or challengers, one by one. One of his first military actions was directed against a senior member of his own Qiyan clan, who

Portrait of Chinggis Khan (in the National Palace Museum, Taiwan)
(Wikipedia *Commons*: retrieved on 26 November 2023 from
https://commons.wikimedia.org/wiki/File:YuanEmperorAlbumGenghisPortrait.jpg)

was accused by Chinggis of violating their tribal alliance by not having sent troops to support Chinggis' campaign against the Tartars, undertaken to avenge an ancestral wrong. The accusation was a pretext used by Chinggis, who wanted an opportunity to eliminate an internal rival. Striking against the Tartars, ostensibly to avenge his grandfather's wrong, just when the Tartars were being routed by a Jin force, was another opportunistic act. In addition to acquiring booty by defeating the Tartars, he was also given an official title by the Jin dynasty as a reward. This Jin official post, though only a nominal one, gave Chinggis prestige and entitlement to govern others.

For several years, Chinggis fought alongside his old mentor Toghrul Khan as his subordinate and tried latterly to form a marriage alliance between Toghrul's granddaughter and his own oldest son. Toghrul Khan and his son, mistrustful of the increasingly powerful Chinggis, decided to kill Chinggis at a sham engagement feast. Two slaves of an ally of Toghrul Khan alerted Chinggis to the secret plot. Soon afterwards war broke out between them. Chinggis' force, being outnumbered, had to retreat and regroup. Keeping himself informed of Toghrul Khan's movements, Chinggis surrounded his enemies' camp when they were unprepared. He prevailed, after battling continuously for three days. The destruction of the powerful Kereit Mongols sent a shock wave to the remaining Mongol tribal groups, the Naimans and the Merkits. The chief of the Naiman challenged Chinggis and was utterly defeated. After Chinggis routed the forces of the Merkits, he held hegemonic power over all the tribes of the Mongolian plateau.

In the spring of 1206, having destroyed all other nomadic tribal powers in the region after a series of campaigns, Chinggis called a great meeting (*quriltai*), during which a shaman, who spoke for heaven, declared him to be the Khan over all others under heaven. It was at this point that Temujin, the leader of the Qiyan tribal alliance, became Chinggis Khan, the paramount ruler of all the nomadic tribes of that region.

Prior to this time, these nomadic tribes had separate identities. Chinggis changed that by setting up new institutions. Instead of being divided into areas controlled by the different tribes, the entire territory he had conquered became a single entity: the Mongol empire. The people of the various tribes all became Chinggis' subjects whatever their previous status or rank, with a new identity as members of the unified Mongol empire and having a stake in its fortunes. Previously some of the heads of the tribal alliances were elected, whereas Chinggis' appointments were hereditary, passing to direct descendants.

As the head of the Mongol empire, Chinggis treated the entire country as his own domain to parcel out as he saw fit. He systematically organized all the people in it into 95 units of 1,000 households each, under which there were two lower administrative levels of 100 households and 10 households. The 1,000-household unit was to be the basic military and administrative entity, each governed by a *nayan* (lord), appointed by Chinggis. Grazing land was assigned to each unit of 1,000 households under their *nayan*. The *nayans* were thus members of the ruling class, and their positions were also hereditary. Chinggis gave the post of *nayan* as a reward to the leaders of tribes who joined him as allies or became his vassals early in the course of his military campaign for ascendancy, and who remained steadfastly loyal to himself or faithful to his cause. Leaders of tribes who came to his side of their own accord rather than being conquered were also made *nayans* over units of 1,000 households of the people of their own tribes. His meritorious comrades-in-arm and loyal servants were allowed to gather the peoples they had captured, together with those from the conquered tribes, to make into units of 1,000 households, and they would each be put in charge of one such unit as a *nayan*. Those granted much larger numbers of households, such as 10,000 or more, were the highest military commanders and Chinggis' sons and brothers. Chinggis divided the empire into subordinate khanates as territories belonging to each of his sons and brothers, except for the central part. This part was the original tribal area of his clan, and it was the seat of the Great Khan, Chinggis himself. Chinggis together with his sons and brothers and their descendants, were the true lords of the land, while the military aristocrats, such as the *nayans*, were all their subjects or servants, who ruled on their behalf.

Having set up these institutions, Chinggis laid down the laws (*jazaq*) of the land to buttress the new social and political order, and to define the boundary between acceptable and criminal behaviour. These laws were a collection of his commands and edicts, which were recorded in writing as the Great Jazaq. The Great Jazaq would be brought out and read during meetings of the khans of the various khanates to elect the Great Khan, and other important meetings or celebratory occasions of the heads of the empire. For general law enforcement, Chinggis created the post of a Supreme Judge, who presided over a judicial organization, conducting hearings, and passing judgements on cases. These were written down as permanent records, not to be altered (*koko debter*).

The Mongols had no written language prior to Chinggis' rule. He was quick to appreciate the usefulness of a written language for empire-wide administration and communication, not to mention the need for writing down his edicts and commands, and for keeping records of all kinds. A Naiman captive with a golden seal carved in the language of the Uyghur Turks appears to have been instrumental in Chinggis' adoption of the Uyghur script for transcribing the language of the Mongols. During the thirteenth century, the civilization of the Mongols took a great leap forward, as they created a state, acquired a written language, and began to write their own history.

To buttress his personal power and to ensure greater security for the Great Khan and his family, Chinggis upgraded and reformed the imperial guards from a few hundred to ten thousand. They were composed of healthy, strong, and talented youths selected from the sons of the *nayans* and from the common people. They were organized into twenty-four-hour shifts to guard the tents of the royal residents. Some of them were needed for specialized roles, such as scribes, drafters of edicts, cooks, wardrobe attendants, falconers and so on. As personal servants of the Great Khan, they were close to the centre of power. Politically and administratively, they functioned as the inner court. Militarily they were Chinggis' own elite troops. Their positions were above those of the *nayans* placed over 1,000 households. This system served many purposes as regards the Great Khan and his household. Those *nayans* who had contributed a son were less likely to rebel against him. It also gave the participants a stake in the regime.

Shortly after Chinggis set up the structure, the institutions, and the laws to consolidate his rule in the empire he created on the East Asian steppe, he embarked on an open-ended career of conquest. It is properly called a conquest, not simply a raiding and looting of the neighbouring countries, although invading accessible cities and towns to capture and enslave the people and to take away their possessions was certainly a part of the process. (Chinggis is said to have once remarked to his generals that a man's greatest happiness lies in suppressing disorderly crowds, winning victory over his enemy, despoiling his property, riding his handsome horses, and possessing his beautiful wives and concubines. The same source relates that when his sons quarrelled about their inheritance, his advice to them was that 'here are plenty of lands and rivers in the world, you could each enlarge your own territory by conquering other countries'.) Like Alexander, Caesar and other conquerors in the West, these Mongols regarded conquest as a glorious endeavour.

Chinggis Khan's campaigns

His military campaigns were carried out in a deliberate and calculated way, avoiding risk. It appears that he chose to fight only when the odds were in his favour. At the beginning, the size of his army was not extraordinarily large. The total number of his troops, estimated on the basis of a total population of 95,000 households with each 1,000-household providing 1,000 fighting men, would be 95,000. With the addition of 10,000 of his guards, he would have an armed force of 105,000. His soldiers, the most battle-hardened and warlike nomadic cavalry, were peerless fighters. He and his fellow commanders, after nearly twenty years of warring and winning battles against combative militaristic tribesmen like themselves, had become masters of the art of war, and were professionals at conquering. They had developed a first-class war machine using military tactics that had served them well and brought them phenomenal successes. They were receptive to new military technology and promptly utilized new weapons, such as firearms with explosives, after witnessing their use by the Song. They employed craftsmen and people with special skills from the conquered regions to produce a variety of weapons for them. They lost no time in augmenting their armed forces with conquered peoples. The inclusion of Turks, Persians, and Chinese greatly swelled the size of the Mongol army as time went on. At times captured enemy soldiers were put in the frontline to lead an attack and wear out the opposition on the battlefield, before the elite Mongol troops entered the battle to deliver the final blows.

The Mongols were patient conquerors. With a few exceptions, once they targeted a country, they would persist in attacking it, even if it took them many decades to complete the process. If they had difficulty in advancing into one area, they would try a second, and reserve the option of returning to the first later. They used terror to frighten their enemies into submission. When their army approached a city, which could be the capital city of a state, or a well-defended stronghold of a region, the Mongol commander would send an envoy ahead to ask the authorities concerned to surrender. If such a request were accepted, the Mongols usually let the existing authority continue to rule as a vassal, who would be obliged to pay tribute or taxes to their Mongol overlords, and who might sometimes be asked to send troops to fight with the Mongols or fulfil some other Mongol demands. Should the request be refused, and the Mongols take the city or the region by force, the vanquished would suffer a terrible fate. The invaders would set fire to buildings, plunder, and slaughter the inhabitants mercilessly. In 1257, when Hulegu's army was marching towards Baghdad, he sent a representative to ask the city to surrender. After being refused, Hulegu's soldiers laid siege, and then broke into that city in 1258. An orgy of killing, looting, and burning went on for ten days, with 800,000 people reportedly perishing. The Mongol army's fearsome reputation was surely the reason many cities opened their gates, and commanders of opposing forces went over to the Mongols without a fight.

The Mongol conquests under Chinggis

The rise of the Mongols under Chinggis Khan marked the thirteenth century as an era of the Mongol conquest and empire building. His expansionist drive began in 1205, the year before he proclaimed himself the great overlord of the Mongol tribes. During this period, he sent a raiding party to Western Xia - a close neighbour and, therefore, the first in the line of foreign states to be subjugated. The raid resulted in the seizure of many captives and much livestock. In 1207, he again sent troops, but retreated after discovering Western Xia's strong defensive posture. Finally in 1209, Chinggis' forces inflicted a major defeat on the Western Xia, and then marched to the capital of that country to besiege it. Chinggis also sent an envoy to negotiate terms with the ruler of the Western Xia. He withdrew after the ruler of the Western Xia offered him his daughter and agreed to become a vassal and pay annual tribute to Chinggis as his Mongol overlord.

Having subjugated the Western Xia into submission, Chinggis' next target was the Jin dynasty, whose empire extended over the region in which the Mongol tribes roamed. His contemplation of an aggressive move was supported by the intelligence he received. Certain disaffected members of the ruling clans of the former Liao dynasty who became Jin officials informed him that the Jin was ripe for destruction, because of ethnic tensions and many other serious weaknesses within this empire. Some of Chinggis' ancestors had been put to death by a ruler of the Jin dynasty for rebelling. On the pretext of seeking revenge for his ancestors, Chinggis waged war on the Jin in 1211. From that year to 1213, Chinggis' forces broke the Jin lines of defence north of the Yellow River, killing many of the 300,000 Jin combatants in a few decisive engagements.

The Mongol forces, divided into three lines of command, traversed back and forth combing through a large region north of the Yellow River, leaving some ninety prefectures in ruins, the people massacred or scattered, and their children and valuables carried away. In 1215, the Mongols captured part of present-day Beijing, the Jin 'Middle Capital', letting it to burn for a month. In 1217, Chinggis delegated further advance against the Jin to a subordinate, who was instructed to continue to attack the Jin on the one hand, and on the other to attract local magnates and Jin officials to come over to join the Mongols, with the land and the forces under their control. Many responded and were given hereditary offices by the Mongols, who allowed them to control certain territories and keep soldiers. The Jin also tried to adopt a similar policy, but more of their subjects chose to side with the Mongols, and fight on the instructions of their new masters. As a result, by 1226 all of the present-day provinces of Hebei and Shandong, that were a part of the Jin empire, fell into Mongol hands.

Though preoccupied with military campaigns against the Western Xia and the Jin, Chinggis did not neglect to send envoys and troops to the western parts of Eurasia, to demand the tribes and kingdoms there to acknowledge him as their overlord, and offer him tribute and services, such as sending soldiers to fight with his forces. Many at first agreed but later rebelled. From 1217 his focus turned westward. His forces crushed the rebels, and by 1218 they completed the conquest of Western Liao and the kingdom of the Western Uyghurs. This brought the Mongol-controlled territory right up to the Central Asian Empire of Khwarizm (Khorezm). In 1219, Chinggis led 200,000 troops himself to punish its ruler, after the merchants on the trade mission, as well as the envoys he sent to that kingdom, were either murdered or humiliated. The Sultan of Khwarizm, after losing cities such as Bukhara and Samarkand to the Mongols, was chased by Chinggis' forces to an island near the Caspian Sea, where he died in 1220. His son and heir, Sultan Jaial al-Din, gathered a force of 100,000 which resisted the Mongols for a while. At the end of 1221 he escaped to India, after the Mongols pursued him to the banks of the Indus River and defeated him there.

Although the empire of Khwarizm was destroyed, Mongol military expeditions to the west did not end there. Chinggis himself returned home with some of the forces in 1225, after staying in Samarkand to organize garrisons for the conquered territory in the west. Another branch of his army continued to march westward, sacking many cities in central and western Persia. From 1221 to 1224, these Mongol forces then swept through the northern Caucasus, Ukraine, Crimea, southern Poland, and European Russia, crushing resistance, and looting and pillaging even on their homeward journey.

After returning from his triumphal expedition to the west, in 1226 Chinggis led an army to punish the Western Xia because its ruler did not appear to him to be a sufficiently loyal and obedient vassal. In the spring of 1227, when the fall of the Western Xia, with its capital surrounded by the Mongol troops, was only a matter of time, Chinggis let his subordinates deliver the final blow, while he turned his attention once more to attacking the Jin. However, he died soon afterwards of an illness in July 1227, at age 65, when the Mongol conquest and empire building was still a work-in-progress.

During Chinggis' return journey from his expedition to the west, he had left his second son, Chagatai, with a garrison to secure the 'western regions', which referred to the territory adjoining the western border of the then Mongol empire, westward as far as the Amu Darya River and the Aral Sea in Central Asia. After Chinggis' death in 1227, Chagatai endeavoured to establish a khanate for himself and his heirs that would incorporate those lands in Central Asia with the domain given to him by Chinggis earlier, since these two areas were situated conveniently next to each other. Because the Central Asian territory was officially under the jurisdiction of the Great Khan (then Chenggis' third son Ogodei) who would not relinquish his control, Chagatai was not able to achieve his ambition during his lifetime. From 1260 onwards, some of his strong heirs managed to defy the Great

Khan and established a semi-independent or independent empire in Central Asia. Frequent violent internal power struggles, over succession especially, as well as numerous wars against external enemies, caused the empire of Chagatai to split up during the fourteenth century. The eastern part became fragmented into individual domains, while the western part became the empire of a usurper, the powerful but ruthless warrior Tughluq Temur, better known in the West as Tamerlane. Tamerlane became a believer in Islam soon after he became Khan in 1348. He commanded other Mongol aristocrats to adopt Islam as their religion.

Chinggis' military expeditions covered a vast area, subjugating or destroying many regimes along the way. Apart from leaving a garrison here and there, he did not attempt to organize regimes to replace the existing ones, or to divide the conquered territories into satraps for his heirs, as he had done in his Mongolian steppe land. He bestowed his legacy on his four sons and their direct lines of descendants and commanded his heirs to divide the fruits of the conquest and not to fight over the spoils. The four sons did indeed inherit khanates, but not altogether peacefully.

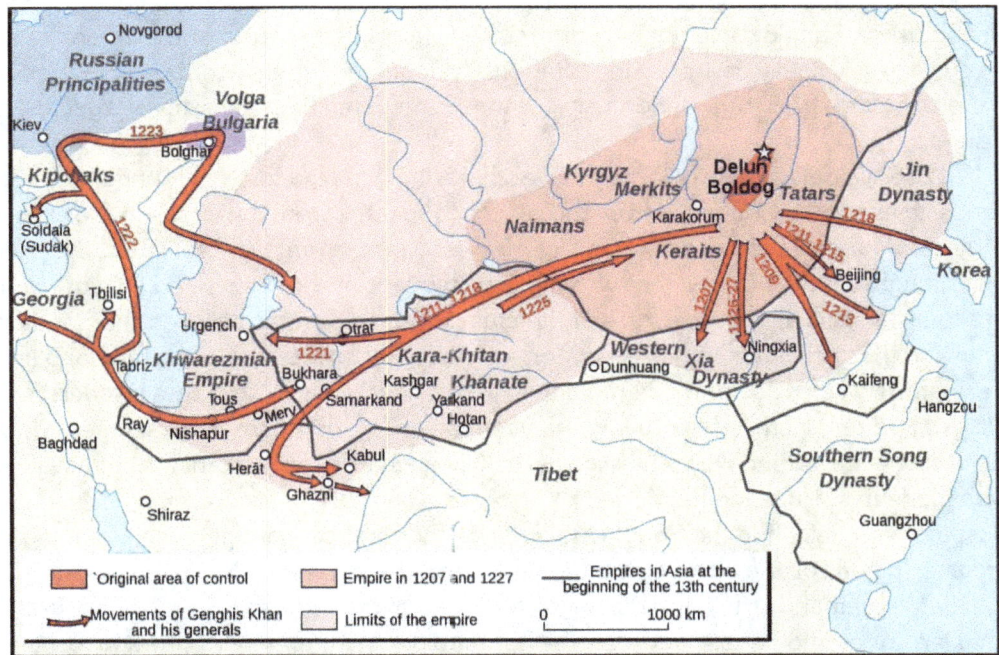

Map showing the Mongol campaigns (*World History Encyclopedia*: retrieved on 26 November 2023 from https://www.worldhistory.org/image/11221/map-of-the-campaigns-of-genghis-khan/)

The Great Khan Ogodei

Chinggis' death did not diminish the impetus of the Mongol drive towards expansion. His third son, Ogodei (1186-1241), succeeded him as the Great Khan in 1229 to take charge of the next round of the conquest. Soon after his accession, he received news that Jalai al-Din, the Sultan of Khwarizm, who had escaped to India, had returned to resume his office. Ogodei despatched a Mongol commander, Chormaqan, with an army of 30,000 to overthrow him and install local leaders who would submit to the Mongols. Cormaqan succeeded in doing so in 1231. Thereafter he set up camp southwest of the Caspian Sea, and from there he set out to conquer the surrounding areas in present-day Georgia and Armenia.

Ogodei's own first objective was to complete the conquest of the Jin as Chinggis had intended. Having lost most of its territory north of the Yellow River, the Jin had built strong defensive positions south of it. In 1228, putting up stiff resistance, the Jin forces even won a victory over the Mongols. The Mongols tried a flank attack and solicited help from the Southern Song. For six years the Mongol and Jin forces were locked in fierce combat. The Southern Song did eventually support the Mongols with soldiers and food before the Jin dynasty was finally destroyed in 1234. This brought the Mongol-controlled area south to the border of the Southern Song, whose wealth rendered it an irresistible target for the Mongols.

In 1235, Ogodei sent two of his sons, each leading a mixed force of Mongol and Han troops, to attack the Song, one from the east and the other from the west. On the eastern front, the Mongols won some initial victories. However, from 1237 to 1241, the Song forces fought so valiantly that they were able to recover some lost cities and fight the Mongols to a standstill along the shores of the Huai River, the border between the Southern Song and the former Jin empire. The Mongols had more success attacking the Song from the west. Between 1235 and 1241, Sichuan was seriously mauled by these invaders, who pillaged and massacred at will, before they retreated. The Southern Song seemed a hard nut to crack, and during Ogodei's reign as the Great Khan, no significant further advances were made in subjugating the Song.

Apart from defeating the Song, Ogodei had other preoccupations, such as setting up a regime to control and exploit the conquered territory. He had Chinggis' 1206 model of a military command structure with the Great Khan at the very top of a pyramid, distributing territories and people - reckoned as households - in his empire for the support (economically, politically, and militarily) of close relatives and meritorious military leaders, who formed a military and political aristocracy below him, and who were bound to the Great Khan as vassals to a feudal lord. These leaders were in command of their own loyal vassals, who had been given lesser amounts of land and number of households as support, and so on down to the commoners at the very bottom of the structure. Or, he could follow

an even older tradition bypassing distribution, and simply establish an overlord-vassal relationship with the existing rulers, or the ruling elite of the subjugated lands. These political
structures had been developed in the setting of the steppe. But at this point, Ogodei controlled a large expanse of fertile agricultural land that could support dense settlements in
the former Jin territory in north China. A new approach to govern this region and to extract its wealth therefore seemed an attractive option, indeed a necessity. Yelu Chucai, a
former Jin official and a descendant of the Liao royal clan, came to his aid. Ogodei took
Yelu Chucai's advice to organize a centralized administration for this region, with different
tax districts, and to register the households in each district to collect different kinds of
taxes at predetermined rates for the government of the Great Khan. He also awarded
specific tax districts and tens of thousands of households in those districts to his heirs, his
royal relatives, and meritorious officials, for them to collect a limited amount of taxes for
themselves, and to receive some benefit of the taxes collected from their area by the centre.
However, these aristocrats were accustomed to viewing the land and the people attached
to them as their private properties, and they made frequent collections at will. The dual
taxation became exceedingly burdensome to the people.

To enhance the prestige of the Great Khan and the glory of the Mongol empire, in
1235 Ogodei ordered the building of a capital of the Mongol empire at Karakorum, with
royal palaces (modelled on the Han Chinese style), official residences, temples, shops and
special quarters for other purposes. Since the Mongols had no cities, the capital had to
be constructed from scratch, with architects and skilled craftsmen drawn from different
parts the empire. Court rules and etiquette were also established, with the help of Yelu
Chucai, for assemblies at the court of the Great Khan.

While the Mongol armies were advancing against the Southern Song in the east, Ogodei did not forget about building empires in the far distant lands in the west, where the
armed might of the Mongols had had dramatic successes in overcoming local resistances
during Chinggis' western campaigns in 1220-25. Ogodei called a top-level meeting in
1235, when it was decided to send a second major military expedition to the west with a
large force of 150,000 troops under the leadership of Batu Khan, Chinggis' grandson
from the line of his eldest son. The eldest sons of other lines of Chinggis' direct descendants, as well as all Mongol aristocratic families, were obliged to raise troops and lead
them to join this expedition, which was dubbed 'the eldest sons' expedition to the west'.
The Mongol invaders left Karakorum in 1236. From 1237 to 1242, Batu's forces broke
the defences of many cities in present-day European Russia, including Moscow. They captured Kiev, and trampled over many areas of Poland, Hungary, Spain, Austria, Serbia,
and Dalmatia. In 1242, Europe was saved from further Mongol attack, when the news of
Ogodei's death a year earlier finally reached Batu, who withdrew his army eastward and
encamped around the lower Volga.

The election of Guyuk, and then of Mongke

Ogodei's death necessitated once more the election of a successor Great Khan. During his reign, Ogodei had extracted a promise from his imperial relatives that the Great Khan should forever be chosen from his line of descendants. Ogodei had favoured his grandson, Shiliemen, but his imperial consorts, who held the reins during the interim period before the election, chose Guyuk, his eldest son. Unfortunately, Guyuk had offended Batu by being disrespectful to the latter as his commander during the time when Guyuk was taking part in the 'eldest sons' military expedition to the west'. The gathering for the election was delayed for four years because Batu continually made excuses for not being able to attend. Finally in 1246, the imperial clans concerned met without Batu to vote for Guyuk to be Great Khan (r.1246 - 48), Shiliemen being considered too young during this round. As the Great Khan, Guyuk was mainly occupied with gathering troops and leading his imperial guards westwards, ostensibly to recuperate from an illness. In reality, his plan was to launch a surprise attack against Batu. A widow of Tolui, Chinggis' fourth and youngest son, sensed the covert plan and sent a warning to Batu, who consequently led his troops eastward to counter Guyuk. Before any engagement took place, Guyuk died in mysterious circumstances in 1248.

After Guyuk's death, Batu dominated the next round of elections for the Great Khan. He took it upon himself, as the heir of the branch of Chinggis' eldest son, to call the imperial clans to assemble at his military camp, far from the Mongol homeland in the west. The purpose was to elect Mongke, Tolui's eldest son and a close ally of his, as the Great Khan in 1248. Ogodei's line, refusing to attend the meeting, sent a representative to revive Shiliemen's claim to this position, a claim rejected by Batu, Mongke, and their supporters. Many of Ogodei's, and some of Chagatai's, lines of descendants refused to accept the legality of Mongke's election, because it did not take place at Chinggis' great yurts in the Mongol homeland. Batu then asked his brother to lead an army to accompany Mongke to return there and hold a meeting to legitimize Mongke's election. The refusal of the members of the other two lines to participate delayed such a meeting until 1251, when Batu coerced his imperial clansmen to meet and to acknowledge Mongke as their Great Khan. During the celebration of Mongke's accession, Shiliemen and some of his other relatives plotted against Mongke, but Mongke's falconer discovered the plot. A bloodbath against all the principals and their subordinates ensued. Most of the plotters lost their lands and their lives. Those deemed to be uninvolved retained the domains Chinggis had granted to Ogodei's line originally, in addition to some lands given to them by Mongke. Ogodei's descendants were not pacified by Mongke's gesture. During the second half of the thirteenth century, a strong and ambitious member of Ogodei's line, Kaidu, who was particularly resentful, kept encroaching on the territory of the empire of Chagatai, and waged nearly half a century of war against the empire of the Great Khan. In the early decades of the fourteenth century, after Kaidu's death, his heirs were unable to prevent their empire from being destroyed and their territory being absorbed by the rulers of the empire of Chagatai, with support from the Great Khan.

For enabling Mongke to become the Great Khan, Batu received the handsome reward he desired, which was to be the recognized ruler of the immensely large empire of the Golden Horde, which he was instrumental in conquering and founding. The official acknowledgement by the Great Khan at this point, before the Mongol empire became effectively split up, was important, because the Great Khan inherited Chinggis' mantle as the overlord of the empire. Batu (r. 1251- 1255) represented the line of Chinggis' eldest son, Jochi, whose descendants ruled their own domains carved out of this large territory through local vassals. This empire flourished for about one hundred years. It declined from the middle of the fourteenth century, starting from weakness at the centre. From the 1420s it became fragmented into several khanates ruled by Mongols, but with a Turkish cultural complexion. The Mongols who migrated to the empire of the Golden Horde were relatively few. Many settled on grasslands, mingled with Turkish speaking nomadic tribes, and eventually became assimilated by their Turkish subjects who followed Islam. In 1502, after being decisively defeated by Ivan III of Russian, the empire of the Golden Horde came to an end.

For Mongke as the Great Khan, another major unfinished task of empire building was that of the conquest of the Southern Song in the east. Related to this more challenging enterprise was the acquisition of areas at the periphery of the Southern Song, and one of these, in its southwest, was Tufan (present Tibet). Earlier incursions had suggested Tufan as an easier target to incorporate into the Mongol empire than its far larger neighbour. In 1252, soon after his accession, Mongke sent Mongol and Han forces to invade Tufan. The Mongol rulers were able to build a kind of feudal benefactor-subject relationship with the Buddhist religious authorities, who dominated this region. In 1253, Tufan became a part of the Mongol empire. Mongke had its census taken, based on which he granted large land domains, with households attached to them in groups of ten thousand, to his two brothers, Khubilai and Hulegu, while reserving the richest area for himself.

Mongke then assigned the challenging task of conquering the Southern Song to Khubilai. Because of the Southern Song's formidable defence build-up, Khubilai decided on a strategy of first invading the kingdom of Dali (Yunnan), which was located on the southwest of Southern Song, and then executing a flank attack on the Southern Song from this direction. Between 1252 and 1255, Khubilai accomplished the goal of overthrowing the ruling house of Dali, without the usual wanton slaughter of the defenceless local inhabitants, and he integrated this region into the Mongol empire. There are two notable contemporary consequences of that historical event: first, Yunnan became a permanent part of China; and secondly Islam, introduced to this part of the world under Mongol rule, is still practised there.

After taking over Dali, Khubilai did not rush to attack the Southern Song. He wanted to formulate a long-term plan for holding north China securely, and for overcoming the Southern Song's defences in the most effective way. He arranged for some Han advisors to join him in his own territory in Shaanxi, including the outstanding Liu Bingzhong. These advisors told Khubilai that too much killing and extortionate exactions were turning the area bordering Southern Song into a wilderness. The people of the Southern Song who had witnessed such desolation would strongly resist surrendering to the Mongols. This situation also deprived the Mongol rulers of taxes and soldiers. They suggested that Khubilai should establish a sound administration with the rule of law and equitable taxation, and promote agriculture and sericulture. They also advised him to strengthen and rebuild the defences of the ruined cities in that area, set up agricultural colonies, store grain, and pacify the people there to prepare for a long struggle against the Southern Song. Khubilai accepted these suggestions and advice and, with Mongke's permission, acted upon them with positive results and popular support. However, the new measures antagonized the Mongol aristocrats and greedy officials because they were obliged to curb their demands on the population. His seemingly ambitious activities also aroused the suspicion of Mongke, his older brother. In 1257, Mongke stripped Khubilai of his political authority, took away his military command, and ordered him 'home to rest from an illness'.

Mongke then despatched another royal relative with an army to attack the Southern Song from the front, while he himself was to advance on Sichuan in the southwest with his own forces. Although Mongke had successes in Sichuan, both armies later failed to take the fiercely defended cities in the heartland of the Southern Song. In 1258, Mongke decided to ask Khubilai to come out of his forced retirement to take over the command of the assault on the Southern Song. Khubilai, delighted to regain military power, sent an advance corps south with instructions to spare the civilians from burning, looting, and killing, while he consulted his Han advisors as to the most effective strategy. As he was proceeding south with the bulk of his troops, he received news of Mongke's death in September 1259, and was requested to return north to take part in election politics. He did not want to do so without some demonstrable successes in his military campaign, so he continued south to surround a Song city on the other side of the Yangtze River. The Song general defended the city stoutly. After two months of siege, Khubilai's soldiers were short of rations and nearly half of them had fallen, leaving Khubilai's side vulnerable to an attack. The Southern Song prime minister, Jia Sidao, instead of taking the opportunity to attack, chose to appease Khubilai by offering to cede certain territory and pay a tribute of 200,000 taels of silver and 200,000 rolls of silk to the Mongols in exchange for peace.

After Ogodei had consolidated Mongol rule after retaking Khwarizm, most of the territory west of the Amu River all the way to the border of Syria became theirs. However, some independent authorities in Persia as well as the Abbasid Caliphate in Baghdad remained unconquered. Not long after his accession, Mongke had ordered his brother,

Hulegu (the third son of Tolui), to lead an army to subjugate these and any other states outside the Pax Mongolica. After crossing the Amu River in 1256, in three years until 1259, Hulegu's forces broke the defences of many cities, including Baghdad, slaughtering, plundering, and burning with impunity. Early in the 1260s, Damascus surrendered to Hulegu, after his forces captured the Sultan of Syria, when he tried to escape to Egypt. At this point, Hulegu received news of Mongke's death in 1259. He led his forces back to Persia, while leaving 20,000 troops to his subordinate, Kitbuqa, to continue the military campaign in Syria and beyond. Kitbuqa sent an envoy to the ruler of Egypt, asking him to surrender. Qutuz, the Sultan, who was a Mamaluke usurper of the throne, killed the hapless envoy, and moved his own army to Palestine to fight the advancing Mongols. When the two armies met in September 1260, the Mamalukes won overwhelmingly. Kitbuqa was killed in this battle, with all his troops. The triumphant Mamaluke forces then went on to take Damascus and the rest of Syria. This battle was significant for halting further Mongol advances in the Middle East.

The Yuan Dynasty (1279-1368)

Khubilai becomes the Great Khan, and emperor of the Yuan dynasty

Let us now take up the story of Khubilai[9] and how he became the Great Khan and emperor of the Chinese Yuan dynasty. We left him receiving from the Southern Song prime minister Jia Sidao substantial concessions in exchange for peace. At that point, his wife sent a messenger to hasten him to return north because his younger brother, Arigh Boke, was raising a large army at Karakorum and appointing someone to govern northern China, in preparation for becoming the Great Khan. Jia Sidao's peace offering came as a timely gift for Khubilai, to take back north as a tangible achievement. He accepted Jia's terms for peace and brought his troops immediately northward to the vicinity of Yanjing (Beijing), the northeren China power base he had developed over the years. He did not go to Karakorum, where he feared that he might be outmanoeuvred by Arigh Boke. The two brothers negotiated between themselves as to which one should become the Great Khan, with neither prepared to give way to the other. Then in April 1260, Khubilai decided to take the initiative by proclaiming himself as the Great Khan in Kaiping, the new city he built for himself, after obtaining the support of several of the imperial relatives who had a say in the election of the Great Khan. Adopting the Han Chinese tradition of having a new reign period, he began his reign as the first year of Zhong Tong, abbreviated from the phrase *zhongchao zhengtong*, meaning legitimate rule from the centre. At the same

---

[9] As a reminder to the reader: he was the third son of Tolui, who was the fourth son of Chinggis.

time, he issued an edict justifying the changes by stating that the 'shortcomings in civil governance mandated the present change from the ancestral way', including the adoption of some of the traditional institutions of dynastic rule of the central plain (the northern China plain). Soon afterwards, Khubilai sent out requisitions for soldiers, horses, and food grains from all over north China, and set up a strong corps of imperial guards for himself. These preparations were made against an invasion from the north, rather than in preparation for reactivating the war against the Southern Song, even though Jia Sidao did not fulfil any of the terms of the peace treaty.

Khubilai's pre-emptive move took Arigh Boke by surprise. In the summer of 1260, he hastened to assemble a group of the imperial relatives partial to his claim, in a camp in the Altai Mountains, and they voted for him there as the Great Khan. With two claimants for supremacy, a military contest between them became inevitable. The war lasted four years, with Karakorum changing hands three times. During this period Arigh Boke lost the acquiescence or support of Hulegu (the empire of the Il-Khan) and Alghu (the empire of Chagatai). Since he had confirmed Alghu in his position as the head of the empire of Chagatai, Arigh Boke became angry at Alghu's failure to deliver grain to support his war effort and attacked Alghu. Khubilai took this opportunity to win over the heads of these two western branches of the Mongol empire by recognizing their right to rule their respective areas as suzerain states inside the Mongol empire, rather than as representatives of the Great Khan, which had been the case up to that point. In the spring of 1264, famine hit the region of Ili, the resource-rich area of northern China where Arigh Boke's soldiers had set up camp after plundering and killing the local population. The hungry soldiers had little will to fight, and Arigh Boke was obliged to surrender to Khubilai. Given that both contestants were reared in the military tradition of the steppe, Khubilai's systematic management of the richer resources of North China was a major factor in his favour in this contest.

In 1264, after Khubilai won the contest, he officially conferred the title of Il-Khan on his brother Hulegu. This gave rise to yet another vassal state in the west, the empire of Il-Khan, within the Pax Mongolica. Like the other Mongol vassal states, the relationship between its ruler and the Great Khan, the overlord of the entire Mongol empire, was mostly that of being dependent in form but independent in substance. The Mongol rulers here were relatively more involved in governing this empire in the tradition of this region, and they also maintained fairly close contact, through the postal relay system, with the court of the Great Khan. Towards the end of the thirteenth century, the Il-Khan Ghazhan (r. 1296-1304) changed his name to Muhammad and declared that he himself and all the Mongols in this empire were to practise Islam. He introduced comprehensive administrative reforms, prohibited the Mongol lords from arbitrary exactions, encouraged commerce and industry, and promoted the development of science. He fought against the Mamaluke empire in Egypt over Syria, and wrote to the King of France, Philippe le Bel, asking the latter to ally with him against the Mamalukes, but without success. The empire of the Il-Khans did not last long. In 1335, the central authority collapsed, to be followed by civil wars and an invasion from the empire of the Golden Horde. Its successor regime was destroyed by Tamerlane towards the end of the fourteenth century.

Portrait of Khubilai Khan (*World History Encyclopedia*: retrieved on 26 November 2023 from https://www.worldhistory.org/image/11204/portrait-of-kublai-khan/)

Khubilai's victory marked the shift of the centre of power of Mongol rule from the northern steppe, as represented by Karakorum, southward to northern China. It also strengthened the hands of those who were in favour of making changes in the Mongol ancestral traditions by adopting certain Han institutions to facilitate Mongol rule in north China. In 1271, Khubilai adopted a Han Chinese dynastic name, Yuan, meaning first. The Chinese accepted the legitimacy of the Mongol-ruled Yuan dynasty, and its history formed a part of the official historical chronicles of China. In 1272, Khubilai sited his capital at Yanjing (Beijing), where a new imperial quarter had been built. A rebellion by a hereditary Han military aristocrat led to Khubilai stripping all such aristocrats of military power. He reorganized the government administrative system with reference to the models provided by the Jin and earlier Chinese dynasties.

The final defeat of the Southern Song

Now secure in his position as the Great Khan, Khubilai could focus his attention on the unfinished conquest of Southern Song. The Mongols had first attacked Southern Song over thirty years previously in 1235, during the reign of Ogodei, soon after the destruction of the Jin empire. During Mongke's reign, Khubilai's initial attempt at taking one of its cities, in 1260, had not been exactly a success. Khubilai therefore had doubts about being able to subjugate this seemingly indomitable foe. He sought assurance that it was the will of heaven for him to take over an empire that had been ruled by the Zhao family for over three hundred years. While Khubilai hesitated, his generals were keen to go. War offered many opportunities: loot, promotions, and even ennoblement were the rewards of military accomplishments. On the Southern Song side, many of its officials, military commanders, and the ordinary soldiers, motivated by patriotism or loyalty to the dynasty, or fear of the Mongols, were prepared to fight to the death. But the prime minister, Jia Sidao, and other high officials were corrupt and complacent. They relied on the broad expanse of the Long River (better known as the Yangtze River) as a natural moat, and on their navy and their long experience in defensive warfare to shield them against their fearsome foe. A jealous and oppressive commander-in-chief led to the defection of a very able Southern Song general, Liu Zheng, who subsequently gave Khubilai useful information and strategic advice on the way forward. He also helped his new chief to train naval forces, a weak link in the Mongol war machine, but vital for warfare in an area full of rivers and lakes, and with the seacoast nearby.

In 1268, Khubilai took his advice and ordered his troops to invade the two key cities on the opposite side of river, as suggested by Liu Zheng. It took more than five years to capture one of the two cities. As soon as the first one fell, the defenders of the other lost heart and surrendered. In 1275, the Yuan court directed a force of several hundred thousand troops against the Southern Song, which lost a series of major battles and many of its cities. Thereafter the pace of the war quickened, and as the main Yuan forces streamed down the Yangtze towards Lin'an (Hangzhou today), many of the defending forces along the way either surrendered or absconded. Although Khubilai exhorted his generals to refrain from killing the people, the populations of some Southern Song cities suffered almost total annihilation. In 1276, the Southern Song court, preparing to surrender, left its capital at Lin'an undefended. The Yuan forces marched in and took the five-year old emperor Song Gongzong, and the dowager empress to Khubilai, who gave the child emperor a ducal title. Song Gongzong later went to Tufan and immersed himself in Buddhism, while the dowager empress became a Buddhist nun.

Even at this stage, the Southern Song dynasty refused to concede defeat. Its loyalists rallied around the captured emperor's two brothers, who were spirited out of the capital before it fell, to a coastal city named Wenzhou, where the eight-year-old Zhao Shi was declared emperor in 1276. Fleeing from the Yuan forces, the Southern Song court retreated to a ship, under the protection of several armed vessels, and moved further and further south to a small island atoll south of Guangdong. When Zhao Shi died in 1278, his younger brother Zhao Bing was made emperor. After the Yuan pursuers caught up with Southern Song remnants, a fierce battle between the belligerents proceeded late into the night, amidst roaring cannons and the battering of heavy seas. With the rest of the empire gone, this hopeless final struggle, at what seemed like the ends of the earth, concluded with the last emperor of the Southern Song plunging into the sea on the back of his prime minister. Soon afterwards, Khubilai's forces mopped up other scattered pockets of resistance, and completed the conquest of the Southern Song in 1279.

The failure to take Japan

Khubilai's expansionist drive did not end with the overthrow of the Southern Song, although the eastern extremity of the Mongol empire, except for the Korean peninsula, was by then surrounded by sea. Korea had not been spared the unwanted attention of the Mongols who, during the reign of Chinggis Khan in 1218, had extracted tribute from its rulers. Khubilai's predecessors had despatched troops to invade Korea on several occasions, turning to slaughtering, looting, and kidnapping when the rulers of Korea did not satisfy their demands. It was Khubilai who stabilized the Yuan empire's relationship with the kingdom of Korea, as that between a suzerain and a vassal. Khubilai also initiated the custom of marriage between Mongol princesses and Korean kings or heirs to the throne.

The control of Korea greatly facilitated the passage of naval forces between Japan and the East Asian mainland. In addition to the steppe nomad's hunger for conquest, Khubilai, possessing by then the Mandate of Heaven as emperor of the Yuan dynasty, also coveted the role of a universal sovereign in the long tradition of northern China, who would unite all under Heaven and receive the homage of rulers of many kingdoms. The Japanese, however, were not willing to be recruited into such a system. They repeatedly rebuffed Khubilai's attempts to contact them with the help of the Koreans, which began in 1267. Official letters from the Yuan court remained unanswered, and Yuan envoys were turned back even before they reached the Japanese capital, and some were killed. By 1274, his patience exhausted, Khubilai sent an expeditionary force against Japan, consisting of 2,000 Mongols, Han Chinese, and Koreans with 900 warships requisitioned from Korea. Meeting stout Japanese resistance, the landing party returned to the ships, which had to retreat after being damaged by a typhoon.

His next attempt to invade Japan was a much bigger affair of several thousand warships, mainly from south China, and a mixed force of 40,000 Mongols, Han Chinese, and Koreans, as well as 100,000 troops from south China under two separate commands. The leaders of these forces had trouble agreeing on an overall strategy and procrastinated

for a month, with their vessels stationed near a Japanese island. The delay was fatal because the typhoon season was approaching. Before any invasion took place, an immense
storm buffeted the ships, causing the fleet of vessels tied together or anchored near each
other to crash into one another with great force. Although some of the leaders managed
to sail away with a fraction of their troops (about one fifth), most of the ships were
wrecked and the soldiers and sailors were either drowned, killed, or captured by the Japanese. So Khubilai's second invasion of Japan ended in total disaster. He was persuaded
against any further attempt by his ministers, and by the opposition of the people from
southern China, who, having supplied the ships and manpower, bore the burden of the
losses. Between 1292 and 1293 Khubilai mounted a far smaller seaborne military campaign against Java, whose king was supposed to have insultingly turned away Khubilai's
envoy. This invasion also ended in failure. However, during this period of Khubilai's attempt to expand overseas, Liuqiu was incorporated into the Yuan empire without incident.

The Mongol empire under Khubilai

Khubilai had developed a regular routine for extending his universal empire. He normally started with diplomacy by sending an envoy to 'summon' or 'instruct' the ruler of
the country he wished to dominate to come to his court, bearing tributes in the manner
of an inferior to a superior lord. Should the ruler come, or if not, at least send his son and
heir in his place, Khubilai would confer (ce feng) upon the ruler a kingly title to rule his
country and give him gifts to take back home. This would be the initial step in establishing
the official relationship between the Yuan emperor as the suzerain and the foreign king
as a vassal. As a vassal, the foreign ruler would be required to send envoys with tributes
at regular intervals, annually or less frequently if agreed. He might have to send his sons
or other relatives as hostages to the Yuan court. He or his representatives would be required to kneel and perform the kowtow as a mark of subjection. Before his heir came to
his throne, the Yuan emperor had to be approached to confer the kingly title on the heir.
There might be demands additional to these standard ones if circumstances warranted
them. Should the foreign ruler refuse to enter into such a relationship or reject the Yuan's
demands either from inside or outside this system, the Yuan would settle the matter by
force. With the rulers of Vietnam, Champa, and Burma, Khubilai tried to consolidate the
suzerain and vassal relationship through sending envoys, or by force. At times he even
endeavoured to rule these areas directly through the military and administrative regimes
he had established.

The rulers of some states were unwilling to comply with the conditions of vassalage.
But the Yuan forces sent against them, weakened from the start by the sultry climate, the
densely wooded jungle-like terrain, and the tropical insects and diseases, found it difficult

to overcome the determined local resistance. The defenders in Vietnam used ambushes and guerrilla tactics against the Yuan invaders with devastating effect. Following these setbacks, internal opposition obliged Khubilai to rely on diplomacy rather than force when dealing with these countries. After the military threat from the Yuan receded, the rulers of these countries, eager for peace and trade with the Yuan empire, observed a nominal tribute relationship with the Yuan by sending envoys with tributes to the Yuan court at regular intervals. By the end of Khubilai's reign in 1294, the momentum of the Mongol expansionist drive, powered by his grandfather Chinggis a century ago, had run out of steam. His successor, Yuan Chenzong (1294-1307) ushered in a policy of conserving and protecting what had been achieved (*shou chen*). Keeping the peace (*wei he*) rather than expansionist war became the new agenda.

When Khubilai ruled as the Great Khan, the territory of the Mongol empire - including the empire of the Great Khan and the other great khanates ruled by the descendants of three other sons of Chinggis and his principal wife - reached its greatest extent. It stretched from the Pacific Ocean in the east to the border of Hungry in the west, with a large swath of the Middle East in between. The territory of the empire of the Great Khan covered an area that included the Chinese lands of the former Song dynasty at its peak, the Jin, the Western Xia, Tufan (Tibet), Dali (Yunnan), Korea, Liuqiu (Taiwan), and the homeland of the Mongols in the East Asian steppes (Mongolia). China, north and south, was once more united and subsumed in the Great Khan's empire, the boundary of which was considerably different from that of the subsequent dynasties that occupied China. The Yuan was a decidedly multi-ethnic empire, and its rulers were non-Han. While other non-Han nomadic rulers of Chinese lands became Sinicized sooner or later, and many took pride in attaining a high degree of the cultural accomplishments that were native to northern China, the Mongol emperors remained strangers to the literary culture of the Chinese, though there were a few exceptions during the fourteenth century. The territory of the Sinicized nomadic dynasties became merged with Chinese lands in the course of time, and their subjects became a part of the multi-ethnic inhabitants of China. In contrast, the Mongol ruling elites mostly lived in their steppe homeland north of the Gobi Desert (abbreviated as Mo Bei in Chinese), or kept domains in, or their close ties with, this region, so it was easy and natural for them to keep their culture and tradition alive. They did not become Sinicized. When the Chinese rebels from the south eventually overthrew the Yuan dynasty, the Mongol ruling house and their supporters retreated to Mo Bei. Since the Chinese successor state, the Ming, did not try to impose direct rule over Tibet, Korea, or even Mongolia, the territory of the Ming was a great deal smaller than that of the Yuan.

Characterization of the Yuan Dynasty

Unlike any of the other dynasties that ruled China, the Yuan rulers effectively enforced a policy of treating their subjects according to their ethnic origins in a hierarchical order. There were roughly four major divisions, which naturally placed the Mongols at the top. They were followed by the Se Mu (mostly Muslim Central Asians), with whom the Mongols were familiar through trade contacts; then the Han (including for example former subjects of the Jin and Liao empires in northern China, and some Koreans); and lastly the Southerners (former subjects of the Southern Song, the more remote and the last to be conquered, also called 'the newly–submitted peoples'). Although no edicts or documents have been found that explicitly stated this policy, it was reflected in the law, the judicial processes, in matters relating to taxation, and in official appointments. Marriage was expected to occur within members of each group, and each followed its own custom with the male considered the dominant partner. Marriage between members of the different groups was not prohibited, but the custom of the male side would be followed. However, if a man from another ethnic group married a Mongol woman, the custom of the male side need not be followed. Polygamy was sanctioned because the Mongols wanted their population to grow. Marriage between a free person and a serf or slave was punishable by either a two-year prison sentence against the free man, or the degradation of the free woman to the position of a serf or a slave. The Mongol military aristocrats, like other tribal nomads, thrived on having serfs and slaves. This custom was widespread when China was being conquered and its people captured or displaced. There were slave markets doing a brisk trade.

This social order, which was created and upheld by the Mongols, was designed to serve their interest as the ruling elites. It favoured themselves and their foreign helpers, whom they relied upon for experience and skills in areas such as governing sedentary populations and managing a complex economy, which were not indigenous to the Mongols. These few foreigners did not constitute a threat to the Mongol rulers. The ethnic classifications and gradations were the Mongols' method to preserve and fix their privileged position permanently, with themselves at the top and with the Chinese majority at the base of the social pyramid. Their other tactic for holding society at the existing status quo was to register people (households) in hereditary occupational categories, such as soldiers, farmers, artisans, Buddhist monks, astrologers, miners, Confucian scholars and so on. Members of some of these groups were obliged to give one month's service annually, free to the state, as corvee (a labour service tax).

Yuan dynasty porcelain dish, mid-fourteenth century. (*Wikipedia*: retrieved on 26 November 2023 from https://en.wikipedia.org/wiki/File:Yuan_Dynasty,_porcelain_dish,_mid_14th_century.jpg)

Governance

Although the Yuan took on some of the trappings of a traditional Chinese dynasty, it was essentially a colonial regime, in that the Mongols were the decision-makers, who occupied most of the high offices of the government. The Mongols formed the top layer of the ruling elite and kept military power in their own hands. Below them were Muslim Central Asians, such as Persians and Uighur Turks, who held high administrative positions. There were even a few Europeans who served as Yuan officials, the most famous of whom was Marco Polo, a merchant from Venice. They distrusted the Chinese, who were the majority in their realm, perhaps out of fear that the Chinese might rebel or overwhelm them, being much larger in number. There was, in fact, one case of a Chinese rebellion by a powerful Chinese marquise (*shi hou*), an aristocratic title given by the Mongols to reward Chinese warlords, who had fought on the side of the Mongols in north China against the Jin. This Chinese rebellion, which occurred during the early years of Khubilai's reign, had a strong psychological impact on him, because it was not just a Chinese peasant revolt, such as occurred here and there in southern China: it was seen as a treacherous act by someone who was expected be loyal to the Mongol dynasty. It deepened the suspicion and mistrust of the Mongol ruler towards the Chinese. Thereafter, all Chinese hereditary marquises, even though they had nothing to do with the rebellion, had their troops taken away, and their noble titles ceased to be hereditary.

There were some Chinese high officials during the Yuan, and they were mostly the descendants of the former Chinese marquises. Not until 1313 did the Yuan dynasty make a serious attempt to revive the civil service examination, which had been used not only by the Chinese, but also by foreign-ruled dynasties like the Jin, to select officials educated in Confucian ethics. When this institution was re-established, quotas were set that limited the number of passes from each category of the ethnic groups, in such a way as to discriminate against the Chinese majority. It did not become a highway for entering government service: only around eight percent of officials of Third Grade and above came through this channel. The Chinese clerks did the bureaucratic paperwork necessary for the civil administration of the empire. They had a reputation for engaging in corrupt practices, and the Chinese scholar-gentry class held them in contempt. Nevertheless, they were deemed adequate as lower-level assistants for their Mongol masters because they could read and write, and had hands-on experience of local government procedures. They had opportunities for promotion and filled the lower to middle ranks of the Yuan officialdom.

Being nomadic herders, the Mongols did not have experience in ruling over a country with densely settled sedentary population, some of whom dwelt in cities, while most made a living from agriculture. Turning large tracts of agricultural land into pastures was a possible option that had occurred in northern China, and in other areas in connection with raising horses for the royal relatives, but a better option existed. Since the main objective of the Mongol conquest was to extract wealth, we have seen that Ogodei decided to tax the agricultural population, as advised by Yelu Chucai, accepting it as a better choice for achieving the desired objective. To do so, the Mongols had to adopt certain Han-Chinese institutions and modes of government, known as *Han fa* - literally the Han method – or *wen zhi* (civil governance). Since the reign of Ogodei, and even more so under Khubilai, *Han fa* was used to divide the empire into administrative units from the provincial level down to the counties, to carry out a census of the households in each local district, and to assess the tax liability due from each household. In addition to Han Chinese officials, the *Han fa* had the support of a few Yuan emperors, who wanted to shift the balance of power more to the centre, and to eliminate the unbridled corruption and abuses in government administration. These were the Yuan rulers who had received a Confucian education while growing up in northern China, as opposed to the ones who had spent their formative years immersed in the martial tradition of the peoples of the steppe. One of them, Yuan Renzong (r. 1312-1320), re-established the state examination for official recruitment in 1315, after the system had fallen into disuse from the beginning of the Yuan. Renzong's attempts at reform using *Han fa* were thwarted by his mother, the dowager empress, who placed her own appointees in key positions and opposed any changes to the status quo.

Besides taxing the agricultural population, the Yuan, like its Song predecessor, also taxed commercial transactions and commodities, such as salt, alcohol, vinegar, tea, and various metals and minerals. The taxes on the households were paid in grain, cloth, and labour service. In 1238, these taxes from Mongol-controlled areas in north China were worth 1,100,000 taels of silver. In the following year, an Islamic merchant, Abdulaheman, placed a bid to collect twice the above amount of taxes for Ogodei, and was given the job. From then on, the task of tax-collection was mostly farmed-out to merchants of Central Asia, who operated such a ruinously oppressive tax regime that it forced people to abscond and become outlaws. After the conquest of the Southern Song in 1279, the Yuan found itself in the happy position of seeing the revenue from the farming sector doubled.

There was a problem in shipping the grain from the southern rice-basket to the capital region using the Grand Canal, which fell into disuse early in the twelfth century and was no longer navigable. The Yuan resorted to coastal shipment from the mouth of the Yangtze River to the port nearest to their capital at Beijing, which was Tianjin. When work on the restoration of the Grand Canal was eventually completed near the beginning of the fourteenth century, this inland waterway was used for transporting taxed grain and other products to the north, without diminishing the importance of the sea route.

Reluctant to use their Chinese subjects to help them govern the empire, the Mongol rulers turned to the Central Asians, Muslim merchants mainly, and entrusted them with the vitally important job of managing the financial affairs - fiscal as well as taxation - of the empire. These powerful lords of finance naturally took the opportunity to fill their own coffers as well as those of the state They controlled the issue of paper currency, an innovation of the Song adopted by the Yuan. While the Song had limited the validity of the paper money it issued to certain areas and periods of time, the Yuan made it an empire-wide currency without time limits on its validity. The value of the paper money was based on silver, which the government collected as taxes, and kept in its treasuries at the capital and in some cities in the provinces. Although the value of paper money issued in 1260 fell when its conversion into silver was forbidden, paper currency could still be viable, and its value maintainable, if the government kept sufficient silver in its stores to support the paper money in circulation. As time went on the amount of silver and gold reserves kept by the government to support the currency in circulation continued to decline, leading to inflation. Despite tax increases, the income of the over-spending government fell increasingly short of its expenditure. When the government resorted to printing more money to remedy the situation, inflation only became worse. Bouts of inflation were followed by the government's effort to stabilize the currency, through devaluation or tax increases, without achieving lasting success. Near the end of the dynasty in the 1360s, inflation was so severe that the paper currency became worthless. Forgery was another problem with the printed money. Although the crime carried the death penalty, that did not prevent a large amount of forged paper money circulating around the entire empire, damaging the monetary system. When the empire of the Il-Khan suffered serious financial strain under Gaykhatu Khan (r. 1291-1295), he also issued paper currency at Tabriz, the capital. Merchant refusal led to the abandonment of paper currency, but *chao*, the Chinese word for it, has remained in use in the Persian language of today as *chaw*.

Commerce and trade

The commercial expansion under the Song, both internally and with foreign lands, continued to flourish in Yuan times, particularly during the decades of relative peace after the fall of the Southern Song. The Pax Mongolica rendered the inter-regional overland trade along the silk roads and steppe roads more secure. The renovated Grand Canal facilitated transport of goods between northern and southern China. Cotton became a large export item in addition to the usual silks, ceramics, and lacquer ware. Spices, pearls, and precious stones were among the notable imports. Taxes on commerce were a major source of the state revenue. For example, the levy on salt, the most important commodity tax, yielded over 7,600,000 ingots of silver for the Yuan treasury during the 1330s.

Unlike the Chinese ruling elites educated in the Confucian mould, who generally held merchants and mercantile activities in disdain, the Mongols had the opposite outlook. As nomadic herders of the steppe, trade supplied them such products as grain, metal, cloth, salt, tea, and medicine, which were highly welcome, if not necessary, supplements to what they could derive from their livestock. As the post-conquest wealthy upper class of the society, the Mongols of the Yuan dynasty were able to indulge in their love of luxury goods, such as pearls and precious stones, despite their enormous expense. They valued merchants because the latter could satisfy their need for several basic consumer items, as well as their taste for certain luxury items. The merchants they were most familiar with were Muslim traders from the Middle East and Central Asia, often Iranians, who dominated the inter-regional overland trade along the Silk Road, as well as the overseas trade of the spice routes, which included China. The Mongols favoured these foreign merchants, offering them patronage, preferment, privileges, and opportunities to amass wealth.

These sophisticated inter-regional traders had knowledge of the banking practices of the Muslim world, and they introduced the Mongol ruling elite to usury. The Mongol aristocrats, possessing surplus wealth from exploiting the subjects of their conquered lands, were relative strangers to earning interest from money. The Muslim traders, who could put fresh investments to good use in their lucrative businesses, took to borrowing money from the Mongols, and then rewarded their creditors with high rates of interest on the loans. It was obviously a partnership that benefited both sides. Some of these merchants made fabulous fortunes from purchasing the right to collect a variety of taxes. Some had the licence to trade in pearls and precious stones. This was an extremely lucrative business with a captive market of consumers who were the Mongol ruling elites. During the reign of Emperor Taiding (r. 1323-1328) the sum owed for purchases of pearls reached 400,000 silver ingots, which was equivalent to nearly four times the annual silver budget of the country (110,000 ingots).

Rich merchants enjoyed high social status. Some had the privilege of special access to the royalty, participation in important court ceremonies, and exemption from labour services. Many became officials through appointment or purchase. They did not shy away from conspicuous consumption and ostentatious displays of wealth, a situation witnessed by Marco Polo. Such a lifestyle was anathema to the Confucian scholars, who stressed the virtues of thrift and a simple life. Successful Chinese merchants also benefited from the rise in social status, but they were not competing on an equal footing with their foreign rivals. Chinese owners of merchant fleets participated in the overseas trade of the spice routes, which, like long-distance overland trade, was also dominated by Muslim merchants. Some of the foreign merchants were given special passes in long-distance overland travel, with the privilege of using the services of the government-maintained postal relay stations.

Postal relay stations

Another Chinese institution which the Mongols adopted was the system of postal relay stations that were responsible for the transmission and delivery of official mail, as well as for providing accommodation for the messengers and travelling officials. During decades of wars of conquest and consolidation of power, the Mongols' need for a reliable network of communication, covering the major routes of long-distance information transmission and travel, prompted first Chinggis, then Ogodei and Khubilai, to restore and strengthen the old postal relay stations of their predecessors, and to set up new ones to include the steppe roads and major lines of communication in Tufan (Tibet). A central administration was set up by Khubilai in the capital at Yanjing to oversee the approximately 1500 postal relay stations. The stations were placed at intervals of around 50 to over 100 li (1 li is equal to 0.5 kilometre). The management of the local stations was the responsibility of taxpayers along the routes. Relatively well-to-do households were chosen to supply and run these stations in lieu of the usual taxes and corvee. Once chosen, they were registered as hereditary postal-relay households, over 300,000 of which were scattered throughout the Yuan empire. On these households fell the duty of providing beasts of burden, such as horses, oxen and remounts, suitable vehicles for transport, food and shelter for the messengers and travelling dignitaries, and personnel to operate the stations. Two or three thousand postal-relay households might be needed to support a large postal-relay station, while a few tens might be sufficient for a small station. For urgent official communications, there were special express delivery stations. Postal relay stations were also set up in some of the other khanates of Chinggis' heirs. These postal routes surely facilitated travel and communication in the domains of the Mongols. Couriers, subjects, and officials of the Yuan and other Mongol-ruled khanates, merchants from Central Asia and beyond, envoys of various principalities and powers, Buddhist monks from Tibet, and Christian prelates of Western Europe all had to traverse these routes on their way to or from Outer Mongolia and Beijing. Although long-distance travellers also used the maritime routes, those who had official business tended to take the postal roads.

Religions during the Yuan

Before Chinggis Khan launched his career of conquest, the Mongols believed in Shamanism. It was a kind of pantheism, the believers in which worshipped the sun, moon, water, fire, mountains, earth and especially the everlasting heaven above. The shamans mediated between the human and the spiritual world. They were expert diviners, who could manipulate themselves into a state of trance and transmit messages from heaven. While building their empire, the Mongols encountered many different religious beliefs and practices, which they welcomed with open arms. It was as if they did not want to offend other powerful deities or forego their blessings.

In the empire of the Great Khan, our main concern here, the religions with substantial following besides Shamanism were Buddhism, Daoism, Nestorian Christianity, and Islam. The faithful of all these, as well as others with fewer followers, such as Judaism and Manichaeism, were able to worship in their churches, temples, or mosques, without official interference provided they respected Mongol rule and kept peace with one another. The registered clergy of the various officially recognized sects were exempt from the corvee duty. They also had the privilege of being accommodated at the postal stations on their travels. The leaders of the Daoist and Buddhist sects vied with each other to win the emperors as adherents and patrons of their religious establishments. The different rulers responded differently to the appeals of their religious supplicants. Of the Buddhist sects, the Mongol rulers favoured Tibetan Lamaism with its magical appeal of mantra and mandala, while Chan Buddhism was popular with the general population. The Yuan court appointed the authoritative clerics, or aristocratic believers, of the different religious persuasions to govern their own sects, under the general supervision of the lama favoured by the court. The emperor, being in control of the religious sects through their appointed religious officials, remained the highest authority on all religious matters. For example, Khubilai decided that the only authentic Daoist canon was the Daode Jing and ordered all others to be burned. Fortunately, this order was not thoroughly executed before it was rescinded.

Islam flourished under the Yuan as a consequence of the power, wealth, and high positions of the Muslim Central Asians. One of Khubilai's grandsons, Ananda, who had a domain in Anxi, became a Muslim after being brought up by devotees of Islam. He ordered the 150,000 Mongol troops under his command to take up Islam.

Nestorian Christianity had powerful adherents among the Yuan ruling elites. The Ongud tribe, which Chinggis conquered and absorbed into the united Mongol nation, had already accepted Nestorian Christianity. Early in the Crusades, the possible existence of a Christian kingdom of Prester John in the east aroused western Christendom's hope of finding an ally against the Muslims. The Italian Franciscan, Odoric of Pordenone, who visited the interior of China during the 1320s, associated the Nestorian Onguds with that legendary Christian country. The rise of the religion-friendly Mongols again stimulated interest in the West in winning such an ally, or possibly converts to Christianity, and led Pope Innocent IV to despatch a Franciscan cleric, Giovanni da Pian del Carpine, in 1245 to seek out the Great Khan, Guyuk at the time. Later, at the time of the Sixth Crusade in 1253, the same Pope and the French King Louis IX sent to Mongolia an envoy, William of Rubruck, who had an audience with Mongke at Karakorum. Neither visit achieved the desired outcome.

The appearance in Constantinople and Rome, in 1287-88, of the Nestorian Monk Rabban Bar Sauma, and his disciple Mark from northern China, prompted Pope Clement III to send the Italian Franciscan, John of Montecorvino (1247-1328), as a missionary to Yanjing (Beijing), where he built many churches and baptized some 6,000 people. Some 30,000 Greek Orthodox Christians who had been brought to Yanjing as soldiers, crafts-men, or captives, by the returning Mongol troops from their expeditions to the West, also converted to Roman Catholicism through the efforts of John of Montecorvino, whose great success prompted Pope Clemment IV to appoint him the archbishop of Yanjing. The archbishop despatched some other Catholic missionaries from Rome to build churches in Quanzhou, then the premier port city in southern China. This first wave of missionary activities of the Catholic Church in China subsided without a ripple for over two hundred years. The work of these Franciscans was unknown to the Jesuit mission-aries, who arrived in Ming China from the 1600s.

A permanent legacy of the Mongol interlude was the spread of Islam to China. There are sizable Muslim populations in Gansu and Yunnan today. Mosques are a familiar part of the architectural scene in these provinces, and in Xinjiang in northwest China. The Chinese word Hui refers to a person who believes in Islam, and it also denotes ethnicity in the Chinese definition of national minority. Today there are an estimated twenty-five million Muslims in China[10], approximately half of whom live in Xinjiang.

Diaspora of peoples

During the century of wars of conquest, the lands the Mongols invaded usually suffered massive destruction of the cities and countless loss of life. Some of the survivors were taken by the Mongols as captives and used as soldiers or slaves, and they might spend the rest of their lives far away from their homelands. The Mongols normally spared the lives of craftsmen, technicians, engineers, and clerics of any faiths in the cities they broke into. They valued and respected those categories of people, who might be transported to places where their knowledge and skills could best be used. The dislocation and transfer of people from one part of the Mongol domain to another was a consequence of the Mongol domination. The 30,000 Greek Orthodox Christians mentioned earlier, who were

---

[10] China – The World Factbook. Retrieved from https://www.cia.gov/the-world-factbook/countries/china/#people-and-society on 27 January 2024.

brought to Yanjing, were not the only examples of the massive transfer of people from the West to China. There were also over 10,000 Russians brought to Mongolia and China as soldiers, craftsmen, or slaves. In 1330, the Yuan government ordered them to assemble, and organized them into a special unit of military guards. They were formed into units of 10,000 households and were given farmland to settle as a military-agricultural colony near Yanjing.

The Chinese diaspora continued under the Yuan. During the fourteenth century, there was a Chinese colony at Tomasik, which developed into today's Singapore. Mongol expeditionary forces sent to invade Japan, Vietnam, Cambodia, Myanmar, and Java were largely recruits of the Southern Song soldiers and sailors who submitted themselves to the Yuan. The Chinese survivors of the disastrous campaigns in these countries were most likely to have remained there. There were Chinese hydraulic engineers working on irrigation in the Tigris and Euphrates River basins. A Chinese Daoist Monk, Chang Chun, who journeyed to Kabul to visit Chinggis Khan in 1222, came across Chinese craftsmen in Outer Mongolia and Samarkand, and heard of a settlement of Chinese weavers in the upper Yenisei valley.

Cultural diffusion

During the age of the Mongol ascendancy, the greater movement of peoples between Asia, the Middle East and Europe, together with the writings of the travellers, facilitated the spread of knowledge, technology, and inventions from one part of the world to another. It was before the rise of Europe, and the Chinese and Islamic civilizations were, in many ways, leading the world. A Muslim observatory was established at Beijing. Arab texts were translated into Chinese at the Islamic Academy set up under Khubilai's reign. Influences from Muslim Iran were likely to have stimulated the development of astronomy and mathematics, which continued to advance in China under the Yuan. Chinese astronomers and physicians served at the court of the Il-Khan in Tabriz. Rashid al-Din (1247-1318), a Jewish convert to Islam and prominent official at the court of the Il-Khan, arranged to have Chinese works translated into Persian. The book, known as *Treasures of the Il-Khan on the Sciences of Cathay* (1313), was the result; it is among the library collection in Istanbul in modern Turkey. Chinese influences are detectable in Persian miniatures, ceramics, and music, and in the Iranian architecture of the Mongol period.

It is unlikely to have been accidental that an ancient Chinese invention, the breast-strap for harnessing horses (third to second century BCE), the not quite so ancient wheelbarrow (first to second century CE), and the sternpost movable rudder in ships (first to fourth century CE) appeared in Europe from the late twelfth to the thirteenth century. This was the time of the last Crusades, when the Europeans fought against the Muslims of the Middle East, who already had centuries of political, military, and commercial contacts with the

Chinese. During the Mongol epoch, there was more transmission of Chinese discoveries and technical advances to Europe. For example, paper - originated in China during the first to second centuries CE - was first imported into Europe from the Islamic world during the twelfth century, before it was produced in Italy at the end of the thirteenth century. Bridges with segmented arches (by 610 in China) appeared in fourteenth century Europe. Metallurgical techniques in connection with the making of iron and steel from China's antiquities came into use in the Rhine valley during the fourteenth century. The Mongols introduced firearms into Europe at the battle of Sajo in Hungary in 1241. The origin of printing, wood engraving, and the use of movable type from eighth to eleventh century China gave rise to the development of printing with movable type in Europe during 1430 to 1460.

The last three were important elements that went into the crucible of Europe's modern transformation. In Europe, firearms underwent potent systematic development with major socioeconomic and political repercussions. The new weapons and military organization led to the obsolescence of the warrior aristocracy of medieval Europe. In China, they remained weapons in the arsenal among others, with little impact on the socioeconomic or political sphere. The place of steel in the evolution of modern transportation and manufacturing industry is well known. Paper and printing appeared felicitously during the time of the Renaissance and the Reformation in Europe, facilitating the intellectual ferment and the spread of knowledge - biblical knowledge included - of that age. The attraction of goods from the East and the accounts of European travellers to the empire of the Great Khan, particularly Marco Polo's depiction of the fabled wealth of Cathay, stimulated Western desire for greater contact with the East. It became a part of the impetus behind the drive of the modernizing Christian countries of Europe, eager to bypass Muslim dominated trade with the East, to circumnavigate the globe, and usher in the age of European imperial expansion. The Mongol Great Khans neither joined Western Christendom as allies against the Muslims in the Middle East, nor became converts to Catholicism as the Roman Emperor Constantine had done. Their vast empire benefited the West through cultural diffusion from China, in ways that were unexpected and far reaching.

Effects on China

By taking over a prosperous, though war-torn, Southern Song in full commercial expansion, the Mongols reaped substantial material benefits. Under their merchant- and trade-friendly policy, commerce continued to flourish. However, there were built-in distortions and outflow of resources, because of the special privileges given to the Muslim merchants of Central Asia, and financial collaboration between these merchants and the Mongol ruling aristocrats. The latter had access to the surplus wealth of China through taxation, and through the Great Khans' gifts to them on celebratory occasions. These gifts amounted to a serious redistribution of the wealth of the empire. The Great Khans had to dig deeply into the state treasures to keep the tradition going. While paper money was constrained to circulate in China only, the precious metal silver was transferred to the western part of the continent, such as the Middle East and Europe. This movement of silver accounted for the shortage of silver towards the end of the fourteenth century near the beginning of the Ming dynasty, which succeeded the Yuan.

During the Yuan, Chinese society became impoverished as a result of being involved in a foreign trade from which it drew little profit. In addition to the general immiseration of society, the Chinese suffered alienation, because the Mongol regime discriminated against the Han and Southern Chinese in their own homeland by its policies and laws. It provided very little scope for the educated ruling elites of China, the Chinese gentry, to assume their normal role of participating in governing the country. Since the cultural climate was not favourable for serious literary production, the energy of the educated Chinese channelled itself instead into the production of popular literature, in the vernacular dialects of their regions. Many poems, satirical songs, novels, short stories, and plays were produced. Drama with singing and dancing became highly developed in Yuan times. Although a large body of these works disappeared, fortunately some outstanding examples have remained to this day. The legacy turned out not to be entirely negative in the end.

The Mongol episode in China, from beginning to end, was characterized by war. From Chinggis' campaign against the Western Xia in 1211 to the conquest of Jin in 1234, there were over two decades of war in various parts of northern China. The conquest of the Southern Song, started by Ogodei in 1235, ended in Khubilai's reign in 1279. Although fighting was not continuous throughout those forty-four years, there was intense fighting in some areas of the Southern Song territory during at least half of that period. Hard statistical records or summaries of the death toll, the dislocation of the people, the plunder and destruction of the countryside and the cities are lacking, but there are descriptive accounts of the terrible aftermath of some of the Mongol military campaigns in China. It is not difficult to conceive of the pain and suffering, and the sense of loss the inhabitants of the war-torn land had to endure during that time. There were in addition other wars connected with Khubilai's stewardship. From the 1260s onwards, there were civil wars and rebellions in north China, which he suppressed. His expansionist wars against Japan and other countries overseas, as well his military campaigns against rebellious or encroaching khanates of Ogodei and Chagatai from the west, though not fought directly on the Chinese soil, all had to be supported by the taxes and services of the people of his empire. After a new emperor Chengzong ascended the throne, these wars came to an end around the beginning of the fourteenth century, when the Mongol dynasty decided on a policy of keeping what they already possessed, rather than of continuing to enlarge the empire.

The end of the Yuan

It was not easy for the Mongols to keep their empire stable and viable for very long. The Yuan never organized a powerful centralized government to rule the whole empire with uniform laws and procedures in the manner of Han governance. Its founding emperor, Khubilai, presided over a structure that balanced the power of the Great Khan at the centre with the power of the hereditary aristocrats, who were largely Chinggis' relatives or descendants, and who controlled armed forces and were given landed domains and people to support them economically in accordance with the tradition of the steppe. In addition to these two strata of ruling elites, the rich Muslim Central Asians, particularly those who held high offices, constituted another group of power holders. Should an emperor die without having established a successor in accordance with the rules of Han governance, the royal aristocrats together with the empress dowager, who would temporarily assume power as the regent, would have the right to elect the next emperor from the eligible heirs. This occurred quite frequently, leading to factional fighting and even civil war on one occasion. The emperors so chosen, even when they were not minors, would start their reigns being beholden to those who had elected them. This system did not favour strong emperors, or a sufficiently empowered and well-organized central authority to check and control empire-wide financial malfeasance and abuses of power, particularly on the matter of taxation. The Yuan official tax rates were not unreasonable by past standards, but the taxpayers were ruthlessly exploited by the Muslim tax-farmers, who were free to take their own cut as long as the government got their quota. Despite regulations concerning what the Mongol aristocrats were entitled to collect from the residents in their domains, there were widespread abuses. Since the people were powerless to resist extortionate demands from either the official tax collectors for the central government, or the exaction from the representatives of the largely absentee Mongol holders of the Chinese domains, they would flee when the burden became too much for them to bear and join the ranks of the roving homeless (*liu min*). The incessant wars, the unstable currency accompanied by periodic inflation, together with the highly irregular and oppressive tax regime, rendered the Mongol rule economically unsustainable, even without adding other negative factors such as Han resentment against the ethnic discrimination which was part of the political oppression of alien rule, and the widening gap between the rich and the poor of the land. In the late 1330s, a trickle of rebellions started in south China, and by the 1350s it became a deluge, engulfing all of China.

Although it was illegal for the Chinese to keep horses and weapons of any kind - even the possession of bamboo was prohibited because bows and arrows could be fashioned from it - the Chinese managed to arm and train themselves to fight. In 1351, Han Shantong, a leader of the popular Buddhist sect known as the White Lotus Society, used religion as a cover to incite and gather people for insurrection. Han claimed Song royal descent and led a movement to restore the Song dynasty. His group tried to stir up peoples' resentment against the Mongol exploitation by reminding them of the extreme poverty of southern China, while the northern steppes became rich. Many of the desperately poor longed for deliverance from their life of suffering; they burned incense and prayed for the dawn of the millennium when the Maitreya Buddha would come and bring paradise to earth. Taking advantage of the popular mood, a cloth vendor, Xu Shouhui, rose up in rebellion, also in 1351, with the claim of being the Maitreya Buddha himself. His movement, as well as the one for restoring the Song, expanded quickly, and achieved considerable military success. The leader of another uprising gathered followers with the slogan: 'smash the rich; benefit the poor'. These words encapsulated the anger of the poverty-stricken and reflected the increasing social tension as the gulf widened between the rich and the poor. Most insurgents wore red turbans as their badge of rebellion. Before long, the insurgents captured major cities and occupied large territories. The rebels had demonstrated to the enemies of the Yuan that the Mongol military machine was rusty, and that the dynasty had become too weak to keep order. There was a documented case of three Mongol commanders, who were ordered by the court to take action against certain rebel forces. Softened through leading self-indulgent lives in pursuit of pleasure, they had little stomach for fighting. Even though they had several thousand elite cavalry troops supported by other forces, they were among the first to run away when confronted by a host of armed men with 'red turbans'.

The emperor Shundi (r. 1333-1368) was presiding over a government that was patently corrupt and an empire that had become ungovernable. Early in his reign, he had attempted to strengthen the central government through greater implementation of Han governance, but it was already too late. He was indecisive and easily manipulated by self-serving officials, who were busy conducting poisonous court intrigues and promoting their own narrow interests, rather than working together for the common good when the empire was in grave peril. Mongol military aristocrats commanding large forces in the field defied the emperor's authority with impunity, and often fought more against one another rather than the rebels. The Yuan dynasty had reached the terminal stage of decline. Although some of the rebel groups were destroyed, or their leaders won over to the government side, the surviving ones kept growing in strength. By the 1350s, most of southern China and parts of the north were out of Yuan control.

Toughened by years of military contests with each other, the rebel forces under a disciplined and well-organized Chinese empire-builder, Zhu Yuanzhang, who was an outstanding tactician and strategist, methodically eliminated his Chinese rivals in the south. In 1367 he sent an expeditionary force of 250,000 north 'to recover the country for Chinese rule and to save the people'. In 1368, he established a new dynasty, the Ming (meaning 'bright'), with himself as the emperor and Hongwu (Vast Martial) as his reign period. Meanwhile, his troops were marching towards the main Yuan capital, Yanjing, taking over provinces in northern China in accordance with his plan. In 1369, Yuan Shundi died after fleeing from his capitals, one after another. His heir, Ayushiridara (also known as

Yuan Zhaozong), took refuge in Karakorum, where he was joined by the remnants of Yuan forces retreating from the onslaught of the Ming. Driven back to their homeland, the Mongols saw their domination of East Asia come to an end after ninety-eight years of ruling the whole of China. Their rule of northern China lasted several decades longer. During most of the period under Mongol control, China was either ravaged by war on its own soil or bore the burden of the Mongol foreign military campaigns. The harsh regime of internecine wars and intolerable economic exploitation left China impoverished and many areas depopulated. These legacies of the Yuan were urgent matters for the Ming to address. The psychological impact of the harsh foreign rule might have been an important factor leading to Ming China's striking withdrawal from foreign involvement, as will be discussed in the following chapter.

References

A General History of China (in Chinese) by Bai Shouyi (Shanghai Peoples' Publishing House, Shanghai, 1999).

A History of Chinese Civilization by Jacques Gernet (English Edition, Cambridge University Press, Cambridge, second edition 1996), chapters 16-17.

China: A History Volume 1 From Neolithic Cultures through the Great Qing Empire 10,000 BCE – 1799 CE by Harold M. Tanner (Hackett Publishing Company, Inc., Indianapolis/Cambridge, 2010), chapter 8.

Chapter 4

The Ming Dynasty (1368-1644)

The Rise of Zhu Yuanzhang, the First Ming Emperor

Zhu Yuanzhang (r. 1368-1398)

The founder of the Ming dynasty, Zhu Yuanzhang, was born in 1328 into an impoverished family of landless agricultural workers in the present-day province of Anhui in southeast China. There was a story that around the time of his conception, his mother dreamt that a divine being put a glowing tablet into her palm. After she swallowed it, a fragrance remained in her mouth. When he was born, a red light filled the room. When neighbours saw the flaming red light at night, they came to help the family to put out the fire, but there was no fire. Such tales of supernatural occurrences surrounding men of humble origin who founded dynasties were not uncommon; their invention satisfied popular expectation.

When Zhu was sixteen, he lost his parents and brothers during a time of drought, pestilence, and famine. His distress was compounded by not having the money to afford a burial plot for them. Fortunately, a kind villager came to his aid, giving him a piece of land for the purpose. Left utterly alone, he became a novice at a local Buddhist temple, felicitously named the Temple of the Awakening Emperor. Soon after, he had to leave the temple because it was no longer able to support him. He became a mendicant, wandering about and experiencing fully the bitterness and hardship of such an insecure life at the bottom of society. Another story relates that when he was ill and alone on his travels, two mysterious purple-robed beings attended to all his needs and disappeared when he recovered. This story may have originated with Zhu himself, to support the claim of his heaven-ordained royal destiny, since the colour purple was associated with royalty in traditional China. In 1348, he returned to the temple, where he learned to read, remaining there for the next few years.

In 1352, when he was twenty-four, flames of rebellion against the Yuan were spreading like wildfire in southern China, engulfing the locality where Zhu Yuanzhang was living. The government troops sent to suppress the uprisings burnt down his temple. The Yuan commander, too timid to fight the rebels, seized instead innocent civilians, presenting them as insurgents to claim the rewards. Although Zhu did not express resentment against Mongol rule on ethnic grounds, the authorities' actions destroyed his livelihood and jeopardized his personal safety. For the sake of staying alive, he joined the local band of Red Turbans, a rebel peasant movement seeking to overthrow the Yuan.

Among the Red Turbans, Zhu was in his element, 'like a fish who had found water'. He soon distinguished himself in bravery and resourcefulness. One of the leaders of the movement, Guo Zixing, noticed Zhu's exceptional ability, brought him into the inner leadership circle, and offered him the hand of his foster daughter in marriage. She would become the future Empress Ma, who would exercise a positive, moderating influence on Zhu, who turned out to be an autocratic emperor.

The success of the Red Turbans raised alarm at the Yuan court. In 1353, the Yuan prime minister Tuo Tuo assembled an enormous army, reportedly one million strong, its marching columns stretching for hundreds of miles, with flags flying and the sound of its drums reverberating into the wilderness. He led it himself, in a determined effort to crush the rebels. Just as he was making some progress, the Yuan emperor foolishly yielded to the intrigue of Tuo Tuo's enemies at court, and relieved him of his command. The Yuan forces were instantly thrown into great confusion, while the hitherto hard-pressed anti-government forces immediately took advantage of the situation to regroup, consolidate, and expand their territory.

Not all Chinese who joined the fray were on the side of the anti-government rebels. Several Chinese landlords responded to the court's call to raise vigilantes to defend themselves, and to fight the insurgents. They fought against the Red Turbans, who were deemed 'lawless bandits', threatening the traditional social order from which they benefited. Some who joined up were opportunists, who took advantage of the general disorder to carve out territories for themselves as local or regional 'strong men', without necessarily obeying the command of the court. Although there were still areas held by Mongol military aristocrats in pockets of southern China, they were gradually taken over by the Chinese warlords or militarists, whom the Chinese referred to as *qun xion*, meaning a group of heroes or strong men.

In due course Zhu Yuanzhang emerged as the leader of the movement that had been fighting the Yuan, under the Song banner. In 1356, he took the advice of some of the learned men who joined him, to seize Jiqing (modern-day Nanjing) from the Yuan. After renaming it as Yingtian, he used it as his base. Its superb natural defences, with the Zijin mountain on one side and the great river Yangtze on the other, caused it to be known as the 'city where the dragon nestled with the tiger'. Its location in a rich agricultural area would ensure the supply of grain for Zhu's large army. It was no accident that it had served as the capital for many earlier dynasties in south China. In addition to the material benefits, the symbolic importance of taking possession of a city with such historical res-onance lifted Zhu's confidence in himself, as the Son of Heaven chosen to save the people from the chaos and disorder of their world. By 1363, having captured many important cities around Yingtian, Zhu was poised to lead a new empire.

Zhu found himself in a world in turmoil, where the reigning dynasty, the Yuan, could no longer maintain civil order. In fourteenth-century China, people would conclude that the Yuan had lost its mandate to rule, and that a new dynasty would rise to replace it. This was how it seemed to Zhu when he joined the local rebel group. To gain prominence among the armed bands of insurgents depended largely on an individual's personal qual-ities such as charisma, intelligence, courage, ambition, good judgement, capacity for lead-ership and so on, rather than on his status or class origin in the society. Zhu was amply endowed with such qualities. He was an exceptional soldier and military leader, who in-spired loyalty and respect in his followers through his personal courage, his brilliance at strategic planning, and his mastery of the correct tactics to use in each military engage-ment. Although he worked for over a decade under higher authorities in his movement, he realized, not long after he joined, the importance of having his own personal power base, while remaining attached to the movement as a front. He wisely chose Yingtian (Nanjing) as that base, where some of his military staff developed into outstanding com-manders, and where he recruited distinguished Confucian literati as advisors.

While Zhu came from a poor segment of the society, he was not a social reformer or a revolutionary with a plan to establish an egalitarian society, largely in the interest of the Red-Turbaned peasant supporters. He abandoned early on the outlaw style of seizing the properties of the landlords in the areas he occupied and forcing the people there to supply him with grain for his needs. Looking to the future, he and his politically minded advisors saw themselves as being on the side of law and order, and they organized a regular regime of tax collection. They did not see landlords as their class enemies. Zhu and those who threw in their lot with him had a simple conservative vision: that of uniting China under a new dynasty in the Confucian-Legalist tradition, with Zhu himself as emperor and his supporters as the new ruling elite.

With such a vision in mind, but before he became the actual head of a united empire, Zhu adopted a political strategy that would eventually help him realize his ambition. He promoted an image of himself as a model Confucian ruler, who exemplified the virtues of benevolence, kindness, and loyalty. He maintained very strict discipline over his troops: after capturing a city, the soldiers were forbidden to kill or rob the inhabitants or abuse the women. When Zhu's forces were poised to take over the cities in eastern Zhejiang, he exhorted his generals to keep a tight rein over their soldiers, with the following remarks:

"To capture cities depends on being martial and brave; to pacify disorder relies on benevolence and kindness. Previously when we entered into Jiqing (Nanjing), we wronged no one. That was why we pacified it at a stroke. Whenever I heard that you captured a city without recklessly killing people, I could not contain myself with joy. The army behaves like a burning fire; unless it is controlled, it could burn throughout the wilderness. A general should regard the absence of killing as being 'martial'. Not only would this benefit the country, [your] descendants would also benefit from the good karma."

Zhu kept taxation to a low rate on agriculture, commerce, and salt, exempted many distressed areas from taxation for limited periods, and provided some help to the very poor. These economic measures and his well-disciplined soldiers were popular with the people and helped to win them to his side. Several years before he enthroned himself, he was already taking up the role of the emperor in many ways. He gathered a group of well-educated and able civilian staff as advisors and officials, set up schools, re-introduced the examinations for the selection of officials, paid respect at Confucius' shrines, performed the rituals of ancestor worship, and carried out certain rites, such as the worship of heaven, that were normally the duty of an emperor. To finally realize his vision, more trials of strength on the battlefield were needed.

Zhu's campaign to unite China

During the 1360s, Zhu Yuanzhang began his military campaign to unite China by first eliminating his rivals in southern China one by one, and then marching north to put an end to the Yuan. One of his most powerful enemies was Chen Youliang, whose headquarters were located further along the Yangtze River above Zhu's base at Yingtian. In contrast to Zhu's high moral standing, Chen demonstrated disloyalty by killing the founder of his (Mongol) movement, whose position he had usurped. Many military commanders in this movement deserted Chen to join Zhu. Loyalty was a cardinal virtue in the Confucian code of ethics, and apparently morality still regulated behaviour, even when the political order had broken down. After his repeated attempts to annex Zhu's territory all failed, Chen decided on a naval showdown with Zhu on Lake Poyang, with an army of some 600,000 men and a flotilla of several hundred large three-storey high vessels, all painted red, and tied together into an imposing array stretching far into the distance. Though Zhu had smaller ships and fewer troops, his generals and soldiers were united in high spirits and with excellent morale. During the engagement, Zhu hit upon a winning strategy after witnessing the burning of twenty of Chen's vessels, when one of his generals shot fire cannons at them, When dusk fell after a day of intense combat, with the wind blowing strongly, Zhu called upon his bravest warriors to ram Chen's fleet with small boats packed with explosives and flammable materials. Soon the flames fed by the fierce wind engulfed many of Chen's warships, with fire and smoke rising to the sky, turning the water of Lake Poyang crimson from the reflection. Pandemonium broke out in Chen's camp with much shouting and screaming. Zhu's forces attacked, inflicting a decisive victory over Chen. Several hundred of Chen's boats were burnt, and many of his officers and fighting men were burnt to death, drowned, or killed. The battle of Lake Poyang made military history in term of its scale, use of fire, and the decisiveness of the defeat by an underdog of a much more numerous and better equipped adversary. Chen never recovered from this blow and died in battle a few days later. The Great Han regime, created by Chen, came to an end after his son, who succeeded him, surrendered to Zhu early in 1364.

Zhu's next target was Zhang Shichen, the warlord of a large area in eastern China that included the rich lower Yangtze delta. Zhang, lacking any interest in providing proper governance, presided over a corrupt and exploitative regime of a self-indulgent officers' corps. A few months before Zhu began his military offensive against Zhang in 1366, he published proclamations castigating Zhang as a criminal, whose military activities had done a great deal of harm to the people and urging Zhang's subordinates to 'abandon darkness and turn to light'. Whether it was the result of Zhu's excellent military strategy or his hard-hitting propaganda, his forces rapidly captured many of Zhang's big cities, and some of Zhang's important generals went over to Zhu's side. After ten months of resistance, Zhang's stronghold was finally breached, and his warlord career ended with his death in October 1367.

Soon after destroying his strongest adversaries in southern China late in 1367, Zhu decided that the time was ripe to use the overwhelming force at his command to unite China. The two lesser independent militarists in his vicinity were eliminated within three months of his despatching troops against them. Greater deliberation was required for the conquest of northern China, where the fiat of the Yuan court no longer had any effect on the commanders of large armies, who jealously guarded their own turf and fought continually against one another. Zhu had a thorough grasp of who controlled which parts of northern China, and their relationship with one another and with the court. Having, like a chess master, worked out a grand strategy, before the end of 1367 Zhu launched the long-awaited northern expedition, with a force of 250,000 troops commanded by his ablest generals. The military campaign was accompanied a proclamation stating that the aim of the expedition was 'to expel the barbarians, restore China, establish laws and regulations, and relieve the people in distress'. It gave an assurance that the 'troops would not commit the slightest offences, and the Mongols and the Muslim Central Asians would receive the same treatment as the Han Chinese'.

The conquest of northern China went smoothly, very much according to the plan: cities fell one after another, or surrendered to Zhu's forces, clearing the way to the Yuan capital, Dadu (Beijing). In July 1368, as the army from the south approached Dadu, the alarmed Yuan emperor, Shundi, fled north from the undefended capital and died in the Spring of 1369. Shundi's successor, Ayushiridara, retreated to Karakorum, where the Yuan remnants regrouped.

When Yuan Shundi evacuated from Dadu, Mongol rule of China effectively ended. Although there were still some independent military regimes of various sizes needing to be eradicated before unification could be considered completely achieved, Zhu nevertheless decided, near the beginning of 1368, that the time was ripe for him to ascend the throne, which he did at Yingtian. Zhu named the dynasty he founded Ming, meaning bright, and called his reign period Hongwu, meaning Prodigiously Martial. He later changed the name of his capital, Yingtian, into Nanjing, meaning southern capital.

Characteristics of Zhu's rule

Although Zhu was dedicated to promoting various aspects of the Confucian tradition in governance, he did not rule as a passive Confucian emperor. He turned out to be a domineering ruler, who tried to supervise and control all aspects of government. During his reign of thirty-one years, from the first to the last year of Hongwu (1368-1398), he exemplified an extreme form of absolutist rule.

During the next two decades, the Hongwu emperor continued the drive for unification. His army speedily overthrew the warlord regime in Sichuan in 1371, and the control of Yunnan was seized from a Mongol prince in 1381. Between 1372 and 1388, several large-scale successful military campaigns against remnant Mongol forces in the northwest and northeast of China culminated in the demise of the Northern Yuan, and the splintering among the Mongols into separate tribal groups, who became less of a threat to the Ming.

While consolidation of the Ming empire was underway on the military front, Zhu also began to establish the political and administrative institutions of his dynasty with a view of making it a long-lasting one, first for the benefit of his own family, to maintain peace and order, and to ensure a sustainable way of life for the people of China, especially as regards their material well-being. As regards his family, he ennobled his twenty-three sons and his brother's grandson as hereditary princes and allowed each of them to have their own official staff and an army, varying in size from a few thousand to tens of thousands. They were positioned at strategic points of the empire to defend the realm. This system bore some resemblance to the Mongol military aristocracy, though the Mongol establishment was not restricted to the royals. When setting it up, Zhu rejected the warning of one of his officials, who had the temerity to point out that such empowerment of the princes might create trouble for the court in the future. Trouble indeed appeared soon after Zhu's death, but the institution survived in a somewhat attenuated form, as we shall see later. To make absolutely sure that the empire would remain with his family, he ruthlessly liquidated, on trumped up charges, a large number of his most senior and meritorious generals and advisors, whose support had enabled him to possess the empire. Probably for the sake of pre-empting possible vendettas, those who were related to these unfortunate officials to the ninth degree were also killed. Tens of thousands of people were killed in these fearsome purges.

Such cruelty formed a striking contrast with the Ming founder's frequently expressed pity for people suffering from famine, dislocation, wars, and other disasters, and for whom he repeatedly commanded his officials to offer food, or remission of taxes or land rent. At the beginning of the Ming, there were indeed many distressed people. Decades of civil wars heaped devastation on a China that had already become impoverished through the exploitation and misrule of the Mongol Yuan dynasty. Countless numbers of people became refugees, some to avoid intolerably high taxation and burdensome labour services, others to escape the dangers of war. They would end up as *liu min*, a floating population of dislocated people without means of livelihood. Death and depopulation turned large areas of China into wilderness, particularly in many regions in the north. Dykes, canals, and irrigation works fell into a serious state of disrepair. In addition to bringing peace and order to an exhausted people, the Ming founder had to find ways to restore the economic health of the empire, if he was to properly fulfil his role as the new Son of Heaven, Furthermore, he had himself witnessed how people without a livelihood became lawless bandits or rebels. The Hongwu emperor strongly subscribed to the Confucian view that the economic foundation of the Chinese empire rested on agriculture, and that increasing agricultural production should hold the key to restoring the health of the economy, not to mention its obvious connection with the sustenance of the people. Another compelling reason for strengthening the agrarian economy by helping the farmers was the government's need for taxes. A government could only raise revenue from those who could produce goods and earn income.

From the beginning of his reign, the Hongwu emperor pursued, for nearly two decades, a vigorous program of rebuilding the agriculture of his empire through a series of measures. He advanced a policy urging the dislocated people to return to their native places to grow crops. The poor or landless of many areas were re-located to farm uncultivated agricultural land. Volunteers from many densely populated regions were called upon to resettle in depopulated areas in the north, or to reclaim wasteland. The government provided food, seeds, agricultural tools, and the remission of taxes or land rent for a limited number of years, to help the people transferred under these schemes to get started. The massive resettlement program, involving an estimated two to four million people, continued for a period under the reign of the Yongle emperor (r. 1403-1424) The amount of land reclaimed was impressive: in four years between 1370 and 1380, 8,947,298 hectares were brought under cultivation. The success of the policy was also reflected in the increased collection of grain tax. For example, the grain tax collected by the Yuan amounted to around 7 million hundredweight, while the Ming, in 1393, collected almost 20 million hundredweight.

In connection with the restoration of the agriculture, an enormous effort was put into water control work, such as the building or repairing of reservoirs and irrigation systems. The growing of certain kinds of trees, such as mulberry trees for the silkworms, was often regarded as a subsidiary agricultural activity, but the *Hongwu* emperor made planting trees into a major project. He issued an order in 1392, requiring each colonizing farming family in Anhui province to plant mulberry, jujube, and persimmon trees, 200 of each on their land holdings. In 1394, farming households of the whole empire were obliged to plant 200 mulberry trees and 200 jujube trees. Two years later, 84 million fruit trees were planted in today's Hunan and Hubei provinces. Some historians have estimated that about 1000 million trees were planted during the reign of the Hongwu emperor.

With peace and economic reconstruction under way, the Hongwu emperor set about organizing the empire's taxation in a systematic way. The Yuan household registration being unreliable, he started from scratch, in 1381, ordering the Ministry of Finance to compile 'Yellow Registers', which were records of the households of the people in their districts. The 'Yellow Registers' formed the basis of the labour service duty (corvee) which the people owed to the state. From early in his reign, measurements of the land owned by each of the households were made and graded according to the quality of the land, and the details were recorded, accompanied by drawings of the land units, which recalled the shape of fish scales. These volumes were called 'Fish-scale Registers', and they formed the basis for tax on land. These records were required to be updated every 10 years, but that requirement was not always met. The accuracy of the population records depended on how strictly the court command was executed, and the effectiveness and uprightness of the officials charged with the task. Because the Hongwu emperor was extremely strict, punishing severely those who did not carry out his orders assiduously, the population and land ownership figures were reckoned the most reliable by historians. The census figures were likely to have been understated, with tax evasion as one reason behind this situation. These records and future adjustments on them, though imperfect, formed the basis on which the bulk of the farming population of the empire was taxed.

In addition to registering the farmers and their lands for tax purposes, the Hongwu emperor also had separate registers made by the Ministry of Works for the households of various kinds of artisans. These people were required to offer the state free services as craftsmen at the capital, for periods of three months in every three years, or pay a tax instead. Those who produced items for the military were an exception. They would reside with the garrisoned troops and receive pay for their work. The registered craftsmen who were settled near the capital spent a third of their time working for the state, which compensated them with rice. Registering artisan households as hereditary occupational tax-able units was a Yuan practice taken over by the Ming.

The soldiers represented another large hereditary occupational group, registered by the Ministry of Defence as such during the Ming. Since they were mostly stationed at the frontiers, the logistics of transporting large amounts of grain over long distances to supply them were enough of a problem without considering the cost of the grain. Letting soldiers grow their own food on military-agricultural colonies at the frontiers would solve that problem and save the state the cost of the food and the labour. (Earlier dynasties, such as the Qin and the Han, had already put such an idea into practice at various frontier re-gions.) Early in his reign, the Hongwu emperor enthusiastically adopted the use of mili-tary-agricultural colonies, especially in some frontier regions. He set up the framework and appointed officials to implement the policy on an unprecedented scale. The pragmatic system that was enforced achieved the goal of enabling the military to become self-suffi-cient in food, without further efforts or costs to the state. This institution, being actively supported by his immediate successor and the Yongle emperor, continued to flourish for some decades, before it eventually started to decline from government malfunction.

By registering the households of the farmers with their land, the Hongwu emperor made sure that the state had a regular source of income from the largest occupational group of the empire. Applying a similar system to the artisans enabled the emperor and his personal staff at the capital and the military bases to have skilled workers to produce everything they needed. Keeping records of the soldiers that the state deployed, and en-abling them to produce their own food supply, were positive steps towards strengthening the security of the empire. These administrative measures and the policy of restoring ag-ricultural production, partly by repairing damaged water facilities, and also through a pro-gramme of population resettlement and wasteland reclamation, helped the economic recovery, advanced the healing process, and the return to life's normal rhythm in a country ravaged by decades of war.

As regards the organization of the government, the Ming founder began by taking over the Yuan system, which he then set out to reform. He could tap his scholar-officials' vast store of knowledge on law and government institutions of the past, and adopt what he saw as appropriate, or he could set up new structures according to the requirements of his time. As regards the central government, he adopted a practical administrative division of Six Ministries, three of which were concerned with the affairs of the farmers, the arti-sans, and the military. As for the others, the Ministry of Personnel enforced the regulations pertaining to the officials of the government; the Ministry of Justice took care of judicial matters; and the Ministry of Rites managed official ceremonials and worship services. The arms of the central government reached out to the regions through the local officials, who were the emperor's appointees. The work of local officials was periodically assessed by supervisory officials sent from the court. To assist him in overseeing the affairs of the whole empire, he continued, early in his reign, the Yuan institution of the Imperial Grand Secretariat, together with a Left and a Right Prime Minister.

As already mentioned, the Ming founder had assumed the role of a Confucian ruler, paying respect at the temples of Confucius and performing the rites of the worship of heaven and earth, even before he became emperor. After founding the Ming, he was serious about the periodic performance of these rites, including the worship of his own ancestors, to whom he granted posthumous titles of emperors reaching back five generations. He ordered schools to be built, which provided the lucky few qualified students important instruction on traditional Chinese culture. He re-vitalized the regular government-sponsored examinations for official selection. Having witnessed rampant official corruption and lawless behaviour during the end of the Yuan, the Hongwu emperor placed great emphasis on law, and its enforcement, as a corrective. The Great Ming Code was compiled with reference to the Tang Code but was more comprehensive and more severe in its punishments.

It was the intention of the Ming founder that the institutions, laws, and precedents he had established would be binding on his successors. He often ended his edicts with the clause 'let no changes be made'. He showed a strong desire for his empire to remain frozen through time, in the state in which he had ordained it. Even though that was not to be, his personal character and the actions and decisions he took during his thirty-year reign would have a vital impact on the future development of the Ming, for good or ill.

On the positive side, Zhu restored peace, order, and economic prosperity to the Chinese lands. In external relations, China under the Ming was once more acknowledged as a dominant power in East Asia. However, he fell far short of the Confucian ideal. A model Confucian ruler was someone who ruled passively by his virtuous example. He would not concern himself with the practical details of the politics or administration, which could be taken care of by his subordinates. His role was to embody goodness or benevolence, and thus inspire his ministers to govern in a virtuous manner. The Ming founder, though he acted kindly towards ordinary people in distress, exhibited a malevolent streak towards powerful government officials who, rightly or wrongly, incurred his jealousy or suspicion. The merciless killing of the high officials and their families and friends who had helped him win the empire has already been mentioned. Being an extremely energetic and hard-driven autocrat, he wanted to actively manage and control everything, even the future if he could.

In 1380, he did away with the Grand Secretariat, and abolished the post of prime minister in perpetuity. But he soon found that governing the empire directly by himself, both the central and the provincial governments, which entailed having to read an average of over 200 reports and twice that number of items to deal with every day, was too much even for a workaholic like him. He tried to remedy this situation by selecting a few scholars of the Imperial Academy to assist and advise him, leaving the power of decision entirely in his own hands. This absolutist tendency for bypassing the regular bureaucracy and concentrating the power entirely in the hands of the emperor continued, and became even more pronounced, under his successors. What had been an informal arrangement of enlisting the assistance of imperial academicians by the Hongwu emperor developed, under his successors, into the powerful 'inner cabinet' (*nei ge*, literally meaning inner pavilion) that met inside the palace as distinct from the outer court. The members of the inner cabinet of around five to ten individuals had far greater access to the emperor than the officials of the Six Ministries, let alone the more distant provincial officials. The head of this 'inner cabinet' assumed the role of the prime minister at times. This system, which strengthened the power of the Ming emperors at the expense of their own officials, was sure to emasculate the regular government administration, especially when foolish men occupied the throne.

Another institution set up by the Ming founder also turned out later to be harmful to the Ming polity. This was the Brocade-Uniformed Guards, intended as a security organization not just for protecting the emperor and his household, but even more for subjugating, intimidating, and controlling the officialdom in case of disloyalty or wrongdoing, real or suspected. This institution also served to add colour, pomp, and pageantry on ceremonial occasions. These armed guards formed the palace police, led by those whom the emperor trusted. They eavesdropped, spied upon, and gathered intelligence on officials. Being responsible directly to the emperor, they had the power to arrest, investigate, imprison, torture, and sentence those suspected of serious crimes, such as treason. When the control of this or its successor institution fell into the hands of tyrannical eunuchs during the reigns of several later irresponsible or feeble Ming emperors, Ming governance suffered great damage.

The Accession and Reign of the Yongle Emperor

Yongle (r. 1402-1424)

According to the rule of succession decreed by the Ming founder, the eldest son of the empress would automatically succeed to the throne. If the empress had no son, the first-born of the emperor with another consort would become the heir apparent. Should the heir apparent die before his father, the eldest son of his principal consort would succeed. Since the heir apparent of the Hongwu emperor predeceased his father, following the rule of succession his sixteen-year-old son, Zhu Yonwen, was in line to succeed. In 1398, the Hongwu emperor died, and Zhu Yonwen (r. 1398-1402) ascended the throne. The young emperor felt uneasy about the military power wielded by his princely uncles, amongst whom Zhu Di, the most senior and powerful Prince of Yan, inspired most fear. Following the advice of his officials, he pre-emptively degraded the Prince of Zhou, Zhu

Di's brother born of the same mother, to the position of a commoner, sending him into exile. He then waited for the Prince of Yan to make a false move and incriminate himself. Soon several other princes were convicted of wrongdoing and stripped of their ranks; some were imprisoned, and others exiled. When the news reached Zhu Di at Yanjing (Beijing), he was alarmed and feigned madness while secretly plotted an uprising. Soon he had raised an army to fight the court's forces sent against him, with the justification of 'cleansing the treacherous officials at the emperor's side'. After four years of a bloody war of succession, in which thousands had perished, a stalemate was reached. In 1401, after a disaffected eunuch informed Zhu Di that Nanjing itself was not strongly defended, he promptly marched on the capital. When his troops reached the vicinity of Nanjing, some of his supporters opened one of the city gates to let him in. A fire started in the palace which killed the empress, but the young emperor disappeared without trace.

In due course, the princes and officials at Nanjing presented Zhu Di with official documents and the emperor's seal and offered him the royal coach to ride to the palace to be enthroned. In 1402, Zhu Di, the Ming founder's fourth and most grandly ambitious son, who was a gifted military commander and strategic thinker like his father, ascended the throne with Yongle (Forever Happy) as his reign period.

One of the first acts of the Yongle emperor (r. 1402-1424) was to punish the 'treacherous' officials, who had given his predecessor the advice on curbing the power of some of the royal princes including himself, as well as those who would not submit to him on account of their loyalty to the former emperor. Not only were the principals killed in extremely cruel forms of execution, their relatives, even remote ones, were not spared from death. He also promptly released his princely brothers from prison or exile and restored their titles and estates to them. While not depriving the princes of the imperial line their wealth and lofty status, he curtailed their military and political powers to such an extent that they would cease to be a future threat to the monarch.

Despite those four years of destructive war, the Yongle emperor presided over a prosperous and powerful country. At the beginning of the fifteenth century, the Ming was still reaping the benefit of the founder's policy of letting the people and the economy of China recover from years of wars, exploitation, and misgovernment. On the foundation of a flourishing economy and strong military force, the Yongle emperor was able to embark on several ambitious projects and campaigns during his reign of twenty-two years. Although these undertakings were enormously costly in terms of financial and human resources, their successful achievement brought him honour and glory, and the empire greater prestige and security.

Almost from the beginning of his reign, the Yongle emperor decided to transfer the capital to Beijing. He had to remain in Nanjing, which would later become the Southern capital, while the new palace at Beijing was being remodelled at the site of the old Yuan palace. Although nostalgia for the city that had been his base as the Prince of Yan might have contributed to his desire for the move, the more important considerations were likely political and security. Since the empire was most at risk from the aggressive nomadic tribes outside its northern frontiers, it made sense to shift its nerve centre further to the north, to manage this threat better. For several years after this decision was made, around 300,000 people, including merchants and rich families from well-developed prefectures in both north and south China, moved to Beijing, thereby increasing the economic and population weight of the capital. Along with this migration, large quantities of wood were shipped to Beijing from the south as building material. The reconstruction of the palace complex at Beijing, itself the size of a small city[11], took seventeen years. In 1408, when the rebuilding was still in process, emperor Yongle transferred himself and his government to Beijing, leaving the heir apparent to preside in Nanjing. Finally in 1420, when the rebuilding was completed, Beijing was formally declared to be the capital of the Ming.

Part of the Forbidden City complex, in today's Beijing (*wendywutours*: retrieved on 26 November 2023 from https://www.wendywutours.co.uk/blog/china/photos-of-the-forbidden-city-on-show-at-the-palace-museum/)

Another great construction project under the Ming was the repair of the Great Wall, the massive defensive structure against the nomadic tribes. For a period of roughly four hundred years from the eleventh to the fourteenth century, while nomad dynasties ruled northern China and then the Yuan dynasty ruled all of China, the Great Wall fell into disrepair because it no longer served any purpose. But after driving the Mongols back to their homeland, the Ming empire of sedentary peoples was once more vulnerable to nomadic incursions from the north. In addition to keeping the nomads out by offensive military expeditions, the rulers of the Ming also decided on a defensive strategy of repairing the existing wall, making new extensions, and putting up inner walls in certain areas. The massive reconstruction work started with the Hongwu emperor, who built forts at strategic

---

[11] Indeed, it is called the Forbidden City.

passes, which included the Jiayuguan fort that guarded the Silk Road at the western extremity of the Great Wall. The Yongle emperor sponsored the work on a long stretch of the wall in certain provinces north of Beijing. It took well over one hundred years and many reigns to complete the entire Ming Great Wall. It was roughly 17 to 35 feet high, 13 to 20 feet wide, and over 4000 miles long. It was made of pounded earth, faced with bricks or stones along certain sections, and dotted with watchtowers. Much of this imposing structure is still standing today.

Did it keep the nomads out? When the empire was strong, it probably protected the Chinese farmers at the border area from small raiding parties and kept larger invading armies at bay until rescue arrived. Near the end of the Ming, when it was severely weakened by peasant rebellions, it seems to have deterred the Manchus, until a disgruntled Chinese general let them in through the strategic pass at Shanhaiguan at the north-east terminus of the wall. The Great Wall might have served as a supplementary security shield for a Chinese empire during its period of strength, but a weak and declining Chinese dynasty could not rely on the Great Wall alone to keep its land and people secure.

The western extremity of the Great Wall, at Jiayuguan (*playingintheworldgame*: retrieved on 26 November 2023 from https://playingintheworldgame.com/2013/06/08/the-brick-story/)

Presiding over a strong and prosperous empire, emperor Yongle was not content with merely keeping a defensive posture. He energetically pursued diplomatic, political, and military actions to confirm the position of the Ming as the pre-eminent power in East Asia – a stance most of the preceding dynasties, when they ruled a strong and united Chinese empire, tended to assume. Although the three million or so Mongols 'north of the desert' had not been able to unite to threaten China as they had done a century before, the more actively aggressive tribal groupings, such as the Oirats in the northwest and the Tatars in the northeast, at times posed significant military challenges to the Ming. Emperor Yongle rose to the challenge, leading 5 military expeditions personally, and won overwhelming victories against them.

What was to be done with the Mongols who surrendered after being defeated? It was not feasible to govern directly the territories where nomadic herders roamed by setting up Chinese-style prefectures and administering them as such. Genocide does not appear to have been an option. The Ming resorted to the age-old 'tribute system', which characterized the relationship between a dynasty ruling a united China and its weaker neighbours. Applying this diplomatic and political device, the Ming bestowed (*feng*) titles like 'Righteous-Sagacious' Prince, or 'Happy-Peaceful' King, on the Mongol chieftains. This act gave the titleholders symbolically or actually the authority to rule over the territory and peoples concerned. This suzerain-vassal relationship would be maintained by periodic tribute embassies by the vassals to the court of the suzerain. The visitors would offer gifts such as horses and other native products and receive sumptuous gifts in return. Peace prevailed for a couple of decades until the tribes revived, and another aggressive Mongol khan rose to power.

The extension of the Ming empire

One of the Yongle emperor's major projects was to use tribute relationships to draw more and more overseas countries into the Ming fold. In fact, the institution had already been flourishing during the Hongwu era. For example, soon after emperor Hongwu ascended the throne, he sent an imperial edict to the King of Gaoli (Korea), a vassal of the previous (Yuan) dynasty, proclaiming the establishment of the Ming. The King of Gaoli responded by sending a delegation to congratulate the Ming emperor, with a request to be made officially the King of Gaoli. In 1370, Emperor Hongwu sent envoys, bearing a gold seal and appropriate documents, to invest him as the King of Gaoli. In 1371, tribute embassies arrived at the Ming court from many countries nearby that included present-day Japan, Thailand, Java, Vietnam, and Korea. When the Yongle emperor moved the Ming capital to Beijing, which was much closer to Korea than Nanjing, ties between the Ming and the Kingdom of Gaoli, which had by then changed its name to Chaoxian, became even closer, with annual tribute embassies and additional ones on special occasions. During the reign of Emperor Wanli (r. 1572-1620), Japan twice invaded Chaoxian, once in 1592 and again in 1597, but was repelled, largely due to military support from the Ming.

To the south lay the Kingdom of Annam with which a suzerain-vassal relationship was established between it and the Ming early in the reign of Hongwu. Soon after emperor Yongle came to the throne, a coup by Annam's prime minister, coupled with the new regime's expansionist drive into Ming territory, led Yongle to send troops to that country and eventually annex it. Subsequently, obstinate and prolonged local armed resistance rendered it very costly for the Ming to keep the territory as a Ming province. As a result, in 1426 the Xuande emperor (r. 1425-1435) decided to restore the earlier suzerain-vassal relationship, to which Annam was eager to return.

To the west lay U-Tsangang (Tibet), where Indian Buddhism took firm hold during the Chinese Middle Ages. It became a theocracy when the monks won the struggle for power between the secular and religious authorities. Unlike Korea and Vietnam, which were vassals, Tibet was incorporated into the Yuan empire. The Yuan acknowledged the power of the Tibetan Buddhist establishment by conferring a princely or kingly title on the head of the strongest Tibetan Lamaist sect. After founding the Ming, emperor Hongwu issued, in 1369, an imperial edict to the leaders of Tibet, requesting them to proceed to the Ming court, then at Nanjing, to be granted titles and offices by himself. Recognizing the fact that the dominant sect in Ming times had lost its monopoly of power, the Ming bestowed florid titles of respect on the leaders of all three of the most prominent Tibetan Buddhist sects, capping the titles with the addition of 'Princes of Law' (*Fa Wang*), indicating their level of authority. Of the three, the 'Yellow Hat' sect, which gave rise to the Dalai Lama of today, developed close relationships with the leaders of the Tatar Mongols as well as the Ming court. From the time of Emperor Yongle, the Ming supported the 'Yellow Hat' strongly. In the course of a few generations, the Dalai Lama gained ascendancy over the other 'Princes of Law.' He became revered as the 'Living Buddha' and the sole theocratic ruler of this region under the Ming.

The Ming retained the power of official appointments and dismissal for ranks below the level of the 'Princes of Law'. Since these latter officials were already the local ruling elite, the act of appointment had the symbolic meaning that the Ming had authorized them to rule on its behalf. The Ming court also appointed roving officials (*liu guan*) to supervise the local administration but left religious matters entirely to the Tibetan Buddhist church. The Tibetan Princes of Law and other officials regularly paid homage to the Ming emperor, bearing tribute items and receiving lavish gifts in return. The Ming kept garrisons overseeing the security of this region and endeavoured to keep the postal relay stations on the routes between Tibet and the Ming capital in good order. Commercial exchanges of Tibetan horses for Chinese tea flourished at several cities in the west designated for such trade. The way Ming governed what is now called the Tibetan Autonomous Region (TAR) did indeed give this region a certain degree of self-rule and autonomy. However, the sovereignty of this region still resided with the Ming. Even when the power of the Ming declined, Tibet remained an integral part of the Ming empire.

During the first sixty years that covered of the reigns of the two outstanding emperors, Hongwu and Yongle, the Ming reached the apogee of power and territorial extent. During the war of unification, the Ming founder's territorial drive seems to have been directed towards recovering the full extent of the Yuan empire, a goal he largely achieved, apart from the Mongol homelands in the north. In strategic areas along the empire's long borders, emperor Hongwu organized garrisons or military-agriculture colonies. In border regions populated mostly by ethnic minorities, he pursued a policy of appointing as Ming officials the existing local powerholders, who were required to pay homage periodically to the emperor with tributes, and who were supervised and checked by roving Ming officials from the central government. The situation in Tibet illustrated this policy, apart from the fact that the powerholders in other regions were secular, while those in Tibet were monks. Emperor Yongle continued the military drive and the consolidation of the border regions, using the same political and administrative policy as emperor Hongwu, except for Vietnam, which he annexed for a limited period. The territory of the Ming reached its greatest extent during the reign of Yongle and remained so for about a decade afterwards.

Admiral Zheng He's Voyages to the 'Western Oceans'

In addition to using the wealth and military prowess of the Ming to enlarge the territory of the empire, the Yongle emperor devoted enormous resources to an unprecedented maritime enterprise: sending Admiral Zheng He with a fleet of 'treasure ships' (bao chuan) and other vessels on a major voyage to the 'western oceans' (xi yang), meaning oceans to the west of the South China Sea. Soon after Yongle came to the throne in 1402, he initiated an ambitious ship-building programme which doubled the capacity of the already huge Longjiang dry-docks near Nanjing, for constructing large numbers of ocean-going wooden sailing ships known in the West as 'junks'. By 1405, a fleet of 317 such vessels, the largest in the world in terms of the total number and size of the individual ships, was assembled for a mission to establish or consolidate diplomatic and commercial relationships with overseas countries, and to explore the world. A eunuch called Zheng He whose surname, like many Mongol converts to Islam, was originally Ma (being the first syllable of Mahomet), was chosen to command the fleet, with 27,800 crew members, and to represent the Ming emperor as his chief representative to these countries.

Zheng He was captured as a child by the Ming forces fighting the Mongols in Yunnan. After undergoing castration, he became a eunuch attached to the household of the Prince of Yen who gave him the Chinese surname Zheng. He grew into a man with an impressive presence, towering in physique as well as in personal attainments. He served the prince

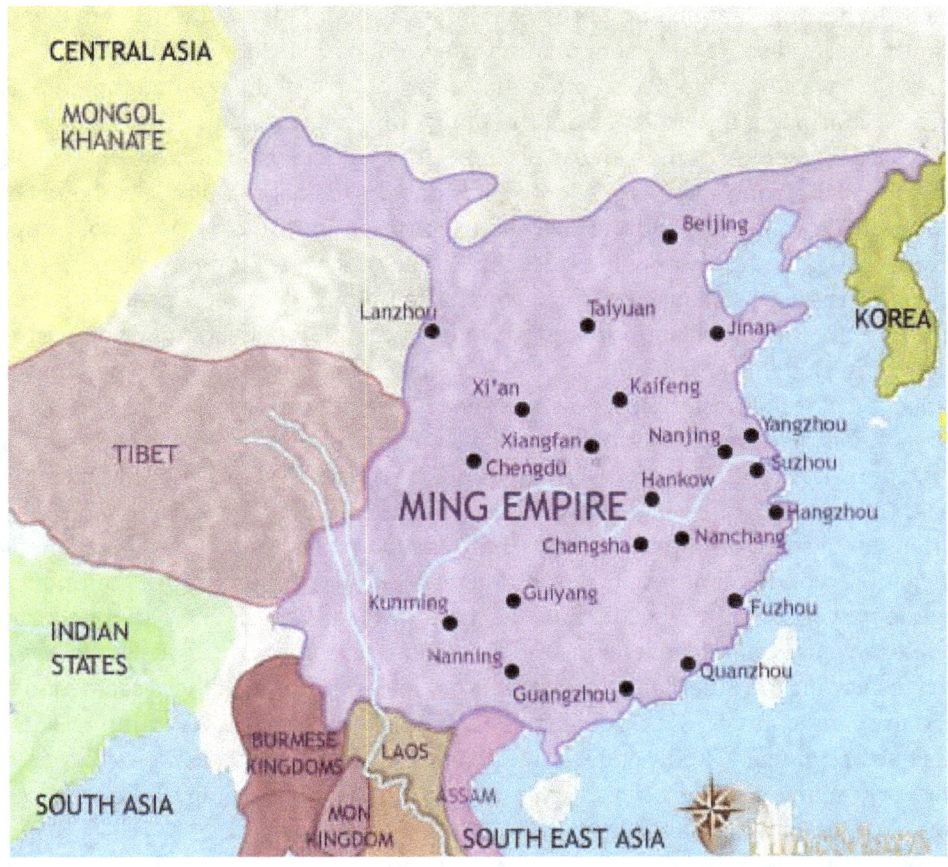

Map showing the Ming Empire, c. 1450 (*TimeMaps*: retrieved on 26 November 2023 from https://playingintheworldgame.com/2013/06/08/the-brick-story/)

loyally and distinguished himself as a military commander fighting for the prince in the war over succession. For his meritorious services he was promoted to be the Grand Eunuch. He was commonly known as the San Bao (Three Treasures) Grand Eunuch. This referred to his merit as a Buddhist, the Three Treasures standing for the Buddha, doctrine, and meditation. Like many Chinese, who were able to combine elements from different religious beliefs and practices to construct their own personal spiritual world, Zheng He, though a devout Moslem, worshipped the Buddha, and Ma Zu, the Daoist goddess of the sea, as well as Tianfei, the Celestial Consort and patron saint of sailors. When the prince became the Yongle emperor, he set aside the Hongwu emperor's injunctions that forbade eunuchs to become literate and participate in government affairs; many were given important posts, and some were sent on ambassadorial missions to foreign lands.

Zheng He was an eminently suitable choice for the role of the commander-in-chief of the Chinese armada, and to represent the Ming emperor in foreign states on the routes of his voyages. He had demonstrated his capacity as a leader of men on the battlefield, and as one of the Yongle emperor's inner circle of aides; he had acquired first-hand knowledge of politics, state protocol, and civil and military administration. The Yongle emperor was willing to give this thoroughly trusted aide the power to act as his plenipotentiary. Zheng He's Islamic heritage, combined with his faith in Buddhism, rendered him a wise choice to build friendly relations with the states in the Middle East and Southeast Asia, where Islam, Buddhism or Hinduism were the dominant religions. With these excellent qualifications for the post, his lack of experience in seafaring was apparently excused.

While Zheng He was a newcomer to naval command and sea voyages, Ming China was the most advanced sea power in the world, possessing the most sophisticated maritime technology and knowledge of shipbuilding and seafaring. This development was the contribution of some of China's coastal ethnic groups, who sailed their well-designed and strongly-built wooden craft over great distances along the coasts or into the open seas, using the power of seasonal winds such as the monsoon, with the help of the mariner's compass, an early Chinese invention, and their knowledge of the positions of the heavenly bodies, especially the Pole star, to direct their movements. Some of them seemed to have settled in many countries of Southeast Asia or further afield. Those who remained in China had accumulated knowledge and experience of shipbuilding, as well as ocean navigating, over many centuries. This heritage paved the way for Admiral Zheng He's successful voyages with his giant ships.

The Ming 'treasure ships', the largest and the most reliable ships of that age, were the culmination of these developments. Their name was derived from the enormous value and quantities of goods − 2,000 tons - they could carry in their capacious holds. Each of these vessels, made largely of teak, was approximately 440 feet long and 180 feet wide, with nine to twelve masts to which were attached huge sails of red silk, a material noted for its strength[12]. Around this time in Europe, Venice had the most powerful navy. The biggest Venetian galleys, about 150 feet long and 20 feet wide, were built for rowing by oarsmen in calm waters. They had a cargo carrying capacity of 50 tons at most. Christopher Columbus' eighty-five feet long Santa Maria, which reached America in 1492, was tiny by comparison.

---

[12] The author took the figures from *Ming Shi*, volume 9, p. 6212, which describes these ships as 44 *zhang* in length and 18 *zhang* in width. Since 1 *zhang* equals 10 *chi* (feet), the dimensions are as given above. They agree with those given by Gavin Menzies in his book *1421 The Year China Discovered the World* (Bantam Books, London, 2002). There is, however, some uncertainty surrounding the length of the Chinese *chi* used in building these ships.

A treasure ship of Zheng He, with an ordinary vessel for comparison
(*Patch*: retrieved on 26 November from
https://patch.com/massachusetts/stoneham/zheng-he-whos-he)

The large Chinese junks were ingeniously designed and constructed to give them the stability and robustness to survive severe storms at sea, such as typhoons. They could remain afloat even when partially damaged by a collision with an iceberg or punctured by hidden reefs, because they had watertight bulwark compartments – sixteen in the larger ships – that were built in sections, like the structure of a bamboo stalk, within strong frames. One or two of these internal compartments might even be flooded on purpose for divers' use, or for trained otters, held on long cords, to herd shoals of fishes into nets for the ships' kitchens. They were equipped with reinforced bows to withstand the battering of the waves, and their 'balanced' rudders, centred at the sternposts, enhanced the vessels' stability and ease of steering. These flat-bottomed and wide-beamed vessels, with enclosed cabins on decks of four levels, were sufficiently commodious to accommodate over a thousand persons. Their sumptuously appointed grand staterooms and spacious apartments, with windows, balconies, and railings for looking out to sea, provided luxurious quarters for foreign dignitaries, who were regularly accommodated on these ships.

A fleet would be composed of many other types of vessels in addition to the 'treasure ships'. It would include somewhat smaller 'horse-ships' for transporting horses for the cavalry, and 'supply-ships' for carrying all kinds of necessary supplies, which included ammunitions for possible military actions, and materials for repair of the ships in case of damage, as well as medicine, food, and water for the health and wellbeing of such a large number of people on board. The variety of food carried by the ships provided a nutritious diet. It included rice (the brown kind also), soybeans, tea, a variety of dried, cured, and pickled meat, vegetables, and fruits, and also liquor and sauces produced by fermentation. There were even live pigs kept for meat. In addition to huge tanks holding the water for the ships' needs, the crew could use paraffin wax or seal blubber as fuel to make fresh water, by distilling seawater when the supply became really tight. Other ships included troop transport for the large body of soldiers on board. There were also small and nimble warships, 165 feet long with five masts, in addition to the even smaller patrol boats, 120 feet or 128 feet long, which were fitted with oars. The warships were organized into squadrons and equipped not merely with the conventional weapons of the time. They also had cannons of brass or iron, catapults and explosive firearms that were not commonplace in the armoury of many other nations, including the Europeans. The ships communicated and coordinated with each other through signalling with bells, gongs, drums, and lanterns. Such a well-equipped and provisioned fleet could navigate in the open oceans for more than three months, covering at least 4500 miles, without having to land for replenishment.

Successful command of such a fleet depended on Zheng He's leadership, but he needed the able assistance and support of others with a whole range of skills and experiences. Managing a large number of people on extended sea voyages, often lasting months or years, on missions serving various purposes, demanded a collaborative effort. Under him there were other eunuch admirals, military officers, and civil officials of different ranks, cartographers, skilled navigators, and artisans relating to ships' repair, in addition to medical officers, pharmacists, astrologers, geomancers, linguists, botanists, Buddhist and Daoist savants, and cooks, not to mention the soldiers and crew. For the diplomatic missions, the fleet took Ming envoys for various countries, linguists, historians, translators, and scribes. Foreign kings, princes, and ambassadors, accompanied by their family members and staff, were brought to Beijing and returned to their homeland by the treasure ships, which were laden with foreign tributes, Chinese gifts, and goods for trade such as Chinese silks, ceramics, and lacquer ware, in exchange for tropical spices, south-sea pearls, precious stones, and other marketable products.

The diplomatic missions were apparently not the only reason for despatching Zheng He to the 'western oceans'. The Yongle emperor had a more personal motive: to track down his predecessor, the Jianwen emperor, whose disappearance triggered rumours and suspicions that he had escaped overseas. Trade was another reason, since the Yongle emperor seems to have been more open-minded to the advantages of commerce than the Ming founder, who had the traditional attitude of disdain for trade. Prestige was also an important consideration behind this project. Yongle wanted to show the world the overwhelming might of the Ming that, together with its high cultural attainments, justified its position as the suzerain, presiding over a world order of subordinate states. During the early decades of the fifteenth century, the Ming was at the height of its power and prosperity. With vast resources at his disposal, and given his love of glory as well as other motives, the Yongle emperor did not hesitate to send Zheng He and his fleet on many expeditions.

Before a fleet was ready to leave, the ships would be arranged in a formation with the treasure ships in the centre, surrounded by the smaller vessels, and flanked by squadrons of warships. Such a powerful armada was well able to take care of any groups of pirates or likely military challenges from the states to be visited overseas. A fleet so composed, with brightly painted ships 'resembling great houses', together bearing a forest of masts that were topped with pennants, must have been an awesome sight when they unfurled their great sails of red silk, and glided on the waves with the curved eyes of dragons or serpents gazing watchfully from their majestic prows.

Zheng He's first voyage started in 1405 and lasted for over two years until 1407, during which time he took his fleet to several countries that included Champa (at the east coast of south Vietnam), Java, Sumatra, Siam, Malacca, Ceylon, and Calicut (at the west coast of southern India). On his return trip, he brought back the envoys of many of the countries he had visited, with tributes to pay homage to the Ming emperor. During the reign of the Yongle emperor until shortly before his death, Zheng He was sent overseas six times with a fleet of similar size as the first, at intervals of two years or less after each trip, with each expedition lasting two years or more. During some of the journeys, Zheng He split the fleet up into smaller groups and let his subordinates command these to cover other routes. The Ming fleets controlled by Zheng He alone, together with those commanded by his staff, visited over thirty different countries or kingdoms.[13] Their fleets landed at Hormuz in the Persian Gulf, and many cities along the coast of the Arabian Peninsula, including Muscat, Aden and Jeddah, from where Zheng He could easily reach Mecca for a pilgrimage, which he performed on one of his trips. Some of the fleets sailed across the Indian Ocean to the east coast of Africa, landing in places around Mogadishu (in Somalia) and Malindi (in Kenya) and covering over 6,000 kilometres on the round trip.

Menzies (*op. cit.*) claimed that some of the fleets commanded by Zheng He's subordinates went much further: that one reached Australia and Antarctica, that another sailed to Australia and the Americas, that a third left a settlement in North America and attempted an expedition to the North Pole, while another rounded the Cape – a century before Magellan. Menzies was a retired British submarine commander. He pieced together these epic voyages commanded by the other admirals of the Ming fleet like a detective, starting with the discovery of an old map, reconstructing the fifteenth-century world of Ming China and elsewhere, and suggesting how these voyages could have taken place.

---

[13] The stone stele erected by Zheng He to commemorate his own voyages had 'over 3,000 kingdoms' written on it. Menzies (*op. cit.*) hazarded an explanation for the discrepancy and believed the figure of 3,000 was correct.

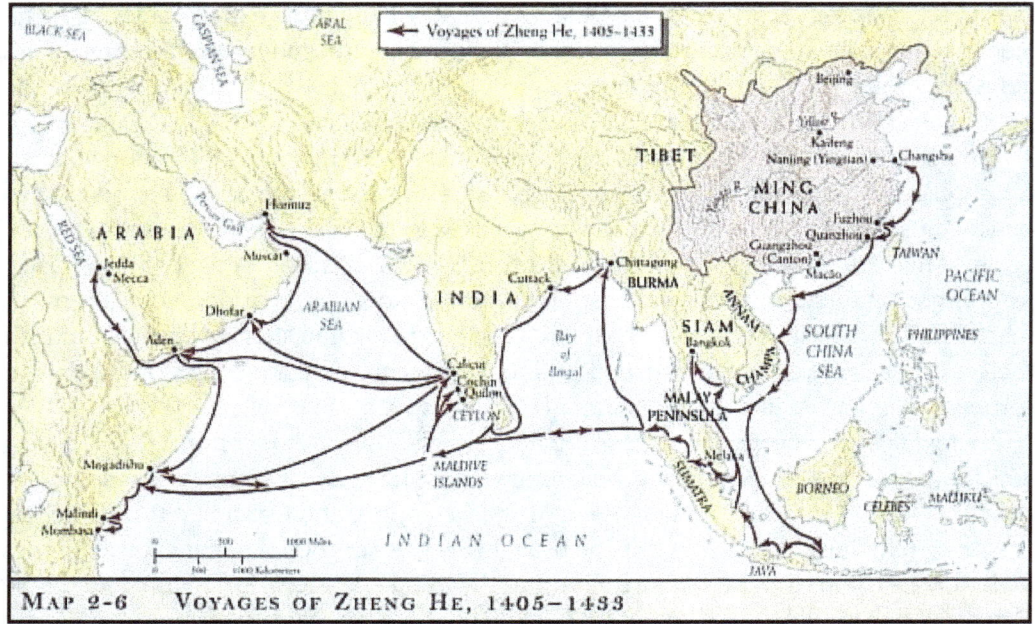

MAP 2-6   VOYAGES OF ZHENG HE, 1405–1433

Map showing the voyages of Zheng He (*Weebly*: retrieved on 26 November 2023 from https://patch.com/massachusetts/stoneham/zheng-he-whos-he)

Realizing that his startling claim would upset those schooled in the tradition of the European maritime exploration and discoveries worldwide, he took great pains to collect evidence and authenticate his case. His fifteen years of diligent research, travelling to actual sites, visiting relevant scholars and experts all over the world, in addition to digging into manuscripts, maps, and various library sources, enabled him to put forward an impressive amount of evidence to support his narrative. Although the claim that 'China discovered the world' has been challenged, Zheng He's seven remarkable voyages are generally accepted as historical.

Although Zheng He never found any trace of the Jianwen emperor, he splendidly achieved the aim of enhancing the prestige and demonstrating the power and wealth of the Ming. His journeys greatly stimulated the tribute embassies from abroad. During the quarter century when Zheng He's treasure fleets roamed the seas, there was a steady stream of envoys and heads of state from the countries or regions where these fleets had visited, coming to the Ming court to participate willingly in the ritualized suzerain-vassal relationship. For example, in 1416 there were embassies from nineteen overseas countries. Even representatives of Mamaluke Egypt came to pay court. Kings from countries including Borneo and the Philippines boarded the treasure ships with their wives and large retinues, going to and fro between their kingdoms and China, some more than once; some even stayed sufficiently long that they died and were buried in China, with the appropriate ceremony. These people were normally honoured and lavishly entertained and provided for by their Ming hosts.

Why did the heads of foreign states and their representatives subscribe to this Chinese world order? The incentives most likely included tourism and material gain: the ships were comfortable, the Ming capitals were worth visiting, the royal banquets and entertainments were enticing, and the gifts of the Ming emperors were often more valuable than the tributes they offered. An added attraction was the opportunities for commerce. Furthermore, there was the comforting protection of the Ming's military might. They probably realized that the submission to a Chinese emperor as suzerain was more form than substance: while the benefits were many, the yoke was light. The kowtows and other signs of subordination were an acceptable price to pay for all the benefits.

In retrospect, it is a striking fact that although the Ming had the military capacity and the naval prowess to conquer many of the states Zheng He visited, it did not do so. Zheng He's instructions from the Yongle emperor were to 'proceed to the end of the earth to collect tribute' from the foreigners and 'to attract all under heaven to be civilized in Confucian harmony'. The Ming had no intention of carving out colonies overseas by wars of conquest, as some of the European colonial powers began to do about a hundred years later in the Americas. It was not aiming to subjugate other states by force, to extract their wealth and exploit their people. The spirit of the tribute system of international relations as promoted by the Ming was peaceful and friendly; the Ming Admirals were enjoined 'to treat distant people with kindness'. This soft power approach contrasts sharply with that of the Portuguese and Spanish empire-builders, who used their superior military power to dominate Mexico and South America by force, leading to massive death tolls, the enslavement of the indigenous people, and the destruction of the native cultures. Although Zheng He's fleets included warships and carried tens of thousands of fighting men and plenty of weapons and armament, these were there to protect the people and valuables carried by the ships, to inspire awe, to impress the rulers of other countries, and to fight only if a situation arose that warranted the use of force. These fleets were not primarily a collection of warships, unlike the massive armadas assembled by Khubilai Khan to invade Japan.

To be sure, Zheng He did use force on several occasions. Some of these incidents were in connection with local chieftains behaving like pirates, or rebels against a regime which China recognized, attempting to rob his ships by force. After defeating them in battles, he took them back as captives to present them to the Yongle emperor. On another occasion, he used force to settle a local succession issue. The lack of colonial intention was further borne out by the fact that Zheng He did not leave sizeable garrison forces in the lands he visited. In many cases, the exchange of documents and gifts, and the bestowal of kingships by the Chinese emperor to rulers of these distant countries, was a form of recognition of the legitimacy of these rulers, as the heads of the independent and sovereign states concerned.

Besides the diplomatic successes and the increased prestige of the Ming, the disappearance of the Japanese pirates during the first half of the fifteenth century was another positive consequence of the Ming naval dominance, through the activities of Zheng He's fleets. The surveys of the coasts, and the charts of sea routes and ocean currents recorded by members of these fleets, increased the knowledge of geography, cartography, and ocean navigation of the whole early modern world, not just for the Chinese, but also for the European explorers. Research carried out by Menzies (*op. cit.*) brought to light evidence that the Portuguese explorers, Vasco da Gama (1460-1524) and Ferdinand Magellan (1480-1521), and even Christopher Columbus (1451-1506) and Captain James Cook (1728-1779, did not sail into the unknown, but were equipped with the knowledge of world maps and navigational charts based on the information painstakingly gathered by these Ming seafarers who preceded them.

Other benefits of Zheng He's voyages included contributions to advancements in scientific knowledge, cultural exchanges, and the welfare of humanity through the propagation of fauna and flora from one part of the world in another. Two examples in the area of food may be instanced: the spread to Asia of maize cultivated in America, and the introduction to the Americas of a distinctive type of Asiatic 'melanotic' chicken that had black flesh, skin, bones, and curly black feathers, and that was considered a more nourishing food in China than the more common types of chicken. Exotic animals like zebras and giraffes from Africa were brought back as gifts to the emperor. A giraffe was fancifully identified by the Yongle emperor as the mythical *qilin* - an animal like a cross between a deer and a unicorn. But apart from the political advantage he gained by its being taken as a sign of heaven's approval of him, no lasting consequence came from importing such a creature. Other significant results of the voyages were the stimulation of trade, and the immigration of Chinese to Southeast Asia and India.

We may ask: was the Ming court pleased with the achievements of Zheng He and his fleets? The Yongle emperor was delighted that so many foreign heads of states and envoys came to honour him as their overlord, and many of their tributes, particularly the exotic, precious, or rare ones, must have had a more than purely symbolic appeal to him. He was also pleased with Zheng He's military triumphs abroad. As the sponsor and driving force behind Zheng He's maritime enterprise, he would not have sent Zheng He and his fleet repeatedly out to sea if he had not valued it.

The ending of the Ming fleet's expeditions

However, in 1424 the Yongle emperor died during Zheng He's sixth voyage. His son and successor, the Hongxi emperor (r. 1424-1425), disapproved of many of his father's costly projects, one of which was Zheng He's overseas missions with the enormous fleets. He listened to his Confucian advisors, who despised eunuchs and disparaged Zheng He's achievements. When Zheng He returned with his fleet at the end of his sixth voyage, instead of the triumphant receptions and rewards which he and his colleagues had formerly enjoyed, they were spurned and cold-shouldered by the new regime. The new emperor, who had no use for the treasure ships, ordered all the building and even the repair of them to be stopped. Zheng He was effectively retired from seafaring: in 1425, his was ordered to be stationed, with his troops, at Nanjing to guard the southern capital.

The Hongxi emperor died after a short reign of only two months, and was succeeded by his son, the Xuande emperor (r. 1425-1435). He continued to pursue his father's policy of retrenchment, but after several years on the throne, he noticed a decline in the tribute embassies from distant lands. In a bid to restore the Ming's sagging influence abroad, in 1431 he ordered the nearly sixty-year-old Zheng He to command a fleet of over 300 ships and 27,000 men and undertake one more major overseas voyage. Another, and a more narrowly targeted mission, was to persuade the King of Siam (Thailand) to cease hostile acts against the King of Malacca (in the present Malaysia), such as impeding the latter's passage to China. In connection with this, Zheng He brought an imperial edict from the Xuande emperor to the King of Siam stating:

'You, Oh king, should follow my orders and treat your neighbour well and instruct your officials not to invade and humiliate others without provocation. If you do this, we will regard you as one who respects Heaven and brings peace to people and makes friends with your neighbours. This is in accord with the benevolent principles I hold in my heart'.

This was Zheng He's seventh and last journey, for he died at sea in 1433 when the fleet was on its way home. This expedition was again a success, as it demonstrated once more the naval supremacy of the Ming and revitalized the tribute relationship and the official trade between the Ming and the coastal states, from the South China sea to the Arabian Peninsula and Africa. In addition to the large number of foreign envoys who came to Beijing on the fleet's return journey, visiting dignitaries from over a dozen countries sent tribute embassies to the Ming court during the years immediately following this voyage, the Malaccan king among them.

Two years after Zheng He's death, the Xuande emperor, who had sponsored Zheng He's last voyage, also passed away. It was the end of an era. The later generations of Ming emperors were no longer interested in the policy of pursuing prestige on the high seas. There were no more sightings of huge Ming fleets with cloud-like red sails in the Indian Ocean. Since the reopening of the repaired Grand Canal for grain transport from the south to north, Beijing in particular, the shipyards were producing more junks for river transport, while fewer and fewer ocean-going ships were being built. A regional rebellion in the southwest, and the resurgence of the Mongol threat in the north, led to the court to concentrate its resources for military campaigns against these foes, during the middle of the fifteenth century.

In 1477, a powerful eunuch named Wang Zhi, who headed a branch of the 'Brocade-Uniformed' palace police, made a last attempt to renew interest in a tribute voyage, and asked for Zheng He's logs. Tribute trade and palace procurement were a monopoly of the Ming eunuchs, which provided many opportunities for corruption and personal enrichment. Zheng He and his fellow eunuch admirals, who commanded the treasure fleets, were outstandingly upright and dutiful in their service to their emperors. They were unlike the later generations of manipulative eunuchs such as Wang Zhi, who deceived their emperors, amassed fortunes, and abused their power. A high official of the Ministry of War named Liu Daxia, after taking possession of Zheng He's documents, took it upon himself to hide and destroy them, and then reported to his superior that these records were 'lost'. In Liu's opinion 'the expeditions of San Bao to the West Ocean wasted tens of myriads of money and grain'. Referring to the shipwrecks and loss of lives, he said 'The people who met their deaths may be counted in myriads'. He considered the eyewitness accounts of foreign lands by Zheng He and his men to be 'deceitful exaggerations of bizarre things far removed from the testimony of people's eyes and ears'. Noting that the treasure ships brought back 'betel, bamboo staves, grape-wine, pomegranates, and ostrich eggs and suchlike odd things', he commented that 'these contributed nothing to the country'. As regards the 'wonderful and precious things' carried back by Zheng He, he asked 'What benefit was it to the state?' He condemned Zheng He's expeditions as 'an action of bad government for which ministers should be severely reproved'. He believed that the 'old archives should be destroyed in order to suppress [a repetition of these things] at the root'. Liu's opinion, thus expressed, was likely to be representative of the views of the Confucian bureaucrats, who were hostile to the eunuchs and feared their unbridled power. Zheng He's unique archives fell victim to the long-standing feud between the literati and the eunuchs. Fortunately, books relating to these journeys had already been published and remained in the public domain, so not all accounts were lost. But the bulk of the valuable information contained in the painstakingly kept logs of Zheng He's voyages did not survive this purge.

The Decline and Withdrawal of the Ming

While the official tribute trade was left to find its own level, ordinary maritime commerce between merchants of China, Japan, and other countries flourished as never before. A certain amount of such trade, conducted through the ports authorized to trade with the merchants of the countries concerned, was legal, but there was a large and growing clandestine trade, and much flouting of the very restrictive Ming regulations on such commerce. The Ming government's response was to revive the ban on overseas trade and travel (*hai jin*) that the Ming founder had resorted to, as a measure against the collaboration of Chinese smugglers and Japanese pirates, who were ravaging the Chinese coasts. By 1500, the building of boats with more than two masts was strictly forbidden. In 1525, the central government ordered the coastal authorities to destroy all ocean-going vessels and to detain the merchants who sailed in them. In less than a century, the most powerful navy in the world had been destroyed by imperial decree.

These measures did little to stop the illegal trade because it was lucrative for all those involved - rich Chinese merchants, desperately poor peasants, and the Japanese pirates who were known pejoratively as *wokou*, meaning 'dwarf bandits'. A different approach, more in keeping with the burgeoning commercial activities of the time, would have been to liberalize coastal trade with more opened ports, and at the same time strengthen coastal defence against smugglers and pirates. This would have had the additional advantage of enabling the authorities to collect more trade tax. This was not the way favoured by the ideologically anti-commercial Confucian literati, who persuaded some of the emperors of the post-Yongle era to issue edicts prohibiting Ming subjects from engaging in foreign trade and overseas travel. The ban made outlaws of those who dared to contravene it.

Because the Ming had allowed its strong navy to wither away and had neglected to keep its once vigilant coastal defence system in good order, the latent Japanese pirates, who were ever ready to pounce, became rampant and bold. During the middle decades of the sixteenth century, they ravaged the whole of the Chinese coast like invading forces, with hundreds of boats and thousands of men, causing enormous damage to the Chinese coastal towns and villages. Sometimes they even set up bases on the Chinese coast. For example, 20,000 of them once based themselves near present day Shanghai, from where they robbed and pillaged nearby towns. These Japanese marauders were aided and abetted by local lords in Japan, as well as by Chinese smugglers and outlaws. There were frictions between the authorities of the two countries, when the Ming suspended Japanese trade at a port where such trade had been permitted, on suspicion of complicity between the Japanese authorities and the pirates. These factors, in addition to commercial growth, led to a phenomenal increase in piracy. During the ten years between 1555 and 1565, the Jiajing emperor (r. 1521-1567) enlisted a number of outstanding generals, who made a determined effort, with the help of crack troops and ample material support, to deal mortal blows to the pirates and remove their threat permanently from the Chinese coast. The price the Ming paid for this success was an empty treasury. During the reign of the Long Qing emperor (r. 1567-1572), the court must have recognized some of the negative aspects of its restrictive policy on trade, and it began to lift the ban, at least partially.

The Ming provides a classic illustration of the phenomenon of the dynastic cycle. The founder and his capable adult son, the Hongwu and the Yongle emperors, were heroic figures, who arrived at the pinnacle of power by overcoming great obstacles. They were outstanding in their personal capabilities and leadership qualities, with outsized ambitions, great force of personality, and strength of will. Presiding over a strong and prosperous country, they greatly extended the territory of their empire. Their era fit the description of the genesis and growth phase of a dynastic cycle. But this state of affairs was not to last.

The Yongle emperor's successors pursued a conservative policy of preserving what their forebears had won, to save costly expenditures and give the people respite from the burdensome demands of the state. However, even just to preserve the status quo, the Ming authorities had to have the political will, and maintain sufficient military strength to resist foreign aggression and to prevent secession by a subject state. As we have seen, the Xuande emperor was prepared to let Annam secede, rather than prolong costly military actions in that area.

There were also threats from the Mongols. In 1449 the Oirat chief Esen emerged after a series of tribal wars as the new Mongol strongman, and he invaded the Ming with a large army. The young Zhengtong emperor (r. 1435-1449 and 1457-1464) was encouraged by his favourite, a vainglorious eunuch named Wang Zheng, to play the war game by himself leading a huge force, reportedly 500,000 strong, to fight the invaders. Esen outmanoeuvred the Ming forces and captured the Zhengtong emperor at Tumu, after inflicting a catastrophic defeat on the Ming. The battle of Tumu was significant because it changed Ming policy from offence to defence. The empress dowager Sun authorized the installation of a new emperor, the Jingtai emperor (r. 1449-1457), who empowered the new minister of war, Yu Qian, to strengthen the defence of the capital as Esen marched on Beijing, bringing with him the royal Ming captive. A series of military setbacks outside Beijing led Esen to retreat. He decided that his best interest lay in agreeing to return to the regime of tribute relationship with the Ming, provided that the Ming would again allow trade at certain designated market towns. He returned Zhengtong, by then a powerless deposed emperor, and peace was restored based on the trade agreement and through tribute embassies.

From the time of its defeat by the Mongols at the infamous battle at Tumu in 1449, the Ming gave up a large amount of territory in the north, retreating behind the inner Great Wall as a line of defence. By the mid-fifteenth century, a slow and gradual dynastic decline had already begun. Its lack of interest in maintaining a strong navy to ensure its position as a dominant maritime power provided further evidence of its waning vigour.

This was a turning point. There were major structural weaknesses in the political and fiscal system that needed to be addressed. Periodically, such efforts were made, but with limited success. One example was Zhang Juzheng's[14] Single Whip taxation reform of 1580 (to which we shall return). But without another strong leader at the top like the Yongle emperor, the Ming moderated its ambition, and withdrew into itself. The dynasty shrank into a passive defensive posture in its relationship with neighbouring and overseas

---

[14] Senior Grand Secretary in the late Ming.

countries and its territory contracted.

The Ming withdrawal was dramatically out of step with the European maritime expansion and exploration that would reach this part of the world a few decades later. This and other developments in Europe would usher in a new world of breath-taking changes, just when China had decided to turn inward and conserve its heritage. This choice was destined to leave China far behind the European powers, in the race to become wealthy and powerful modern nations. It also rendered China vulnerable, later in the Qing dynasty, to European imperial ambitions. In late Ming times, European development was still only a distant rumble, reaching the Chinese shores when the Portuguese established a foothold at Macau, and when the Jesuits arrived in China.

The start of European incursions

Towards the end of the fifteenth century, the Portuguese sea captains Vasco da Gama (1460-1524) and Ferdinand Magellan (1480-1521), through the foundation laid by Prince Henry the Navigator (r. 1394-1460), led the European drive to find a direct sea route to tap the wealth of the lands far to the east, and to trade in their spices, silks, porcelain, and other desirable products, so as to avoid having to operate through Arab middle-men. Following their success in rounding the Cape of Good Hope in Africa and in circumnavigating the world, the Portuguese set up a colony in Goa (on the west coast of India), from where the coast of China was within easy reach. In 1515, the Portuguese landed at an island near Guangzhou, and from then on they sought permission from the Ming authorities to trade. They were not successful, because Portugal was not among the states with a tribute relationship with the Ming, and Ming subjects were still forbidden to trade privately with foreigners along most of China's coast, except at certain ports opened to merchants of specified countries. The Portuguese then resorted to force, occupying and attacking many cities along the coast. The Ming forces successfully repelled their attacks and ejected them from the occupied territories. Despite having eliminated their own navy, the Chinese during the sixteenth century were able to repulse European invaders, and thus save themselves from the fate of the indigenous peoples of South America. Notwithstanding these setbacks over several decades, the Portuguese never abandoned their goal of establishing a foothold in China. In 1553, they bribed a Ming official to let them land at Macau, with the pretext of having to dry out their ships after encountering severe storms at sea. In reality, their plan was to establish a permanent presence after landing, build residences, set up administrative offices, and encourage the immigration of Portuguese people. Around 10,000 individuals did come to settle at Macau. When the Wanli emperor (r. 1572-1620) ascended the throne, he imposed a customs duty on the Portuguese at Macau, collecting more than 20,000 taels of silver annually. Since the Ming government was desperately short of money, it tolerated the Portuguese *de facto* occupation of Macau, on account of its income from the customs duty.

The Spanish followed soon after the Portuguese, with Magellan claiming the Philippines for Spain in 1521. The small overseas Chinese communities there acted as an interface, facilitating trade between the Spanish and continental China. The Dutch also arrived with their armed fleet. They tried to dislodge the Portuguese from Macau, but without success. The Ming stoutly defended its coast without letting the Dutch gain any foothold. The Dutch found a haven in southern Taiwan, where they defeated the Spanish, who had occupied the north of the island since 1626. In 1642, the Dutch took over the entire island, but only briefly.

The Catholic authorities in Rome strongly supported the overseas colonial expansion of the Catholic countries Portugal and Spain, since their thrusts helped to spread Catholicism to other parts of the world. Jesuit missionaries came to China on the heels of the Portuguese and used Macau as a beachhead to advance into China. The Jesuits were highly educated in the arts and sciences of a West which was on the eve of a scientific revolution. They acquired a high degree of proficiency in the Chinese language and became knowledgeable about Chinese culture, so that they could communicate with the educated Chinese at a sophisticated level on matters relating to both Chinese culture and Western science and technology; in this way they hoped to make them more receptive to the Christian gospel. After preaching for many years in southern China, an Italian Jesuit priest, Matteo Ricci (1552-1610), pioneered an approach that rendered Christian texts more understandable and acceptable to the educated Chinese. He linked Confucian 'ancient ethics' with Christian moral precepts, and accommodated Chinese ancestor worship as 'civil rites', while rejecting Buddhism and Neo-Confucianism. He began to make converts of scholar-officials, and he finally moved north to the capital. In 1601, the Wanli emperor gave him a stipend as a Western scholar and permitted him and his fellow Jesuit priests to stay and preach at Beijing. Other Jesuit missionaries adopted the same approach, and some also tried to reach the common people. By the end of the Ming dynasty in 1644, there were around 40,000 Catholic Christians in China.

The court officials valued the Jesuits' knowledge of science and technology. Some were employed by the court to work on chronology in the newly established Bureau of the Western Calendar to revise the calendar, and they, together with Chinese scholars, produced many books on astronomy and chronology. Others introduced western knowledge of physics, mathematics, mechanical engineering, and geography, as well as many arts subjects, to the educated Chinese through learned discourse, and by translating western texts. The Ming authorities even tapped the Jesuits' know-how on making 'western' cannons. It is noteworthy that the society that had invented gunpowder and firearms centuries earlier fell far behind in further development of these weapons until it was threatened by external foes. The next time the Chinese needed to import western technology on weaponry would be in the nineteenth century, when the Qing dynasty that succeeded the Ming was seriously threatened, by both internal rebellion and external aggression.

We may wonder why this early round of valuable transfer of western knowledge failed to make a lasting impact on the Chinese society. One reason was that the Jesuit mission in China was limited in scale, and its main objective was religious conversion rather than cultural transfusion. Perhaps the underlying reason for China's imperviousness to foreign influence must be sought in its political structure, its economy, and its own deep-rooted cultural tradition.

There was transfer in the opposite direction too. The Jesuits brought back to Europe their knowledge of China, which inspired the appearance of 'Chinoiserie' as popular collectibles, found among ceramic products, furniture, and landscape design used in homes or for public display. The early European Enlightenment thinkers like Montesquieu and Voltaire, who were searching for a political model of ethical government founded on virtue without appeal to religion, saw Confucian China as the example they were looking for. This cross-cultural exchange between China and Europe appeared to have more impact on Europe, because of the receptive response of the great European philosophers to Confucianism, and the influence of their ideas on a Europe already in the throes of political change.

The Europeans were spreading by sea to distant shores, building colonial empires first in the Americas, and soon thereafter endeavouring to establish bases in East Asia and Southeast Asia. In contrast, Ming China, having destroyed its own navy, tried to steer clear of outside entanglements, and become self-contained within its own borders. Inside the empire, despite the weakening of the political superstructure, the society underneath showed plenty of vitality. The population nearly doubled from an estimated 70 million during the early decades of the Ming rule to around 130 million at the end of the dynasty. The Ming official population figures, collected for taxation purpose, were notoriously inaccurate, mainly because people tried to minimize the tax obligation, and also because the method of census-taking was not as rigorous as a modern census collection. Although there were more mouths to feed, there were also more hands to work. The economy expanded considerably in many directions: agricultural, commercial, and industrial. More labour-intensive farming, land reclamation, cultivation of new crops from the Americas such as sweet potato, peanut, maize, and tobacco, and improvements in agricultural machinery, technique, and irrigation, all contributed to significant increases in food and other farm products. The surplus of primary products and labour led to a boom in craft production, either as a cottage industry or in factories.

Economic and cultural developments

Trade, both internal and external, flourished. The commercial demand provided stimulus to industrial production. In the richer parts of southern China, factory production of various commodities for both the internal market and export thrived, as wealthy merchants and landlords used their capital accumulation as investments in both industry and commerce. Considerable advances were made in weaving, fabric dying, papermaking, metallurgy, and in the making of ceramics and lacquer wares, and cloisonné. Although there were domestic improvements in firearms, the European cannons made by the Jesuits were considered more devastating. A fourteenth century Ming official was the first person to experiment with a rudimentary rocket-propelled flying machine. Silver imported from abroad and mined by the Chinese replaced the ever-depreciating paper money as the main currency of exchange and tax payment.

Some modern Chinese Marxist historians like to look at this type of economic development in the Ming as 'budding capitalism'. But in fact, there was no flowering of capitalism in Ming China. Among possible explanations, a modern economic historian, Mark Elvin, has suggested[15] that a 'high level equilibrium trap' kept the highly developed labour-intensive agricultural economy of China from being able to lift itself by its own bootstraps to achieve a capitalist market economy.

The dynamism of the Ming economy was reflected in its lively cultural scene. Popular literature, novels, and short stories flourished during the Ming, in response to the demands for culture and entertainment by the growing urban middle class. A similar phenomenon would occur in Europe much later. A booming printing industry and a brisk book trade helped to satisfy these tastes. Theatrical performances also grew in popularity. The traditional art forms such as painting, sculpture, music, and dance continued to find expressions among the gentry and the common people in diverse ways. The study of the Classics continued to attract those who wished to achieve higher social status or gain official posts, or for self-improvement. During the early decades of the Ming, the court favoured Song Neo-Confucianism. As time went on, prominent Ming thinkers did not feel bound by the Song interpretation of the Classical texts: their syncretistic brand of Neo-Confucianism was deeply influenced by Zen Buddhism and Daoism. They believed that moral knowledge or innate goodness (*liang zhi*) was inherent in the human mind, and they were concerned with recapturing this pristine state of the self before its corruption by egoistic thoughts and desires. They practised 'quietism' and stressed 'absolute spontaneity' and 'perfect accord between the mind and the world'.

Many works were published which presented practical knowledge on a wide range of subjects from medicine to dietetics, geology, the geography of China and foreign countries, encyclopaedias of agricultural techniques, and illustrated treaties on the technology of ceramics, iron, and steel. The Tiangong Kaiwu was one of the most comprehensive works on applied science and technology. The illustrated text covered mining with machinery, the building of boats and carts, the making of bricks, ceramic and metallic products, and many other industrial products. A remarkable book on botany and pharmacopoeia was

---

[15] *The Pattern of the Chinese Past,* by Mark Elvin (Stanford University Press, Stanford CA, 1973).

Ben Cao Gang Mu. It was printed in 1596 with 'magnificent plates'. It had notes on over one thousand plants and one thousand animals, with medicinal uses. It recorded a method of smallpox inoculation, similar in principle to that developed in the modern science of immunology.

The seeds of governmental decline

There were many reasons for the Ming's decline, including poor leadership at the top, systemic weaknesses, and financial crises. The Ming governance suffered from too much concentration of power in the hands of the emperor. If such an absolutist ruler delegated his power to the wrong people, or let his power be usurped by them, or if he were himself incompetent, the polity could be harmed. The extraordinary concentration of power originated with the founder who, after abolishing the prime ministers' office, tried to govern the entire country single-handedly with the help of a small number of scholars working from the inner courts or pavilions inside the palace. He terrorized the regular bureaucracy by setting up a fear-inspiring palace police, the Brocade-Uniformed Guards, to exercise surveillance over his officials and bend them to his will. It is ironic that his less capable heirs strengthened this absolutist tendency, though they lacked the founder's capacity for work, or his talent for making the day-to-day decisions on the business of running a vast empire.

The Ming dynasty was unusual in allowing eunuchs to participate in every area of government, civil and military, and the abuse of power by eunuchs was a special feature of Ming autocracy. The founding emperor, mindful of the lessons of eunuch abuse of power in history, prohibited eunuchs from handling official documents and meddling in politics. He decreed that the eunuchs should be treated as lowly servants, doing merely menial tasks, and be kept in their place through fear of law and discipline. The Yongle emperor, who seized the throne from his nephew with the eunuchs' help, overturned this ancestral injunction. From then on, those eunuchs who gained their emperors' trust and affection could become members of the ruling elite. Many held high official positions, acquiring great wealth and exercising enormous power or influence. Although there were a few towering figures among the Ming eunuchs, such as Zheng He, who served their emperors and their country admirably, many others were prodigiously corrupt and notorious for their abuse of power. While there were established institutions to assess, check, and supervise the work and the conduct of the regular officials, no such controls existed as regards the eunuchs. The emperor was the only one who could curb the eunuchs. If an official called an emperor's attention to eunuch misbehaviour or abuses, he might well put his own live at risk, should the emperor side with the eunuchs.

Not all the Ming emperors were endowed with the wisdom and good judgement to enable them to exercise their autocratic power justly and benevolently. Many of them were not even interested in managing the affairs of the state. They regularly failed to hold court audiences or respond to official communications. Their negligence led to usurpation of power by unscrupulous people close to them from inside the palace, who were either members of the inner cabinet or eunuchs. These people tended to be corrupt and to misgovern the country. The Chenhua emperor (r. 1464-1487) was exploited by his eunuch Wang Zhi whom he had appointed him to head a section of the palace police. The Jiajing emperor devoted himself entirely to practising Daoism during the later years of his reign, from which he did not wish to be distracted by his duties as the head of the state. Power fell into the hands of Yan Gao who, for many years as the head of the inner cabinet, was notorious for corruption and acting unjustly towards officials outside his inner circle. The personal servants of the emperors knew the likes and dislikes and personal weaknesses of their masters, whom they could manipulate to gain power, wealth, or official posts for themselves and their henchmen.

The Zhengde emperor (r. 1505-1521) and his eunuch Liu Jin illustrate fully the lethal combination of an irresponsible emperor and a tyrannical eunuch. This ruler came to the throne as a teenager of fifteen. He was so fond of hunting, fishing, and all kinds of amusements and games that he had no time for the official business of government. This gave an opportunity to Liu Jin, the leader of a gang of eight eunuchs, known as the 'eight tigers', to take over the job of receiving all official documents - letters, reports, and petitions - from all parts of the empire, while keeping the young monarch intoxicated with entertainments. Liu Jin craftily presented these documents to the emperor just when he was most distracted. The emperor once waved him away irritably with the remark 'this is what am I using you for, yet [you] come to disturb me'. From then on Liu Jin made the decisions for the emperor, and sometimes even changed laws at will. After Liu Jin and his gang were put in charge of the palace police, and the East and West Depots, officials who opposed or offended Liu Jin either lost their jobs or their lives. Extremely cruel punishments that could led to death were meted out, even to high officials, on trivial offences. He put his supporters, or those who bribed him heavily, in key government posts. Offering or solicitation of bribes became the order of the day. Those who did not satisfy him in every respect would be accused of crimes and suffer imprisonment, torture, and even death. With Liu Jin in charge, rampant corruption and a reign of terror prevailed. When Liu Jin discovered an anonymous letter accusing him of misdeeds on a street where the emperor had just visited, he ordered all court officials to kneel in front of the Feng Tian gate for questioning. and to listen to his day-long tirade. It was a scorching summer day, and some officials died from heat and thirst on that occasion. Finally, the crimes of Liu Jin were exposed, and he was arrested and convicted of treason. After his property was seized, hundreds of thousands of gold and silver ingots, four thousand jade belts, and many precious stones and other treasures were found in his house. All these ill-gotten gains were obtained during only a five-year tenure as the emperor's surrogate.

The corruption and misrule served only to exacerbate the financial difficulties that the government began to experience, along with administrative decline, from the middle of the fifteenth century. The institution of self-sufficient agricultural-military colonies gradually disappeared. The land and population registry of the early Ming became less and less reliable. The land that belonged to small independent farming households, which provided the mainstay of the government's taxes, decreased alarmingly as time went on. The reason lay in the encroachment of peasant land by the wealthy merchants and landowners, a significant number of whom were royal relatives. The Ming founder had 23 sons; and his descendants that were recorded in the 'Jade Register' might have numbered about 300,000 by the end of the dynasty. They formed an unproductive 'super class' of powerful and privileged people, who tended to use their special connections or influence to take into their possession ordinary peoples' land. Land grabbing was also a common vice amongst greedy local elites and high officials, eunuchs included. This abuse impoverished the small farmers or turned them into landless labourers who might become rebels or bandits. It also removed a large amount of land from taxation, partly because the land that belonged to many special categories of privileged people was not registered for tax, and also because the mighty had ways and means of avoiding land registration and paying taxes. By 1529, the eighth year in the reign of the Jai Din emperor, the amount of land subject to tax had shrunk to less than half of that recorded at an earlier period. Even though the tax burden was increased on the remaining taxable land and farming households, the tax revenue was nevertheless drastically reduced. The government had trouble paying its officials, as well as supporting its military.

Feeble attempts at reform did not rectify the situation significantly until the early years of the Wanli emperor, who ascended the throne as a boy of ten. Still under the supervision of his mother and the dowager empress, he followed their advice to allow Zhang Juzheng to lead the inner cabinet, and to run the country. Zhang happened to be a capable and strong-willed leader of government. During the ten years, starting from 1573, when he wielded almost dictatorial power, he rendered the bureaucracy more effective through measures that promoted able officials, while weeding out the ineffective and corrupt ones. He greatly increased the amount of taxable land by having the empire's agricultural land measured district by district, without interference from powerful landowners. His 'Single Whip' reform unified the various categories of taxes, such as in labour or in kind, and commuted them all into silver currency, which was to be collected by the local officials directly. His tax reforms turned the government's financial deficit into a surplus, and reduced the tax burden on those who were least able to bear it. It appears that Ming decline could have been arrested, even at such a late date, if given effective leadership at the top. Because Zhang's reforms on taxation impinged on the interests of the rich and powerful, they did not last beyond his death in 1582, when the Wanli emperor dishonoured him posthumously.

After the Wanli emperor assumed control of the government himself, seizure of peasant land by the rich and powerful returned with a vengeance. He set a bad example by granting his imperial relatives unusually large estates, with land that had been seized from his helpless subjects. From the middle period of his reign at the beginning of the seventeenth century, the Ming state was in crisis, politically, economically, and financially. A loose-knit group of scholar-officials or ex-officials, who were deeply concerned about the critical situation the country had fallen into, started a political movement that stood for clean government. Because prominent members of this group met for political and philosophical discourses at the site of the old Song dynasty Donglin Academy in the city of Wuxi, they and others with similar views came to be known as the Donglin Party. They were so vehemently opposed to the corrupt and lawless behaviour of those in power that they were not afraid to criticize or attack high officials if their conduct did not come up to their standards of integrity or uprightness. Unfortunately, their political impact was limited by a system in which all power flowed from the monarch. They might have had some influence on public opinion, but unless the emperor gave them the authority to implement their ideas, they could only remain powerless bystanders. The Wanli emperor had no inclination to employ these people in key posts.

The Wanli emperor's actions served only to make a bad situation worse. To raise funds, he authorized a project to open up new mines by eunuch officials all over the empire, and to have the eunuchs collect taxes from these enterprises. From 1597 to 1605, although 3,000,000 taels of silver had been collected for the emperor, a large part of the profit went to the eunuch officials, their assistants, and the local bullies who became involved. The eunuch officials behaved arrogantly, with utter disregard of law, oppressing the local people in criminal ways, and exploiting them as free labourers in the name of the labour service tax. The mining enterprises, which gave rise to new opportunities for corruption and abuse of power by eunuchs, were deeply resented by the people in the localities concerned. Many rose in rebellions against the government.

Even with eunuch abuse of power, and the damages associated with it so much in evidence, the Tianqi emperor (r. 1620-1627) facilitated the rise of another lawless eunuch, Wei Zhongxian, who held dictatorial power for seven years. Wei was an illiterate gambler. He decided to neuter himself to improve his life's chances as a eunuch. He schemed his way into the heart of the emperor's wet-nurse, known as Madame Ke, of whom the emperor was particularly fond. Wei's close relationship with Ke helped him to become a favourite of the emperor also. Before long he was given the post of handling official documents for the emperor. This gave him the opportunity to write edicts, with the help of his more literate collaborators, in the emperor's name. Since his ambition knew no bounds, he murdered or sent into exile those who stood in the path of his rise. He trained a personal force of ten thousand armed men in the confines of the palace, without the emperor sensing any personal threat. After being put in charge of the palace police, he tried to subdue all opposition by using the terror tactics of secret spies, imprisonment, and torture. He dismissed many of the officials, including members of the Donglin Party, who dared to impeach him. Some were imprisoned and tortured to death. He put his followers and collaborators in power, while mercilessly persecuting members of the Donglin Party, which stood for all those who opposed him. Officials who petitioned the emperor to condemn Wei's crimes were liable to get short shrift. The Tianqi emperor was so prone to listen to Wei and his supporters' stories and excuses that in the end the accusers became the accused. Wei's crimes were not exposed until the beginning of the reign of the Congzhen emperor (r. 1628-1644), who finally put an end to Wei Zhongxian's tyrannical regime.

The raging misrule during the Tianqi period did nothing but aggravate the late Ming crises. Peasant uprisings that had been sporadic throughout the Ming grew larger, more persistent, and more difficult to quell. It was as if the dynasty was losing its mandate to rule. As it had been towards the end of the Yuan, ambitious rebel leaders tried to use secret religious organizations as a cover to appeal to people suffering from economic distress, social injustice, or political oppression, to gather followers and then foment rebellion. The White Lotus Society had a long lineage as a vehicle for this purpose. It made its reappearance during the Wanli period in 1514, and in 1622, during the reign of the Tianqi emperor, its leaders, with nearly 200,000 adherents, decided to raise the flag of armed rebellion. Although this anti-government movement was suppressed, violent peasant unrest spread like wildfire, particularly in the Shaanxi province in northern China where, in 1627, a severe famine occurred. By the 1630s, small bands of rebels grew into armies of two or three hundred thousand, sweeping across the countryside and capturing towns and provincial cities.

The Ming authorities tried both to fight the rebels and to win them over by offering inducements, but two resilient rebel leaders, Zhang Xianzhong and Li Zicheng, each controlling an independent army of his own, survived all the government's effort at suppression and pacification. Despite some military setbacks, by the 1640s each had successfully occupied several provinces. In 1643, Zhang made himself the Great King of the West, and set up an orderly administration to rule from the city of Wuchang in central China. The following year, after Zhang had captured Chengdu in Sichuan and transferred his capital there, he made himself an emperor.

Also in 1643, Li, calling himself the Heaven Serving and Righteousness Promoting Great Generalissimo, set up a government at Xiangyang, with the help of disaffected members of the scholar-gentry. Li's literati supporters also advised him to adopt policies which were calculated to win more peasant support for his regime, such as giving the land seized by landlords back to the peasants and getting rid of unreasonable and burdensome taxes. After capturing Luoyang, Li distributed the gold, silver, and grain from the store of an imperial prince to the people. These and other popular measures helped his movement to grow. In 1644 Li took Xi'an, which became the capital of his kingdom of Da Shun (Great Accord). Here he established an elaborate government administration, with laws and regulations.

When Li saw that the Ming was too weak to defend its realm, he marched with a large, well-disciplined force from Xi'an to Beijing early in 1644. All along the way, county after county surrendered without a fight, and he was able to capture Beijing within two months of the start of the march. After the fall of his capital, the Chongzhen emperor took his own life. At Beijing, Li sought to set up a central administration by recruiting lower ranking Ming officials to supplement his own. Higher officials, those above the Third Grade, were forced to contribute money to the new regime, because they were presumed to have become rich by corruption. At this point, the Ming seemed to have reached the end of its dynastic cycle. Evidently the time had come for the Ming to be replaced by a new dynasty, which was again to be founded by a rebel leader of underprivileged peasant origin, like the Hongwu emperor of the Ming. However, subsequent events showed that the mandate of heaven had passed Li Zicheng over, and his movement was soon to be swept away by a rising tide from the steppes.

References

1. General references:

A General History of China (in Chinese) by Bai Shouyi (Shanghai Peoples' Publishing House, Shanghai, 1999).
History of Chinese Civilization by Jacques Gernet (English Edition, Cambridge University Press, Cambridge, second edition 1996), chapters 18-21.

China: A History Volume 1 From Neolithic Cultures through the Great Qing Empire 10,000 BCE – 1799 CE by Harold M. Tanner (Hackett Publishing Company, Inc., Indianapolis/Cambridge, 2010), chapters 9-10.

2. The voyages of Zheng He:

1421 The Year China Discovered the World by Gavin Menzies (Bantam Books, London, New York, 2003).

When China Ruled the Seas: The Treasure Fleet of the Dragon Throne 1405-1433 by Louise Levathes (Oxford University Press, New York, Oxford, 1994).

Chapter 5

The Foundation and Rise of the Qing Dynasty

The Defeat of the Ming, and the Founding of the Qing

Nurhaci and the Later Jin dynasty

The founders of the Qing dynasty were members of the Nuzhen (or Jurchen) tribe that inhabited the forests and steppes of northeast Asia. During the early decades of the twelfth century, the scattered Nuzhen tribal groups became united under a strong leader, who established the Jin dynasty, which lasted for about a century. After the Ming dynasty (1368 – 1644) took over from the Mongol Yuan dynasty (1271 – 1368) in China, it tried to control the vast territory inhabited by the Nuzhen tribes outside the Great Wall and placed military garrisons at strategic places. At the same time, the Ming made the leaders of the different Nuzhen tribal groups its vassals, giving them official titles to govern their own people. These tribal leaders were expected to demonstrate their loyalty to the Ming through participating in the 'tribute' relationship, visiting the Ming court periodically to acknowledge their fealty and to exchange gifts. They were also expected to cooperate with the Ming officials to capture fugitives and offenders. This was the normal policy that had been enforced by the Ming in its relationship with the tribes or states along its borders.

The spectacular rise of the Nuzhen in late Ming not only formed a sharp contrast with the precipitous decline of the Ming: the two movements were actually closely connected. In earlier Ming times, the Nuzhen people were fragmented into tribal groups of various sizes that carried on continuous fratricidal wars of raids and vendettas against one another. They had long felt the oppression of Ming officials and resented the Ming policy of 'divide and rule'. To throw off the Ming yoke, they needed to unite, and strengthen themselves politically and militarily under a strong leader.

Nurhaci (1559-1626), who sensed this need, emerged as just such a leader around the middle of the corrupt and self-indulgent reign of Emperor Ming Wanli (r. 1573 – 1620). Nurhaci began his career as the head of an insignificant Nuzhen tribal group. He had only a few tens of fighting men under him. He was, however, an ambitious and gifted man, in the mould of an empire-builder or dynastic founder. He also harboured a personal grudge against the Ming for the death of his father and grandfather. His lack of military manpower did not deter him in the least from attacking and overcoming far more numerous foes. Besides being a brave and skilful warrior, he was also a brilliant military strategist and tactician, often winning battles against overwhelming odds. When going to war, he took the initiative of when, where, and whom to attack, and chose his targets carefully, to overpower the weak and avoid premature confrontation with a strong enemy. Little by little the territory and people under his control grew. Besides conquering other tribal groups, he also built alliances as a peaceful means of expansion. Many leaders of small tribal groups flocked to him with their followers. attracted by his reputation for invincibility in war and benevolence towards those who came to join him. Their motives might have been to seek a protector, or for upward mobility. Nurhaci's patient build-up of power and influence, and his persistent pursuit of increasing the territory and the number of people in his domain, bore fruit. Ten years after he started his expansionist movements, all the Nuzhen tribal groups in his ancestral region of Jianzhou came under his rule. This provided him with a far more promising foundation to challenge the relatively strong and numerous Nuzhen communities further away.

Before he was ready to challenge the Ming, he avoided arousing Ming suspicions of his intentions by personally bringing tribute to the Ming court and paying homage to the Ming emperor on many occasions. He also cooperated with the Ming officials in apprehending and even killing Nuzhen tribal chiefs who plundered Han settlements, and by returning the Han captives. He volunteered to fight Japanese pirates on the side of the Ming. Because of these acts and his persistently professed loyalty, the Ming court promoted him to become the highest official of his region, thus conferring legitimacy on the dominant position he had achieved among the Nuzhens. This development was a result of his judicious policy because he was aware that the high status and power given to him by the Ming greatly enhanced his authority and prestige in the eyes of his own people.

Between 1601 and 1625 Nurhaci displayed his organizational genius through establishing and perfecting the Banner system, whereby the entire Nuzhen population was grouped into Eight Banners of different colours, each with its own leader and a hierarchy of subordinate officers under his overall direction. This apparently militaristic organization was also political in terms of authority, and financial as regards taxation. This system not only provided him with a formidable fighting force with clear lines of command and ease in mobilization; it also gave him a rough-and-ready functioning government, managing the affairs of a population which was in the process of being moulded into an orderly society, obeying the rules and regulations laid down by him.

Recognizing the need for a written language, at least for governmental administration if not for other purposes also, he authorized the adoption of the Mongolian alphabet to express the Nuzhen native tongue. He prescribed a hair style for men that required shaving the hair from the crown and the two sides of the head, while leaving the rest to grow long enough to be braided into a plait at the back. Women were forbidden to bind their feet in the manner of the Han Chinese. He also laid down rules on the style of dress for the people in his territory because he apparently saw clothing as a matter of identity or solidarity rather than merely fashion. After more than three decades of ceaseless struggle, military as well as political, he accomplished the seemingly impossible task of uniting the fractious Nuzhen tribal groups into one cohesive ethnic entity, spreading over a vast territory in northeast Asia. In 1616, the 57-year-old Nurhaci proclaimed the establishment of the Later Jin dynasty (1616 – 1636) - or simply Jin as it later became - with himself ruling as the Yingming (meaning wise or sagacious) Khan (r. 1616 – 1626) of this new and expanding empire.

Map showing the location of the Later Jin Empire (*Wikipedia*: retrieved on 30 November 2023 from https://en.m.wikipedia.org/wiki/File:Map-Qing_Dynasty_1616-en.jpg)

In 1618, as the head of a unified Nuzhen tribe controlling the formidable army of the Eight Banners, Nurhaci decided that the time was ripe to challenge the Ming, by openly declaring his hatred for the Ming, and his intention to attack them, and by capturing several Ming towns with tens of thousands of people and livestock. The Ming responded with an army of 100,000 including 10,000 Koreans, supported by canons, against 60,000 Banner troops. The high morale of the Banner troops, fighting for ethnic survival and ascendancy, together with their superior military tactics, won the day. This major victory whetted Nurhaci's appetite for making further advances into Ming territory. In 1621, he captured the important garrisoned cities of Shenyang and Liaoyang, which enabled him to control a large swathe of the territory of the Liaodong (meaning Eastern Liao) peninsula, together with its people and resources. During the same year, Nurhaci moved his capital to Liaoyang, and four years later to Shenyang (later to be known as Mukden).

After these important victories against the Ming and having brought more Han population into territory under his control, Nurhaci showed a tyrannical side of his character. He became mistrustful of the Han people, persecuting his own Han official staff and mercilessly slaughtering large numbers of people in Han villages and towns. Those who were not killed were made into slaves of the Nuzhen aristocracy, working on the land taken away from themselves or other Han landowners. This was a radical change from his previous policy of being benevolent to the Han people and of employing the Han elite as officials. The enslaved Hans tried to escape if they could, and many fled in advance of an approaching Jin army. Within a few years, more than three million people had left Liaodong.

In 1626, Nurhaci decided it was time to make further inroads on Ming-controlled territory. With 130,000 troops he marched towards the Ming garrisoned city of Ningyuan outside the Great Wall. The Ming official in charge of the security of Liaodong, Sun Chengzong, was a very able and patriotic man. He made thorough and painstaking preparations to defend against attack and was ready to resist the enemy strenuously. However, he was removed from office, at the instigation of the powerful eunuch Wei Zhongxian, and was replaced by a man who had 'the courage of a mouse' and was as 'fearful of the enemy as if they were tigers'. The new head ordered the defenders, together with the people of a large surrounding area, to retreat behind the Great Wall. A relatively low-ranking but courageous Ming official, Yuan Chonghuan, defied his superior's order and took over the defence of Ningyuan himself. He and other like-minded officials, after putting in place many strong defensive measures, were ready to lay down their lives for their country. As Nurhaci moved rapidly with his troops towards this city without any interference, he expected an easy victory against a relatively small force of less than 20,000 defenders inside the city. The over-confident Nurhaci ordered wave after wave of his infantry and cavalry to advance against heavy barrages of well-directed salvos from Western cannons and other types of firearms. After sustaining heavy losses, he had to retreat, because the defenders had scorched the earth of the surrounding areas to make sure that there was nothing to sustain his troops. For the first time in his 42 years at war Nurhaci suffered defeat. It was a first great victory for the Ming, and a serious setback for Nurhaci. He died later that year at age 68.

Hong Taiji (Emperor Chongde)

Nurhaci's death left the Jin in a perilous state, not least because he had not appointed a successor. In the Jin domain in Liaodong, good arable land became wilderness, because the Han majority, the sedentary tillers of the soil, continued to flee as a result of Nurhaci's policy of turning them into landless agricultural slaves. This situation led to famine, high inflation, and social disorder. The hitherto fearless Jin forces seemed to suffer a loss of nerve. The Jin's enemies - the Ming to the west, the kingdom of Korea to the East, and hostile Mongols to the north - were all poised to deliver it a crushing blow.

In the face of these challenges, the heads of the Eight Banners agreed to appoint Nurhaci's eighth son, Hong Taiji, as the head of a collective leadership. The social stability and the economy of Liaodong improved after Hong Taiji gave the land back to the Hans and ended their slavery. Then he proceeded to tackle his enemies one by one. He led his troops inside the Great Wall, attacking the Ming at its weaker points rather than stoutly defended cities such as Ningyuan. The easy victories raised the morale of the Jin troops. The Jin cause was no doubt helped by the death of Yuan Chonghuan, who had hurried back from Liaodong to the capital to organize the Ming defence. Hong Taiji, wishing to avoid another hard fight with heavy losses, plotted to eliminate Yuan by framing the latter as someone who had a secret agreement with him to betray the Ming. The Ming emperor fell into the trap, and executed Yuan Chonghuan, wrongly, as a traitor.

In 1627, the Jin forces rapidly occupied a large part of the Korean peninsula. The king of Korea was forced to sign a treaty with the Jin, whereby the king of Korea or his representative was obliged periodically to pay respect to Hong Taiji at his court with tributes. This was the procedure used by the Ming to maintain symbolically the suzerainty and vassal relationship between itself and its less powerful neighbours, a system the rising Jin empire also found it convenient to adopt. This treaty also obliged Korea to sever all contact with the Ming, its former suzerain. The Ming, hardly able to keep its own borders intact, was in no position to defend its former vassal.

Hong Taiji next focused his attention on subjugating various Mongol tribes, particularly those in northeast Asia, by force and diplomacy. This was a challenging task: it took eight years of fighting and negotiating for him to unite all the Mongol tribal groups in Nan Mo (south of the desert) under Jin leadership. These eastern Mongols became Jin loyal allies or subjects because the Mongol aristocrats were allowed to join the Nuzhens as ruling elites. Hong Taiji established a set of laws and regulations to govern the Mongols through their own leaders. The setting up of an Eight-Banner Mongol force greatly strengthened the military power of the Nuzhens.

Hong Taiji realized that during the military campaigns, the collective leadership proved, at times, an obstacle to unified command and decisive actions. He found ways to concentrate power in his own hands at the expense of the other collective leaders. After having so successfully increased the position, power, and territorial extent of the Jin, Hong Taiji became dissatisfied with his own title and position. In 1636, he became formally the Emperor Chongde (r.1636-1643), thus elevating himself far above those who had been almost his peers during the collective leadership phase. He changed the dynastic name from the Jin to the great Qing (meaning pure). He also changed the name of his ethnic group nation from Nuzhen to Manchu, the name of the tribal group that formed Nurhaci's core supporters at the start of his campaign for unification. Emperor Chongde made the most powerful and meritorious Manchu military commanders into princes. Several Mongol and Chinese military leaders were also given princely titles.

Although conquering China and replacing Ming rule with his own was his ultimate goal, Chongde needed to proceed step by step. A priority at that point was to strengthen his rule politically, economically, and administratively over the Qing domain, which had by then expanded to cover a considerable area northeast of Ming China and northward deep into the lands of the Mongols, while sharing a common boundary at the Yalu River with Korea at its southeast. To do so, he set up a central administration with six ministries, or boards, with rules and regulations modelled on those of the Ming and run by top Manchu aristocrats. He enlarged the number of soldiers in the Eight Manchu and Mongol Banner forces by incorporating suitable males of each of these ethnic groups from newly acquired territories. He also formed an Eight Banner Han force from the Han population in his domain. The building of an enlarged military force, particularly the inclusion of the Hans, undoubtedly improved his chances of accomplishing his ambitious enterprise. Although the Ming could muster armed forces many times those of his, Emperor Chongde, a keen student of the history of the Middle Kingdom, must have taken courage from historical precedents of the successful conquest and subsequent rule of the Middle Kingdom by dynasties established by nomadic or semi-nomadic peoples, who had also started from relatively small domains of limited population and with greatly outnumbered military forces.

Having put his own house in order, Emperor Chongde's plan against the Ming was first to take over any remaining pockets of Ming garrisoned cities in China's northeast, and then conquer the territory north of the Yellow River, before attempting to conquer all of China. Before he was ready to proceed with this plan, from 1636 to 1640 he despatched tens of thousands of his troops several times to invade Ming territory through weakly guarded points of the Great Wall, further to the west. The purpose of these military expeditions was not to capture Beijing and overthrow the Ming at this stage, but to gain riches through looting, to wreak havoc on the targeted areas, and to probe the enemy's strengths and weaknesses. To prevent too much sacrifice of scarce manpower, the Qing commanders were instructed not to try to capture strongly defended cities. Their armies ranged far and wide, inflicting defeat on Ming forces that dared to fight them. Many Ming officials commanding thousands of troops would shelter behind city walls rather than engage the invaders in combat. After several months, the army would return to the Qing capital at Shenyang with much treasure (gold and silver), and large numbers of captives and livestock, while leaving the Ming cities and villages through which they passed in ruins.

Between 1641 and 1642, the Qing emperor fought the fierce Battle of Song-Jin to take over Songshan and Jinzhou, Ming strongholds outside the Great Wall. The capture of these cities further consolidated the Qing control of China's northeast, and it also removed a major obstacle to the invasion of Beijing through the strategic but fiercely guarded Shanhai Pass, the breach of which would amount to a stranglehold on the Ming. These and further aggressive military actions against the Ming in 1642 demonstrated fully to the Qing emperor the military weaknesses of the Ming, despite the larger forces his more populous neighbour could muster.

In 1643, Emperor Chongde suddenly died before he was able to realize his goal, and without having chosen a successor. Prince Dorgon, one of the most powerful members of the Manchu aristocracy, proposed to appoint Chongde's ninth son, a six-year-old boy, as a compromise candidate, to succeed him as the Emperor Shunzhi (1643-1661), with himself and another prince as co-regents.

Prince Dorgon and the fall of Beijing

Soon after settling the issue of succession, an unmissable opportunity for the Qing presented itself from developments inside the Great Wall. In the spring of 1644, the Ming capital Beijing had fallen into the hands of the peasant rebel leader, Li Zicheng. The closeness of the Shanhai Pass to Beijing - about a week's march - and the tens of thousands of Ming soldiers garrisoned there guarding this vital pass under the Ming general Wu Sangui, prompted Li to send an emissary, bringing 40,000 taels of silver, to persuade Wu to surrender to his new regime. Knowing that the Ming court officials at Beijing had mostly surrendered to Li, Wu did so also to preserve his own position. Then he heard that his father in Beijing was among those who had been forced to hand over money to the new regime. Adding insult to injury, he learnt that one of Li's generals had taken possession of his beautiful concubine, Chen Yuanyuan. Thus outraged, general Wu turned against Li and proclaimed himself as a loyal Ming subject. Aware that his forces were no match for those of Li's, his only recourse for survival was to turn to his erstwhile enemy, the Qing, for military support. He contacted the Qing, as a Ming official, offering an alliance with the Qing to fight the peasant army, and adding the inducement of 'splitting territory' with the Qing. The plan he put forward to the Qing was to let the Qing army enter China, not through the Shanhai Pass guarded by himself, but through other weakly defended points to the west, to engage Li's main forces stationed in northern China. If the Qing proceeded with this plan, he planned to keep his own army intact and wait for opportunities to display his strength after the belligerents had exhausted themselves.

Shortly before general Wu approached the Qing, Prince Dorgon had already recognized the fall of the Ming at Beijing as destiny, calling for the Manchus to fulfil their ancestral ambition of ruling China. He accepted the advice of his Han official, Fan Wencheng, who urged him to despatch troops to inside the Great Wall, this time not to loot and pillage, but to win the people over to the Qing side, and to fight the *liu kou* ('roving bandits') - a derogatory term for the peasant army - for mastery of north China. Still avoiding the Shanhai Pass, the quickest route to Beijing, the Manchu troops were again going to use the weak spots where they had entered northern China many times previously. The Qing plan happened to coincide with General Wu's suggestion.

At this point, the initiative passed from Wu to Li. After Li Zicheng realized that general Wu was not going to surrender after all, he led several thousand troops himself, starting on 13 April 1644, to the Shanhai Pass to fight Wu. Alarmed at the news that Li was coming towards the Shanhai Pass, Wu was forced hurriedly to alter his plan. Aware that he might well be defeated and meet his death in combat against Li's forces, he realized that asking the Qing to fight the peasant army in north China would not save him from the danger he was facing. In desperation, he sent one letter after another, asking and then begging Prince Dorgon to move the Qing troops speedily, not in the direction he had originally suggested, but towards the southeast, straight to the Shanhai Pass, where the gate would be opened to welcome them in. This invitation was almost too good to be true - one Dorgon was certainly not going to refuse. Because it had been so strongly defended in the past, the Manchus had not even attempted to force their way through this pass for some time, for fear of heavy losses. It was the ideal route to invade Beijing. Dorgon quickly accepted Wu's invitation, promising a princedom to Wu and his descendants. Gathering all the Manchu forces, Dorgon promptly changed the direction of their march to the Shanhai Pass.

Li had not considered the possibility that Wu might seek help from the mighty Manchus outside the Great Wall. Had he anticipated Wu's move, he might not have tried to force Wu's hand so lightly. He probably would have moved much more of his force stationed in northern China and made more thorough preparations for taking on the combined forces of the Qing and general Wu Sangui. En route to the pass, Li met elders from there sent by Wu, who pretended to surrender so as to delay the progress of Li's army, in case it arrived at Shanhai too much in advance of the Manchu rescue force. When Dorgon's forces did arrive at the Shanhai Pass on 21 March 1644, the armies of Li and Wu had already been in battle for one day. Dorgon massed his troops a few kilometres outside the gate, behaving more like an observer than a participant. The next day, after fighting resumed between the two sides, Wu's side was showing signs of being overwhelmed and disintegrating. Sensing Wu's desperate plight, before Dorgon would agree to help he pressed Wu to accept terms of surrender to the Qing as a subject, rather than representing the Ming as an ally. Wu had no option but to comply. When Dorgon threw his army into the fray the next day, the combined forces of Wu and the Qing outnumbered those of Li's, which were defeated decisively. Li hurriedly retreated to Beijing, with the victors following close behind. Back in Beijing, Li hastened to ascend the throne of his new dynasty, the Great Shun (Shun Dynasty), and left the very next day, taking his army westward to his old base at Xi'an. Thereafter, his movement declined. Had Li reached the Shanhai Pass without the delay, and crushed Wu before Dorgon's arrival, the history of China might have turned out very differently.

Shortly after Li left Beijing, but not before he had set the palaces on fire, Prince Dorgon entered the city with his soldiers under strict orders not to loot or plunder the inhabitants. The Qing prince took the advice of his Han official, Fan Wencheng, to use a 'softly, softly' approach towards the ex-Ming officials. To this category of people, the prince offered, if they would surrender to the Qing, to give back to them their official positions, and their land and properties taken away by Li Zicheng, regardless of whether they had surrendered to that regime. Many surrendered gladly. In northern China, several of the ex-Ming generals, who had surrendered to Li Zicheng earlier, responded positively to the Qing invitation to surrender, bringing with them their troops and the cities they were guarding to the Qing side. Then Dorgon sent out armies to destroy Li Zicheng.

This first stage of the Manchu conquest of China went extremely smoothly. The gentle approach adopted by Prince Dorgon stabilized the situation and made Beijing and a large part of northern China sufficiently secure to enable the Emperor Shunzhi (r. 1643 – 1661) to ascend the dragon throne, on 8 October 1644, as the first Manchu ruler of the Qing dynasty in China. It would be the last of the Chinese imperial dynasties.

Unifying the Country Under the Qing

Ming resistance

The most important task now facing the Qing was to unite China under its rule. Among its major enemies, besides the peasant-led regimes of Li Zicheng and Zhang Xianzhong, there was also the Southern Ming, formed by loyalists, who rallied around a Ming Prince Zhu Yousong as the Emperor Hongguang (r. 1644-1645), reigning at the old Ming capital of Nanjing from June 1644. Without sufficient manpower to fight on all fronts, Dorgon concentrated his military efforts first on crushing Li Zicheng. Although Li still had a multitude of troops in his movement – an estimated total of over 200,000 at one point – Li did not have a breathing spell to work out a coherent strategy, and continued setbacks had lowered his soldiers' morale. The combined forces of the Qing commanders and Wu Sangui continued to take the initiative, attacking, pursuing, and beating Li's army until Li retreated to a mountain south of Wuhan, where, in May 1645, a group of peasants or local vigilantes killed him (the exact cause of death was unconfirmed). The Southern Ming regime at Nanjing lasted only a year to June 1645, despite the heroic effort of the patriotic Shi Kefa to salvage the situation. It was defeated first by the old habits of corruption, starting with the emperor himself who sold offices to raise money, and by factional squabbles, before being overwhelmed by the Qing military force. The Qing then concentrated its attention on conquering Zhang Xianzhong's regime in Sichuan. Although Zhang was killed by an arrow fired from the Qing side in 1647, his generals continued to lead peasant armies to resist the Qing.

The deaths of the Emperor Hongguang and the rebel leaders did not end resistance to Qing rule. One after the other, three other Ming princes became (some very briefly) the emperor of the Southern Ming, with temporary capitals driven further and further south or southwest. The last one, the Yongli Emperor (r. 1646 - 1662), lasted the longest – for sixteen years. The remnants of Li Zicheng's and Zhang Xianzhong's rebel armies came over to Yongli in large numbers to fight against the Qing army, who were increasingly looked upon as alien invaders, because the Manchus were trying to submerge the Han identity in a brutal way. The power struggle between the two army commanders, and lack of cooperation between the armies of the peasants and officials, severely weakened this resistance movement. Qing military pressure forced Yongli to retreat to Burma in 1658. In late 1661, the Burmese handed him over to general Wu Sangui, who was in charge of the territory bordering Burma as a princely vassal of the Qing. Wu had him executed. His death ended the Southern Ming, but still not all armed resistance or revolt against Manchu rule.

Before the remnant of Li Zicheng's peasant army was completely wiped out, many fresh uprisings broke out against Qing rule. These were precipitated by Dorgon's policy of forcing his Han subjects to dress and wear their hair like the Manchus. Ever since Nurhaci had laid down rules for clothing and hairstyle for men and women in his domain, the dynasty forged by his descendants forced all peoples under their rule to dress and wear their hair like the Manchus. The Han men found it objectionable to have to wear their hair in the peculiar and distinctive Manchu style. But the Manchu rulers took their conquered subjects' willingness to make this change in their appearance extremely seriously. Those who complied were deemed submissive, while those who refused, or were just slow to make the change, would be regarded as enemies, punishable by death.

In 1644, after the Qing took over Beijing, sensing the Han peoples' strong sentiments against shaving their heads, Dorgon decided it was expedient not to force the issue at that point, and risk antagonizing the people whose support he needed. A year later in June 1645, after the Qing's victories against Li Zicheng and the Southern Ming regime at Nanjing, the overconfident Dorgon no longer felt any constraint on the matter. He decided to impose the Manchu style of hair and clothing in all the area under Qing rule. Edicts commanding men to shave their heads went out everywhere, with a limit of up to ten days at most for compliance, and a threat of 'killing those who would not follow the regulations of our dynasty'. The choice, as it was put succinctly to the public, was between 'keeping your hair, or your head'. This demand stirred up enormous anger among the people. Reactions were particularly violent in the newly conquered Yangtze River region. Outraged residents of several cities in that area rose up in revolt with cries of 'take off our heads, but not our hair'. They killed many Qing officials, manufactured weapons, and organized armed resistance movements to fight the Qing armies sent to suppress them. Dorgon's reply was brutal: he sent in troops to crush the uprisings and butchered the people of these cities en masse.

There was another Qing policy that was even more tyrannical. As the Qing army advanced into northern and central China in 1644, Dorgon adopted a policy of 'enclosing' huge areas of land belonging to the Han people and making them into estates for the Manchu royal family and their relatives, the Manchu military aristocrats, and the Banner forces. About one million people were thus rendered landless and reduced to working as agricultural slaves on estates owned by others. As mentioned previously, this practice, which was introduced by Nurhaci after he successfully invaded large areas of Han settlements in the northeast outside the Great Wall, was discontinued under Hong Taiji, because the economy of his state was seriously damaged by the loss of such slaves escaping in large numbers. Dorgon's reintroduction of this extremely oppressive policy, but now on Han lands inside the Great Wall, was on a much larger scale. Once again many of the enslaved attempted to escape, despite the risk of terrible punishments if caught. There were also severe reprisals against those who gave shelter to, or were even suspected of aiding, the escapees. These harsh measures, brutally enforced, added fuel to the fire of Han resistance, and may have delayed the unification of all fragments of the broken Ming empire under Qing rule for over a decade.

During the critical first seven years of Manchu rule, since Shunzhi was in his minority, prince Dorgon had managed the affairs of the state on his behalf. As we have seen, the harshness of some of the Qing measures introduced during this period alienated the Han population and rendered it more difficult for the new dynasty to unify the country. Although the Manchu conquest was for the benefit of their own people, and their military aristocrats formed an uppermost stratum of ruling elites, they were too small in number to administer and control the vast Chinese lands without Han Chinese collaboration. Soon after the takeover, many Ming officials in both the central and local government were temporarily retained. Examinations were held as soon as possible to replace the old Ming officials with a new crop of candidates who had gained their degrees under the Qing. The transition was made easier by the fact that the Qing had adopted, by and large, the Ming political and administrative institutions even before the dynasty established itself in Beijing. This was achievable because the Manchu dynasty already had the service of its own loyal and well-educated Han subjects, who had settled outside the Great Wall and who threw in their lot with the Manchus. Later, the Qing rulers introduced important changes and innovations according to their lights. Even the oppressive prince Dorgon tried to win Han support by propagating the idea that 'the Manchus and the Han were members of one family'. To supplement the Banner forces, he organized a new military force, known as the 'Green Battalion', made up of surrendered Han soldiers and officers. This Han army later played an important part in the war against Wu Sangui.

Soon after Dorgon's death in 1651, when Shunzhi himself began to rule, he tried to give the Han officials more authority, even though he continued to uphold the principle of Manchu dominance. Throughout the Qing, the dynasty enforced a policy of having its government offices, both central and provincial, run in tandem by both Manchu and Han officials. However, the system discriminated in favour of ethnic Manchus, who were often in a position of greater authority over their Han colleagues until the second half of the nineteenth century, when many Han officials gained dominant positions at the court and in the provinces. Those who had resisted Manchu rule were treated more leniently by Shunzhi. Rather than resorting to military suppression and killing all rebels, especially the 'small bandits', he preferred to offer them pardon if they would surrender. His reign, however, did not last long, for he died at age 24 of smallpox. His heir, who became Emperor Kangxi, was chosen partly because he had already had smallpox. The choice, however, turned out to be very good one. In 1669 Kangxi (r. 1661-1722) would order an end to the inhumane practice of 'enclosing' Han land, as well as the return to its owners of the land already seized. He cited his pity for the suffering of the victims as a reason for this act. For an astute ruler like Kangxi, he must have been aware that by freeing the 'enclosed land' and the labour force, his government stood to collect more tax revenue.

Although unification was effectively achieved in 1663, after the elimination of the last of the peasant rebel forces that once fought under the banner of Li Zicheng, the peace that prevailed was fragile and tentative. Less than a decade later, the 'Rebellion of the Three Feudatories' (*san fan zhi luan*) flared up in the outlying provinces. The *san fan* referred to the three Han princely commanders of garrisons, Wu Sangui in Yunnan and Guizhou, Shang Zhixing in Guangdong, and Geng Jingzhong in Fujian, who were elevated to the position of princes by the Qing in recognition of their meritorious services during the Manchu conquest. They were exceptional because their princely positions were combined with having possession of their own troops as well as territory bases, which they each ruled and taxed as if these were their own fiefdoms. Of the three, prince Wu Sangui was the most powerful, with 90,000 troops and a network of high officials over whom he exercised control. Financially they were a burden to the Qing central government, which, in addition to being deprived of the tax revenues of their areas, had to support them with large subsidies. Besides, their military power and lawless behaviour were posing a threat to the central government. In the interest of the dynasty's security, Kangxi decided to remove these princely, semi-independent, 'military governors' from their posts, even if doing so might lead them to revolt, which indeed they did.

In 1673, Wu Sangui was the first to raise the flag of rebellion. Later, from 1674 to 1676, the other two princes, as well as many other disaffected Han military officials, joined Wu in revolt against the Qing. The rebel forces made rapid progress at first: in a little over a year, most of the territory south of the Yangtze River was lost to the Qing. Kangxi used the strategy of isolating Wu Sangui. He successfully induced Wu's collaborators to return to the Qing fold with rewards, while focusing the main military thrust largely on defeating Wu Sangui's own forces. Although the plan worked well, the Qing failed to crush the rebel regime entirely until 1681, three years after Wu's death. While the initial phase of the Manchu conquest - the establishment of Qing rule in Beijing in 1644 - had been relatively easy, the later phase, that of unifying the country, was an uphill battle, full of challenges. Wu Sangui's rebellion was the most serious threat the Qing had to face up to this point.

Taiwan

But there was yet another threat to Qing rule, and it came from the direction of Taiwan. The last bastion of anti-Qing movement was based in Taiwan, the large island off the coast of the Fujian province. The Ming did not try to occupy or colonize this island, though it had the military capacity to do so. Both the Dutch and the Spanish did colonize it, the Dutch forcing out the Spanish in 1642. In 1661, Taiwan was drawn into the military conflicts of the Ming-Qing transition, because Zheng Chenggong retreated there with his armed forces after having failed in his military campaign against the Qing. Zheng, the son of a powerful pirate chief turned Ming loyalist, raised a 'righteous army' to fight for the Southern Ming, motivated either by opportunism or patriotism, or both. Emperor Longwu, delighted with Zheng's support, granted him the use of the royal surname Zhu. Since Taiwan was in Dutch hands at that point, Zheng - known to the Dutch as 'Koxinga' (the lord with the royal surname) - and the Dutch fought over the possession of the island. Both sides used cannons, and the Dutch also had other types of firearms. Having a naval force of 200 ships and 25,000 troops under his command, Zheng overwhelmed the Dutch, whose forces were outnumbered and whose reinforcements from the Dutch East India Company in Batavia failed to materialize. The Dutch survivors of a nine-months' siege were allowed to depart from Taiwan with some money, while leaving the bulk of their treasures and weapons behind them.

In Taiwan, Zheng Chenggong ruled under a princely title granted by the Southern Ming. He continued to use restoration of the Ming to legitimize his regime, and to gain Ming loyalists' support. After his death in 1662, his son Zheng Jing succeeded him. Zheng Jing's army invaded the mainland whenever an opportunity arose. Unable to dislodge the Zhengs from Taiwan, the Qing pursued at first a scorched earth policy along the shores of the five coastal provinces, stretching from Shandong to Guangdong, to make the coasts secure, and to prevent collaboration between the local inhabitants and the Zheng regime. To enforce this *hai jin* (sea ban) policy, the residents along these coasts were forced to move from 15 to 25 kilometres inland, and they were also forbidden to cross a fixed line of defence to reach the sea. This was a draconian measure that inflicted great economic hardship and personal losses on a multitude of people who depended on fishing and trade. In recognition of that, from 1664, during the reign of Kangxi, fishing was allowed to resume in certain coastal towns in Shangdong, and in 1668 the *hai jin* was relaxed altogether.

Having so much difficulty in achieving peace and stability after taking over the Ming Empire, the Qing court put off resolving the Taiwan question until after it had suppressed Wu Sangui's rebellion in 1681. Before that time, after typhoons foiled various Qing attempts to invade the island, the court supplemented a defensive policy with repeated attempts to send people there to persuade its leaders to surrender to the Qing and return to the mainland peacefully. As China became increasingly united and stable under the Qing dynasty, the hope of restoring the Ming grew dim. Over the years, many military commanders leading tens of thousands of soldiers accepted the Qing offer to return to the mainland.

In 1681, Kangxi decided the time was ripe for a military solution, and appointed Shi Lang, who among the surrendered military officers was exceptionally qualified, as Marquis Jinghai to command a naval force to capture Taiwan. Combining his knowledge of the conditions of the weather, wind, and ocean currents, with his experiences of naval warfare off the straits of Taiwan, he adopted, in June 1683, an appropriate strategy to fight and win a decisive battle at Penghu, a small offshore island that provided a stepping stone to Taiwan. Then at Shi Lang's urging, the government in Taiwan surrendered to the Qing. In August 1683, the Qing troops went ashore, and they were welcomed by the people there.

Then the question arose at the Qing court as to whether to keep Taiwan as a part of the empire. Such a question would have surprised those at the courts of European countries then striving to carve up the world into their possessions. There were many officials, particularly those controlling provinces opposite Taiwan, such as Fujian and Zhejiang, who argued for abandoning the territory, probably because they did not want the responsibility of having to defend it. Shi Lang presented a strong case for keeping the island, and several other high officials also favoured keeping Taiwan. Kangxi, at first hesitant, was eventually persuaded by the merits of the case for keeping Taiwan. This island, about the size of Belgium, became a Qing prefecture to be administered by the provincial government of Fujian, with military garrisons stationed both in Taiwan and on the island of Penghu. With the pacification of Taiwan, the Qing was at last enjoying a period of internal peace and stability, almost forty years after its army had marched into Beijing to put Shunzhi on the throne as the first Manchu ruler of China.

The High Qing Era: the Kang-Qian 'Age of Prosperity'

Let us now return to the start of the reign of Emperor Kangxi (r. 1661-1722). Like his father, Emperor Kangxi also ascended the throne as a child, at seven years old in his case. A panel of Regents chosen by his father managed the affairs of the state on his behalf until 1669, when at the age of fifteen, he officiated at the early morning daily court meetings, and took over the reins of power personally. After suppressing the revolt of the 'Three Feudatories' and taking over Taiwan, Kangxi was the first Qing emperor to reign over a united China with internal peace. He was an outstanding ruler, who, in his sixty-one-year long reign, effectively consolidated the dominant position of this foreign dynasty in the economic, political, and cultural life of China. We will now consider several of his important policies.

In the economic sphere, Kangxi presided over a country the agricultural economy of which had been seriously damaged by over a century of war. This situation left an enormous amount of uncultivated land accompanied by a large floating population without reliable means of livelihood. He set about restoring the damaged agricultural economy to health by encouraging people to return home, or to move to remote regions, to cultivate land or to reclaim wasteland. People who had done so were generously rewarded with three to five or even more years of tax remission, and possession of the land in perpetuity. Those who responded to the court's initiative, but lacked the means, were aided with seeds, cattle, and ploughs, and in some cases with money for the journey. Those who had the capacity to reclaim more than thirty acres of land had the opportunity to serve as local officials if they were sufficiently literate. As a part of the programme of stimulating agricultural production, the estates of the Ming royals and aristocrats were sold cheaply to the public. Although his successors, Emperors Yongzheng (r. 1722-1735) and Qianlong (r. 1735-1796) continued to pursue this policy of land reclamation and the promotion of agriculture, the most striking results occurred mostly under Kangxi's auspices. In a little less than 40 years, from 1685 to 1724, cultivated land increased by more than 116,000 *qing*, or the equivalent of over 2.6 million acres. By 1726, four years into Yongzheng's reign, the land under cultivation exceeded that at the end of the Ming by around 20.6%.

Other measures that enhanced agricultural production included the above-mentioned prohibition against 'enclosing' land belonging to the Han people by Manchu aristocrats. Another was large-scale work on flood control. Kangxi allocated large sums of money and appointed a very able official to successfully accomplish the task of restoring the flow of the Yellow as well as the Huai River, each through its former bed, and to prevent the frequent inundation of enormous areas of fertile crop land from the flooding of these rivers and their tributaries. His two successors concentrated their efforts on large scale repair of coastal embankments against flooding from the sea.

From the time of Kangxi's reign, agricultural production grew enormously, no doubt greatly helped by the increase in the amount of cultivated land and by effective flood prevention. There were other factors that contributed to this period of over one hundred years' time of plenty, celebrated as the 'High Qing era' or the 'Kang-Qian Age of Prosperity', which spanned the reigns of Kangxi through Yongzheng, to the last twenty years of that of Emperor Qianlong. There was a drive to increase the productivity of the land through refinement and improvement in agricultural techniques. Chinese agriculture had reached the most advanced level of development before the arrival of modern agronomy. The spread of early ripening rice led to twice-yearly harvests that doubled the yield of rice in southern China. There were fruitful experiments with drought-resistant rice. Farmers from the south successfully grew rice in many areas in northern China. Food became more plentiful through the widespread propagation of foreign food crops – maize, sweet potato, sorghum, and peanuts, some of which had high yields, or ripened at different seasons to achieve a year-round harvest, or thrived on marginal land. The increase in the production of industrial crops such as cotton, tea, tobacco, sugar cane, and mulberry trees (for silkworms) led to an expansion of craft production as cottage industries or in workshops, and to factories processing these products as raw material. Trade flourished under these circumstances. Commerce, both internal and with foreign countries, grew to an unprecedented scale.

In summary then, China in the eighteenth century was by no means an economically backward country. Its economic and population growth was the most rapid in the world, according to Jacques Gernet[16], who also held the view that the Chinese peasants were more comfortably off and better educated than their counterparts in the France of Louis XV.

These Qing emperors' energetic promotion of agriculture naturally benefited the state treasury in terms of the increased collection of taxes, and its success also conferred greater legitimacy on their (albeit non-Chinese) rule, as they fulfilled so well their traditional leadership role in strengthening food production and water engineering. The acceptance of their rule was surely helped by the fact that they also adopted a policy of exceedingly generous tax remission, not just to start people off on land reclamation, or in areas hit by droughts or other natural disasters, but as a regular measure for improving the livelihood of the people. These rulers certainly understood the link between economic wellbeing and social stability.

Despite the lenient tax regime and heavy military expenditures, the Qing treasury remained in surplus during this period of unprecedented economic boom. The expansion in agricultural production and its subsidiary industry and trade enabled the Qing treasury to retain a balance of over 50,000,000 *liang* (1 liang = 50 grams) of silver in 1706 under Kangxi. During the middle period of Yongzheng, the surplus increased to over 60,000,000

---

[16] See *A History of Chinese Civilization* by Jacques Gernet, Second Edition 1996, Cambridge University Press, Cambridge and New York.

liang. From the thirtieth to the sixtieth year (1766 - 1796) of Qianlong, the surplus remained above 60,000,000 *liang*, reaching over 80,000,000 *liang* at times.

This early Qing period of relative peace and prosperity enabled the population of the empire to grow by leaps and bounds. The population of China recovered somewhat from 152,500,000 at the end of the Ming in 1644 to 160,000,000 in 1679 during the eighteenth year of Kangxi. Less than one hundred years later, in 1776, it had nearly doubled to around 311,500,000. Even after the economy and administration of the empire started to decline towards the end of Qianlong's reign, the momentum of population growth continued from this large base. By 1851, during the reign of Emperor Xianfeng (r. 1850-1861), the population in China had reached a record 436,000,000.

In the political sphere, although the Qing government modelled itself on the Ming, the early Qing emperors including Kangxi had to share power to some extent with the Manchu military aristocracy, particularly those on the Committee of the Princes. This committee was normally made up of the most powerful Manchu aristocrats, with whom the emperor consulted and deliberated on important political matters, both legislative and judicial. The power of Ming emperors had been unconstrained by such a group of hereditary aristocrats. The early Qing emperors exhibited a tendency towards enhancing their own autocratic power at the expense of the hereditary Manchu aristocrats and other high officials. Although Emperor Kangxi managed the affairs of state with the Committee of the Princes, Emperor Yongzheng bypassed it by the creation of the *Junji Chu* (The Grand Council), where all important affairs of the state, including military matters where speed and secrecy were at a premium, were decided by the emperor with the assistance of its members. This relatively unstructured office was made up of high officials from the regular bureaucracy, both Han and Manchu, chosen, dismissed, or changed at will by the emperor, to advise him and to assist him in drafting and transmitting edicts. This Grand Council had neither a regular office building nor an address. Its meetings usually took place somewhere in the inner palace near the emperor's actual residence, at any time when the emperor felt the need to call a meeting. By exercising power through an instrument entirely under his direction and in his control, the emperor's autocratic power was greatly enhanced.

In 1791, Emperor Qianlong abolished the Committee of the Princes, which had in fact become obsolete. The cabinet, also known as *dorgi yamum*, that had been powerful under the Ming lost its monopoly to transmit memorials to the emperor. Many high officials were given the privilege of transmitting their memorials directly to the emperor, for his eyes only. The route and procedures for transmitting edicts and memorials were tightened and institutionalized, to protect confidentiality and prevent tampering, through a succession of reforms carried out by each of the Qing rulers since Shunzhi. The lessons of the Ming eunuchs' intercepting and tampering with edicts and memorials were apparently taken to heart by the Qing rulers, who did not give eunuchs much opportunity to abuse power. The Qing was relatively free of examples of eunuch usurpation of executive power. The reforms that created the *Junji Chu*, and which facilitated direct communication between the emperor and any of his high officials in private, gave rise to an unprecedentedly high degree of concentration of power in the hands of the emperor. The cabinet effectively became redundant. These measures, in addition to the use of the traditional devices of surveillance and control, such as the censors for checking up on the officials, made the Qing emperors even more absolutist than those of the Ming.

Nevertheless, these early Qing autocrats successfully pursued enlightened policies which benefited the people through unprecedented economic growth coupled with an extraordinarily mild tax regime. They might be described as *ming jun* (enlightened despots). Before the onset of administrative decline during the last decades of Qianlong's reign, the authors of the Kang-Qian age of prosperity made serious efforts at reforming the bureaucracy, with a view to curbing corruption and abuse of power, with considerable success. Other enlightened measures included Kangxi's edicts against agricultural slavery, and Yongzheng's decision to elevate various hereditary categories of *jian min* (debased people), such as entertainers, bonded servants, and people who lived on boats or shacks, from their lowly classification. Their inclusion in the general population registers helped to remove the stigma and the social and judicial discrimination traditionally attached to them.

As a foreign dynasty that lasted 267 years, the Qing had far greater staying power in comparison with the Mongol Yuan dynasty which ruled all of China for only 89 years. It compared well with the 276 years of the indigenous Ming. While the Mongol rulers were relatively alien to the Han Chinese culture and employed Han governance only to a limited extent, the Manchu emperors embraced the Chinese Confucian culture wholeheartedly, and broadly took over the Ming or Han Chinese governmental institutions before they inserted their own modifications. By the same token, the Yuan had failed to support in a serious way the Chinese traditional state-sponsored system of examinations. In contrast, the Qing appreciated the vital importance of this institution and made full use of it for recruiting officials and qualifying the gentry. This policy served the interest of the foreign rulers by providing them with a pool of well-educated Chinese to run the state in addition to the Manchus; it also won them the support of the Chinese gentry, whose cooperation was essential for the smooth functioning of the state. Furthermore, the rulers' control of the content of the examination helped them to promote a cultural orthodoxy they favoured. The enlightened measures of the early Qing rulers, together with the foreign dynasty's ability to win the Chinese gentry's cooperation, must have contributed to the longevity of Qing rule.

Challenges to the Qing, and Territorial Expansion in the Nineteenth Century

Xinjiang and Tibet

In contrast to an image of weakness and decay which China presented to the world by the middle of the nineteenth century, China in the seventeenth and eighteenth centuries under Qing rule was a vital country rising to its zenith of wealth, power, and territorial expansion. It was strong politically and powerful militarily, possessing a thriving economy that supported a rapidly growing population. But even though the Qing originated as a power from the steppe zone, it was not spared the usual military harassments and threats from China's restless nomadic neighbours, who, during this time, were the Dzungar Mongols of China's northwest. The Mongol tribes in the northeast of China, known as the Khalkha, were no longer troublesome to the Qing, because they had been subjugated or won over by the Manchus during their rise to power, as previously discussed. The western Mongols began to pose a challenge for the Qing when an ambitious and aggressive empire-builder called Erdeniin Galdan or Galdan Boshugtu Khan (1644 - 1697), rose amongst Dzungars, one of the four subdivisions of western Mongol tribes known together as the Oirats. Galdan allied himself to the eastwardly expanding Czarist Russia, and mounted, in 1688, a major invasion of the territory of the Khalkha Mongols. Being obliged to protect the Khalkha Mongols, the Qing had to act. After his warning to the Russians and his request to Galdan to withdraw westward were ignored, Emperor Kangxi personally led, from 1689 to 1697, three victorious military expeditions against him. During the last of the Qing military campaigns, Galdan ended his own life after his movement disintegrated.

Galdan's defeat and death did not end the Dzungar challenge to the Qing. During the first decades of the eighteenth century, Tsewang Rabtan, Galdan's nephew, established a huge empire that ran from southern Siberia through to the south of Lake Balkhash and to the frontiers of Tibet, covering the valley of Ili and western Mongolia. During this time and for over a century previously, power politics among the western Mongols were intimately bound up with the control of Tibet, because Buddhism of the Tibetan Lamaist variety had grown, since Yuan times, into the dominant religion of the Mongols. The power vacuum in Tibet left by the decline of the Ming, and before the Qing asserted its authority in this region, made this theocratic land vulnerable to Mongol military invasions and political domination. Since the middle of the seventh century, Tibet had been overrun and controlled first by the Khoshut Khanate and then by the Dzungar Mongols. There was enormous prestige attached to the Mongol leader who became the protector of the Dalai

Lama. After the Dzungars occupied Lhasa and other important centres in Tibet in 1717 and 1718, the Qing saw the importance of wresting Tibet from the Mongols as a part of the effort to contain the Dzungars. In 1720, a Sino-Manchu force from Sichuan ascended the high Tibetan plateau in the company of the seventh Dalai Lama and drove the Dzungars from Lhasa. The challenge posed by the Dzungars continued until, in 1756 and 1757, Emperor Qianlong waged the ferocious military campaigns that resulted in their near extinction.

After the destruction of the Dzungars, the Moslem Uyghurs, newly emerged from Dzungar domination, took up arms against the Qing in 1758. The Qing force sent to suppress this movement eventually took over control of the Islamic oases of the Tarim basin. Qing victories in the wars against the Uyghurs and the Dzungars greatly enlarged the territory of the Sino-Manchu Empire in its northwest towards Central Asia. This vast area was given the name of Xinjiang (New Territory). For over a century, the Qing placed it under military rule with garrisons at many strategic points. Its remoteness made it a place for exile of those who committed criminal or political offences. During the latter half of the nineteenth century, the Qing hold on this territory was rendered insecure by large scale Moslem rebellions and Russian incursions. After suppressing the rebellions, the Qing made it into a province and lifted the ban on Han immigration to that region. Today it is known as the Xinjiang Autonomous Region (XAR).

After removing the Mongol overlords from Tibet by force, the Qing set about re-establishing control over this snow-bound region of high plateaus that had been incorporated into the territory of both its Yuan and Ming predecessors. In 1751, the Qing quelled an armed rebellion by a Tibetan prince with the help of the Dalai Lama. The lesson of the rebellion taught the Qing the importance of curbing the power of the Tibetan aristocracy. To prevent any single individual from having too much power, in 1751 the Qing abolished the old institution of the King or Prince of Tibet. In 1787 and again in 1791, Nepalese Gurkhas invaded Tibet. On receiving the news, Emperor Qianlong mustered an impressive force that drove the invaders back to Nepal. This move was very popular with the Tibetans, and it helped the Qing court win local cooperation to put forward the *'29-Article Ordinance for the More Effective Governing of Tibet'* in 1793, which the Qing had long considered necessary for bringing order to this region, and for consolidating the Qing's hold on it.

This document, which set down in writing the framework for the governance of Tibet, was the result of mature considerations based on over one hundred years of Qing experience of dealing with this region. In brief, it spelt out that Tibet was to be governed by a group of three leaders of equal status: the Tibet Amban (a Qing imperial commissioner-resident appointed by the emperor), together with the Dalai and the Panchen Lamas, who were respectively the first and second highest ranking lamas of the *Gelug* (Yellow Hat Sect) which had dominated Tibetan Buddhism since the Ming. On the matter of appointing government officials of Tibet, a list of candidates, drawn up by the Amban and the Dalai Lama, was presented to the Qing government, which made the actual appointments. Although the act of appointment itself was a formality only, it nevertheless signified that the Qing central government was the ultimate authority on Tibetan affairs. The Amban also held the power to promote, transfer, reward, and punish these officials. On security matters, a force of three thousand troops was to be stationed as a permanent garrison distributed among several important cities in Tibet. On foreign affairs, only the Amban had the authority to deal with foreign countries. It was also his job to audit the income of the local government and supervise the minting of silver currency.

Clearly the sustainability of the Qing control over Tibet was not entirely a matter of its miliary prowess, although being able to protect Tibet against its powerful neighbours and to keep its internal peace and order was important for the Qing to gain a foothold there. The Qing was able to consolidate its dominant position in Tibet through establishing practical institutions and regulations, and through exercising its authority in a judicious manner.

Perhaps the most important element that sustained Qing control over Tibet was the support of the Dalai Lama. From the beginning of the dynasty, the Qing tried to build a special relationship with the Dalai Lama of whichever reincarnation, investing him with florid, honorific titles and recognizing his position as the highest religious authority in Tibet. A visiting Dalai Lama was normally received with great pomp and ceremony and showered with gifts. The Qing recognition strengthened and reinforced the position and authority of the Dalai Lama, and the *Gelug* headed by him. After the Qing court did away with the Prince of Tibet in 1751, the Dalai Lama no longer needed to share power with a temporal head of Tibet. This was during the time of the Dalai Lama of the Seventh reincarnation. From then on, he and his successors became the theocratic rulers of Tibet, along with the Amban. His *Gelug*, already enjoying a position of predominance, squeezed out or absorbed other competing Buddhist sects such as the Red Hat to become, with Qing support, the sole spiritual authority of Tibet. Since the Amban, being an outsider, had to rely heavily on the cooperation and support of his Tibetan colleagues and underlings, the Dalai Lama and his establishment were left to manage the internal affairs of Tibet with a good deal of autonomy. Since the Qing presence and power ensured peace, security, and stability of a theocratic social order in his favour, the Dalai Lama and his flock willingly cooperated with the Qing to remain under its protective umbrella. What did the Qing get out of this? Stability and peace in this border region, and the prestige of extending the territory under its control. The Qing, however, did claim sovereignty over Tibet. The mere fact that all those who governed Tibet, from the highest officials downwards, received their appointment or authority to rule from the Qing court justified this claim, which ultimately originated from military conquest. From the point of view of seventeenth century Tibetans, the lack of sovereignty might not have seemed a high price to pay, considering that from the middle of the twelfth century onwards, Tibet had been subject serially to the Yuan, the Ming, certain Mongol tribes, and from 1720 onwards to the Qing.

Colliding with an eastwardly expanding Russia

The seeds of the Russian conquest of Siberia starting from the sixteenth century had long been sown by the Mongol conquest of Russia in the thirteenth century. The empire of the Golden Horde that subjugated the Russians had established steppe routes with postal stations which facilitated communication and trade between European Russia and China. The easy flow of products from China over vast distances on land routes rendered safe and secure by the Pax Mongolica whetted the Russian appetite for luxury goods, such as silk and tea, from the east. In due course, the Russians, like the Europeans who circumnavigated the world to trade with the east by sea, went directly to the source of the goods themselves, cutting out those who collected taxes or took profits in the middle.

Besides opening up communications and trade, the Mongol conquest was credited with the transmission to Europe of an extremely potent Chinese invention – gunpowder. The result of the acquisition of this knowledge by the Europeans was to have far-reaching consequences that tipped the balance of power between the steppe and the sown in favour of the latter. The Europeans were amazed by the explosive force of cannon balls, which had been used in siege warfare by the Mongols. Recognizing the potential of gunpowder, the warring Europeans strove to develop the technology of manufacturing firearms. Their success soon led to the spread of a variety of firearms: muskets, handguns, cannons and so forth. By the middle of the fourteenth century, firearms became as familiar as any other kind of arms in Europe. The Russians used cannons in 1376 for the first time, and in 1450 they were producing light handguns in Moscow and Tver. By the end of the fifteenth century, the Europeans were better at making cannons than the Chinese. This revolution in military technology rendered the military supremacy of the warriors of the steppe a thing of the past, since bows and arrows were no match for guns. In 1558 the Russians, under Ivan IV (r. 1547-84) also known as Ivan the Terrible, overthrew the last of the Khanates of their erstwhile Mongol overlords, and were poised to expand eastward into the Siberian steppe, the heartland of the pastoral nomads, including the Mongols.

The spearhead of the Russian expansion into eastern Siberia was formed by bands of Cossacks rather than the regular Russian government troops. But the lands which the Cossacks had tamed would sooner or later be claimed by Russia, which would set up a government apparatus to administer and control, and then tax, these areas. In Russia, the Cossack communities developed around the sixteenth century from groups of people on society's fringe – outlaws, deserters, peasants fleeing from the oppression of serfdom, and spirited individuals who would not bend to the Russian autocracy. These people banded together for mutual protection and support. Some had settled along certain stretches of the Dnieper and the Don rivers, and others wandered around Russia's borderlands, where policing was relatively relaxed. Their ethnic origins were diverse: Russians, Ukrainians, nomads of different tribes, or people of mixed races were all included. Those who had drifted to the wide-open spaces of Siberia, could lead a freewheeling existence, and make a living from trading, hunting, river piracy, or even agriculture. Some ranged far and wide along the rivers of Siberia on wooden rafts and built their *ostrog* and *stanitsa* (log fort and settlements of wooden huts) as bases from which to spread out further. The Cossacks brought with them firearms, especially muskets. When they came into close contact with nomadic tribal peoples, their 'magic bullets' often prevailed, even when they were outnumbered. Despite their spreading in this diffuse fashion, in less than 100 years from the time of Ivan IV, Cossack pioneers had reached the shores of the Pacific and sailed into the Bering Straits that separated Asia from America. By the 1640s, advance parties of the Cossacks had been traversing the river Amur. They reported back to the Czar, enthusing about the agricultural wealth and the abundance of game of this region, and strongly recommending Russian occupation.

Conflicts soon broke out between these two expanding empires, because the territory the Cossacks would like to claim for Russia was already a part of the Manchu empire. Before the arrival of the Cossacks, Hong Taiji's armies, starting in 1634, had reached this region, and the inhabitants there, being similar in language and culture to the Manchus, readily submitted themselves to his rule. In 1650, reports of Russians burning, looting, and kidnapping from the local population alerted the Qing to send troops to repel the intruders. Over a period of ten years starting from 1652, several skirmishes took place between the Qing forces and the Russians until, by 1660, the latter were driven away from the middle and lower reaches of the Amur.

In 1665, the Russians returned and redoubled their efforts to take possession of this region. They recruited more Cossacks and built more forts. One located strategically at Yaksa (known also as Albazin), a centre of transportation or communication, was made into a military command post. After Emperor Kangxi took over the reins of the state in 1667, he did not want a piecemeal response: an endless replay of Russian incursion and Qing repulsion. Furthermore, he found that the Russians were sheltering a rebellious Mongol chieftain and his followers, who had escaped in 1667, and had been helping the Russians. This was a provocative act, because it undermined the peace and order the Qing had established in the territory of its Mongol subjects. Kangxi sought a permanent resolution of the frontier conflicts with Russia through diplomatic negotiation. For this purpose, he sent letters repeatedly to the Czar, requesting the latter to keep the Russians in check, stop the incursions, hand over the fugitives sought by the Qing, return the occupied Qing territory, and send representatives to negotiate a peaceful settlement of the issues raised.

Moscow ignored Kangxi's requests but kept on sending embassies to Beijing for trading purposes, the beginnings of which could be traced back to 1619 during the reign of the Ming emperor Wanli. The Russian court eagerly sought trade with China because the Chinese products, such as silk and cotton goods, and tea (starting from late seventeenth century), were in great demand in Russia. Those who were sufficiently privileged to be included among the Russian delegations could make handsome profits, and the Russian authorities could raise significant amounts of taxes, from the process of exchanging the Russian products, such as fur, skins, woollens, and clocks, for those from Qing China. From the 1660s to the 1750s this trade grew from 4500 roubles to over 1.4 million roubles. Although the Qing court had little need for these Russian goods, it permitted the Sino-Russian trade exchanges to use this trade as an incentive for Russia to settle the border issues raised by the Qing. Dismissing the Russian fondness for sending large embassies at frequent intervals, the Qing government limited the frequency, size, and the length of stay of the Russian delegations to Beijing: for example, to 200 people once every three years, staying no longer than 80 days. The embassies to the court of Kangxi had been a disappointment to him because Russian delegates focused so narrowly on trade that they had neither the interest nor the authority to discuss the border issues he wanted raised.

Frustrated by the lack of positive response from the Czar towards his proposals, Kangxi was prepared to use force against the Russian-occupied Yaksa. He was not going to do it precipitately, but in a decisive way to convince the Russians that the Qing had the military capacity to defend its territory against their aggression. In 1681, he even visited this border region personally to inspect the situation. He made preparations for the supply of an army of 3,000, complemented by a newly trained maritime force, and transported firearms - cannons and guns - for a prolonged military struggle against an enemy which, though not numerous, might prove formidable. In 1684, the Qing commander assaulted Yaksa with both land and marine forces after warning the Russians of the coming attack unless they retreated to Irkutsk. The outnumbered and severed battered Russians surrendered. After burning Yaksa, the Qing forces retreated to nearby towns. They clearly had no plan to advance further into northern Siberia. In 1685, Russian reinforcements and the remnants from Yaksa reoccupied the town. The Qing forces returned and surrounded the town tightly in all directions for five months, inflicting heavy losses on the Russians. Those who surrendered to or were captured by the Qing were incorporated into the Banner forces. When the 800 Russian defenders had dwindled to nearly 100, and the town was on the point of being taken, messengers from the Czar hastily arrived and begged the Qing to raise the siege, while promising to send negotiators to discuss the border problems. Thereupon Kangxi ordered the siege to be lifted.

Why did the Russians drag their feet on negotiating a border settlement? Before the time of our contemporary interest in oil and mineral extraction, most of Siberia was an under-populated wilderness, not worth the cost of sending an army to conquer it and then keep it secure. But it suited the Russian government to support the self-financed informal expansion of the Cossacks into this region, and their nibbling away at, or advancing by stealth into, the territory of the neighbouring Qing. Kangxi's strong stance and the Russian interest in trade eventually prompted the Russian authorities to abandon this approach during the reign of the Russian Czar, Peter the Great (r. 1682-1725), and negotiate in earnest with the Qing.

The first item the negotiators had to agree upon was the common border between the two states. After much haggling over a period of three years, the multilingual Treaty of Nerchinsk, signed in 1689, fixed the frontiers at the far eastern end of the two countries from the Heilong Jiang (Amur River) to the Pacific, although there was a small area south of the Wusuli (Ussuri) River that remained to be settled. In addition, it also addressed the issues of concern to both sides. Two decades later, the Qing, troubled by the intrigue between Russia and its Dzungar enemies at its frontier further to the west, recognized the necessity for a well-defined boundary between the two countries in that region. The problem of Russian protection of Mongol escapees was also an issue. The Qing court stopped the Sino-Russian trade after its request for a negotiated settlement made little headway. Russia's desire for a resumption of the commercial relationship led it to conclude, in 1727, the Treaty of Kiakhta with the Qing. This treaty determined the Sino-Russian boundary further to the west in present-day Mongolia. It also gave the Russians access to commercial exchanges at the border town of Kiakhta, in addition to the regular trade missions to Beijing. On Russia's request, it included a new provision allowing delegations of Russian Orthodox clergy to visit and stay in Beijing. During the negotiation of both treaties, the Qing negotiators yielded a certain amount of territory to Russia for the sake of clinching the agreements on the boundaries concerned. These treaties concluded between the Qing, at the height of its power, and Russia, in the throes of modernization, on the basis of equality and mutual respect for the sovereignty of one another, were unprecedented and constructive. They brought about 150 years of peaceful relationship at their mutual borders, and regularized the commercial, diplomatic, and cultural exchanges between the two countries over that period.

The zenith of Qing power

Having gained control over Mongolia, Taiwan, Tibet, and Xinjiang, and having fixed its frontiers with Russia, Qing China's territory from the 1760s to the 1840s covered around thirteen million square kilometres. The Qing possessed more territory than any dynasty preceding it, with the sole exception of the Yuan, another alien conquest dynasty. Its domain included Mongolia in the north, Lake Balkhash, and the land south and east of it through the Pamirs to the Himalayas in the west, and along its east seaboard, the islands of Taiwan and Sakhalin. The Qing might well have been able to extend its boundary further north into the relatively empty Siberian steppe at the height of its military might in the 1750s. It could have insisted on preserving the land on which it had a reasonable claim, instead of yielding to Russia's demands during the negotiation of the above-mentioned treaties. But the Sino-Manchu empire had reached a point of conservative self-containment and consolidation rather than expansion. The smaller countries around, and some beyond, its borders, such as Nepal, Burma, Siam, Ryukyu, and Korea acknowledged its influence or suzerainty by maintaining the tribute relationship with the Qing, until it became engulfed in a series of catastrophic events coming from within as well as from abroad from the 1840s onwards. After its military weakness was revealed during the First Opium War (1840-42), the territory of the Qing shrank considerably due to foreign aggression, as we shall see.

The Qing dynasty acquired its vast domain by its military prowess, subjugating both the sedentary Han areas as well as the homeland of the nomadic herders. Many Han Chinese dynasties had been able to conquer the regions where the nomadic herders roamed, but they had difficulty in retaining control over enormous stretches of arid to semi-arid or forested areas, where the people they wanted to tax would vanish with their livestock, and then return to attack their garrisons. Chinese rulers from the Tang to the Ming all had to relinquish territory they had acquired by force in the steppe zone when it became too costly for them to keep it. The Yuan had no trouble holding on to their Mongol homeland, whence the Mongols returned when their dynasty came to an end in China. The steppe origin of the Manchus probably helped the Qing to retain permanent control of the vast regions of Mongolia, Manchuria, and much of western China through institutions such as the Mongol Banners, and through establishing long-term bonds using patronage and loyalty as cement between the dynastic house and the tribal ruling elites. These bonds were formed from special audiences for the tribal chiefs, leading celebratory gatherings of nomadic peoples in steppe settings, marrying Manchu princesses with the heads of the nomadic tribes, and cultivating good relations with the powerful theocratic leaders of Tibet, the Dalai Lama in particular.

Despite the brutality of the original conquest, the alleviation of tax burdens and economic growth under the High Qing era must have gone a long way to win Han acquiescence to Qing rule among the general population. The dynasty also tried to gain popular support through its involvement with popular religions. It deified folk heroes and heroines, elevating their worship into state-sponsored cults, which flourished. The popularity of these cults was indicative of a level of integration of the state and the society, as well as popular acceptance, at least initially, of their rulers from outside the Great Wall.

As regards the Chinese gentry, they were mostly won over by the Manchu rulers' wholehearted adoption of Han governance and imperial Confucianism. Although the dynasty openly discriminated in favour of the Manchus, it supported the traditional examination system, thus fortifying the social status of the Chinese gentry as well as providing the scholar-gentry opportunities to participate in government. The Qing emperors, particularly the early ones from Kangxi to Qianlong, immersed themselves in the Chinese cultural tradition and endeavoured to play the part of proper *Tianzi* (Sons of Heaven) in the Confucian mode. They became the guardians and upholders of the China's traditional Confucian social and moral order. Peace and stability depended in the first instance on this self-regulating order imbedded in tradition and culture, before resorting to the strong arm

Map of the Qing Empire and adjoining lands (*Wikipedia*: retrieved on 30 November 2023 from https://en.m.wikipedia.org/wiki/File:Qing_Empire_circa_1820_EN.svg)

of force. For example, in 1670 Kangxi issued the Sacred Edict as a 16-maxim embodiment of orthodox Confucianism for instructing people how to behave in an ethical manner. Later, in 1724 Yongzheng issued an amplified instruction. These were read by local officials at public gatherings accompanied by music, incense, and audience participation, such as bowing and kneeling as in services in Christian churches. While the alienated Chinese gentry had remained aloof under the Yuan, they mostly cooperated and supported the Qing, and played the traditional and important role of being the interface between the government authorities and the people.

The early Qing rulers took seriously their role as guardians of China's cultural heritage, and they provided energetic leadership, outdoing even Emperor Yongle of the Ming, in sponsoring major projects involving the collecting, compiling, cataloguing, copying, and printing of valued written works. The writing and publication of the voluminous Ming history, an enormous illustrated encyclopaedia, and the famous Kangxi dictionary, among others, under Emperor Kangxi was succeeded by an even more ambitious undertaking that resulted in the *Siku Quanshu* (Complete Books of the Four Imperial Repositories), during the reign of Qianlong. The material of the *Siku Quanshu* was gathered, over a period of thirteen years, from all manuscripts and printed works preserved in private collections all over the country, as well as those kept in the public libraries. The entire work contained 79,070 volumes divided into four subject categories: canonical, philosophical, historical, and literary. These projects, in addition to their cultural benefits, provided much employment for scholars.

However, there was another and more negative side to the early Qing emperors' involvement with cultural matters. This was their prerogative in determining what was culturally acceptable and what was not. Subversive writings were weeded out and the writers punished. The exercise of this prerogative was by no means peculiar to the Qing: it went as far back as Emperor Qin Shi Huang, the first unifier of China. But because of the origin of the Manchu dynasty, the early Qing emperors were extremely sensitive to any suggestion in a piece of writing that could be construed as questioning their legitimacy, or being disloyal to the dynasty, denigrating nomadic peoples in general and Manchus in particular, and being disrespectful in the slightest way to themselves. The 'literary inquisition', or the search for offensive written works and the imprisonment and investigation of their authors, started in the reign of Emperor Kangxi and increased in intensity and thoroughness under Emperor Qianlong. During the more than one hundred and thirty years of their rule, the number of people affected ran into thousands. Not only did most of those convicted of such cultural 'crimes' lose their lives: their close relatives, scholarly associates, or even printers of their works suffered the fate of banishment, enslavement, or even death in some cases. These tyrannical acts of the Qing autocracy caused not only personal suffering of the victims; they also created an atmosphere of fear and an unhealthy intellectual climate, where many scholars would play safe, limit their intellectual horizons, and go along with the soporific orthodoxy of their rulers. In addition to destroying the authors, works were condemned as 'banned' books, which were gathered for burning or alteration. The books that were burned or 'revised' ran into tens of thousands, roughly equal to the variety of subjects and number of volumes of the *Siku Quanshu*. This was a serious and irredeemable loss to China's cultural heritage.

References for the Qing will be found at the end of chapter 7.

Chapter 6

External and Internal Challenges to the Qing

The Initial Impact of European Trade and Empire Building

The Qing rulers of China, who practically closed China's door to the world outside its recognized tributary states, were not aware of the fact that from the sixteenth century onwards the maritime powers of Europe had begun carving out colonial empires and spreading their peoples out of Europe to rule other regions of the world. The power which knocked most forcefully on China's door was Britain. By the mid-nineteenth century, Britain ruled India and was the dominant maritime power.

The control of India gave the British great advantages over their European rivals in developing trade with China – incomparably more than the Portuguese enclave at Macau. It provided British merchants opportunities to develop a lucrative local carrying trade along the coast of the Indian subcontinent. The geographical proximity of India and southern China, and the ease of communication between the two areas by sea, enabled this trade to be readily extended to China. Moreover, the possession of India greatly facilitated the logistics of British military intervention in China. It is worth remembering that in this age of imperialism, Britain was ever ready to use force to protect its commercial interests, if these were threatened by a local regime. In fact, British overseas traders were accustomed to look to their home government for military and other forms of support for their foreign commercial ventures.

After having taken possession of India, the British mercantile community tried to develop the triangular trade between Britain, India, and China. During most of the Qing dynasty, maritime trade between China and countries overseas was confined to the single port of Canton (now Guangzhou) in Guangdong, the southernmost province of China. At this port there was a special maritime customs office, the Hoppo (Administrator of the Canton Customs), to levy duties on imports and exports. Also located at this port was a group of merchants who were licenced to conduct foreign trade as a monopoly. They belonged to an association known to the British merchants as the Cohong (*Gonghang*) or Thirteen Hongs of Canton. These Chinese Cohong merchants worked closely with the East India Company, their British counterpart. They acted as an intermediary between the foreign merchants and the Chinese authorities, who found it convenient to rely on the Cohong merchants to collect the taxes and control the foreign merchants. Finding this regime too restrictive, in 1793 the British East India Company sent an embassy, led by Lord George Macartney, to Beijing for the purpose of asking the Qing court to open more ports for trade, to have a fixed and reduced tariff, to allow a British representative to be stationed at Beijing, and to cede a small offshore island and some land near Canton to Britain to maintain as a base.

This embassy brought out the fundamental differences in outlook between Great Britain and Qing China on international relations and trade. An audience was arranged for Lord Macartney with the aging Emperor Qianlong. A difficult situation arose immediately be-

Lord Macartney and the emperor Qianlong (*New World Encyclopedia*: retrieved on 30 November 2023 from https://www.newworldencyclopedia.org/entry/Macartney_Embassy)

cause of the Qing court's woeful ignorance of the developments that had transformed Europe into a collection of powerful modern nation-states, which were in the process of reshaping the world through imperialism. The court officials were not able to see the writing on the wall regarding the fate of the East Asian civilizations centered on China, which operated on the tribute relationship developed by China in its commercial and diplomatic relationships with the smaller and less powerful neighbouring countries, or local maritime environs. Their limited knowledge of the world beyond East Asia led them to treat the British embassy as a tribute-bearing mission, whose representative would be required to perform the kneeling and kowtowing in the presence of the Qing emperor, as a ritual acknowledging China's suzerainty. The gifts and samples of goods the British brought were received as tributes. But Lord Macartney, representing a modern sovereign state, could not possibly have any dealings with Qing China except on the basis of one sovereign power with another. The Qing officials were not aware that Great Britain, as the most powerful nation in Europe, was already in possession of a colonial empire that spanned continents. In this global context, the Qing presumptions seemed preposterous. Because of these differences, and Britain's unacceptable request to the Qing to cede to it two small parcels of territory, the embassy was a non-starter, and the British requests were refused. Another British embassy in 1816 under Lord Amherst was equally unsuccessful. The Qing court's out-dated idea of international relations, its low esteem for trade, and China's self-sufficiency in cottons and woollens, which were the main British goods then imported into China, together put a temporary brake on the British drive to open more of the Chinese market for overseas trade. Britain did not resort to the use of force after these rebuffs, but that restraint would soon be abandoned.

The First Opium War (1841-1842)

During the eighteenth century, while the Chinese market for British exports was limited, there was considerable demand for Chinese tea, silks, and cotton goods in Britain and Europe. As a result, the balance of trade was very much in China's favour, with a net flow of silver currency in tens of millions of dollars into China. Eventually, as we shall see, this situation was changed by the growth in the import of Indian opium into China by the East India Company. This joint-stock company, founded in 1600 as a monopoly on Indian trade, went on to govern India as a British colony two centuries later. The British found that the opium grown in India, being light and compact, could be easily shipped to China, where a high profit could be made. The market for opium in China was not initially large. During most of the eighteenth century, a few hundred cases (each containing 65 kilograms) per year had been imported into China, where the importers could net 400 to 1,000 dollars per case. However, because of the high rate of profit, the government of

British India taxed the trade at more than 300% above cost.

Starting in 1729, the Qing court issued an edict banning the smoking and trading of opium. It considered this highly addictive drug to be a poison, and a social evil that seriously harmed the users and damaged society's moral fabric. The prohibition in China had no effect on the activity of the East India Company. Working closely with the Cohong merchants, it was smuggling into China increasing amounts of the opium it cultivated in India. Besides the East India Company, other British and foreign merchants also participated in this illegal trade. By 1819 more than 4000 cases per year were being shipped into China. Competition from British 'free traders', who were putting pressure on the British government to abolish the monopoly of the East Indian Company, prompted the company to speed up the opium trade while the going was good. More opium was grown in India, and its shipment to China was stepped up from 1819 onwards, as the following table illustrates.

Import of opium into China during the nineteenth century

Years	Number of cases
1729	200
1790	400+
1817-1819	4,228 (average)
	Acceleration of opium imports
1821	5,959
1826-1829	12,851 (average)
1829	16,257
1830	19,956
c.1836	30,000 (roughly)
1838	40,000 (at least)
c.1850	68,000
1873	96,000
1893	Imports began to decline because of price rises
1917	Imports ended; opium produced in China was sufficient for the market

The escalating opium trade, with its enormous profit, was a financial bonanza to the East India Company. For example, in the years before 1818, its revenue of less than one million GBP was more than tripled by 1822. From the 1820s, its receipts from opium alone were growing to equal the interest payment on its debt in Britain. After the 1840s its income from opium kept on rising and dwarfed the debt interest. This business was effectively a means for the transfer of wealth from China to Britain. British India also benefited from the increased tax collected from this rapidly growing trade. For example, between 1829 and 1830, the British-Indian government was estimated to have collected over one million GBP of taxes on the opium exports, an amount equivalent to 10% of its total annual revenue.

The rising opium imports eroded China's favourable balance of trade to such an extent that by 1825, the value of China's imports exceeded its exports. This situation was occurring despite increasing amounts of tea, silks, and cotton cloth that had been exported to Britain and Europe. The result was an accelerated net outflow of silver currency. Between 1800 and 1820, China netted ten million *liang* (tael) of silver in its maritime trade, while between 1831 and 1833, ten million taels of silver were shipped out of China. The imbalance was largely due to opium imports. For example, from July 1837 to June 1838, the British exported 5,600,000 GBP worth of goods to China, of which 3,560,000 GBP (around 60%) was opium. During the same period, the British imported 3,100,000 GBP worth of goods from China. The balance of trade was a deficit of 2,50,000 GBP on the Chinese account. But for the opium imports, China would have been in surplus. From 1820 to 1840, around 100,000,000 dollars of silver left China. This figure was equivalent to 1/5 of the total silver currency in circulation during that period. The net outflow of silver currency caused the depreciation of the copper cash, which was the currency used in the daily business transactions of the people. But silver was the currency of taxation. Towards the end of the eighteenth century, one tael of silver could exchange for approximately 1000 copper cash. In 1838, it took 1600 copper coins to exchange for one tael of silver – a roughly 60% increase in the tax rate.

The flood of opium into China, as well as the increasing net export of silver from China from the 1820s, was causing alarm in the court of Emperor Daoguang (r.1820-1850) and many high provincial officials. Edict after edict had been issued prohibiting its trade and use by his predecessors, without any effect on curbing, let alone stopping, these illegal activities. On the contrary, the import of opium through smuggling, and the illicit networks in connection with this trade, grew enormously, and with it the bribery and corruption of officials at various levels of the government. Opium smoking spread from the south coast to over ten provinces inland, including Beijing. Shortly before the Opium War, over two million people had succumbed to it. Opium smokers came from all walks of life: gentry, officials, shopkeepers, Daoist priests, day labourers, and soldiers. It was beginning to be seen as an unprecedented disaster for the country, where so many people succumbed to this slow-acting poison that sapped their will, and ruined their health and family life, before killing them. Faced with this critical situation, Daoguang asked the court officials and the governors of the provinces what actions to take.

One option was to continue the prohibition and find ways of making it effective. One high official, who had no illusions as regards the difficult of enforcing such a policy, wrote a memorial to the emperor proposing the opposite - that is, relaxing the ban. Morality aside, as a practical solution to a complex problem his suggestion of lifting the ban had the merit of allowing the government to tax it. On the matter of stopping the outflow of silver, he suggested bartering between the imports and exports without resorting to the use of silver money. He was also in favour of relaxing the ban on the cultivation of opium poppies in China, so that eventually the locally produced drug would replace the foreign import. While he did not think people should be penalized for opium smoking, he was against letting government employees indulge in this 'evil habit.' Although the Viceroy of Liangguang (Governor-General of Guangdong and Guangxi provinces) approved of this way of dealing with the problem, many of the high officials the emperor consulted denounced this 'preposterous' approach. Most of them were for tightening the enforcement of the ban and increasing the penalty, against not only the dealers in opium but also the smokers. A few were even in favour of the death penalty against those smokers who could not or would not shake the habit, after a period of grace.

Among the most forceful spokesmen for the most stringent and active enforcement of the ban was Lin Zexu (1785-1850), the Viceroy of Huguang (Governor-General of Hunan and Hubei Provinces}, an official known for his integrity and uprightness. Lin had achieved some success in opium prohibition in the area under his jurisdiction. He did so by seizing all equipment used for opium smoking and severely punishing those who sold opium, offered facilities, or made equipment for the smokers. In 1838, he addressed cogent pleas to Emperor Daoguang, urging the latter to use strong and extraordinary measures to stem the flow of this poison; otherwise, in the not too distant future, there would be neither silver left to pay for the troops, nor soldiers fit enough to fight the country's enemies.

Towards the end of 1838, Emperor Daoguang, persuaded by those who agitated for effective implementation of the ban, despatched Lin Zexu to Canton as the Imperial Commissioner for the purpose of putting an end to the importation of opium. Shortly afterwards, he drew up a set of new regulations on opium prohibition with severe penalties against offenders. These he sent to the provincial governors, enjoining them to follow the directives strictly, with the aim of rooting out the evil entirely. When Lin reached Canton in March 1839, he lost no time in arresting Chinese opium dealers and the officials who took bribes. After destroying the network of the Chinese dealers in opium, he had to contend with the foreign importers to stem the flow of opium from its source. He ordered the foreign merchants to hand over their stock of opium by a fixed date. Under his new regime, foreign vessels had to give a guarantee never to import opium into China again.

He even addressed two letters to Queen Victoria appealing for her help. His demands being ignored, he resorted to coercion, by cordoning off the 'Thirteen Factories' outside the city wall of Canton where the small foreign (mainly British) community of 350 traders resided. However, he allowed them their daily necessities, but not the services of their Chinese employees. The British representative, Captain Charles Elliot, was among the residents. He asked the merchants to hand in their stock, with the assurance that he would take responsibility on behalf of the British government for the surrendered stock. After over 20,000 cases of opium were handed over to the Chinese authority, the foreigners were allowed to go free. Then Lin destroyed the opium by burning it for days, as a spectacle in public view. Daoguang was delighted with the action Lin had taken, and soon afterwards appointed him as the Viceroy of Liangguang to take care of the aftermath. Two months later, Captain Elliot and the British merchants retreated to Hong Kong – a relatively uninhabited island south of Canton - from where they continued to trade freely.

In Britain, even before Lin's drastic action to enforce the opium ban, the British mercantile community, bristling from Qing China's restriction on foreign commerce as their trade with China grew, were clamouring for 'free trade.' The interest of the free traders also clashed with that of the East India Company, whose monopoly was terminated in 1814. Where China was concerned, the political campaign for free trade gathered momentum when the British manufacturers, caught up in the industrial revolution and the search for new markets, were also putting pressure on the British government for the opening of the Chinese market for overseas commerce, by force if necessary. Since the British diplomatic efforts had failed to move the Qing to accept trade on the British terms, the use of force to achieve this goal was being considered as a practical option.

Lin Zexu's forceful seizure and burning of opium in 1839 was an act born of desperation rather than a calculated move to precipitate a war with Britain. In fact, soon after he had done so, he declared to the British that the port of Canton was open to trade as usual, but not to trading in opium. He did not know that what he had done played into the hands of the British mercantile and manufacturing communities, who were already pressing for Britain to take a strong stand against China, and who were eager to see China's gates blown open by force. His action provided the British with a *casus belli*. Early in 1840, Lord Palmerston, the British Foreign Secretary, was preparing for war and instructing Captain Elliot, who had become the British plenipotentiary, regarding the conduct of the war and Britain's demands. With the support of the British Parliament, a British expeditionary force was sent in April 1840 to take military action against China.

Lin must have been aware that his action might lead to war. At the beginning of 1840 he started to strengthen Canton's defences. He drilled troops, drafted physically fit locals, and trained them in maritime warfare. He purchased Western boats and cannons and placed more wooden fences with iron chains around Humen, also known as the Bogue, at the entrance to Canton, where additional cannons were positioned. He also tried to understand the British and the world outside China more, by organizing teams of translators to translate foreign newspapers and books. Thus prepared, he waited for the British to attack.

When the British fleet did arrive in the vicinity of Canton in the summer of 1840, and saw the tight defensive arrangements there, they avoided an engagement and sailed north instead. After overcoming the defences of a coastal city along the way, the fleet began to threaten Beijing from a river nearby. The court grew alarmed, and Lin came under attack by a party of appeasers. A Manchu grandee, Qishan, replaced Lin and coaxed the British back to Canton to conduct peace talks, with the assurance that Lin would be punished, and that the British demands were all negotiable. The patriot Lin was made the scapegoat, although Daoguang had agreed with what he did and had encouraged him to be strict. Found guilty of mishandling the opium prohibition, the aged Lin was sent into exile far away in Xinjiang.

At Canton, Qishan demolished Lin's defences and dispersed the soldiers and sailors to please the British. Intimidated by talk of the British restarting the war, Qishan agreed (verbally) to the British demand of 600,000 dollars (Mexican silver) for compensation, to the reopening of Canton, to diplomatic equality, and to the cession of Hong Kong - a virtually uninhabited island with excellent harbours and a smallish mountain sheltering it against typhoons. But Qishan had agreed to more than he could deliver, because the terms exceeded the limits of what Emperor Daoguang could countenance for appeasing the British. Under British pressure, and without modern communication devices such as telephones or telegraphy, there had been no time for him to consult the court, located about 1500 miles away. After the British occupied Hong Kong in January 1841, the party for resistance got the upper hand. Qishan was removed from office, and the court decided for the first time to fight the British by despatching generals with troops to Canton.

While the Qing court regarded the British demands put forward by Captain Elliott as excessive, the British government rejected them as insufficient. He was recalled and replaced by a new British plenipotentiary, Sir Henry Pottinger. The British government was determined to protect and promote the already considerable commercial interest Britain had developed in China, by forcing the Qing court to yield to its terms through a decisive demonstration of its military superiority. With the benefit of the industrial revolution and the accumulated experience of centuries of naval warfare in Europe, the British warships of the nineteenth century, iron-clad, steam-driven, and armed with the most powerful cannon and shells, were the most advanced and formidable in the world. 'Britannia rules the waves' was no empty claim. For several months in 1841, the small mobile force of British gunboats, initially less than fifty vessels, and several thousand troops (before reinforcement from India), sailed north along the coast of the provinces of Fujian and Zhejiang, destroying batteries, and taking cities with little difficulty. The Qing defenders were intimidated by the *chuan jian pao li* (solid boats and piercing cannon shots) of the seemingly invincible invading force. They were at a loss when confronted by the modern naval force of an alien invasion. By comparison, the Qing's own ships and weapons were hopelessly antiquated. Its navy was virtually non-existent. Like its civil administration, the Qing military was in an advanced stage of decay. The commanding officers were often corrupt and irresponsible, while the poorly paid and badly trained soldiers were better at victimizing their own defenceless people than fighting an enemy. There were individual exceptions, particularly among middle-ranking officers, who defended their cities bravely, but hopelessly and sacrificially against the superior firepower of the British.

A British ship destroying Chinese war junks in the Opium War (*Wikipedia*: retrieved on 30 November 2023 from https://en.wikipedia.org/wiki/First_Opium_War)

However, the royal relative whom Daoguang sent from Beijing to engage the British was not one for risking his life and limb. On the way south, he was more interested in amusing himself than studying his unfamiliar enemy and making proper strategic combat plans. During the spring of 1842, he became battle shy after his ill-prepared troops suffered a resounding defeat, when they attempted to recover three cities lost simultaneously in Zhejiang. This turn of events softened Daoguang's resolve, and he sent emissaries south to negotiate with the invaders. The British, however, did not think that the Qing emperor had been sufficiently intimidated to accept all their terms for peace, and took their fleet into the Yangtze River valley. After capturing Shanghai and Zhejiang, the British fleet paused in front of the city of Nanjing. At this spot, on a British gunboat, the Qing government yielded to all the terms dictated by the British, and signed, on 29 August 1842, the first of the 'unequal treaties' - the Treaty of Nanjing (Nanking). (The English-language historical document of that period used 'Nanking', which was the earlier Wade-Giles system of transliterating the name of that city into English, while 'Nanjing' is the Pinyin system of transliteration.)

The Unequal Treaty System and the Second Opium War (1856 – 1860)

The Treaty of Nanjing

According to the terms of the Treaty of Nanjing, China was to

1. Open five coastal ports, those of Shanghai, Ningbo, Xiamen, Fuzhou, and Guangzhou (Canton) for trade

2. Cede Hong Kong Island to Britain

3. Pay Britain a compensation of 2,100,000 dollars (silver) of which 600,000 were for destroyed opium, 300,000 for compensating the merchants, and 1,200,000 for military expenses. There was an additional payment of 600,000 dollars as ransom for the city of Canton.

Although this treaty allowed China to retain the right to levy import and export duties, the rates for these had to be approved by the British representative. It meant that China lost the important right to fix its own rate of tariffs on foreign trade. During the two years that followed, a supplementary Treaty of the Bogue, signed in 1843, fixed the import/export tariff rates at a uniform 5%. It also included a clause on *extraterritoriality*, a word we will hear again, meaning that British subjects in China were exempt from Chinese legal jurisdiction. It also allowed British fleets to be stationed at the opened ports. The most-favoured-nation clause enabled the British to enjoy any concession wrung from the Qing by any other country. The British were allowed to lease land in the treaty ports for businesses and residences. The *Zujie*, meaning leased territories or concessions, were governed by the representatives of the British, and developed into small self-contained foreign-run enclaves within China. These foreign concessions were unlike the enclaves of Arab merchants in Canton during the Tang, or Turkish traders from Kokand in Xinjiang in the 1830s, or the Portuguese settlement in Macau, where the Chinese authorities found it convenient to let the foreign communities govern themselves in accordance with their own customs and usage, but where the Chinese authority retained sovereignty over these areas. China had effectively lost its sovereignty as regards the foreign concessions at the treaty ports covered by extraterritoriality. There was no mention of opium in this treaty, the trade for which simply continued, and grew like it had done before Lin tried to stamp it out.

Other Western imperialist nations were not slow to follow the British example. In 1844, under the threat of force, the Qing concluded the Treaty of Wanghia with the United States, and a separate treaty was also concluded with the French, who were more interested in supporting the Catholic missionary movement in China than in trade. With the most-favoured-nation clause, each of these nations enjoyed the same rights and privileges in China as Britain, except for the indemnities and the ceding of territory. The French forced the Qing to remove the ban on Catholicism that began in 1724 under Emperor Yongzheng, after he discovered that the foreign pope also had jurisdiction over his Chinese Christian subjects and the Jesuits in his service. Under the treaty regime, the French won the right for Catholic missionaries to build churches and proselytize their religion from the treaty ports. Protestant missions, particularly British ones, pressed their national representatives to gain similar rights as the Catholics. They also asked to be allowed to build schools and hospitals in China.

Once the Qing court had been shown to buckle under the threat or the use of force by the foreign powers - Britain, France, the United States, and Russia - there was a tendency for them to encroach more and more on China through an increasing number of new treaties, and to exact ever greater concessions from China. In 1856, when the Qing was preoccupied with major internal rebellions, Britain, allied with France and encouraged by America and Russia, took the opportunity to wage the Second Opium War. It was also called the Arrow War because the Chinese authorities boarded a smugglers' boat of that name, to catch Chinese pirates on what they thought was a Chinese-owned vessel. The British, however, claimed that it was a British boat flying a British flag. The alleged insult to the British flag was used as a pretext for invading China. The French pretext for war was that a French Catholic priest was killed in Guangxi. In 1857, the British laid siege to and then occupied Canton. In 1857, an Anglo-French fleet hurried north to capture Dagu (Taku) near Tianjin, and threaten Beijing.

The Treaty of Tianjin (Tientsin) and the Convention of Beijing (Peking)

By the summer of 1858, the Qing court yielded to the foreign pressure and signed the Treaty of Tianjin. This treaty obliged the Qing to open many more treaty ports. In addition to the original five, the coastal ones were to be extended further to the north and across to Taiwan, while many inland cities along the Yangtze River also became treaty ports with foreign concessions and consular jurisdiction. Foreign merchant fleets were permitted to travel freely along the Yangtze River. Foreigners were allowed to travel into the interior to trade and to preach. Opium, its trade and smuggling having spread further in China, was legalized. An indemnity of around 4,000,000 taels of silver was to be paid to the British and around 2,000,000 taels was to be paid to the French. While confirming that the import and export tariffs were to remain at 5%, a transit tax of 2.5% was fixed on foreign goods travelling into the interior from the treaty ports. America and Russia were also able to acquire the additional rights conferred to the British and the French. This treaty also obliged the unwilling Qing court to allow foreign diplomats to open legations in Beijing.

Shortly afterwards, it became clear that the European powers were still not satisfied. They sought to expand the war by insisting on taking their fleet up to Beijing to exchange the signed treaty at the court. The Qing did not refuse the requested exchange but asked the Anglo-French party to land in Beitang and to proceed to Beijing from there by land. Instead of doing as requested, in 1859 the Anglo-French forces fired at the battery in Dagu, the strategic fort that defended the mouth of the Peiho (Hai River), a river near Tianjin on the route to Beijing. The defending Qing forces returned the fire, causing several hundred casualties and sinking several ships from the attackers' side.

This provoked a punitive Anglo-French expedition. At the start of 1860, more than 20,000 Anglo-French troops landed in Beitang, after receiving intelligence from the Russians that the place was undefended. The invading force overpowered China's defensive positions along their way to Tianjin. After Tianjin fell, Beijing was in peril. Emperor Xianfeng (r. 1850-1861) fled with the court to Rehe, where he died in 1861. From Beijing, the Russian representative hastened to meet the leaders of the invasion to offer them a map of Beijing and advised them on the weakest point to assault and take over the city. Having control of Beijing, the Anglo-French forces thoroughly looted the 150-year-old Yuanmingyuan, the imperial Summer Palace built in a unique Sino-European style with the help of the Jesuits. After burning for three days, the once magnificent palace was reduced to a pile of rubble, as it remains to this day. With the invaders threatening artillery bombardment of the Imperial Palace in Beijing, the Qing court once more succumbed to the might of superior weaponry.

In the autumn of 1860, prince Gong, a member of the imperial family left in charge at Beijing, formally exchanged the Treaty of Tianjin with the British and French representatives. At the same time, he also signed the Convention of Beijing (Peking) with these two imperialist powers, as well as Russia and America. The Convention of Beijing forced China to cede to Britain the southern part of the Kowloon peninsula and add it to Hong Kong, which by this time had already developed into a major entrepôt. Tianjin was opened to foreign trade. The indemnity in the Treaty of Tianjin was increased to 8,000,000 taels of silver to be paid to each of the British and the French. There were also additional charges of hundreds of thousands of taels of silver as compensation for the British and

The ruins of the Summer Palace (*China Daily*: retrieved on 30 November 2023 from https://global.chinadaily.com.cn/a/201910/21/WS5dad5c03a310cf3e35571b46.html)

the French armed personnel. The French demanded the opening of the interior for the French Catholic missions to buy land and build churches, naturally under French jurisdiction. Hoping to dump cheap machine-produced textiles in China, the British demanded the import of textiles to China free of duty. All these demands were incorporated into this treaty. Subsequently, in 1898, the British forced the Qing to lease an area known as the New Territories, the northern part of the Kowloon peninsula, for 99 years.

The establishment of the Imperial Maritime Customs Service

Regarding the administration of customs at the treaty ports, the framers of the Treaty of Tianjin took into account the problems that had been encountered, and how they had been resolved, in implementing the Treaty of Nanjing. The Chinese customs officials at the different treaty ports opened after the Treaty of Nanjing had great difficulty in collecting the fixed rate of customs duty, already set at a low level, from foreign merchants, because their authority was not respected, even though China had not given away the right to impose and to collect customs duty. In addition, extraterritoriality left Chinese authorities no means to use the normal sanctions, such as fines or confiscation of goods, to coerce the foreigners to pay. All they could do was to complain to the foreign consuls who had jurisdiction over the foreign merchants involved. The same was true when the foreigners committed an offence against customs regulations, such as smuggling.

As Shanghai was fast becoming the premier port for foreign trade, the British Consul, Rutherford Alcock, had a vexing time settling disputes between the British traders and the Chinese customs. He stood for strict enforcement of the treaty tariff, and he also disliked the laxity and irregularity associated with the Shanghai customs. As a practical solution to these problems, he hit upon the idea of introducing Chinese-speaking foreign nationals, paid by the Chinese, to assist and supervise the Chinese administration of customs. In 1854, he was instrumental in setting up, with Chinese cooperation, the Foreign Inspectorate of Customs in Shanghai. The inspectors were drawn, one each, from the British, American, and French Consular Services. The support of the foreign consular and other authorities enabled this ad hoc customs office to function successfully during the initial phase of its introduction. The local Chinese Superintendent of Foreign Trade accepted it because it was easier for him to let foreigners manage foreigners and bring in the much-needed revenue. At its inception the status and authority of the foreign inspectors were not clearly defined. Whether they were agents and subordinates of the foreign consuls, or officials of a branch of the Chinese government, was a question that had to be clarified when their status and authority were challenged by some foreign merchants and their consuls.

With this history in mind, the Treaty of Tianjin called for a uniform system of customs administration to be established in all the treaty ports. It further stipulated that the high Chinese official responsible for foreign trade was free to appoint any British subject to assist him in customs administration, prevention of smuggling, defining port boundaries, serving as a harbour master, and in the distribution and maintenance of lights and beacons and so forth, all to be financed by the tonnage dues which were collected from foreign shipping. These treaty provisions could only be realized if the Shanghai Foreign Inspectorate of Customs was extended to all the treaty ports under a central administration. The conditions for setting up and governing such a centralized customs administration had yet to be put in place on both the Chinese and the foreign sides.

Because the Qing court did not anticipate that the tiny income from its tax on foreign trade at that point was going to grow into a much more significant source of revenue as time went on, it was less agitated about the possibility of foreigners taking over the Chinese Maritime Customs than by the establishment of permanent foreign legations in Beijing. The Treaty of Tianjin obliged the Qing court to prepare itself to face the thorny issue of having foreign ambassadors residing in Beijing, and possibly intruding on the Qing ruler, without observing the traditional protocol of paying obeisance to him like members of the tribute embassies. Besides the question of court etiquette, and after almost two decades of dealing with foreign authorities by proxy through the provincial authorities as matters arose, the Qing indeed needed an office at the central government level to take charge of its intractable relationship with the imperialist powers. In 1861, a 'general office for the management of the affairs of various nations', known in its abbreviated form as the *Zongli Yamen* (Romanized as *Tsungli Yamen* prior to the introduction of the Pinyin system), was created at the capital for this purpose. The officials of this new office would meet with the foreign ambassadors at Beijing to settle all official businesses as equals, without the necessity of the emperor being present. As a result, the issue of court etiquette was no longer a pressing concern.

In addition to foreign relations, this office was to take responsibility for international commerce, tariffs on foreign maritime trade, and the foreign-managed customs service. As China began to modernize, it became involved with many of the modernizing sectors, such as the building of railways, construction of steamships, and the opening of mines, as these were often connected with foreign investment or debt. Prince Gong, who signed the Treaty of Tianjin, believed that the best way to deal with the Westerners was through courtesy and good faith. His conciliatory attitude towards the representatives of the Western powers won warm praise from the British ambassador, Sir Frederick Bruce, with whom he developed a cordial personal relationship. During the first two decades after the founding of the *Zongli Yamen*, prince Gong was a prominent leader of this establishment. Though he provided crucial help to the Empress Dowager Cixi in her coup to gain power, he was too independent-minded and not sufficiently subservient to please her. In 1884, she sent him home after stripping him of all offices.

Because future treaties were to be written in English, in 1862 prince Gong initiated, with court approval, the establishment of a school at the capital for training English-language translators, which was called the *Tongwen Guan* (School of Combined Learning). This school, funded with revenue from the maritime customs, broadened its curriculum later to include French, Russian, and modern scientific subjects in its curriculum. Similar schools were also set up in Shanghai and Guangzhou under provincial auspices.

Just as these first steps in framing new institutions for the Qing foreign relations were taking place, Emperor Xianfeng died in August 1861. Before his death, he appointed eight high officials to act as Regents to help his successor, Emperor Tongzhi (r. 1861-1875), a six-year-old minor, to conduct state affairs. The mother of Tongzhi, an extremely ambitious and ruthless woman, who became the Empress Dowager Cixi (1835-1908), carried out a coup with the support of prince Gong, as well as several other powerful political figures, to bring down the Regents and seize supreme power.

As a deeply conservative ruler, Cixi feared and resented the aggression of the imperialist powers and the modernizing challenges they presented to China. On the other hand, her narrowly focused self-interest and her passionate concern for holding onto the reins of power by whatever means, prompted her not only to appease these powers, but also to seek their military assistance to suppress the Taiping Rebellion (of which more later) which raged from 1850 to 1864. The same impulse led her to work with the group of officials who, like prince Gong in Beijing and Zeng Guofan, Zuo Zongtang, and Li Hongzhang in the provinces, favoured a conciliatory approach to the foreign powers. They believed that to save herself from continuing foreign aggression, China needed to learn from the West: at the very least to overhaul its war-making capacity, build its own modern gunboats and armaments and train soldiers and sailors who could operate such equipment and conduct modern warfare. The Empress Dowager Cixi went along with their efforts at limited modernization. These officials, dubbed the 'foreign affairs' clique, were strongly opposed by some ultra-conservative and reactionary officials, who harboured deep-seated suspicions and hostility to the foreigners and their 'strangely ingenious' techniques. They stubbornly resisted change. Cixi played one side against the other to keep her ascendancy over any one group of her ministers. Her own ambivalence toward this key issue of the time prevented her from giving strong, decisive, and unwavering leadership towards modernizing China.

By the early 1860s, to save the dynasty Qing China had been beaten into a receptive mode regarding treaty implementation, for which the imperial powers held it responsible to the last letter. Like all legal documents, the provisions of the treaties were capable of differences in interpretation when applied to actual situations. Sometimes they provided only bare outlines, leaving the details to be worked out. The interpretation of extraterritoriality was an especially thorny issue. After the Treaty of Tianjin and the Beijing Convention, the British desired peace to enjoy the fruits of what they had extracted from China by the wars and treaties. The American government also favoured a policy of `making an effort to substitute fair diplomatic action in China for force'. The conditions were therefore ripe for the two sides - the *Zongli Yamen* and the ministers of the legations in Beijing - to cooperate in earnest to realize the terms of these treaties, particularly those on the administration of customs for the whole country. Although the French and the Russians had other designs on China, such as encroaching on the territory along China's frontiers, they also stood to gain from the Sino-British negotiation on treaty implementation.

As regards the customs, the most pressing item on the agenda was the extension of the foreign Inspectorate of Customs in Shanghai to all the treaty ports. Before doing so certain issues which arose needed to be settled if it were to continue to function effectively. One was the status and authority of the foreign customs inspectors. Were they officials of the Chinese government or were they agents and subordinates of the foreign consuls? Another was whether the Qing government retained the right to collect tax on foreign trade, and to enforce Chinese customs laws and regulations on foreigners covered by extraterritoriality. The Qing government had no reason to assume that it had lost these rights. The Qing officials maintained that extraterritoriality did not mean that foreigners were permitted to violate Chinese laws, customs laws included, with impunity. It did, however, give the foreign offenders the opportunity to be tried in their own consular courts according to the laws of their own nation. It was also assumed that the foreign consuls were adequate for the judicial role and would conduct their judicial function in good faith. The *Zongli Yamen* had noticed that some foreign merchants doubling as consuls were not sufficiently disinterested or trained to assume the role of judges in consular courts.

In an age of merchant adventurers, some British merchants behaved as if the Chinese government had lost the above-mentioned rights. The British merchants were not pleased when the British inspector of the Chinese customs, Horatio Nelson Lay, tried to establish a new order at the customs house in Shanghai by enforcing the customs law and collecting the treaty tariff 'strictly and impartially' as required by treaty. They particularly objected to his extensive use of legal sanctions such as fines and confiscations against smuggling, fraud, and other illegal acts. They lodged complaints against him with the British consul, D. R. Robertson, who succeeded Rutherford Alcock. Called upon to defend the interests of the British merchants, consul Robertson was offended by Lay's unwarranted independence of action and lack of consultation with himself, given that Lay was his subordinate. He also thought Lay was too zealous in upholding the authority of the Chinese customs. This and other disputes, centring on the status and authority of the British inspector of the Chinese customs, as well as on China's right to collect customs duties itself, brought the British consuls and the Chinese superintendent of customs into conflict.

Partly with the help of the British inspector, these issues were brought to the attention of the British Foreign Office. The successive British Foreign Secretaries, Lord Clarendon and his successor, Lord Russell, both took the view that the British inspectors were Chinese officials, and as such their authority was derived from the Chinese government. In Lord Clarendon's opinion, the British inspectors could be tried in the consular courts as British subjects, but not as Chinese customs officials. Disputes arising when they were performing their official duties would have to be settled politically with the Chinese superintendent of customs, not judicially by the British consul. Lord Russell supported the interpretation of authoritative British legal opinion (consulted by Lay when he was on leave in England) that, in the light of the treaties, China retained her sovereign right to make customs laws and to enforce them through lawful sanctions such as confiscations. But fines, being directed against the person, requiring possibly imprisonment in case of non-compliance, would require consular intervention when extra-territorialized foreigners were involved. The above opinions expressed the official position of the British Foreign Office regarding Chinese customs. The American minister, Anson Burlingame, took a similar stand. The British position enabled the nascent foreign-managed inspectorate of customs to avoid being made into an appendage of various foreign consular services. As such, the foreign inspectors would have been torn between performing their Chinese customs duties and following the bidding of various foreign consuls. Under such circumstances, no uniform system of customs administration would have been possible at even one treaty port, let alone all of them.

The clarification of the British Foreign Office's position on extraterritoriality concerning the Chinese customs and the foreigners working in it paved the way for the authorities of Britain and China to implement the customs provisions of the Treaty of Tianjin. For this purpose, the *Zongli Yamen* summoned Lay to come to Beijing. Lay had been given the title of Inspector General of Customs by the Chinese authorities for him to act as the head of a centralized customs service, to be extended to all the treaty ports as required by the Treaty of Tianjin. As Lay had already decided to take home leave, Robert Hart, one of the two British customs officers who were to stand in for Lay in his absence, was asked to go to Beijing instead.

The youthful and Chinese-speaking Robert Hart, of Northern Irish origin, turned out to be admirably suited for this work as well as for the role of a moderator, which he was called upon to play, between the *Zongli Yamen* and the foreign legations. For a start, the expertise he possessed regarding the operation of the treaty provisions and customs regulations was invaluable for both sides to draw upon. Perhaps even more important was his ability to shape Western requirements into what was practically realizable in Qing China, as he demonstrably had a rare combination of inside knowledge of both foreign, particularly British, objectives, and Qing politics and administration. To undertake the work successfully required administrative skill and political acumen of a high order, with both of which he appears to have been richly endowed. Unlike many treaty port Westerners of this period, he was not contemptuous of the Chinese. He did not consider it beneath his dignity to work, though only nominally as it turned out, as an official of the Chinese government. He had an attitude of sympathy and good will towards the Chinese and a willingness to see the Chinese point of view. Having a historical perspective, he took a long-term view of the situation in China. Although the China before him was extremely weak, he nevertheless entertained a vision of China as a strong modern nation taking her rightful place in the comity of nations. He saw himself as someone working towards that goal. It was, therefore, not surprising that he soon won the good opinion and trust of the leaders of the *Zongli Yamen*, prince Gong in particular.

The British minister, Sir Frederick Bruce, was extremely appreciative of the part played by Hart in treaty implementation. He wrote to the Lord Russell that without Hart and the foreign-managed customs service, he would 'abandon as hopeless the task of realizing the indemnities and of working out the commercial innovations introduced by the Treaty into China'. He believed that this organization led by people like Robert Hart had a key role to play in helping to effect gradually 'by persuasion such a change in the view of the Imperial government as will admit of the exigencies of foreign commerce, and of foreign treaties, being worked harmoniously with Chinese administration'. The American minister also strongly supported Hart and the new foreign-led Chinese Maritime Customs Service (to be abbreviated as the MCS), that grew out of the Shanghai Foreign Inspectorate of Customs to cover other treaty ports.

The Imperial Maritime Customs House (first building)
(*Wikipedia Commons*: retrieved on 30 November 2023 from
https://commons.wikimedia.org/wiki/File:Imperial_Maritime_Customs_House_%2
8first_building%29.jpg)

The increasing importance of the Maritime Customs Service (MCS)

In 1863, upon his return to China, Lay was dismissed in connection with his attempt to control the gunboats he purchased from England for the Qing government. Hart was appointed the Inspector General (abbreviated as I.G.) of Customs by the *Zongli Yamen* with the support of the ministers of both Britain and America. To facilitate his role as an interface between the Legation and the *Zongli Yamen*, Hart set up the headquarters of the MCS with a small staff in Beijing. From there he built up the MCS as a uniform system of customs administration with customs houses at most of the treaty ports. By 1905, there were 33 treaty ports with customs houses collecting tariffs on Sino-foreign coastal and riparian trade amounting to around 35,000,000 *Haikwan Tael*, out of which 9% was used for the upkeep of the MCS. With the *Zongli Yamen* giving him virtually a free hand, Hart structured and managed the MCS as a modern centralized hierarchical administrative organization. It was staffed, in its upper echelons, by well-paid foreign personnel each with well-defined authority and capacity, who operated strictly according to a body of rules and regulations laid down by him, to govern every aspect of the organization and its functions.

In charge of each customs house the I.G. installed a foreign commissioner of customs, who was responsible to the I.G. for all the official business transpiring at his port. The I.G. controlled the customs houses of his far-flung empire through regular two-way correspondence, with circulars, directives, reports, and accounts going to and fro between the head office and the ports, and with all the records carefully kept. Being familiar with the modern British civil service, Hart established a regular career structure with attractive salaries and fringe benefits, especially for the elite foreign staff of the MCS. They were selected by examination and recommendation. The number of foreign staff rose to more than 1,000 after 1885. At the base of this organization were several thousand Chinese in clerical or menial positions. Since their pay and their opportunities for career advancement were limited, they were far less costly to employ than the foreigners. The MCS so set up was a semi-colonial establishment, by virtue of the autonomous behaviour of its foreign management vis-à-vis the *Zongli Yamen*, and the powerlessness of its Chinese staff. However, it was an effectively centralized customs administration that functioned efficiently, performing its duty of collecting the treaty tariffs and allowing no leeway for the irregularities and grafts that had characterized the Qing native customs. As an administrative organization, it fitted remarkably well the description of a modern 'rational bureaucracy', or 'legal authority', as categorized by Max Weber in his classic study of social institutions and their historical development. According to Weber, members of this type of organization normally operate more efficiently and with greater financial probity than members of a traditional 'patrimonial' administrative organization like the Qing customs. (The Weberian categories refer to the general principles and actual characteristics applicable to each type of organization, and one should not expect the MCS to be a perfect example of the Weberian categories.)

Although the MCS was a semi-colonial civil service imposed on China, the leading member of the *Zongli Yamen*, prince Gong and his successor, prince Qing, accepted it and worked closely with Robert Hart, who remained as its I.G. until the Qing dynasty ended in 1911. An important reason for this was that the Chinese authorities had the benefit of the use of the surplus the MCS collected from the revenues of certain ports during the initial decades of its establishment, after deducting the maintenance cost for the MCS and the indemnity payments to foreign countries. Before 1912, the maritime taxes collected at each port were kept and lodged by the Chinese superintendent of trade at the local customs bank of the port concerned, while the MCS handled the assessment of the duties, the examination of the goods, the keeping of records and accounts, and the making of periodic reports to the *Zongli Yamen* of all duties collected and expenses deducted. Being thus informed of the size and location of the revenue, the *Zongli Yamen* was able to direct its use. The cost of the maintenance of the MCS would come out of the superintendents' funds at certain ports. As regards the revenue from the ports to which certain foreign indemnity was attached, such as the Anglo-French Indemnity imposed by the Treaty of Tianjin, the commissioners of customs at those ports would sign as witnesses to the scheduled transfer of the instalments from the Chinese superintendents to the foreign consuls concerned. The sources of revenue directly collected and controlled by the MCS were tonnage dues, which were required by treaty to be used for the lights and aids for navigation, in addition to income from special permits, licences, fines, and the sale of confiscated goods.

The MCS came into existence before the time when China had a diplomatic corps, with foreign language expertise, knowledge of international law, and experience in international affairs. Prior to its establishment, the Qing government was reduced to relying on the advice of Western diplomats who represented the very nations that had aggressive designs on China. From the early 1860s, the Qing were able to turn to their own more trustworthy foreign civil servants in the MCS, the I.G. in particular, for advice and assistance on issues concerning foreign relations. The MCS became their 'window on the West'. Hart participated in the negotiation of many Sino-foreign treaties and conventions, starting with the implementation of the commercial and customs provisions of the Treaty of Tianjin mentioned earlier. He was credited with the successful conclusion of the Protocol of Paris of 1885 that ended the Sino-French War and gave Vietnam to France. He played an important part in the Chongqing Convention of 1890 that opened the upper Yangtze River to foreign trade by steamships. His brother, James Hart, represented China in the negotiations with British India on the opening of Yatung (Nyatong) as a trade mart between India and Tibet in 1893. Before China had permanent diplomatic missions abroad, Hart used his influence in moving the Qing government in this direction. In the 1870s, when the *Zongli Yamen* decided to send representatives to England and France and an ambassador to America, the MCS facilitated these moves by assuming responsibility for making arrangements for their financial support. To the Western governments and public, Hart tried to present the Chinese case, appealing for moderation in foreign demands and warning against forcing changes on China too rapidly. In several cases that turned upon the interpretation of extraterritoriality, he succeeded in limiting further encroachment of China's sovereignty by the foreign merchants and officials at the treaty ports, through appealing to British legal experts and the British government.

In connection with the competition of the imperialist powers for economic and political advantages in China, the British I.G. of the MCS, being a loyal British citizen, naturally strove to serve the British interest. It was generally recognized that the British interest in China was essentially economic: at first centred on trade, industrial and other investments later also played an important part. Of all the powers, Britain had the largest foreign investments in China. The commercial treaties and the MCS were the necessary legal and administrative structures to support the British objectives. By contrast, the territorial ambitions of Russia, Germany, and Japan, in addition to their economic interests, seemed much more threatening to China, and Hart was fearful and suspicious of these countries' designs on China. He believed that his efforts to advance British interests were also beneficial to China, and he hoped that Britain and China would cooperate closely to resist the other three. Hart used his influence on the ministers of the *Zongli Yamen* in Britain's favour. During the Sino-Japanese War of 1894-95, Hart advocated British participation in the ownership of the profitable Kaiping coal mines in north China, to pre-empt a possible Japanese takeover, should Japan win. He was instrumental in transmitting to the British minister the message from the Qing government expressing its willingness to lease the north China port of Weihaiwei to Britain, presumably as a counterweight to balance the leasing of Port Arthur to Russia. Foreign procurement for gunboats and armaments in connection with China's modernization, if entrusted to the MCS, went to British firms. The I.G. had posted a resident agent in no other capital city but London. The MCS recognized a superior British claim with respect to its staff appointment: the British occupied 50% or more of the foreign staff positions, the leading ones included. English was the language of internal administration in the MCS.

The British government recognized the MCS as an important British asset in China and gave it British protection and support throughout the Qing. In keeping with the semi-colonial character of the MCS, the I.G. lived and worked in the foreign Legation Quarter in Beijing and belonged in the same social circle as the foreign diplomats. At a lower level, a parallel existed between the foreign commissioners of customs and the foreign consular officials at the treaty ports. This situation enabled Robert Hart and the British ministers, as well as the foreign consuls and commissioners of customs, to have easy access to one another so as to confer and communicate freely without having to inform, or be supervised by, the Chinese authorities. The commissioners of customs of course had to report their important financial or political dealings to their chief, the I.G.

The British domination of the MCS provoked the jealousy of the other treaty powers, though all of them, as well as citizens from some other Western countries, were represented among a foreign staff of some sixteen different nationalities. To keep the support of the other treaty powers, the I.G. made a point of maintaining contact with the ministers of the other legations, as well as 'a fair attempt' to give the nationals of the chief treaty powers a stake in MCS. Because of the services rendered by the MCS to foreign trade and finance, it was supported by the powers as a common interest.

Robert Hart's desire to be more than a mere collector of customs, and his visionary hope that the MCS would become a dynamic centre for the progressive modernization of China, led to his participation in many endeavours in that direction. Initially from the position of an adviser, he went on to act as an agent for purchasing gunboats and arms from Britain, and for recruiting personnel for the building of China's modern Beiyang Fleet during the 1870s. His ambition to become the Naval Inspector General of a modern Chinese Navy under the Qing central government was thwarted by Li Hongzhang, the powerful Grand Secretary and the Superintendent of Trade of the Northern Ports, who preferred to build his own regional power base. Partly also to counterbalance British predominance in China, Li used Gustav Detring, a German commissioner of customs in Tianjin, to import German technology and personnel to China.

The MCS assumed a host of ancillary functions not closely related to customs collection.

These included provision of lights and aids for navigation, hydrographic surveying, the regulation and licensing of pilots, management of harbours with construction of wharves and jetties and the conservancy of the approach to the harbours through dredging. It also dealt with the control of smuggling, administration of quarantine, registration of foreign trademarks, and the organization of trade exhibitions abroad, some of which functions would have been assumed by other specialized departments of the government of a modern country. The MCS organized itself internally to take charge of some functions as required by treaty - examples being the Marine Department for hydrographic surveying, and the sighting and maintenance of lighthouses and other aids for navigation - and others which might need the skills or the personnel of a modern semi-foreign organization.

In addition to the above, the MCS was asked by the *Zongli Yamen* to take responsibility for the conveyance of mail matters between the foreign legations and their consular establishments in the treaty ports. Having established steamship lines for its own internal correspondence between its headquarters at Beijing and the treaty ports, the MCS easily extended this service to include the foreign diplomatic post. Later the MCS extended the postal facility to the public along the same routes. It was Robert Hart's fond hope that a unified state-managed modern postal service would emerge from the service's postal department. To accomplish this the new organization would have to replace the existing official courier service (*Yizhan*), as well as the privately organized traditional courier networks (*Minju*) for the general public, not to mention the foreign postal agencies already set up by foreign residents of the treaty ports. Such a development was strongly resisted not only by the Chinese with a vested interest in the *Minju*, but also by the foreigners of the treaty ports. The customs administration's steadfast pursuit of this goal, in addition to pressures for administrative reform from other quarters of the Qing government, led eventually to the establishment of the Imperial Post Office in 1896. This new office continued to be located inside the MCS, where it was managed by a Postal Secretary under the I.G. The MCS also subsidized it financially. It became independent of the MCS in 1911, when it came under the jurisdiction of the Ministry of Posts and Communications, which was established as a part of administrative modernization inside the Qing government. This was how the modern Chinese postal service emerged out of the MCS.

The clamour for reform of the antiquated Qing institutions, in connection with rising Chinese nationalism and foreign pressure, led to changes in the supervisory organs of the MCS during the first decade of the twentieth century. In 1901, the *Zongli Yamen* became the *Waiwu Bu* (Ministry of Foreign Affairs). In 1908, the *Shuiwu Jiu* (Chinese Maritime Customs Service) was created, and the jurisdiction over the MCS was transferred from the Ministry of Foreign Affairs to this fiscal office. During the same year, a new Customs College was also set up to advance the position of the Chinese staff inside the MCS. Robert Hart, who was preparing himself for retirement after nearly half of a century as the I.G., saw this as an irresistible process of Chinese eventually gaining control of the MSC.

For half a century before the Qing dynasty ended in 1911, its finances were severely strained, partly by the payment of the indemnities imposed by the imperialist powers, and on account of the heavy military expenses required in wars against internal rebels and foreign invaders, in addition to many military modernization projects. Because of the lack of facilities for fund raising from internal loans like those which existed in modern nation states such as England and France, foreign loans were introduced by using the surplus of the maritime customs revenue of certain ports as security for repayment, after the foreign indemnities tied to it were met. Because of the supervision of the foreign-controlled MCS in collecting the revenue, the foreign investors, banks, and banking syndicates looked upon these loans as sound investments. During the three decades from 1861 to the time of the Sino-Japanese War of 1894-95, Qing provincial and local authorities contracted, mostly with the approval of the central government, twenty-five small, short-term foreign loans, each individually secured on the maritime customs revenue of certain ports.

After the Sino-Japanese War, the financially exhausted Qing central government, having to pay Japan a crushing indemnity of 230,000,000 taels, was obliged to borrow from foreign sources. Between 1895 and 1898, it raised three foreign loans of 16,000,000 GBP each: one from a Russo-French syndicate of some half a dozen banks, and the others from an Anglo-German syndicate composed of the Hong Kong and Shanghai Banking Corporation (the HSBC of today) and the Deutsch-Asiatische Bank. These loans were issued below par, from 83 to 94 1/8. The interest of 4 to 5 percent was considered high for these long-term loans, which ran for between 36 to 45 years. All three were secured on the maritime customs revenue, which had increased because of the growing Sino-foreign trade. For example, the customs revenue had more than doubled from just under 10,000,000 Hong Kong taels in 1869 to over 21,000,000 Hong Kong taels in 1895. Although most of the terms on these loans were financial, there were political conditions also. For instance, the Anglo-German loans included a condition that required the status quo of the MCS to be preserved during the duration of this loan. Since the Anglo-German Loan of 1898 ran for 45 years, it would secure the MCS as it was then constituted until 1943.

In 1901, the Western powers and Japan, which had sent troops to China to crush the Boxer Rebellion, imposed in the Boxer Protocol a devastating indemnity of 450,000,000 taels ($333 million at the exchange rate then current) on a prostrate Qing China, the entire annual revenue of which was estimated at around 250,000,000 taels. Since the Qing government was obviously without the resources to pay this sum as a single payment, arrangements were made for it to be paid in instalments over a period of thirty-nine years with 4% interest until the debt was amortized on 31 December 1940, when the principal and interest would reach a total of 982,238,150 taels. Since what was left of the maritime customs revenue after all obligations attached to it were met was insufficient to cover the instalments and interest, revenues from certain Chinese native customs within 50 li (about 16 miles) of several major treaty ports were also used for these payments. As a result, the I.G. of the

MCS controlled these native customs as well. While the Chinese taxes were collected in silver, this Boxer indemnity and the Japanese indemnity were paid in gold, which continued to appreciate against silver. This made the debt burdens even more onerous to the Chinese. Hart's proposal to adopt a gold base for maritime customs collection was not supported by the foreign trading nations in China. From 1901 to the end of the Qing dynasty in 1911 and beyond, the primary concern of the MSC in fiscal administration was the collection and repayment of the foreign indemnities and loans.

Internal Challenges: Early Uprisings, the Taiping, and Other Rebellions

Signs of internal decline in the Qing

The Opium Wars and their consequences were the first major challenge to the declining Qing. We must now turn our attention to serious internal challenges, stemming from corruption and laxity in the court, the civil administration, and the army. The frugal regime of the Kangxi and Yongzheng periods gave way to the highly lavish and extravagant lifestyle of the Qianlong (r. 1735-1796) era, with the court setting an unhealthy example in conspicuous consumption. There was rampant corruption. The emperor's favourite Heshen was a notable example. In over twenty years as a high-ranking Manchu official, he amassed a fortune of about 800,000,000 *liang* (Chinese ounce = 1.75 oz. avoirdupois) in silver currency. This sum was equivalent to 50% of the state income during that period. To accumulate such an inordinate amount of wealth, he developed a network of corrupt collaborators. Together they created a predatory climate of squeeze, proliferation of fees, extravagant gifts, and general financial malfeasance that spread like an epidemic in officialdom. The generous stipends to encourage official integrity introduced by Emperor Yongzheng, and various strict measures to control official corruption instituted by all early Qing emperors, were undermined by the middle of the Qianlong era. The civil administration became increasingly lax, ineffective, and irresponsible. As the malaise spread to the military, the erstwhile formidable Banner forces lost their capacity to fight. The Green Battalions suffered the same fate. The once overflowing government treasuries were showing signs of being largely run down, through fraud and corrupt practices. Taxes were increased and fees of all kinds proliferated to make up for the shortfall in government revenue. Selling official posts had once been a rarely used means to raise funds by the Ministry of Finance. During the Qianlong era, it had become a very common practice, or malpractice, which helped to fuel corruption from that time on.

Like several previous dynasties during their time of decline, land became progressively more concentrated in the hands of the rich and powerful through seizure or purchase. The smallholders were reduced to either joining the ranks of a floating population of the dispossessed, or becoming grossly exploited tenant farmers, paying 40-50% of their income as rent to the landowners, on top of the government's land and capitation taxes. But unlike previous dynasties, the unprecedented population growth during the previous one hundred or so years meant a decrease in the amount of arable land per capita. In a country where the per capita share of land was already very small, further shrinkage was bound to lead to economic hardship. The increasing rural economic distress as a result of these developments led to social unrest. Secret anti-Qing movements became active and drew growing support, with or without needing to hide under the cloak of a religious movement. One such movement, the non-religious Heaven and Earth Society, spread in the coastal provinces and in Taiwan. In 1786, their members in Taiwan started an uprising aimed at overthrowing the Qing, restoring the Ming, and redistributing land. This revolt took the Qing over a year to suppress at a cost of over 10,000,000 *liang*.

In 1796, the first year of Emperor Jiaqing (r. 1796-1820), members of the subversive White Lotus Cult, with Buddhist inspiration, rose up in a large co-ordinated rebellion in several provinces in the interior. They stood for the restoration of Han rule and land redistribution. This religious cult had existed as far back as the Song dynasty and had been involved in anti-Yuan rebellions before the beginning of the Ming. The nine year long military campaigns against the rebels exposed the general corruption in the Qing military administration, where large amounts of funds allocated for the troops went into the pockets of the generals and commanders who became rich, while the soldiers were underpaid and clothed in rags like beggars. The armies – both the Banner forces and the Green Battalions – sent out to fight the rebels were battle-shy. They preferred to follow the rebels from afar rather than engage them in combat. Jiaqing had first to address the weaknesses in the Qing armed forces before an effective strategy could be devised to isolate and annihilate the rebel forces. The cost of 200,000,000 *liang* for the suppression of this rebellion was a heavy burden on the already strained Qing finances.

Although the Qing Court continued to be troubled by smallish uprisings from this time onwards, the major rebellions did not occur until the nineteenth century. Of these, by far the largest was the Taiping Rebellion.

Hong Xiuquan and the formation of the Taiping

The Taiping Rebellion began on 1 January 1851 in Thistle Mountain, a remote mountainous region of Guangxi province in southwest China. Before the leaders of this movement decided to rise, they had already spent several years in this lawless region that harboured many rebel movements on account of its poverty, the presence of significant numbers of ethnic minorities, and the weakness of the local authorities. During the period from the mid-1840s onwards, they tried to gather and indoctrinate adherents, to bond with each other and with their followers, to train a well-disciplined army, to store weapons and other supplies, and to develop an agenda for a radically new social, economic, and political order, with a strong religious tinge that promised to establish the Heavenly Kingdom of Great Peace on earth. If some of the above activities in preparation for an uprising did not entirely differentiate the Taiping from the White Lotus type of traditional rebel movements, which endeavoured to draw those who were disaffected with the status quo with promises of a utopian and millenarian future, the Taiping had many features that set it apart, largely on account of the personality, character, and personal experiences of their founder, Hong Xiuquan (1814-1864).

Hong was born into a modest farming family of Hakka origin from a village in the southern coastal province of Guangdong. The Hakka, transcribed from the Cantonese 'guest people', were Han Chinese who had migrated from the north during troubled times in the past. Over the centuries, these people retained their separate identity and northern dialect (a variant of Mandarin) and maintained an uneasy relationship of mutual competition and hostility with the original inhabitants among whom they had settled. Having to farm the more marginal or hilly areas, their hardy women toiled on the land and kept their feet unbound. Because Hong was noticeably bright, his family exempted him from farming chores, and made sacrifices to enable him to get an education, hoping that he might raise the economic and social status of himself and the members of his family, if not also the entire Hong lineage group or clan in his village, if he passed the state-sponsored examinations. As a teenager, he showed promise in a qualifying exam, so he was encouraged to continue his studies of the Confucian classics well into adulthood.

In order earn a living, he became a schoolteacher in his own or other villages nearby. This profession gave him the leisure to prepare for future examinations that took place once every three years in Guangzhou. Should he pass, he would get his entry level degree of *Shengyuan*, popularly known as *Siucai* (refined talent) before the next hurdle of a higher degree. Having failed the examination twice, and already in his thirties, he travelled to Guangzhou for the third time with a desperate urge to succeed. While he was in Guangzhou, he came across a foreigner wearing a long gown, and sporting a hairstyle that made him look like a Daoist priest or a fortune-teller. He and his Chinese companion were handing out pamphlets to the examination candidates. Hong approached them hoping for words of encouragement, which he apparently received along with several of their pamphlets, which he perused casually and then put aside.

After his failure for the third time, he fell seriously ill by the time he reached home, travelling in a sedan chair. In the course of an illness that lasted forty days, he first lost consciousness and then became delirious. This was followed by a prolonged semi-conscious trance-like state, during which he saw vivid visions of himself being taken up in a beautiful sedan chair to a luminous place, where he was saluted by a multitude of fine men and

women with expressions of great joy. After he left the sedan, an old woman took him to
a river and washed him clean. Then he was led to a great hall, the beauty and splendour
of which were beyond description. In this resplendent setting, he was received by a man,
who was 'sitting with an imposing attitude upon the highest place'; he was 'venerable in
years, with a golden beard, and dressed in a black robe'. The venerable old man bestowed
upon Hong a sword and a seal, objects that symbolically stood for power and royal authority. He then revealed his anger and sadness to Hong because the people of the world,
who were all produced and sustained by him, had turned away from worshipping him
and had rebelled against him. They took his gifts but worshipped demons instead of him.
Then the old man commanded Hong to exterminate demons and overcome evil spirits.
There was also a middle-aged man whom Hong called his elder brother, who would aid
Hong in slaying evil spirits in all corners of the earth. There was, besides, an episode involving the 'venerable old man' rebuking Confucius, who appeared at one stage, for having misled the people by his teachings.

After he recovered from this illness, Hong did not forget the extraordinary visionary
encounters he had experienced. His personality, demeanour, and even to some extent
his appearance became drastically altered. From being a lively character fond of poking
fun at others, he turned into a distinctly solemn, unsmiling, and taciturn man, who took
himself extremely seriously. Instead of being quick-tempered, he became truculent and
imperious at times. He bore himself with great dignity, walking always with measured
steps and holding his body erect while sitting. He struck others as having become a resolute and uncompromising person. As a tallish man with large penetrating eyes, a long
sandy-coloured beard, and handsome features, he had become strikingly impressive to
look at. He spoke with a sonorous voice and an authoritative air. As a well-educated person with all these characteristics, Hong had the aspect of someone who readily commanded respect.

The visible changes reflected his new inner life and preoccupations. He changed his
given name from Huosiu (meaning fire refined) to Xiuquan (meaning completed refined).
The character *quan* was made up of two radicals (the basic building blocks of Chinese
characters), one being *wang* (the king) and the other *ren* (the people). This new name
contained the hidden meaning of 'king of the people'. Although he intimated some of
his thoughts to members of his family, such as telling his perplexed father that 'the venerable old man above had commanded that all men shall turn to me, and all treasures
shall flow to me', the exalted vision of himself as a king with a mission to save the world
contrasted starkly with the reality of his humdrum life as a member of a humble farming
family. Not being able to believe in his 'visions' entirely, or without the means to realize
them, he subjected himself to the examination ordeal once more after another six years
in school teaching and studying Confucian classics. After all, what other outlet was there
for a thirty-nine-year-old village schoolteacher, with a burning ambition to move upwards

on the social and economic ladder? Faced with failure again, he did not suffer another nervous breakdown this time, but became very angry. In a defiant spirit Hong denounced the Manchu government and its examination system as corrupt. He vowed never to take the Qing examination again, or ever to wear its official vestments.

After Hong returned home, he had an experience which. together with his visions, truly changed his life. A visiting cousin's curiosity was aroused by the pamphlets given to Hong at Guangzhou, which were lying about. When Hong himself decided to investigate the set of nine pamphlets which had the title 'Good Words for Exhorting the Age', he became extremely excited. He probably did not realize that these were Christian tracts because Christianity was banned in 1836, when he had received them, and so it remained in 1843, when he discovered them again. The tracts spoke of a Sovereign on High (*Shangdi*), a Chinese term for God, first used by the Jesuit Father, Matteo Ricci, and later used in the Protestant Bible translated by Charles Karl Gützlaff. While the Protestant missionaries in the nineteenth century endlessly debated which of half a dozen Chinese terms was the most appropriate one for God, the Catholic Pope Clement XI issued a papal bull that forbade the use of *Shangdi* and *Tian* (Heaven) in referring to God but approved the word *Tianzhu* (Lord of Heaven), which since then became the Chinese Catholics' name for God. According to the tracts and the Bible, which Hong later acquired, the Lord on High was humanity's Heavenly Father, who created the world, and from whom sinful humanity had turned away. Hong immediately recognized this figure as the Venerable Old Man of his 'visions' and concluded that he was the son of this exalted Lord on High. Regarding the tracts, he was quoted as having said that they were 'purposely sent by heaven to me to confirm the truth of former experiences'. Otherwise, he would not have dared to believe in his visions alone, as they could have been construed as 'mere productions of a diseased imagination'. In these Heavenly tracts, he found the objective proof of the validity of what he had experienced in his visions, and the divine revelations specially directed at himself. He became assured that God in the 'sacred work' was his Heavenly Father, who had in his visions commanded him to save the benighted Chinese people and turn them back onto the path of righteousness with a Heavenly regime of his own, and with him as the ruler. Had he not been given a sword and a seal? These were Chinese symbols for royal authority. In a moment, Hong had transformed the ancient Chinese belief in the Mandate of Heaven into a belief in the Will of God. He also identified the middle-aged man, who helped him to slay evil spirits, as Jesus Christ, his elder brother, who had already come into the world to save mankind. These revelations made Hong 'feel as if awakened from a long dream', and he 'rejoiced to have in reality a way to heaven, and a sure hope of everlasting life and happiness'.

Hong was not aware that the two men, the bearers of the good news, were missionaries: one of them was thought to have been an American Protestant missionary named Edwin Stevens, and the other was an early Chinese convert to Protestantism called Liang Fa (or

Afa), who was the author of the tracts. In missionary activities, Liang had been closely associated with Robert Morrison and many early Protestant missionaries sent to China.

Liang's tracts contained the most essential messages of the Bible and many of the important elements of orthodox Christian beliefs and practices. First, it was imperative for
mankind to believe in God, the universal Father and Creator of all things in Heaven and
on earth, and in Jesus Christ as the Saviour of fallen humanity. Then it followed that
human beings must worship God, the one and only Lord on High, and must obey God's
command to do good and reject evil. The worship of all idols and other gods and spirits
was strictly forbidden. They must observe strictly the Ten Commandments of God and
lead a moral life. The good people would have God's blessings and protection in life, and
thereafter would enjoy eternal bliss in Heaven. The unbelievers or evildoers, on the other
hand, would suffer calamity on earth and the punishments of hell hereafter. Baptism was
a necessary rite for rebirth and regeneration. This summary encapsulated the essential
tenets or the religious ideology of the rebel movement Hong was later to establish. He
was not troubled by the omission in this work of any mention of himself as God's second
son and the younger brother of Jesus, because he had received that revelation when he
was 'taken up to Heaven'. Neither was he troubled when he later learned about the sim-
ilarity between the messages contained in these works and Christianity, because the sim-
ilarity only confirmed what he knew was the universality of the truth. Since Hong's
religious experience emphasized God the father, other items such as the celebration of
Christmas, the Holy Eucharist, Jesus's resurrection, the doctrine of the Trinity, and the
New Testament emphasis on love and forgiveness were all omitted. Hong's God was the
wrathful jealous God of the Old Testament, who had been much sinned against, and was
ready to strike down all idols and fiercely sweep away any other forms of worship.

From that point onwards, Hong's secret life came out into the open. He had become
a passionate and unshakable believer in a syncretistic new religion that combined many
important elements of Christianity with his own eccentric personal additions and interpretations. He told his cousin, who had already acquainted himself with the contents of
the pamphlets, about his visions, and the connection between the two. His cousin became
a convert to this new religion. The two prayed to God, promising solemnly 'not to worship
idols, not to practise evil things, but to keep the heavenly commandments', and then
poured water over their own heads with the words 'purification from all former sins, putting off the old and regeneration'. Although a modern psychiatrist has diagnosed Hong
as someone who had suffered an episode of mental disorder which exhibited symptoms
of hallucination, paranoia, and delusions of grandeur, he was clearly sufficiently in possession of his faculties a few years after his recovery to tell his story coherently, and with
enough passion and conviction to persuade his cousin to believe in the fantastic construction he had made from this mysterious experience and the Christian tracts.

Although Hong would have put his own life and those of his relatives at risk if the Qing authorities had got to know that Hong was destined, or even believed that he was destined, to found a new dynasty, it was relatively safe for him to spread his new religion while leaving out the political implications. He tried to persuade his relatives to accept the new faith and went about preaching in earnest to the people of his own and neighbouring villages. He made a number of converts: two of his cousins, Feng Yunshan and Hong Rengan were among them. Like Hong himself, both were educated but unsuccessful scholars as regards the state examinations. They were such enthusiastic neophytes that they went about 'with a spirit of joy' to spread the new gospel, each in his own village. In the summer of 1843, after attracting an initial following, Hong established the Society of God Worshippers for recruiting new members.

Before long, Hong's iconoclastic monotheism was bound to come into conflict with the long-established Chinese polytheistic religious beliefs and practices, if not also the Qing authorities. China's popular pluralistic religious culture accommodated many different belief systems. As a result, it was commonplace to have ancestor tablets at the family shrines, Confucian tablets at schools, and the Kitchen God might rub shoulders with the God of Wealth in peoples' homes. Buddhist or Daoist temples with their own pantheon of deities dotted the cities and the countryside, not to mention that here and there were shrines with well-known or obscure deified personages. The concept of religious freedom from state interference had not evolved in China through historical experiences as it had in Europe. It had been taken for granted that the state had a right to regulate and intervene on religious matters, ranging from patronage to prohibition. During the Qing, the state supported an orthodox Confucianism and certain popular cults. Emperor Yongzheng banned Catholicism in 1724 but did not otherwise intrude into the people's religious beliefs and practices unless sedition was suspected. In China's long history, many rebellions were fomented by religious cults, because religious gatherings provided good camouflage for those seeking recruits for seditious activities.

Hong was an example of someone who was using a religious cult with a hidden intention to start a rebellion. His exclusive monotheism was revolutionary for China because it meant that the entire slate of religious beliefs in China's tradition had to be swept away, and the sacred objects associated with them destroyed. While propagating his new faith, he started to denounce idolatry of any kind, including the worship of ancestors and Confucius, and he also sought out idols in the countryside and carried out violent physical attacks on them. The parents of the school where Hong taught kept their children away, because they strongly objected to his removal of the tablet of Confucius. Early in 1844, he lost his teaching post through clashes with the elders of his village on religious issues.

Without employment, Hong decided to leave home together with his cousin Feng Yunshan, who had been let into the secret of his political agenda. Although Feng came from a prosperous farming family, he was ready to throw in his lot with Hong in pursuit of a venture which was enormously risky, because the penalty for sedition was death, not only for those directly involved but also for all relatives several degrees removed. Together the two of them trekked as itinerant preachers, looking for a more suitable place, a remote area sufficiently distant from the surveillance of authorities, where they could find receptive people to build a nursery for their new religion, as well as for the 'great enterprise'. After wandering for several months and visiting some relatives of Hong's in Guangxi, Hong and Feng went in separate directions.

Hong headed east to return home, where he produced a body of writings of religious precepts and verses such as the 'Ten Commandments' and 'Ode for Youth' for the education and edification of his followers. There was a brief interlude of a couple of months, when he and another cousin, Hong Rengang, went to study the Bible in Guangzhou in response to an invitation from Rev. I. J. Roberts, a Southern Baptist Minister of a Protestant mission there. This visit did not seem to have much effect on Hong's basic beliefs, even though he had the full use of the Bible, both the Old and the New Testaments. The lessons he learned from this visit that were going to be useful for his movement were the printing and distribution of Christian tracts, and the conduct of public worship services.

Feng went westward into the remote Thistle Mountain area of Guangxi, where he successfully pursued, with great persistence and effort, the goal of winning followers for the new faith. By the time Hong returned to Guangxi in 1847, he was received with great reverence in Thistle Mountain as the spiritual head of some 3,000 members of the Society of God Worshippers. Even though the establishment of this society was the fruit of Feng's labour, the pre-eminent place in it had been reserved for Hong, because Feng had told the congregation about Hong's experience of being taken up to Heaven to be received by God as his son.

Together, Hong and Feng intensified the indoctrination and established rituals, 'heavenly regulations' (based on the Ten Commandments), and disciplinary measures to govern a society that had taken on a militantly puritanical character. The members had to observe the Ten Commandments strictly and abstain from drinking alcohol and from smoking, not just opium, but also tobacco. Hong and Feng also sent out converts to establish branches of the society in many other parts of both Guangxi and Guangdong.

During the late 1840s, the Qing authorities were unable to maintain law and order in large parts of the mountainous impoverished province of Guangxi. Banditry was rife. Although some bandits were of local origin, many moved into the lawless Guangxi region from around Guangzhou, which had suffered an economic decline following the shift of foreign trade to Shanghai after the Opium Wars. Large gangs of several thousand men might be emboldened to sack small towns. Apart from gangs of outlaws, different communities banded together to advance their common interest, for settling scores, and for mutual protection; in case of serious disputes, they would fight and take the law into their own hands. The rapidly growing Society of God Worshippers became a prominent local group that fought outsiders, with notable success, to defend the interest of their members, or to seek redress against any wrong inflicted on any of their 'brothers' and 'sisters'. Protection and mutual support prompted many vulnerable people to join this society, in addition to religious or other reasons. As the society gathered strength in numbers and other resources, Hong's identity as God's son with a divine mission to establish a new dynasty was coming more and more into the open in his recruitment drive. He had also been openly denouncing the Manchus as alien oppressors, who had robbed the Chinese of their estate and ruined the Chinese economically. Although taking up arms to establish a new dynasty was an extremely risky undertaking, those with little means of economic support, or who had been alienated by the Qing authorities because of corruption or other grievances, might have found joining such a movement an opportunity to improve their lot, or to avenge themselves.

There was a small inner circle of members whom Hon took into his confidence. They had been identified by him as the top echelon of leaders, whose support he needed as generals and ministers of his new kingdom. They were Yang Siuqing, Xiao Chaogui, Shi Dakai, and Wei Changhui, in addition to Feng Yunshan. Hong, re-enacting a celebrated Chinese tradition whereby the head of the Kingdom of Shu became sworn brothers with his two top generals, bonded with these five as a group of sworn brothers. Following Hong's political agenda, they pledged to overthrow the Manchus and establish a new kingdom according to God's command. Their motives in being a part of this movement were clearly socio-economic and political because they would belong to the aristocracy or ruling class of the new regime.

The God Worshippers' hostility to traditional beliefs and their iconoclasm, while intimidating to many, provoked the active hostility of a member of the powerful local gentry, who led a militia to arrest and imprison Feng in 1848. After Hong left for Guangzhou to seek Feng's release through petitioning higher authorities, the leaderless society was becoming fractious and uneasy. A prominent and exceedingly ambitious member, Yang Siuqing, circulated a story that one day he became deliriously ill when God descended to earth and took possession of his body. God made him His Spokesman as well as the Redeemer of Sickness, so that he would take on the sicknesses of others who would then be spared. A spirit possessing the body of a person and speaking through this person was a role normally assumed by a medium, who might be hired by someone wishing to contact an ancestor. Yang shrewdly exploited this common superstition as a means to gain authority, not just equal to but even higher than that of Hong's. Soon, Yang's close ally, Xiao Chaogui, announced that Christ had also descended on him and made him His Spokesman too. Before long, many society members were falling to the ground in a state of delirium and speaking in tongues, each claiming to be God's Spokesman. After Feng was released, and returned to base with Hong in the summer of 1849, the society was divided into factions, some supporting one and some another of those who had claimed that God had spoken through them. Hong settled the matter with his judgement that the experiences of Yang and Xiao were of God, while the others were of the devil. Hong's decision unified the members of the society at a critical juncture when the leaders were preparing for an uprising, but it would licence Yang and Xiao to use the same claim to trump Hong's authority in the future.

By the middle of 1849, the society's membership had grown to around 10,000. It was not an organization that people joined singly. When a prominent member of a family joined, he often brought into the society his entire family, if not most members of his lineage or clan, which might number in tens or hundreds. In one case over one thousand miners from a certain mining district joined the movement. Because the leading members of this society were Hakkas, and because Guangxi had large settlements of Zhuang and Yao minorities, many Hakkas and these minority people became members. By this time, the society was attracting not just poor peasants, but people from different social levels and walks of life, including rich merchants, wealthy landowners, miners, local militia, and ex-soldiers. Anticipating their uprising, Hong and Feng intensified their recruitment drive to boost their future fighting force. Famine, pestilence, and the increasing communal violence during this time drove many to seek refuge in Hong's organization. Since all comers were welcome provided they would practise the new religion and obey the society's puritanical regulations, gangs of pirates and bandits, when pressed by government authorities, sought shelter under the powerful protective umbrella of this society. Among them were two well-known women bandit leaders, who joined with a few thousand followers. However, many found that they could not abide by the society's strict rules and discipline, and they left. As regards many of the actively seditious Triad secret societies in this part of China, Hong would not associate with them, finding their aim of restoring the Ming, their folk religious practices, and their low moral standards incompatible with his own.

With the number of God Worshippers growing by leaps and bounds to over 20,000 sometime during 1850, and with the escalation of violent conflicts between members of this society and other armed communities, particularly some of the local gentry and militia, the chances of a clash with official government troops became increasingly likely. Had it not been for the Guangxi governor's abdication from his duty to keep order, the clash would probably have occurred much sooner. Sensing the possibility of having to fight government forces sent against them before very long, the leaders of the God Worshippers accelerated their preparation for military actions. In May 1850, Hong and Feng arranged to have their families in Guangdong join them in Guangxi. In the autumn of 1850, Hong commanded the leaders of all branches of the society scattered in other areas to gather all their members with their families, and what belongings they could take along, and to assemble in Jintian (Golden Field), a place near Thistle Mountain, for 'collective camping'. This was effectively an order for a general mobilization of the whole society.

In Jintian, Feng Yunshan, with the help of another scholar, had already drawn up an impressive master plan supposedly derived from the military tradition of the Zhou dynasty (c.1030-207 BCE). Following this plan, they registered all the able-bodied men and assigned them to fill units of a systematically organized army. From corporal to the commander-in-chief, each level of the hierarchically structured army command had a certain number of soldiers with the appropriate number of officers. Through an assignment designated by one of the five elements, a number, and the colour of the vest or flag, each person knew his unique place in the command structure, and his superiors whose orders he was obliged to obey. The men were given printed manuals on camp construction and the different battle formations, together with regulations for troops on the march. A strict code of sixty-two rules had been laid down to govern the conduct of military personnel, with regulations covering not only their behaviour on the battlefield, their relationship with their colleagues and those ranked above and below them, and their treatment of the civilian population, but also their personal and religious life. Penalties for infraction ranged from demotion to death. To show defiance against the Qing, the men were ordered to stop shaving the top of their heads, and to keep their long hair in place with a red turban around their foreheads. While they were known as the 'Long-haired Bandits' on the Qing side, they abusively called all those associated with the Qing 'imps' (imperialists). After this preliminary process, they underwent military training and drilling.

This movement was unusual for having female battalions, partly because of the need to have as many soldiers as possible, and partly because of its ideology regarding the equality of the sexes. Women were given the opportunity to be combatants, but they constituted only a small auxiliary force to the main body of male fighters. They had separate living quarters and were governed by a hierarchy of female officers. The strong Hakka women with their unbound feet made this situation possible. The non-combatants at Jintian were put into camps of their own, where a strict regime of segregation of the sexes was put into practice. Husbands and wives living in different camps might see each other once a week for a short time under the watchful eyes of chaperons. A hierarchy of officers with various titles managed these camps.

All those who responded to the call of 'collective camping' at Jintian gave up not only their family life, but also all their private property. Their land and houses were sold for cash where possible. All their money and other valuables were put into the Holy Treasury. Many of them probably were poor with few means, but there were rich merchants, and some very wealthy people. For example, Shi Dakai's family contributed 100,000 taels to the community chest. Wei Changhui and another rich landowner turned over their huge stores of grain which could sustain a largeish army for several months. In return, the community supplied the members' basic material needs, such as food and clothing.

Because openly buying weapons for so many soldiers, even if it had been possible, would arouse suspicions, Wei Changhui purchased iron from any source, ostensibly for making agricultural implements. The mountaineers gathered wood and made charcoal.

At Wei's village, volunteers worked round the clock to hammer the iron into weapons. They used a large flock of honking geese to mask the noise of these activities. They also made crude cannons, muskets, and explosives. Women were enlisted to make uniforms, flags, and other equipment. They buried all the finished products until needed.

In Beijing, the new emperor Xianfeng (r. 1850-1860), who succeeded Daoguang, did not receive any news of the seditious religious community in faraway Guangxi from the governor of Guangxi, who paid no attention to matters of internal security. After reports from other officials and a delegation of representatives of the gentry sounded the alarm, the emperor dismissed the governor and appointed other civil and military officials to control the crisis. In the winter of 1850, government troops were moving into Jintian and the inevitable armed clashes between Hong's followers and the local soldiers and militia sent against them took place, with the defeat of the government side. Soon after, the Qing sent two larger bodies of troops, one led by a Manchu Brigadier General and the other by a commander from a neighbouring province, to root out these 'religious rebels'. The day before hostilities began on 31 December 1850, four groups of God Worshippers of over 10,000 people arrived for the 'collective camping'. With these reinforcements, the God Worshippers thoroughly routed the Qing forces. Having killed so many Qing soldiers and officers, for the God Worshippers there was no looking back, even for those who had not joined the religious community to engage in a rebellious movement. What had occurred accorded with the plan of Hong and the other leaders of the movement.

On 11 January 1851, on Hong's thirty-eighth birthday - reckoned the Chinese way, which counted from conception so that a person is one year old on the actual date of birth - he assembled all the God Worshippers in Jintian to proclaim himself as the Heavenly King, the supreme leader of a theocratic kingdom, the *Taiping Tianguo* (Taiping Heavenly Kingdom, often abbreviated as the Taiping). From his knowledge of Chinese Classics, Hong chose the word *Taiping* as it referred to a stage of the world where everlasting peace and prosperity reigned, and this was to be the stage which his *Tianguo* (Heavenly Kingdom) ushered into China by the Will of God. He also appointed Yang Siuqing, the naturally gifted military strategist and tactician, to be commander-in-chief of the entire military force, as well as the commander of the Central Army. The other four of his sworn brothers were appointed commanders of the Front, Rear, Right and Left Armies.

The military campaigns of the Taiping and their establishment in Nanjing

Having declared themselves as the enemies of the Qing, the Taiping could not stay in any spot for long. They had to keep on breaking through encirclements by enemy troops or suffer being pursued by them as they marched in their thousands with their elders, and their women and children, first towards the west and then north. The strictly disciplined

Taiping soldiers fought bravely. Unlike their Qing counterparts, they did not victimize the civilians of the towns they fought over by looting, burning, raping, and killing. The Taiping on the move had their appeal, and many joined them to start a new life or for other reasons of their own in the areas they traversed. As a result, the movement's fighting complement continued to be strengthened. Because they dealt honestly, vendors willingly sold them supplies they needed. Finally, in September 1851 they captured Yongan, their first walled city, where they stayed until April the following year. They took a breathing spell to structure their civilian government with a system of offices and court etiquette based on those of the Zhou dynasty. Hong's sworn brothers were made kings, with Yang Siuqing leading the others as the East King and Shi Dakai the most junior as the Assistant King. They also created their own solar calendar, rather than the traditional lunar based one. This was another of Feng Yunshan's innovations. They stocked up on supplies and recruited new members. Their total reached almost 40,000, with half that number in the fighting force. For several months, the Qing forces did little to dislodge the Taiping until the Spring of 1852; then over 30,000 Qing soldiers laid siege to Yongan.

The rebels managed to slip out of the besieged city, and attempted to capture Guiling, but without success, though their fighting force had increased to over 60,000. They then proceeded north to the province of Hunan, where they sustained heavy losses at an ambush staged at a narrow ford by a scholar-official leading a quite small militia. The Taiping failed to capture the provincial capital of Changsha after a siege of more than two months, thanks to a large concentration of troops inside the city and the determined resistance of the gentry and officials gathered there. They did succeed in breaking into many county seats where they gathered an enormous number of weapons, ammunition, guns, gunpowder, and other supplies. In Hunan, the Taiping started to issue inflammatory anti-Manchu proclamations urging people to join them and adopt their religion. Although their anti-Manchu revolutionary propaganda won them many recruits amongst the disaffected, outlaws, and the desperately poor, their militant Christianity and their animosity towards Confucianism and other popular religions, together with their iconoclasm, provoked the antagonism of the gentry and scholar-officials, who became their most formidable enemies. In their march north through the watery region of Lake Dongting and the tributaries of the Yangtze River, their fighting force grew to 100,000, and they were able to commandeer thousands of boats to enable them to become waterborne in a fleet, sailing along the Yangtze, to invade the triple city of Wuhan. Thanks to the lack of preparedness of their Qing enemy and the skill of the Taiping miners for exploding city walls with underground tunnels, all three cities fell into the hands of the Taiping within a short time.

The capture of this centre of transportation, communication, and commerce on the Yangtze River was their greatest prize so far. Their Holy Treasury was filled with several million taels of silver from raiding the government offices, and from confiscation of the wealth of the rich. They also collected a large amount of grain. In addition to those who voluntarily joined, they started to conscript people into their army. They had now reached a turning point, where they could drive north to Beijing or east to Nanjing. Their decision not to march rapidly to take Beijing, when they had the revolutionary momentum, was considered a strategic mistake by some, because defensive measures for blocking a Taiping march on Beijing were not in place, and the militia from Hunan, the Xiang army led by scholar-officials, which would eventually defeat them, was not yet in existence at that point. They decided to go east, following the Ming example of siting their capital at Nanjing. This city had been the capital of many dynasties in the past, partly because of its location in the rich and populous lower Yangtze region, and partly because the mountains, and the Yangtze River surrounding it, rendered it easy to defend.

With a fleet of over 20,000 vessels, and a force numbering 500,000 even without ten percent of the conscripted men and over eighty percent of the conscripted women, the Taiping flotilla sailed downstream towards Nanjing on 8 February 1853, with the Heavenly King on a boat decorated with a dragon's head at its bow and tail at its stern, accompanied by the massive army. Along the way through the province of Jianxi, the Taiping carried away the valuables of the city of Jiujian, its residents and defenders having fled on news of the approaching Taiping. The next major city along the Yangtze was Anqing, the provincial capital of Anhui province, which was also deserted apart from its governor, who awaited his death alone outside the city, after its wall was breached by Taiping artillery fire. From Anqing, the Taiping collected over 300,000 taels of silver in government offices, over one hundred cannons, and an enormous amount of food and other supplies. En route through Anhui, many people came forward to offer money, food, and sometimes themselves, boosting the Taiping army to nearly 750,000. All along the Taiping's journey to Nanjing, there were sympathetic uprisings of the Triad secret society, whose members then joined this movement. From 6 March 1853, wave after wave of the Taiping arrived at the outskirts of Nanjing, their 'Little Heaven', a little over two years since the uprising had begun in Jintian, over 1000 miles away.

Nanjing, situated on the south bank of the Yangtze River, was a large city with 10 gates protected by 15,000 battlements along a winding 30-mile-long city wall that was thick and high. From the gates of the city, the Taiping presented the awe-inspiring sight of a sea of red-turbaned men covering an area of several square miles. After attacking the city for 13 days, some of the Taiping, who had infiltrated the city, by a stroke of luck killed the governor, and others dressed as monks set fire to houses near the gates, to signal those outside to advance into the Outer City. They then captured the well-guarded Inner City of the Manchu Bannermen by brute force and massacred everyone in sight. After taking possession of Nanjing, the leaders discussed once more whether they should leave a garrison there and proceed north to strike Beijing while the iron was hot. Again, the seductive wealth of the lower Yangtze region caused them to choose Nanjing as their capital, though a British friend of the Taiping, Alexander Lindley, considered this choice a fatal mistake that lost Hong the empire.

On 29 March 1853, amid great pomp and pageantry, the Heavenly King and the other Taiping Kings, together with their families and dignitaries, carried either on resplendent sedan chairs or on the back of horses, accompanied by heralds, musicians and bodyguards, followed by a long line of holy soldiers, entered in triumph into Nanjing, where they were greeted by hundreds of thousands of kneeling soldiers and crowds. Here the Taiping rulers built palaces, laid down defensive measures, organized their government and other institutions to govern the areas under their control, and sent out armies to wrest the rest of the empire from the Qing. They had established in the south a dynasty to rival the Qing in the north.

Had the Taiping marched north immediately after they took Nanjing, overwhelming the resistance the Qing could muster in a short period of time, and capturing Beijing with their huge army of 750,000 before the onset of the cold winter, their Heavenly King's wish might have been fulfilled. Instead, two months after the Taiping entered Nanjing, Yang Siuqing, the Taiping commander-in-chief, despatched two meritorious commanding officers leading a force of about 80,000 to capture Beijing. Although this force was sufficiently large to capture cities and win battles, it suffered losses and defeats as the Qing concentrated troops from all over the north to block the invaders' advance. The Taiping army struggled against many obstacles and challenges to reach within 3 miles of Tianjin, 70 miles from Beijing. However, shortage of ammunition and other supplies, and the failure of the reinforcements to reach it, together with the harshness of the north China winter, forced it to retreat. On its southward journey the army was split up, continually harassed, often surrounded, and finally destroyed by an elite cavalry force led by the Mongolian Prince, Sengge Rinchen (Senggelinqin in Pinyin) (1811-1865).

Leadership struggles in the Taiping

Cracks began to develop in the Taiping leadership. In terms of military and administrative capacity, Hong Xiuquan could hardly be compared with Emperor Hongwu, Zhu Yuanzhang (r. 1368-1398), the founder of the Ming. The credit for the establishment of the flourishing Society of God Worshippers at Jintian, and the setting up of the Taiping military systems, belonged to Feng Yunshan. Feng's early death was a great loss for Hong and the Taiping movement. Happy to retire into his literary and religious pursuits, Hong gave the East King, Yang Siuqing, unfettered authority to direct the civil, military, and religious affairs of the Taiping. Yang took the opportunity to concentrate power into his own hands and built up a cohort of supporters. He also became arrogant and oppressive towards other officials, including his brother kings. Despite the disastrous Northern Expedition, Yang gained personal kudos through his success in directing the Taiping forces to make Nanjing secure by capturing certain key cities nearby, and by reclaiming the cities and territories along the Yangtze River all the way to Wuchang and Hanyang, giving the Taiping thereby access to the resources, and the facilities for transportation and communication, of this stretch of the Yangtze valley. Hong's poor judgement of character, and his misplaced trust in Yang, was to cost him and his movement dear.

Not satisfied with the power, position, and the string of honorific titles Hong had already bestowed on him, Yang decided, in the middle of 1856, that the time was ripe for him to make a bid for the leadership. Threatened and alarmed, Hong played for time, and secretly recalled the North King, Wei Changhui, back to the capital to help him. To keep Wei away from the capital during the intended coup, Yang had despatched Wei to the west on a military campaign. As soon as Wei slipped back into Nanjing without Yang's knowledge early in September 1856, he contacted a group loyal to Hong, and they made a plan to kill Yang and his two powerful brothers. Hong approved of this plan. Once the killing started, the situation got out of hand. Out of fear of revenge by Yang's cohorts, Wei and his henchmen initiated a bloodbath, with the killing going on for many days, leading to the death of several tens of thousands of Yang's relatives and associates, including those suspected of being pro-Yang. Hong was appalled. With his own life threatened by Wei, who had fallen out with him, he sent for Shi Dakai, the Assistant King, whom Yang had also sent away to the west ostensibly on a military expedition, but also to keep him out of the way. Before Shi reached Nanjing, Hong's supporters inside the city managed to capture Wei, who was executed by Hong.

Shi was welcomed as a saviour when he appeared, early in the winter of 1856, in the Heavenly Capital which was still shrouded in gloom after the fratricidal frenzy. A young man in his early twenties, Shi had already distinguished himself both on the battlefield and in civil administration. He had a reputation for being lenient, kind, and conciliatory towards the people in Taiping-controlled areas, where taxes were collected at a lower rate than under the Qing. At that point, Shi had the dubious distinction of being the only surviving sworn brother of the Heavenly King. Recognizing that Shi was the only one who could take on the job of managing both the civil and military affairs of the government, Hong honoured Shi and asked him to direct state affairs. Shi promptly set about strengthening the military position of the Heavenly Kingdom and retrieving lost territory in Anhui Province.

Unfortunately, the euphoria did not last long. Hong's two older brothers, being jealous of Shi, succeeded in destroying Hong's trust in Shi, who had been steadfastly loyal to Hong. Soon Shi felt frustrated and thwarted by Hong's mistrust. With his life possibly in jeopardy, in May 1857 Shi decided to leave the Heavenly Capital and take his army of approximately 200,000 to Sichuan and remain there. It was a journey easy to conceive but difficult to accomplish, because by then a new generation of better-trained provincial militia, and the battle-hardened Xiang Army led by scholar-officials under the leadership of Zeng Guofan and his associates, were determined to suppress the Taiping rebels wherever they might be found. After wandering through fifteen provinces and covering almost 6000 miles, Shi and his dwindling army of 7,000 were trapped by Qing forces at a river crossing in Yunnan Province in June 1863. To save his soldiers, he gave himself up. He was executed in August 1863 after writing his confession. The fratricidal bloodletting, and Shi's defection with a substantial Taiping army, were mortal blows to the Taiping Rebellion from which it never fully recovered.

The imperial powers intervene

Thanks to two young and gifted generals, Chen Yucheng and Li Xiucheng, who did not defect with Shi Dakai, the existence of the Taiping Heavenly Kingdom was prolonged for another seven years after Shi's departure. Both rose up from the ranks of humble foot soldiers to become top commanders, each with a kingly title, after the first generation of Taiping kings, except for Hong and Shi, lost their lives. Chen was the Heroic Prince (the Brave King) and Li was the *Zong Wan* (the Loyal King). When they cooperated and co-ordinated in certain strategic military campaigns together, which they did during the period between 1858 and 1860, they recovered a lot of the territory the Taiping had lost in the west after Shi's departure, and they also won a signal victory over the Qing by destroying the two large Qing military camps, the Great Northern and Southern Barracks, which had put the Taiping capital under siege, one from the north and the other from the south bank of the Yangtze River. Without a sufficiently prestigious and experienced military leader such as Yang Siuqing or Shi Dakai to function as a unified commander in the central government, these two younger generals tended mostly to work separately in their own theatres of war. The *Gan Wang* (Shield King), who was also the new Prime Minister, and the cousin of the *Hong Rengan* (Heavenly King), finally reached the Taiping capital in 1859 after many years trying to do so, but they did not have sufficient experience in military affairs to fill this role adequately. Subsequently, Li sought to expand further to the east to conquer Zhejiang Province and the rest of Jiangsu Province, two of the richest provinces of the Qing. He was successful until the foreign powers decided to intervene.

The naivete and ignorance of the Taiping regarding the imperialist powers was another major factor contributing to the ultimate downfall of their kingdom. Soon after the Taiping settled in Nanjing, the representatives of Britain, France, and the United States each visited their Heavenly Capital on separate occasions to become acquainted with this competing new Chinese regime, which projected power along the Yangtze River. The visitors became aware of the friendliness of the Taiping towards Westerners, whom the Taiping regarded as their 'foreign brethren' because of the perception of their shared Christian faith. However, the foreign diplomats were offended by the Heavenly King's pretension to be a universal ruler, and they would not cooperate with any diplomatic protocols that reinforced it. Concerned that the Taiping were some new kind of militant Protestants, the

French received the assurance they sought that the Taiping were not persecuting Catholics. While not recognizing the regime in Nanjing as legitimate, all the representatives of the foreign powers informed the Taiping authorities that their governments adopted a policy of neutrality in the civil war. The positive attitude the Taiping maintained on trade, including foreign trade, which flourished in Taiping-controlled areas prevented friction between the Taiping and the powers, which kept their neutral stance until after the Treaty of Tianjin (1858, discussed previously).

After having wrung such extensive concessions from the Qing through the Treaty of Tianjin, the powers were tempted to abandon their policy of neutrality towards the civil war, in favour of supporting the government in China that had given them the concessions. The Taiping aided this shift in policy when Li Xiucheng led an eastward expansion in the early 1860s, captured the treaty port of Ningbo, and threatened Shanghai. When the Taiping armies attempted to invade Shanghai, the British, French, and Americans in the foreign Concessions were fully ready to cooperate with the local officials, who solicited foreign help to fight against the Taiping. Witnessing the foreign and the Qing forces together attacking Li Xiucheng's army at the outskirts of Shanghai, the Taiping felt betrayed by their 'foreign brethren', for they had hoped that the foreigners would allow them to invade Shanghai. They had appealed to the foreign representatives for understanding the necessity for them to recover Shanghai for God's people and had repeatedly promised not to harm foreigners or damage their property. Although the Taiping fought bravely against superior foreign weaponry and even won some skirmishes, they had finally to abandon their goal of capturing Shanghai after their fourth attempt in 1862, particularly as the formidable Xiang Army under Li Hongzhang, a protégé of Zeng Guofan, was appointed by the Qing to direct the fight against the Taiping in this theatre of war, with foreign support.

Having abandoned their neutrality, the naval forces of Britain and France joined the war against the Taiping to recover Ningbo and many cities in the vicinity of Shanghai and Ningbo during the early years of the 1860s. The British and the French also helped the Qing by giving some of their army officers leave to lead foreign mercenary forces to fight against the Taiping in this eastern war zone. Among these was Major Charles Gordon, who became a celebrated figure in nineteenth century England as the 'Chinese Gordon', and later as the hero of the siege of Khartoum. Major Gordon became the commander of the 'Ever Victorious Army', a foreign mercenary force operating under Li Hongzhang. This force had been created in Shanghai by an American adventurer called Frederick Townsend Ward, who later perished in action fighting the Taiping near Ningpo. Often supported by the pounding of heavy artillery from British gunboats, Gordon helped the Qing to recover many Taiping-occupied cities, the most famous of which was Suzhou. The French performed similar services for the Qing over the recovery of the city of Hangzhou. The Taiping made a grave mistake in attacking the treaty ports, a consequence of their ignorance of the world outside China and of the power politics between the Qing and the foreign powers.

The Taiping's anti-Confucianism, the development of the Xiang Army by Zeng Guofan, and its defeat of the Taiping

Not the least important of the causes of the Taiping's failure lay in the movement's militant anti-Confucianism. This was probably the result of Hong's own failure in passing the state examination, which was based largely on the Confucian classics. Hong never explained the basic philosophical issues he had with Confucianism. In fact, he interpreted the Lord on High (*Shangdi* or *Huang Shangdi*) in Chinese classics as the Christian God, because the Bible translated by Gützlaff used those Chinese terms for God. In the areas of ethics and morality, similarities between these two different worldviews could easily be found. The problem lay in the militantly exclusive monotheism Hong had fastened upon from reading Liang Fa's pamphlets. The worship of the spirits of ancestors and of Confucius himself was therefore idolatry, a crime punishable by death in the Taiping Kingdom. The militant anti-Confucianism of the Taiping that led them to burn the Confucian classics and destroy Confucian temples, and the tablets of Confucius in schools, was deeply offensive to the scholar-gentry officials. Having witnessed the uselessness of the regular Qing military forces, these scholar-officials strove to create more potent regular armies out of regional militias. Most of them started their career as scholars, not military officers. There was inevitably some trial and error before they were able to bring these powerful new regional forces successfully to the rescue of their cultural heritage against its destruction by the Taiping. In doing so, they destroyed the rebel dynasty, and gave the Qing a new lease of life. Had Hong adopted the tolerant Jesuit attitude towards Confucianism and the traditional Chinese rites, and kept his armies away from the treaty ports, the Taiping Heavenly Kingdom might have lasted a few more decades as a rival dynasty to the Qing.

This was not to be the case, thanks to the scholar-officials. Foremost amongst those who led the war against the Taiping was Zeng Guofan, the creator of the Xiang (another word for the Hunan province) Army. Like Hong, Zeng also came from a poor farming family, and struggled with obtaining a good education and passing the state civil service examination. But unlike Hong, Zeng succeeded in getting the highest degree at age twenty-eight and became, as a member of the Hanlin Academy, an official at the court. He was a staunch supporter of the Confucian world order and the dynasty that benefited him.

During 1853, when the Taiping army invaded Hunan, Zeng was sent back to his home province to raise a militia to support the regular Qing forces and fight the rebels. This experience taught him that a new kind of militia, different from the informally gathered and untrained country folk, was needed to save his province, let alone the Qing dynasty, from the Taiping. He and another scholar set about creating from scratch a blueprint for the organization of this new force. Being careful in his choice of the people who made up this force, from commanding officers down to the common soldiers or 'braves', he drew up a list of criteria, such as robustness, courage, physical endurance, honesty and so forth for selection and screening of the recruits. Those who were physically strong but did not pass the character test were used as porters or labourers. The elite group of officers were Confucian scholars of sound moral character, who, after being handpicked and nurtured by Zeng, had distinguished themselves in action. Zeng understood the importance of bonding among the soldiers so they would come to aid and rescue one another. He also laid great emphasis on the personal loyalty of the soldiers to their officers and commanders who picked and trained them. Zeng aimed to develop the Xiang Army into a well-trained and strictly disciplined fighting force with high morale. The soldiers were paid so well that that they could send money back to support their families at home, and they retired after a few years on active duty. Their families were on the army register as surety against defection. Like the Taiping, Zeng also believed in winning the hearts and minds of the people through propaganda. Before he launched what one might describe as a war in defence of China's Confucian cultural heritage, he issued a proclamation denouncing the 'bandits of Guangdong and Guangxi', detailing their crimes.

The presence of many rivers and lakes in his theatre of war prompted him to build a naval force also. Securing a steady stream of revenue for the support of the costly Xiang Army was a challenge to Zeng at the beginning. When the Qing central government authorized the collection of a new 1% transit tax levied on Chinese goods in passing through certain collection points, Zeng was able to rely on this tax to finance his army.

Although the Xiang Army was more of a match for the Taiping than the Qing regular forces, the first few years of its fight against the Taiping were an uphill struggle. Up to 1857, the regime in Nanjing was still the winner in the military competition for the provinces of Hubei, Jiangxi, and Anhui through the control of their major cities. Zeng's forces gained ascendancy in this region only after the suicidal massacre in the Taiping capital, and Shi Dakai's defection with over 200,000 seasoned fighters in the middle of 1857. Thereafter, though there was still much seesawing of cities changing hands between the rebel and the government side, Zeng's strategy of depriving the Taiping of the wealth and supplies from these provinces began to bear fruit after he seized Anqing from the Taiping permanently, after a three-year effort late in 1861. Around this time, the Taiping lost one of its two remaining best commanders, its Heroic King, Chen Yucheng. Chen was about to launch another Northern Expedition, when he was betrayed by one of his subordinates, who delivered him to a Qing general. Chen's elimination made the task of recovering the rest of Anhui, and the drive to Nanjing, much easier for the Xiang Army. When Li Xiucheng's plan of expansion to exploit the rich regions east of Nanjing all the way to the coastal cities of Shanghai, Ningbo and Hangzhou floundered, precipitating the entry of the British and the French on the Qing side in the civil war, the situation for the Taiping became critical. In the Spring of 1862, Zeng was able to make a comprehensive plan of tightening the noose around the Taiping capital. The troops under the command of his brother, Zeng Guoquan, closed in on it from the west, Zuo Zongtang from the south, and Li Hongzhang from the east, as well as some other forces, all under his unified command. Nanjing fell on 19 July 1864, after two years of siege by Zeng Guoquan's forces, who then swept through the city, killing, looting, and setting fire to palaces and houses, and filling the streets with corpses and piles of rubble.

Before the fall of the Heavenly Capital, Hong Xiuquan died of an unknown cause on 1 June 1864, at age fifty-one, after reigning thirteen and a half years. His last decree stated that the 'time has come for the Heavenly King to go to Heaven to petition the Heavenly Father and Heavenly Elder Brother to preserve the Heavenly Capital'. Six months before his death Li Xiucheng counselled evacuation from Nanjing to a more defensible place, but Hong would have none of it. Seeing the desperate shortage of food in the city, Li begged Hong to let the people leave, but Hong balked at the suggestion, and ordered his people to live on 'sweet dew' (grass or weeds), emulating the ancient Israelites living on manna from Heaven in the desert. Li nevertheless let as many leave as possible. After the fall of the Nanjing, Li gathered Hong's three sons, one of whom was the sixteen-year-old Junior Lord, Hong's heir, and a group of Taiping dignitaries and soldiers, all disguised as Qing soldiers, to find a way out of the city. When night fell, they slipped out with their horses through a broken section of the wall.

Their escape was soon discovered, and Zeng sent a party to pursue them. Because Li had exchanged his own excellent mount for the decrepit horse of the Junior Lord, he got left behind. After dismounting from his weary horse, he sheltered himself in a ruined temple. Before long he was found by some villagers, who delivered him to the government camp, hoping for rewards. On completing a 36,100-character confession, he was executed on Zeng Guofan's order on 7 August 1864. The Junior Lord's party, escorted by Hong Rengan, escaped temporarily. His group was captured three months later, after going through several provinces, seeking to meet up with other Taiping troops still operating in southern China. Although the young children in his party were spared, the Junior Lord and the other Taiping dignitaries were all executed. Before his death, Hong Rengan wrote several poems and confessional statements. At this point, there were still tens of thousands of Taiping combatants scattered in several southern provinces under various commanding officers. The Xiang Army pressed them hard: some units surrendered en masse, while a few generals fought doggedly on. The military campaign dragged on until the death of the last Taiping general in February 1866, when the Taiping Rebellion finally came to an end.

Consequences and legacies of the Taiping

Of the countless 'peasant' rebellions in China's long history, the Taiping rebellion was the biggest not only in China but also in the world. Because long periods of intensive fighting took place in the most populous region of China, the estimated death toll of twenty million is probably a very conservative figure. According to Chinese sources, the census figure for the total population of Jiangsu, Zhejiang, Anhui, and Jiangxi provinces was 136,308, 000 in 1850, but it was only 117,138,441 in 1865. Despite immigration into these depopulated provinces after the end of the rebellion, the population in this region did not recover even one hundred years after the cataclysmic event. Beside the loss of lives, the total economic cost to the people caught up in this destructive war was incalculable. The total military expenditure of the Qing in suppressing this rebellion was estimated to be over 200,000,000 taels, which was about five times its annual land tax revenue in the 1840s. It was a major catastrophe and tragedy for nineteenth century China.

Although the Qing dynasty survived - saved by the Chinese scholar-officials turned generals, and the new regional armies they created - power was no longer so heavily concentrated in the hands of the central government. The court made attempts to cut down or disband the regional armies soon after the fall of the Taiping, but it had then to reverse these acts and turn to Zeng Guofan, Li Hongzhang and Zuo Zongtang, and ask them to pacify the rising Nian (1851-1868) and Panthay (1856-1873) rebellions (see the following section) after the Manchu (Mongol) Banner forces again proved inadequate for this task. Able to control major military forces and having access to local sources of revenues from *Lijin* and the growing maritime customs, these powerful regional officials, though still loyal to the dynasty during the nineteenth century, represented a growing shift in the balance of power between the central government and the regional powerholders, in favour of the latter.

Although the scholar-generals were conservative Confucianists, reaffirming their attachment to the traditional state and culture, particularly after having experienced and put down the challenge of the Taiping heterodoxy, they were also modernizers, having witnessed at close quarters the power of the Western gunboats and artillery against the Taiping. Their 'self-strengthening' movement aimed at preserving China's traditional institutions and values, by the selective adoption of elements that appeared to account for the strength and wealth of the Western nations. They wanted a *fu* (wealthy) and *qiang* (strong) China without having to go through more wide-ranging reforms as Japan was doing, let alone wholesale modernization or Westernization. Their modernization projects, especially those in connection with Li Hongzhang, included building shipyards and armament factories to make modern steamships and weapons, sending a small number of students to Western countries to receive military and naval training, setting up a national telegraph system, and establishing capitalist enterprises with merchant management, particularly in spheres where modern foreign enterprises were undermining traditional Chinese economic activities, as well as some other initiatives. Late Qing reformist Confucian statesmen and scholars (Zhang Zhidong, Kang Youwei and Liang Qichao) utilized the concept of *tiyong* (essence-practical use) to characterize their circumscribed modernization as Chinese learning for essence, and Western learning for practical use.

The Taiping Rebellion further weakened the Qing regarding its capacity to deal with the foreign powers, particularly Britain and France. These nations took the opportunity, when the Qing was at a low point in its struggle against the Taiping, to wage the Second Opium War in 1856, and to extract further concessions from the Qing through the Treaty of Tianjin in 1858 and the Convention of Beijing in 1860 (as discussed earlier). Since the emperor and the Chinese scholar-officials looked upon the Taiping Rebellion as a 'disease of the heart or vital organs', but the Western encroachment as a 'disease of the skin', they chose to give way, and cooperate with these powers to fight the Taiping rather than make a strong stand against the foreign invaders. The Qing court was itself a liability as regards China's sovereignty and territorial and administrative integrity because it became a hostage to intimidation by Western diplomats, and succumbed all too readily to threats from Western gunboats and artillery. If the Qing had been as determined to fight the invaders from the West as it fought the Taiping, the court could have made a stand by withdrawing to the interior where gunboats could not reach, and doggedly fighting a prolonged land war if necessary. The cost of such a war and the difficulty of suppling a sizeable army so far away might have discouraged foreign aggression. Once such a seriously threatening rebellion got underway, the Qing had no spare capacity or breathing space to fend off the aggressors from overseas. Instead, the Qing became less resistant and more cooperative with the foreign powers.

Was the Taiping a revolutionary movement that bestowed valuable legacies, or inspired future generations of Chinese people? Apart from the novelty of Christianity, a theocracy presiding over a golden age of justice, purity, prosperity, and peace had ancient Chinese roots. The Yellow Turban Rebellion (184-205 CE) had preached a quasi-religious Taiping Dao (The Way of Great Peace) of Daoist inspiration to support a similar ideal world order, which they strove to establish. The organization of the Taiping military institution, which doubled as their civilian government, as well as their system of land tenure - which existed only on paper - were derived from the leaders' knowledge of history and certain classical literature. But borrowing from the past hardly befits a revolutionary movement.

Those who found the Taiping ideal of equality among men attractive might have become disillusioned, considering the carefully structured hierarchy in their officialdom, which was elevated high above those whom they governed. Theirs was by no means a classless society. However, women did fare better under Taiping rule, for they were allowed to take the civil service examination, hold office, bear arms, and have the same share of land as men. Moreover, foot binding was not allowed. Because the cause failed, these improvements did not become a permanent legacy under the Qing. It might have inspired future movements to improve the position of women in China. But their practice of polygamy, though only those with kingly rank were entitled to this privilege, was a step backward. By limiting commercial activities to take place outside the gates of their cities, they turned their cities into forts. This seemed another backward step, though the ideology of the Taiping was more positive towards merchants and trade than the entrenched Confucian attitude on this subject. Their abolition of private property was a radical communistic type of experiment, but the people's communes in Maoist China, where rural families pooled their land and other resources, and shared the fruits of their labour, arose out of different needs and circumstances. These experiments were ephemeral. As institutions, they had neither historical roots, nor popular appeal in China. Hong Rengan's modernizing reforms were mostly unimplemented plans on paper, better known to historians than politicians or reformers.

It was nothing new to whip up anti-Manchu ethnic sentiment of the Hans, considering that the Triad society was doing the same. However, Hong Xiuquan's stance against Manchu rule apparently became transformed into the nationalism of the great Chinese patriot and revolutionary leader, Sun Yatsen (1866-1924), who came from the same region in Guangdong province as Hong. As a young boy, Sun proclaimed himself as Hong Xiuquan the Second.

Although the Taiping religion incorporated important elements of Christian beliefs and practices, it was significantly different from mainstream Christianity in the West as represented by Roman Catholicism and Protestantism. Since converting the Chinese to Christianity had been such an uphill battle, some Western missionaries and Christians in China welcomed the Taiping movement as a rare opportunity to Christianize China at a stroke. This was particularly the case during its initial successful phase between 1853 and 1855. Many wrote favourably about the Taiping, and published articles and books, as well as letters to the North China Herald, a treaty port press, to arouse the sympathy of their countrymen and the support of their governments for the Taiping cause, despite the 'errors' they had discovered in the Taiping Christianity.

On closer scrutiny, during and after the 1860s, though a few continued to think well of the Taiping, some of those who had been formerly pro-Taiping expressed their disappointment, and new voices hostile to the movement came to the fore. Some Westerners suspected that the leaders of the Taiping were imposters, and their 'fake religion' was used by the leaders to further their political ambition to overthrow the Manchu dynasty, and perhaps to gain foreign sympathy as well. Hong's claim to be God's son and the younger brother of Jesus, and Yang's claim of speaking for God when he was possessed by the Holy Ghost, appeared shockingly blasphemous to these people. They also found Hong's presumption of being the sovereign of all nations deeply offensive. When the Western powers abandoned their neutrality and joined the Qing to attack the Taiping, they had the blessings of many of their missionaries.

Despite having lost many foreign sympathizers, the Taiping had steadfast foreign advocates and friends, even after the movement was crushed. Notable among these were Thomas T. Meadows, a translator of the British Foreign Service, and August Lindley. Meadows' *The Chinese and Their Rebellions*, and Lindley's writings remain valuable sources for those interested in accounts which had first-hand connection and involvement with the movement.

Because the movement failed, China did not become transformed into a Christian nation, however imperfect Taiping Christianity may have seemed from the point of view of orthodox Western Christian establishments. There was yet another negative legacy of this movement after its suppression during the late Qing. As a heterodox religion hated by the Qing officials and the gentry, the Christianity of the Taiping, though more Protestant than Catholic, was ironically linked in the minds of these people with Catholicism, because it was translated into Chinese as *Tian Zhu Jiao* (Heavenly Lord Sect). Although the Qing government was forced officially to tolerate and legalize the Catholic Church and its missionary activities, not just at the treaty ports but all over China, after its treaties with France in 1844 and 1858, the Qing authorities were not able to contain public fury whipped up by Chinese conservatives, which sometimes led to persecution against French Catholic missionaries and Chinese Catholics, with dire consequences.

Jumping forward into our own era, although the Communist government of China is officially atheist, it has settled on a policy of permitting the people of China, whether as members of the Han majority or of an ethnic minority, to believe and practice major religious faiths, such as Buddhism (including the Tibetan Lamaist variety of Buddhism), Daoism, Christianity, including Roman Catholicism, Protestantism, and the Eastern Orthodox variety, Judaism, Hinduism, and Islam. The Chinese authorities seem to find the mainstream orthodox expressions of these faiths easier to accommodate than new offshoots like the more fundamentalist Christian 'house churches'. The Falun Gong was considered subversive, because it resembles the kind of heterodox underground religions, like the White Lotus Sect, the Triads or the Heaven and Earth Society, and the Taiping Christianity, which had tended to destabilize the existing social or political order in China during the last two thousand years. However, contemporary left-wing historians writing from mainland China and Hong Kong find the Taiping praiseworthy, because they regard the movement as a glorious peasant revolution that, irrespective of its failure, left a commendable anti-feudal and anti-imperialist legacy in the history of China.

Other Uprisings: the Nian and Panthay rebellions

Around the time of the Taiping rebellion the Qing was threatened by other rebellions, of which the three most serious will be discussed here. The first was the Nian Rebellion (1851-1868) that erupted in Northern China in the same year as the Taiping declared the establishment of their Heavenly Kingdom, although the two movements were not connected at that point. Unlike the Taiping, the Nian had no religious affiliation, socio-economic ideology, strategic goal, or political organization. They did not have a unified command until 1856, when the separate groups elected a leader to coordinate their forces to strengthen themselves against the Qing. Their origin could be traced back to the 1790s, to groups of bandits roaming in the poverty-stricken border region of several provinces lying north of the flood-prone Huai River. Historically, marshy junctions of provinces were favourite hideouts of outlaws, because they were a no-man's land in terms of law enforcement. Their name, Nian, is likely to have been derived from the torches made from twisted paper, which they carried to rob people at night. Most of them resorted to banditry out of severe economic distress. The late Qing administrative decline led to neglect on flood control work along the Huai and the Yellow rivers, a situation that resulted in more frequent flooding, and crises in the economic situation and physical survival of the people of the areas concerned. By the 1850s, small bands of bandits had coalesced into large armies that rose up in rebellion against the Qing. In 1855, the rebel forces were boosted by the victims of the great flood brought about by the Yellow River breaking its dikes around Kaifeng, and dramatically changing its course of exit into the sea from south to north.

Although the total number of seasoned Nian warriors was not large, ranging from around 30,000 to 50,000, their mobile armies of mixed infantry and cavalry forces, equipped with long spears, swords, and some firearms, wrought havoc by raiding and looting the towns and villages over large, populated areas between Beijing and Nanjing. Many threatened villages fortified themselves and organized militias for self-defence. The Nian also established fortified villages to retreat into after their foraging activities. The united Nian rebels were more than a match for the regular Qing forces sent against them. They developed a kind of guerrilla warfare, whereby they would lead their enemy on a long chase, sometimes over several provinces, and then induce their pursuers to split up into smaller units in some difficult terrain, where they would regroup and pick off their exhausted and divided opponents one unit at a time with overwhelming forces. The Qing found the mobility and guerrilla tactics of the Nian very difficult to deal with. In 1860 when Sengge Rinchen took over the suppression of this rebellion, his formidable Manchu and Mongol cavalry struck hard at the rebels and had the upper hand for a few years. From around this time, the Nian and the Taiping rebels, being both pressed hard by the Qing, sometimes joined forces with one another to fight against their common enemy.

In 1865, even Sengge Rinchen and his cavalry were brought down; he himself and most of his men were killed, and five thousand of his company's horses were captured by the Nian using their guerrilla strategy.

After Sengge Rinchen's death, the court ordered Zeng Guofan, the victor against the Taiping, to suppress the Nian. Because he had been obliged, by the jealousy of the Manchu court, to disband the best of his Xiang Army, Zeng had to use the Huai (or Anhui) Army, which had been recruited and trained by Li Hongzhang, whose native province was Anhui (also known as Huai because this river ran across the north of the province). Zeng gave this job to Li in 1886, after he found that, among many obstacles that stood in his way to success, perhaps the most serious was the difficulty of commanding the loyalty of the officers of the Huai Army. Li also found it hard to pin down and destroy the Nian rebels, who 'moved as freely as mercury' over a large area. Being reduced to waging a slow and patient war of attrition, and by making artillery, guns, and gunboats purchased from the West available to his loyal, well-paid, and well-equipped force, Li was able to overpower the Nian survivors, after having driven them to Shandong, and to bring the rebellion to an end in August 1688.

The two other major upheavals involved Muslims in China's southwest and northwest. The Muslims were a major group of ethnic minorities in China. Those in the southwest grew in number during the Mongol Yuan dynasty and settled in the province of Yunnan. There were also large Muslim settlements in China's northwest, spreading over the provinces of Gansu, Shaanxi, Qinghai, Ningxia, and Xinjiang. These were descendants of mixed marriages between the Chinese and merchants of Islamic faiths, mostly Arabs and Persians, who came to China over the Silk Road through the Central Asian land routes as early as the Tang (618-907 CE). Some also came by sea and settled in some of the coastal cities in south China. It was these Central Asians who brought Islam to China. To their secular Chinese neighbours, these Muslims were known as Hui people, many of whom shared a common surname, Ma. A separate group of ethnic minority Muslims, who settled mainly in Xinjian, were the Uighurs, a Turkish people whose military exploits were well-known in the Tang.

Qing administrative decline and economic distress also affected these ethnic minority communities in the southwest and northwest of China. As ethnic minorities, they had the additional grievance of being discriminated against by the Sino-Manchu authorities. In 1856, the smouldering resentment of the Muslims in Yunnan against the heavy burdens of land taxes and other exactions by the Qing, burst into flames of revolt after clashing violently with the Chinese gentry and officials over rights to the exploitation of gold mines. This was known as the Panthay rebellion (1856-1873). Many rallied to the standard of Du Wenxiu (1823-1872), a local leader of the insurrection, who proclaimed himself as Sultan Suleyman of the Kingdom of the Pacified South (*Pingnan Guo*), with Dali as its capital, after his army captured many cities and overran half the province of Yunnan.

Du's ethnically inclusive regime, which included Chinese and Li minorities holding top level military posts, had the support of the people of Yunnan across ethnic lines. It was also popular because the government was actively trying to develop the economy of Yunnan. After several military setbacks at the hands of Du's forces, the Qing tried to induce him to surrender, which he refused to do. Du sent overtures to Shi Dakai when the Taiping general's forces marched into southwest China, but logistic difficulties prevented them from joining together to fight the Qing. After the fall of Shi and the Taiping, the Qing was able to muster greater forces against Du, whose revolt came to an end after the fall of Dali in 1872.

The Muslim Dungan Revolt in northwest China (1862-1873) was not connected with the turmoil in Yunnan; rather, it was galvanized by the northward intrusion of a Taiping-Nian army in 1862 into Shaanxi, which was already a tinderbox of ethnic tension between the Chinese and the Muslim communities. The revolt spread to Gansu, Ningxia, Qinghai, Xinjiang, and Gansu, where the Muslim leaders of insurrections, among whom was the revered religious teacher, Ma Hualong (1810-1871), had built hundreds of forts surrounded by ditches to defend their communities. The Qing had no effective measures, military or political, to restore order among these turbulent Muslims, until Zuo Zongtang, a meritorious veteran of the wars against the Taiping and the Nian, was given the task of their suppression in 1868.

Zuo planned his military campaign carefully for the long haul, after obtaining valuable advice from Lin Zexu (who as the reader may recall had been exiled to Xinjiang for several years after he had triggered the Opium War with the burning of opium), and another scholar, who had served Lin and had settled in the northwest. Zuo was also able to tap into the knowledge he had acquired in China's northwest, and on farming through an earlier association. Because of the difficulty of obtaining supplies over the long distance to the troubled areas, Zuo planted crops and established military farms to supply his soldiers with food and their horses with fodder, in addition to building an arsenal in the city of Lanzhou to produce arms for his well-trained soldiers. When he was ready, he applied his well-laid plan to the toughest of the four groups of rebels, who were those under Ma Hualong. After Ma's base at Jinjibao was put under siege for sixteen months, Ma was forced by mass starvation to surrender. To strike terror into the hearts of other rebel leaders, Ma Hualong and his son were punished by being subjected to the cruel 'death by a thousand cuts' form of execution, and many of his top aides were also put to death, while his followers were settled elsewhere, 'never to return'. Zuo applied similar tactics successfully to all the other Muslim rebel groups except those in Xinjiang, and by 1873, apart from a unit of about 2,000 who escaped further west with their families to Kyrgyzstan, the remaining rebels either surrendered or lost their lives.

After Zuo's victorious campaigns, there were still certain pockets of Xinjiang outside Qing control. Several Muslim Khans of this region had rebelled against the Qing periodically since the mid-1820s. Jahangir Khoja (?1788-1828), whose forebears had ruled Kashgar before the Manchu conquest, led an army from Kokand, a Khanate west of the border of Xinjiang, to invade this and other oasis cities in western Xinjiang in 1827. The Qing managed to subdue Jahangir's invasion and the insurrections in 1847 and 1857.

During the 1860s, several ambitious local leaders, taking advantage of Qing preoccupation with other rebellions, declared themselves kings or sovereigns of the pockets of territory under their control, in defiance of the Qing. To strengthen his rule, the 'king' of Kashgar asked the neighbouring state of Kokand for military support. In 1865, Yaqub Beg (1820-1877), a princely relative of the ruler of Kokand, came with an army which, by 1870, occupied all of southern and a part of northern Xinjiang, where he ruled as an independent Khanate. Since both Russia and Britain were interested in expanding territorially into this region, both recognized Beg's regime to weaken the position of the Qing. In 1871, Russia invaded Ili in northern Xinjiang, and signed a commercial treaty with Beg's government the following year. In 1873, in competition with Russia, Britain sent an embassy of 300 strongmen to Kashgar, with gifts of military weapons, such as guns and small cannons, and concluded a treaty with this regime.

Beg's rule was not popular with the local people. He and his supporters imposed Central Asian institutions on this region, whereby they concentrated landholding in the hands of the ruling elites, who extracted taxes and labour services from their subjects at will, without written regulations. They also imposed Sharia law, enforced by Islamic courts and religious officials, who were at liberty to whip women who did not veil their faces on the street, and to punish severely those who infringed upon any religious regulations in the slightest way. Non-Muslims who refused to convert to Islam were put to death. Many rose up in revolt against this harsh regime and waited anxiously for rescue to come from the Qing.

At the Qing court, which was trying to deal with the Japanese invasion of Taiwan in 1874 (to be discussed later), there was a heated debate on whether the government should concentrate its limited financial and military resources on defending the east coast or on the far northwest. Li Hongzhang, who was the most powerful Chinese official after the death of Zeng Guofan in 1872, argued strongly in favour of defending the coast, where he had a strong power base after building a fleet of modern gunboats and a naval force at Fuzhou. He was even prepared to abandon Xinjiang. Zuo Zongtang pleaded for retrieving Xinjiang from the aggressor, and he persuaded the court to secure a foreign loan with the help of the Inspector General of MCS, Robert Hart, for defraying the military cost. In 1875, Zuo was authorized by the court to proceed with a military campaign against Beg. On his arrival in Xinjiang, the Uighurs and other ethnic communities greeted him with offerings of food and horses. Zuo's forces repeatedly defeated Beg, who killed himself in 1877. By 1878, Zuo had recovered all of Xinjiang apart from Ili, which had been under Russian occupation since 1781.

After bringing peace to Xinjiang, Zuo tried to reorganize government administration, reform the system of taxation, and retore the economic health of this war-ravaged region. To the returning refugees, he provided food, seeds, and animals, to get agricultural production going. He also developed civilian and military agricultural colonies in Xinjiang. In 1884, the Qing court adopted Zuo's proposal to make Xinjiang a province, providing it with regular civilian administration. Subsequently, the Qing introduced many projects for developing the education, communication, and the economy of this new province, which is now known as the Xinjiang Uyghur Autonomous Region (XUAR).

References for the Qing will be found at the end of chapter 7.

Chapter 7

The Depredation of China by the Imperial Powers and Japan: The Fall of the Qing

Increasing Encroachments on China by the Imperial Powers

International settlements and foreign residents

The suppression of the rebellions brought the Qing a decade of internal peace, but the operation of the unequal treaty system which lasted one hundred years, from 1842 to 1943, and the endless intrusive activities and demands from the foreign powers, did not allow China to enjoy tranquillity for long. The period from 1842 to the early 1870s was a time when the western commercial and cultural interests predominated, and Britain, France, and America strove to enlarge the treaty provisions, to ensure their full enforcement, and if possible to enjoy the rights they had extracted from the Qing in a peaceful environment. The West's cultural penetration was mainly associated with the activities of the Protestant and Catholic missionaries, who did not limit their proselytizing to the treaty ports. International settlements began to be built, mostly on the waterfronts of various treaty ports, where the consular officials of each of the foreign treaty powers governed their own resident nationals, who were largely composed of merchants and missionaries. The foreign officials of the Qing MCS were also prominent members of the foreign society at the treaty ports.

As a treaty port, Canton (Guangzhou), to which all foreign maritime trade had once been confined, did not thrive, because the locals there remained hostile to foreigners and their commerce for many years after the Opium War. Instead, Shanghai rose to take its place and grew rapidly to become the most important entrepôt in China. In 1844 44 foreign ships had entered Shanghai, but in a little over ten years the number had grown to 437 in 1855. The Anglo-American Shanghai International Settlement, with its own elected Municipal Council, and the French Concession, with its European architecture and Western way of life, resembled European colonial enclaves elsewhere in the world. The foreigners kept themselves socially apart, while relying on the services of the locals, such as shopkeepers, servants, and business agents to act as an interface between them and the world of the 'natives'. The residents in these foreign concessions were not limited to the British, Americans, and French. In fact, people of many different European nationalities settled there, as well as others, among whom were Canadians, Australians, South Africans, and Jews of various nationalities.

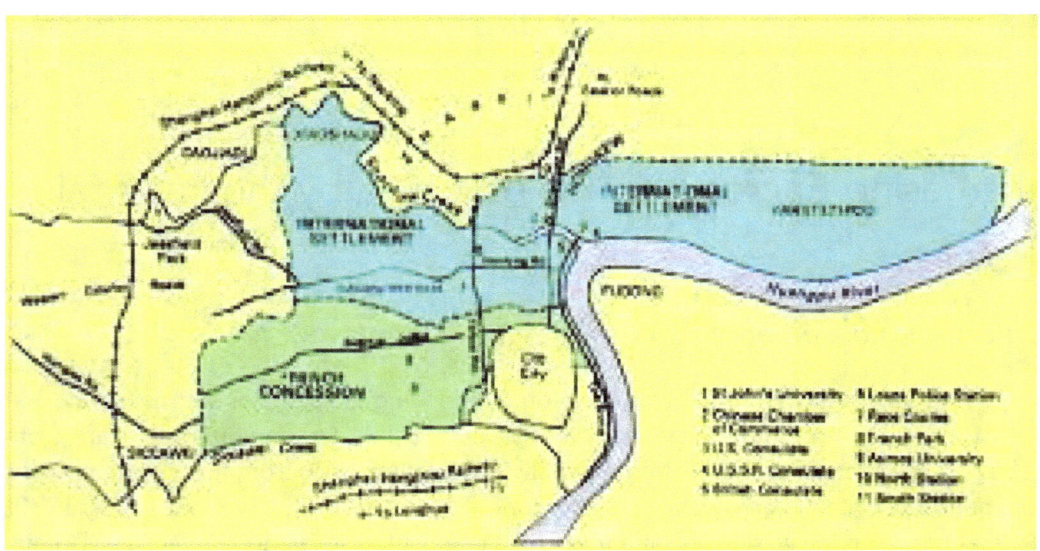

The international settlements and the French concession in Shanghai c. 1930
(*The Asia-Pacific Journal*: retrieved on 30 November 2023 from
chttps://apjjf.org/-Jeff-Wasserstrom/2980/article.html)

Mizrahi Jewish traders from Iraq and British India arrived in Shanghai soon after it became a treaty port, and before long a thriving Jewish community came into being there. Some, like the Sassoons and the Kadooris, made fortunes by developing their businesses and they joined the international social upper crust; others served their community as teachers, doctors, shopkeepers and so on. Because of its openness to immigration, Shanghai became a safe haven where Jewish people suffering persecution elsewhere could freely enter without visas or other troublesome documentation. In the 1900s, many Jews fleeing pogroms in Russian found shelter in Shanghai. There were many Jews among the 8,000 or so Russians who settled in the French Concession after the Russian Revolution of 1917. From the early 1930s to 1941, around 20,000 Jewish refugees poured into Shanghai from Austria, Poland, and Nazi Germany, some with the helped of 'protective' passports issued by Chinese diplomats. The number of Jews who came to Shanghai during the Holocaust was equal to the total who emigrated to all the British Commonwealth countries combined. Although some of these refugees emigrated to America or Australia, most of them stayed in Shanghai. In 1943, the Japanese occupation army in Shanghai moved the Jews into a ghetto in the Hongkou district, where many were accommodated in group homes known as 'Little Vienna'. The people there survived the war, despite the scarcity of food and the lack of amenities. After World War II, during the Chinese Civil War (1945-1949), or shortly after the establishment of the People's Republic of China, most of the Jews of Shanghai relocated themselves either to the West or to the state of Israel, which they helped to found.

In terms of numbers, the Chinese were the largest group in both the International Settlements and the French Concession, where the best residential and retail properties lay, but they had no say in running these foreign- controlled enclaves. There were also a significant number of foreigners in Shanghai not residing in the international concessions. A new type of Chinese business agent, known as compradors, who specialized in foreign commerce, emerged in Shanghai and the other treaty ports. From the middle of the 1840s, starting with a couple of hundred thousand residents living in the Chinese walled city, and a hundred or so foreigners outside it, by 1930 Shanghai had grown into a major modern metropolis of over 3 million people, including nearly 50,000 foreigners of many different nationalities.

Early Western economic impact

Imports entered China through the treaty ports, especially Shanghai, at a rate of duty fixed at 5% of the value of the goods, for all products. They incurred a transit tax of 2% when passing into the interior. Of a large variety of items imported, those of the highest value were opium, cotton textiles, and yarn. During the five years from 1870 to 1874, the total imported goods had an annual average value of 68,869,000 Hong Kong Taels (HKT), of which opium accounted for 25,987,000 HKT (39.2%), and cotton textiles and yarn for 21,451,000 HKT (32.2%). Twenty years later, in 1894, total imports reached 144,233,000 HKT, an increase of 109%. The value of opium imported, though still a high figure at 29,947,000 HKT, decreased to 21.1% of the total. The import of cotton textiles and yarn increased to 49,653000 HKT, or 35.3% of the total. The damage done by the importation of opium to China has already been discussed. The expansion of the Chinese markets for cotton yarn and textiles from Britain and American was something new, for China had been self-sufficient using textiles produced by cottage industries in peoples' homes, or in small workshops or factories. This new development was partly connected with the industrial revolution of the textile industry in these countries, where machine production of textiles in modern factories rendered the end-products cheaper than the Chinese versions traditionally made by hand. Imports were also helped by the low import duty and transit dues. Spinning and weaving were long-established rural handicraft industries, the income from which formed an important part of the income of the farming families. The cheap imports damaged the fragile economy of the Chinese countryside and caused hardship. Other machine-made cheap imports led to unemployment of those engaged in manual fabrication of those products. Another rural industry that suffered was the production of oil and lamps for lighting. This was destroyed by the widespread use of imported kerosene, and lamps from America. All these imports increased rural impoverishment.

The most important Chinese exports were tea and raw silk. The demand for tea from China continued to decrease from the 1890s, due to the increasing export of Indian tea from the maturing tea plantations established under British rule. The export of Chinese silk was also hit by competition from Japan and France, where more modern methods were used in the processing of silk filaments. Although the export of Chinese raw materials and agricultural or craft products increased in volume over the years, they were not a significant source of enrichment for the Chinese, because their added values were low. Furthermore, their export was controlled by foreign firms, which forced the prices of these products down so low as to leave very little margin for the producers. The demands of international markets induced some Chinese farmers to switch to cash crops like tobacco and cotton instead of food crops. With greater exposure to the world market, the Chinese producers for export also became more vulnerable to the upswings and downturns of the globalized marketplace.

From the early 1860s, both the British and the Americans went into the business of transporting passengers and goods on the inland rivers and along the seacoast of China using modern steamships. The foreign companies involved soon monopolized this lucrative line of business. This development took away the livelihood of many Chinese boatmen and owners of junks specializing in this type of carrying trade, and it also hindered the emergence of a modern Chinese steamship business. The Chinese economy suffered under the British-led 'imperialism of free trade', with the Chinese participants becoming passive victims rather than active stakeholders under an economic regime which had hardly been designed for the benefit of the Chinese people. The Chinese government had compromised its nation's sovereignty and signed away its right to determine even its own import and export tariff rate. Its people could not rely on their government to protect them from foreign exploitation.

This initial contact with the Western powers was just a foretaste of worse things to come. During the second half of the nineteenth century, as industrialization gathered pace among the Western nations and in a rapidly rising Japan, the gap between the economic and military strength of these imperialist nations and China grew alarmingly large. Their initial goal of controlling Chinese trade had shifted to exploiting China's natural resources and its cheap labour, and to developing and controlling its modern industries, railways, and financial markets. They also sought to make colonies out of the independent countries on China's periphery, which had been within China's political and cultural sphere of influence for centuries past. Ultimately, they aimed to carve up China into their separate spheres of influence, as a prelude to outright colonial domination of China.

The European Colonization of China's Tributary States

The Sino-French war over Vietnam (1883-85)

Unlike Britain, France's interest in China had been territorial and cultural (in connection with spreading Catholicism) rather than commercial. Instead of going straight for a piece of China in full view of other predatory nations also interested in China, it was easier for France to begin the process by threatening the territory of a smaller country at China's border. During the 1850s, France sent an army to Annam (Trung Ky) in the south of Vietnam, a Qing tributary. Since the Qing was preoccupied with fighting for its own survival against the Taiping, it was in no position to help Vietnam. Later, in 1862, France forced Vietnam to sign the Treaty of Saigon that effectively turned the southern part of Vietnam into a French colony. When France invaded Hanoi in the north in 1873, the king of Vietnam invited Liu Yongfu, who commanded the Black Flags, a remnant Taiping army active on the border between Vietnam and China, to join his own force to fight the French. This mixed force managed to hold the French invaders at bay and to kill their commanding officer, Francis Garnier. In 1882, the French government under Jules Ferry, pursuing more strongly the policy of colonial expansion in Vietnam, sent reinforcements and captured Hanoi. The king once more asked Liu for help and the French were again defeated. The French increased their force further and captured Thuân An. After forcing Vietnam to sign the Treaty of Hué (1883), and the later renewed Patenôtre Treaty (Treaty of Protectorate), making Vietnam a French protectorate, the French asked the Qing to recognize French rule of Vietnam, and withdraw the Qing army stationed in the north of the country.

At the Qing court, there was a debate between a party for war, whose leading spokesman was Zuo Zongtang, and another for peace, headed by Li Hongzhang. Recalling the time before the Opium War forty-one years previously, the present court, with Emperor Guangxu (r. 1875-1908) on the throne and with his aunt the Dowager Empress Cixi as the power behind the throne, wavered between the two policies. An army was sent from the provinces bordering Vietnam, but the commanders were told to be passive and not to make any move 'to give the French a handle', meaning not to provoke the French or give them an excuse to open hostilities. At the same time, Li Hongzhang was instructed to conduct peace negotiations with the French. This 'softly, softly' approach only encouraged the French to overrun the north of Vietnam in 1884, occupying the Red River Delta and advancing towards the Chinese border to attack the Qing army stationed in north Vietnam. This started the Sino-French War of 1884-85. The timid Qing court was again reduced to the familiar peace-at-any-price stance. In April 1884, Li hastened to sign a brief Sino-French Treaty in Tianjin. The terms required China to accept the French demands to agree to all existing treaties as well as any future treaties between France and Vietnam; to withdraw the Qing force from the north of Vietnam; and to open certain trading posts between Vietnam and China.

The French, however, were not ready for peace, for they wanted to weaken the Qing even further. They sought an excuse to drive home the lesson that the modern French naval force could seriously damage Qing China. In June 1884, the French army reached the spot where the Qing garrison was stationed in north Vietnam and issued an ultimatum to the Qing to withdraw within three days. The Qing representative explained that the order to withdraw had not yet been received from the court. The French killed the Qing representative and bombarded the Qing camp with their artillery. Forced to strike back, the Qing garrison fought strongly against the French force, which had to retreat.

The French immediately accused the Qing of breaking the new treaty, and moved their fleet to the Chinese coast, threatening Zhejiang Province, Taiwan, and especially Fuzhou, the capital of Fujian. Located at the port of Mawei in Fuzhou was a modern shipyard, built as a part of its programme of modernization by the financially strained Qing government using what precious resources it could command. The officers of the Chinese fleet, alarmed by the sight of the French fleet sailing straight into the Chinese naval base at Mawei, begged for permission to raise anchor and to prepare for action. The Qing court, desperate for the success of the peace negotiations then taking place in Shanghai, commanded all coastal defence forces to remain where they were and wait, and not make the first move. The officers of the modern fleet at Mawei were ordered not to raise anchor, and they were strictly forbidden to be the first to use their artillery. When the commander of the French fleet notified these officials that his force was going to attack, they had still made no preparations even to defend their own fleet. Instead, they asked the French commander to postpone the attack till the next day, but their request was refused. When the French started to bombard the Chinese fleet, which had prepared itself neither for war nor for self-defence, these senior officials fled. The remaining officers and men of the Chinese fleet fought bravely, but to no avail. Some of the ships were sunk even before they were able to raise anchor, and within half of an hour the entire Chinese modern fleet at Mawei was destroyed. Then the French proceeded to demolish the modern Chinese shipyard and coastal defensive positions at Mawei. At this point, the Qing court had no option but to declare war against the French. Outraged by the French invasion, Chinese people stormed and destroyed French churches along the coasts, overseas Chinese contributed money, and workers called a strike in Hong Kong.

The French success with their naval bombardment at Mawei was not matched by their military operations elsewhere, particularly on land. They met setbacks in Taiwan, Zhejiang, and especially when they invaded a border pass in Guangxi from Vietnam. The Qing troops guarding the pass, led by a seventy-year-old veteran commander, scored a major victory against the French. This disastrous defeat apparently brought down the government of French Prime Minister Jules Ferry. The Qing court, rather than taking advantage of the military success and the confusion in the French capital to take a strong stance, continued to pursue a pro-capitulation policy, but in the face of opposition from some high civil and military officials. Shortly after the armistice agreement signed in Paris on behalf of the Qing government by Robert Hart's London agent, James Duncan Campbell, Li Hongzhang concluded a new unequal treaty with the French Ambassador in Tianjin, the Treaty of Tientsin, in June 1885. The Treaty of Tientsin confirmed the main provisions of the brief Sino-French Treaty signed in 1884, in which the Qing had agreed to the French colonial rule of Vietnam, and the opening of trading posts on the border between Vietnam and certain Chinese provinces. In return, the French agreed to evacuate from certain ports which they occupied in Taiwan. As the powers were competing over the right to invest in building railroads and open mines in China during the closing decades of the nineteenth century, this treaty contained many details of French demands in connection with these new economic developments, as well as provisions on commerce and tariffs. With the French ruling Vietnam, the Qing government had to continually fend off French demands for more and more privileges, including altering the boundary of Vietnam at many points further into Qing China.

Britain, Burma, and China

The kingdom of Burma had a tributary relationship with the Qing, who expected a tribute-bearing embassy to come to Beijing once every ten years to pay homage to the emperor. This low frequency meant that Burma had not been very closely tied to the Qing. The small military skirmishes along the border between Burma and the Qing province of Yunnan were mostly local and easily contained, because both sides preferred peaceful co-existence.

Burma clashed with British-ruled India when Burma expanded westwards into Assam, which the British had deemed Indian. Having won three Anglo-Burmese Wars during the years 1824 to 1885, the British made Burma into a province of India in 1886. Subsequently, the Qing's *Zongli Yamen* signed a treaty with the British minister in China that endorsed the continuation of the decennial tribute embassy from Burma to the Qing court. The same treaty also called for the two sides to meet to discuss trade provisions, and to fix the previously amorphous boundary between China and Burma that had been left as a matter of jurisdictional history and precedents. The tribute embassy never arrived again from Burma, but there was a great deal of pressure from Britain on the Qing to develop trade, and a railroad, between China and Burma with a view to reaping economic benefits for the British. Over the years, during the repeated Sino-British negotiations over the boundary between Burma and China, the British persisted in trying to push this boundary deep into what had been regarded as Chinese territory, either by jurisdictional history or in terms of the natural separation of states by rivers or mountains. The British succeeded in gaining a large amount of Qing territory at the border of Burma in one negotiation, during which a weak Qing negotiator made huge unwarranted concessions to the British.

British and Russian Encroachment Onto Territory on China's borders

Qing China's efforts to retain Tibet

The British control of India also had a destabilizing effect on Tibet. As mentioned earlier, during the eighteenth century the Qing destroyed the power of the Dzungar Mongols who controlled Tibet, and after making this region secure, established a system of governance for it. An Amban was appointed to rule, on equal terms, with the Dalai Lama primarily, and to some extent with the Panchen Lama, the less powerful of the two lamas. Short of ruling Tibet as a province, Qing China had established an incontrovertible claim to sovereignty over Tibet. During the nineteenth century, both Britain and Russia, especially the former through its Indian colony, were interested in pulling Tibet away from a weakened Qing dynasty, which for its part tried to use diplomacy to fend off these aggressors and retain sovereignty over Tibet.

Trouble started when, in 1876, British India leased a part of Sikkim from its ruler for building a road from India through Bhutan for commercial purposes, without the permission of Tibet. The Thirteenth Dalai Lama and the people of Tibet felt aggrieved by this development, because both these countries were Tibetan dependencies in terms of tradition and history. Consequently, Tibet was preparing to go to war with British India. The Qing Amban tried in vain to restrain the Dalai Lama from taking military action. He was also unable to persuade the reluctant and hostile Tibetans to agree to opening Yadong and another city for trade with British India.

War broke out in 1887, and the Tibetan army, no match for the well-drilled troops equipped with modern firearms from British India, was defeated by the Anglo-Indian force, which, after having occupied all of Sikkim, was persuaded by the Qing Resident to stop the war and wait for the pending negotiations on border demarcation and other matters between the Qing and Britain. Negotiations soon took place between the Governor of India and the Qing Amban, supported by James Hart, a commissioner of customs and brother of the I. G. Robert Hart. In parallel with this, peace talks were also taking place between the Qing Ambassador in London and the British Foreign Office. Strongly desirous of peace and not powerful enough to oppose the British militarily, the Qing signed the first Indo-Tibetan Treaty in 1890 with the British, in which the Qing accepted the status of Sikkim as a British protectorate and fixed the boundary between it and Tibet largely on British terms. Later in 1893, the two sides agreed to extend the 1890 treaty to include a provision that opened Yatung across the border from India to British trade, and another that obliged Tibetan nomads grazing in Sikkim to observe British regulations. The Tibetans did not accept this treaty, largely because of the loss of Sikkim to British India. They were also incensed by the provisions that allowed the British to trade freely at Yatung, while they had to abide by British rules when grazing their livestock in Sikkim, where they had once been free to roam.

In 1903, Britain invaded Tibet over a boundary dispute. The Russians, who had approached the Dalai Lama previously, now saw an opportunity to advance their interest in Tibet. The Dalai Lama had been tricked into believing that the Russians, who had come to him dressed in the costume of Mongolian lamas, had the same faith as the Tibetans. He therefore decided to enlist Russian support against the British. The Russians, having trouble with Japan at that time, were not able to engage directly in any military conflict with the British from India. Instead, they sold arms to the Tibetans and encouraged them to fight the British themselves.

The Tibetans once more fought with an Anglo-Indian force, with the same result, partly because their army lacked discipline. The Qing Amban, unable to prevent the war, offered to negotiate with the opposition. The Dalai Lama, still unwilling to negotiate, had no plan other than empowering the lamas of his temple to conduct ritual cursing as a means of causing the deaths of the Anglo-Indian soldiers. As the enemies drew near, the Dalai Lama hurriedly escaped and went into hiding in the neighbouring province of Qinghai. Having occupied Lhasa, the British in 1905 forced the Tibetan official, who represented the Dalai Lama, to sign an agreement that compromised Tibet's authority to govern itself, as well as its relationship with the Qing. The Qing did not accept this agreement and sent officials to India to conduct new rounds of negotiations.

From 1905 to 1908, officials of the two sides met many times, in both India and Beijing, to thrash out additional terms to the Indo-Tibetan Treaty that would incorporate the vital interests and concerns of both. The British had new economic demands and a strong interest in keeping Russia out of Tibet, while China's greatest concern was the preservation of its own sovereignty over Tibet. The agreements that were arrived at during this period included, with some changes, the previous Indo-Tibetan treaties between Britain and China in 1900 and 1903, and the agreement Britain had forced on Tibet during its occupation of Lhasa in 1905. There was an important new provision in which the British agreed not to annex Tibetan territory or interfere in Tibet's political affairs. This was aimed at addressing the Sino-Tibetan concern regarding Britain's ultimate interest in Tibet. It also stated that China had agreed not to permit any other nation to meddle with Tibet politically or territorially; this was targeted especially at Russia. There were provisions for additional trading posts to be opened exclusively for British commerce. At those cities opened for British trade, Britain was to discuss with China regarding its interests in establishing telegraphic communications to India. China agreed to indemnify Britain the sum of 1,200,000 taels, on behalf of Tibet, for military expenses. China also agreed to buy back certain travel lodges, and a telegraph line between Gyantse (Jiangzi) in Tibet and the border of India. Even though the agreements did not explicitly state that Qing China possessed sovereignty over Tibet, the mere fact that Britain signed such agreements on Tibet with China implied admission of China's authority to govern Tibet, which was equivalent to acknowledging that China had sovereignty over Tibet. The detailed commercial provisions of the agreement in 1908 also bore the signature of a Tibetan high official, in addition to the Chinese and British negotiators.

These crises in Tibet prompted the Qing, during 1904-09, to change its existing governance of Tibet, and some areas in Sichuan where Tibetans had settled, to a well-tried policy known as *Gaitu Guiliu* (bureaucratization of native officers). This was a policy that replaced the local chiefs or petty rulers with roving officials appointed by the central government. During the eighteenth century, Emperor Yongzhen, and earlier rulers during the Ming, had used this method to govern many areas with large minority settlements. The introduction of this change stirred up many local powerholders concerned to resist it. The Qing sent a force from Sichuan that rapidly quelled the local rebellions. The Qing then allocated one million taels to open schools, build infrastructures such as roads and bridges, and support irrigation and farming as well as administrative reform in the pacified area, where a new province of Xikang was to come into being. However, a Tibetan invasion of Sichuan put this plan in jeopardy.

Qing officials believed that the Dalai Lama played a key role in fomenting the troubles in Sichuan. After his escape from Tibet in 1905, he remained in China until 1908, during which time he went to Ulan Bator (Ulaanbaator) in Mongolia, where there was a Russian Consulate, to seek Russian support. His disloyal behaviour did not prevent him from being received by the Qing court with the ceremony due to his station. During Dowager Empress Cixi's seventieth birthday celebration he was awarded a new honorific title, and received a gift of 10,000 taels, before being sent back to Tibet.

Having treated the Dalai Lama so courteously and benevolently, the Qing expected gratitude and cooperation from him. Instead, the court heard from officials in Sichuan that the Dalai Lama had bought Russian firearms and hired Russian instructors on his return journey, and they blamed the Dalai Lama for the Tibetan invasions in Sichuan. The Qing court ordered the Dalai Lama to withdraw the Tibetan troops. Receiving no satisfactory response from him, the Qing mustered a force of 3,000 elite troops from Sichuan to restore order. Early in 1909, when the Sichuan troops marched near Lhasa, the Dalai Lama fled to India under the cover of darkness. The series of Qing military campaigns in Tibet with its revitalized New Army from 1909 to 1911 was remarkably successful, conquering part of eastern Tibet and reorganizing it as the province of Xikang. Qing troops occupied Lhasa, removed certain uncooperative princes from power, and garrisoned several towns. They even marched to the borders of Nepal, Bhutan, and Sikkim to demonstrate their prowess to the British. The Qing moves, however, alienated the Dalai Lama, who had become better disposed towards the British. Relying on British support, the Dalai Lama adopted a more defiant and uncooperative attitude towards the Qing authorities after his return to Tibet in 1910.

Russian annexation of Qing territory

After the Russian expansion into the Far East during the middle of the seventeenth to the eighteenth century, the Russian empire and the Qing shared a land border traversing China from the northwest to the northeast, all the way to the sea. During the time of the Kangxi and Yongzhen emperors, equal treaties were made between the two countries on border demarcation from the far eastern end to Kiakhata, and on trade, as mentioned earlier. When the Qing military weakness was exposed during the Opium Wars, the Russians became very active and persistent in their drive to annex Chinese territory all along their common borders, not just in Tibet where the British presence curbed their ambition. Elsewhere, they were spectacularly successful at annexing Chinese territory. During the second half of the nineteenth century, Russia annexed approximately 1,510,000 square kilometres of territory from Qing China, using a combination of force, trickery and intimidation of the spineless Manchu court, and its negotiators, on the various Sino-Russian treaties and 'boundary surveys'.

In determining the borders between them, Russia and China did not use coordinates such as longitude and latitude to arrive at scientifically sound and accurate points and lines in fixing their boundaries: accuracy was not the point, especially from the Russian point of view. The Russian objective was to acquire as much land from their militarily weak neighbour as possible. To delineate borders the Russians favoured the use of mountain ranges, major rivers, and border checking points which were very infrequent, because this method enabled them to gain more Chinese land when a 'survey' or revision of certain sections of the boundary took place. In such an event, they might choose another mountain range or a river further into Chinese territory with non-existent border checking points, and demand to shift the new boundary there.

Starting in 1855, the governor of Russian Siberia revealed his ambition to encroach upon the Amur region of China's northeast. As a part of his plan to develop Siberia, he wished to use this river for transportation and to acquire the coastal land from the mouth of the Amur as a Russian possession. He therefore sailed along the Chinese Amur River with a fleet and demanded the Qing to give the left bank of the Amur River and its mouth to the sea to Russia. His demand was rejected. When the Qing court fled from Beijing to avoid the Anglo-French invading force, the Russians sent an army to occupy Sikhote-Alin, which lay south of the Amur River and east of the Ussuri River, a region that had been a part of the Chinese empire since the thirteenth century. This time they succeeded in forcing the Qing negotiator to sign the Treaty of Aigun, whereby the territory north of the Amur River and south of the Waixingan Ling (Stanovoy Mountains) was to be taken over by Russia, except for a tiny area of sixty-four settlements east of the river, where the Chinese retained jurisdiction and the right of permanent residence. This too was later taken away. The amount of territory involved here was 600,000 square kilometres. Another 400,000 square kilometres of territory at the east of the Ussuri River, including the island of Sakhalin, was to be under the jurisdiction of both Russia and China. The Qing court did not ratify this treaty.

In 1862, during the first year of Emperor Tongzhi's reign, the Russians wished to acquire territory in China's northwest, where Lake Balkhash and the land directly south of it had been a part of Qing China since the time of the Emperor Kangxi in the seventeenth century. The Russian negotiator Babukov insisted on demarcating the Sino-Russian boundary by internal customs checking points in Chinese towns, and two Chinese inland lakes. The talks broke down for a while because of Babukov's unreasonable bullying tactics. When the meetings resumed in 1864, Babukov threatened the Qing negotiator that the Russians were going to use force unless the Qing agreed to the boundary as drawn by the Russians. Soon afterwards, the Russians did send an army to occupy the Chinese territory they claimed. The broken-spirited Qing yielded once more to force, and concluded a Sino-Russian Northwest Boundary Survey Treaty that gave the Russians Lake Balkhash and the territory south and east of it, an area of 440, 000 square kilometres. This was not the only boundary survey treaty. Adding up the territory China ceded to Russia through the Treaty of Aigun, the Convention of Beijing, and a series of Sino-Russian boundary survey treaties up to 1881, the total reached the previously mentioned figure of 1,510,000 square kilometres. Later, Russia started to encroach deeply into China's northeast, until a rising Japan blocked her advance.

The Rise of Japan and Japanese Annexation of Qing Territory

The modernization of Japan

Tokugawa Japan was as isolationist as Qing China before the Opium War, with its doors closed to Western trade and other contacts, apart from a small window in Nagasaki opened for Dutch commerce from Indonesia. Although several Western powers were pushing at the gates of Japan before the middle of the nineteenth century, it was the United States that led the pack in opening Japan for trade. The credit for accomplishing this went to a skilful American negotiator, Commodore Matthew Perry, whose cause was assisted by an array of gunboats aptly positioned outside Edo (Tokyo), the capital of the Tokugawa Shogunate. Although there was an emperor residing in Kyoto from whom the Tokugawa Shoguns derived their authority, he had been reduced to a figurehead centuries before. Since 1600, the Tokugawa Shoguns gained supremacy over all other hereditary feudal lords of domains in the whole of Japan; their government in Edo dominated Japan. The Shogunate made very limited concessions in this first treaty with the Americans in 1854: the opening of two isolated ports for provisioning of American ships, a little trade, and the stationing of a consular representative at one of these ports, in addition to the most-favoured nation clause. Soon after, the Japanese also made similar treaties with the British, the Russians, and the Dutch.

Not satisfied with such small gains, Townsend Harris, the American Consul, succeeded in persuading the Japanese to sign a fuller commercial treaty with provisions similar to the Chinese unequal treaties. His task was made easier by the Japanese awareness of the Opium Wars, and the unequal treaties the Western powers had imposed on China by force. The Harris Treaty, signed in July 1858 between Japan and America, opened six Japanese ports for American trade, fixed low tariff rates for imports and exports, and granted extraterritoriality to the Americans. In addition, foreigners were to be allowed to reside in Edo and Osaka. Shortly afterwards, Japan signed similar treaties with Britain, Russia, France, and Holland. In contrast to China, the powers had not waged wars on Japan, nor had there been payments of heavy indemnities or cession of territories.

This forceful opening of their country to foreign trade by the Western powers sent a shock wave through the 265 autonomous Han or feudal domains of this insular island nation under the overlordship of the Tokugawa Shogunate. Although, unlike China, the Japanese did not suffer from the ruinous imports of opium and exports of silver, the foreign menace roused the well-educated and politically active segment of the population into a heightened state of awareness of the peril their nation was facing, and the need for action. This social segment included the samurai, the Japanese hereditary military caste, which was relatively large, accounting for about 6% of the population in Japan (as compared with about 1% for the scholar-gentry and officials). Even though the Japanese ships and weapons were obviously no match for those of the foreign intruders, there were still many trigger-happy Japanese extremists, who were itching to try to 'expel the foreigners' by force, to keep their homeland pure. Others saw that the only way to save Japan was to learn from the foreigners, to transform Japan into as strong and rich a country as one of the European powers. Caught between these two policy poles, the Shogunate government retreated into inaction.

Faced with the government paralysis, the more militant members of outlying domains invoked the emperor's authority to execute their own impractical but desperate agenda for driving out the foreigners by force, without the sanction of the Shogunate. Their actions led to retaliatory foreign naval bombardments of certain Japanese cities, and punitive financial reparations imposed on the Shogunate government. These sharp lessons persuaded patriotic and politically engaged samurais that the only way for their nation to escape the fate of China and other Asian countries was to learn the secret of Western wealth and strength and use Western technology to create a rich Japan with a strong military. It was significant that the samurai were not the top echelon of powerholders like the daimyos and the Shoguns, who had far greater vested interests in preserving the status quo. Before the samurais could implement policies to realize this vision for Japan as a whole, they needed a unified national government, not the decentralized domains governed by the daimyos and Shoguns. What better and speedier route towards forming a unified national government than to revive the ancient and yet still current imperial authority under the emperor?

With few exceptions, such as in countries with lawful democratic elections, existing rulers of governments do not normally give up their position and power without violent struggles. The Shoguns and their supporters fought for the survival of the old regime, but they were defeated in the civil wars that started in 1864, against forces marshalled by the visionary samurais from two outlying domains, Chūshū (Hagi) and Satsuma, who were bent on restoring the imperial government. The restoration of imperial rule in 1868 under Mutsuhito, better known in connection with his reign period as Emperor Meiji (r. 1867-1912), did not mean that Japan was to come under the personal rule of an autocratic emperor. The Japanese were accustomed to their emperor being a national symbol, a titular head of state, or the source of 'all legitimate authority', rather than the person actually exercising this authority. It did mean that a centralized national government was to replace the decentralized Shogunate, and that local prefectural administrative authorities were to take the place of the domains of the daimyos. It also meant the beginning of modernization of Japan with Emperor Meiji standing as the personal symbol of this movement. The emperor and his court were soon moved to Edo, renamed Tokyo, meaning 'Eastern Capital'. On its way to modernity, the Christendom of Europe had developed, through centuries of wars, into nation-states with their citizens imbued with a sense of self-conscious nationalism. The Meiji Reformation of 1868 was a most remarkable political revolution that accomplished within fifteen years, since the opening of Japan by Commodore Perry in 1854, the ending of centuries of feudalism and the beginning of Japan as a modern nation-state, its citizens consumed by a nationalism that must have been lying dormant.

With the authority of the imperial government behind them, the modernizers, who were mostly the young samurais responsible for the revolution, pushed through a series of major political, administrative, economic, financial, legal, and educational reforms with the goal of transforming Japan into a Western style military and industrial power. Having acquired important aspects of its high culture from ancient China, Meiji Japan, unlike Qing China, had no deep reservations about learning from the West. While the Chinese initially focused their modernization projects narrowly on the military and technology related to it, the Japanese adopted a more broadly receptive approach to things Western, because it was sometimes difficult to distinguish between what was idiosyncratically Western and the modern ideas and innovations that empowered the Western nations' military and economy. Despite the existence of Western models, and because of its different historical, cultural, and social conditions, Japan was launching itself into uncharted territory. Inevitably, engineering appropriate changes involved a process of trial and error, of discarding the unproductive, and of fine-tuning the more successful approaches. Fortunately for Japan, its new leaders were pragmatic, flexible, and goal-orientated rather than doctrinaire or ideological.

Without a tradition of democracy, there had not been significant pressure for popular participation in the political process in Japan until almost a decade after the Meiji restoration. Believing that representative government was a part of the secret of Western strength, the Japanese oligarchs introduced, in 1889 and 1890 respectively, a constitution and a twin-chamber parliament called the Diet (of Anglo-Saxon inspiration). From this beginning, Japan evolved into a democracy in its own fashion. To strengthen its military, the new government brought in universal conscription following the French example, established a separate Navy modelled on the British, and adopted a German-style independent chief of staff answerable only to the emperor. Its centralized modern education system was modelled on that of the French. The government was willing to pay a high price for the expertise of various foreign advisors before they had their own Western-trained students returning from abroad.

Before the financial and economic reforms bore fruit, the Japanese imperial government was severely short of funds. Having to pay compensation to the feudal lords and their samurais as well as bear the cost of modernization, the government was forced to finance itself largely on credit. Except for a small amount of foreign loans, most of the money was raised internally as loans from rich Japanese merchants and as government bonds. Before long, by the mid-1880s, financial reform, changes in land tenure and its taxation, as well as an increase in income from agriculture through technological improvements and by bringing more land into cultivation, especially in Hokkaido in the north, improved the financial position of the government. In Qing China, by contrast, the cost of the suppression of rebellions, large-scale natural calamities, the cost of combating foreign invaders and the increasingly heavy burden of indemnities levied by the imperialists, left the Qing with hardly any financial resources to spare for modernization.

In the process of industrialization, the Japanese government, unlike its Chinese counterpart, took the initiative in investing not only in the military and related fields, but in many other areas of modern manufacturing. Because the government-managed modern enterprises that covered most sectors of the economy did not thrive during the early years, for reasons including lack of experience with modern machinery, the lack of a modern transportation system, and bureaucratic inefficiency, they were sold off as financial liabilities very cheaply to private companies with close links to government during the 1880s. However, the government kept in its own hands the strategic enterprises, such as shipbuilding and the making of ammunition and armaments. The Japanese government also developed modern transportation infrastructure such as roads, ports, and railways, and established telegraphic and postal services. It set up a European-style central bank - the Bank of Japan - to implement its monetary policy, to maintain a sound currency. After initial difficulties had been successfully addressed, the small number of privileged private enterprises that had purchased from the government most of the modern industries took off and grew, through the Japanese way of cartel formation, into the industrial giants of the twentieth century.

The industrialization of Japan was a spectacular success story in which her central government played a vital role in providing political stability, law and order, sound monetary institutions, accessible credit and risk reduction for the private participants, as well as personal encouragement and many other kinds of support for entrepreneurs from different walks of life, so as to establish private enterprises in a range of modern sectors, and to thrive economically in a unified Japan free from internal trade barriers. The impoverished Qing government in China did not have the financial means to play such a role. The modern enterprises sponsored by the Qing government used capital and management provided by the merchants. This category of business that was labelled as *Guandu Shangban*, meaning 'official supervision and merchant operation', was too much hampered by bureaucratic control to flourish. Had Japan remained under the decentralized feudal Tokugawa Shogunate that restricted business and foreign trade, the modern economic transformation would likely not have taken place. Although massive imports of cheap machine-made cotton textiles from abroad led to large trade deficits for a couple of decades from 1869, the trend was reversed after the Japanese adopted foreign technology and formed large cartels in this industry in the 1890s, when the native cotton textile boom began. The much gentler opening of Japan to foreign trade provided the stimulus for the revolutionary changes, and its consequences, on balance, did Japan more good than harm. The impact of the much more violent 'opening of China' was largely negative, particularly in the short term.

In just half a century after Japan's fateful encounter with Commodore Perry, this island nation was well on its way to achieving its dream of building a rich country with a strong military through modernization, and thereby attaining its goal of national security against possible foreign subjugation. No longer willing to be bound by the unequal treaties forced on her, Japan, after having demonstrated her military prowess through wars against China and Russia, was able to negotiate new treaties on terms of equality with the Western powers concerned between 1894 and 1911. By 1905, the Japanese economy had expanded enormously through industrialization, almost stretching credulity, and its population had also increased from 30,000,0000 half a century before to above 45,000,000. Japan was the only country in East Asia, or in the world outside Europe and the United States of America, to modernize during the nineteenth century. From that time onward, on the foundations she had laid, Japan continued to develop, politically and economically, in parallel with the modern nations of the Western hemisphere.

Having leapt into the modern age by learning from the West, Japan also embraced whole-heartedly the Western ideology of imperialism, building empires at the expense of militarily weaker nations. Security from, and equality with, the Western powers no longer seemed to satisfy the ambition of the new militantly nationalistic Japan. Apart from the activities of Japanese pirates along the Chinese eastern seaboard, and the Japanese invasions of Korea during the Ming period, the Japanese had not been in the habit of attacking their neighbouring countries. But in the late nineteenth century, Japan seemed to be in a hurry to get in on the act of imperialist exploitation using her newly strengthened military forces, targeting Korea, Taiwan, which had been a part of the Qing province of Fujian since the eighteenth century, as well as China itself.

In 1874, Japan invaded Taiwan with 5,000 troops, but met stout resistance from the locals. At that time, Taiwan was still administered as a part of Fujian province, before its upgrade into a province itself after the French invasion in the mid-1880s. In response, the court sent an official to Taiwan to organize defensive measures. However, the easily intimidated Qing government, yielding to the advice of the British and American mediators, agreed to a Special Treaty of Beijing with Japan, whereby the invaders were paid 500,000 taels to withdraw their troops.

At about the same time, the Japanese also started focusing their expansionist drive on Korea, which had closed her doors tightly against foreign trade, as China and Japan had once done. Half-hearted Western efforts to open Korea earlier in the nineteenth century came to nothing. In 1875, emulating Commodore Perry, the Japanese anchored several warships off Incheon, a Korean city near Seoul, and demanded that Korea open certain ports for trade. As a tributary of the Qing, the matter was referred to the *Zongli Yamen*, which urged Korea to settle with Japan directly. In 1876 Korea signed an unequal treaty with Japan that opened three ports for trade and declared Korea to be an 'independent state'. Under the guidance of Li Hongzhang, the most powerful Qing foreign affairs official, Korea also signed similar treaties with other Western powers from 1883 to 1886. This strategy was aimed at letting the powers keep each other in check and giving Korea time to modernize through 'self-strengthening' on the Chinese model.

Meanwhile, inside Korea conflicts at the court between the pro-Chinese faction, and the pro-Japanese one sponsored by Japan, sometimes led to military intervention from both countries. Because Japan was not ready for serious military engagement over Korea during the 1880s, she signed the Li-Ito Convention (also known as the Convention of Tientsin) whereby both China and Japan were to withdraw their armed forces and military advisers from Korea, and each was to notify the other before sending them back if trouble recurred. By 1894, Japan felt sufficiently strong to carry out its long-nurtured 'continental policy' of expansion by plunging into an aggressive war against China over the control not just of Korea, but of parts of China also.

The Sino-Japanese War and its consequences

A peasant insurrection early in 1894 prompted the Korean court to ask the Qing for help. Li Hongzhang promptly sent a small force of about 1,500 soldiers and informed Japan of this fact, with a promise to withdraw as soon as the trouble was over. Using the excuse of accompanying the Japanese ambassador to Korea and protecting the Japanese residents there, Japan sent an army to occupy certain strategic points in Korea. Soon the rebellion subsided, and the Qing, preparing to move its soldiers home, proposed that both countries withdraw their troops in accordance with the Li-Ito Convention. The Japanese not only refused to do so but increased the number of their soldiers in Korea to over 20,000, several times that of the Qing, and moved them to Seoul so as to dictate policy to the Korean government through the appointment of a 'regent' amenable to their wishes. Without declaring war, on 25 July 1894 the Japanese suddenly attacked Chinese ships, sinking a transport vessel leased from the British with over 700 soldiers on board. With its hand thus forced, the Qing declared war on Japan on 1 August, when the Japanese also declared war on China.

Although the Qing did declare war, the court was split between a party for war and one for appeasing the Japanese, with the powerful Li Hongzhang, who was a favourite of the imperial powers as well as of the Dowager Empress Cixi, strongly advocating peace. Li had concluded many pro-capitulation treaties that satisfied the desires of the foreign powers for annexing Chinese territory, for exploiting China economically, and for paying compensation by China for the aggressive wars the powers waged against China. Li pleased Cixi because he helped her regime to survive many crises of foreign diplomatic pressure or military intervention, through his adherence to the Qing policy of peace-at-any-price with the foreign intruders. Even when war was imminent, Li refused to send more troops to the Korean front to support general Ye Zhichao, who had wired him an urgent request for reinforcements. Putting his faith in the intervention of the Western powers to rein in the Japanese, Li commanded Ye to make no move until he gave the order to fight. Li, the chief appeaser, controlled both the Huai Army and the modern Beiyang Fleet that could engage the Japanese. This made it almost impossible for these forces to pursue the war, both defensive and offensive, with the energy and initiative required, since they were under Li's orders to avoid military combat.

Ill-prepared and outnumbered, the Qing forces resisted but could not withstand the Japanese onslaught, first on Asan and then on Pyongyang, and the demoralized general Ye Zhichao fled with his troops to China across the Yalu River during the latter part of September 1894. Shortly after taking Pyongyang, the Japanese attacked the Beiyang Fleet on the Yellow Sea near the Yalu River. This fleet was a centrepiece of Qing military modernization under Li Hongzhang's initiative. The opposing fleets, twelve vessels on each side, were similar in tonnage, but the Chinese fleet, being inexperienced in sea battles came out lined up abreast like cavalry troops ready to charge and was outmanoeuvred and encircled by the Japanese vessels. After battling fiercely for five hours, the Chinese lost five vessels, but they inflicted such serious damage on five Japanese ships, including the enemy flagship *Matsushima*, that the Japanese had to withdraw from the scene of battle. Through the courage and determination of the wounded Admiral Ding Ruchang and his subordinates, the introduction of the Beiyang Fleet and its officers to naval warfare was by no means a   disaster. There were still four battleships remaining intact, and ready for the next engagement.

After this naval encounter, Li Hongzhang, for the sake of saving the military base of his political power, ordered all the Beiyang Fleet to anchor in the harbour of Weihaiwei and keep the vessels safe by avoiding the enemy. He instructed the fleet's officers 'not to engage the enemy under any circumstances'. Li failed to foresee that instead of finding a safe haven, the Beiyang Fleet in Weihaiwei were herded together like lambs ready for the slaughter. He had no reason to assume that the Japanese would not attack Weihaiwei. This situation was reminiscent of the Chinese modern fleet anchored in Mawei that had prepared itself for neither defensive nor offensive warfare against the French, because Li Hongzhang and the Qing court were afraid of provoking the French who, indeed, had needed no provocation to make war on China.

Map of South-East Asia at the end of the nineteenth century (*Omniatlas*: retrieved on
30 November 2023 from https://omniatlas.com/maps/asia-pacific/19000616/plain/)

Japan's next move was to invade China on land with a two-pronged attack: one across
the Yalu River from Korea to capture Jiulian and Andong (present Dandong), and the
other to land on the Liaodong Peninsula to occupy Jinzhou, with the aim of taking Lushun
and Dalian. The Japanese achieved these military objectives by late November 1894 with
relative ease, partly because of the lack of fighting spirit of the Qing military, and partly
because Li Hongzhang was, as usual, more ready to sue for peace than to pursue the
war. Li refused Admiral Ding Ruchang's plea to aid Lushen with the Beiyang Fleet. Li's
once formidable Huai Army, which had suppressed the Nian Rebellion two decades earlier, had become as feeble as the Manchu Banner and the Chinese Green Standard forces
when it was deployed against the Japanese. Administrative decline and corruption had
sapped the strength of the military force of the Qing.

In January 1895, the Japanese were ready to advance against Weihaiwei. To attack
the Beiyang Fleet from behind, the Japanese army landed on the Shandong Peninsula

to occupy the shore surrounding its harbour, against which their navy had already imposed a blockade. Then they turned their big guns both from the shore and from their ships on the entrapped Beiyang Fleet. Under fearsome artillery bombardment, Admiral Ding Ruchang and several patriotic officers fought courageously. Refusing to surrender when urged by the Japanese to do so, he ordered his subordinates to break out of the blockade but was unsuccessful. In desperation, he ordered his officers to sink their ships to prevent them falling into enemy hands. All but one of his officers refused to do so. Seeing the hopelessness of the situation, he and some other officers of the fleet committed suicide. After his death, a foreign employee surrendered the remaining eleven vessels of the fleet to the Japanese. Faced with the ruin of its modern fleet, continuing defeats on land, and the desire of Empress Dowager Cixi to avoid having her sixtieth birthday celebration spoiled by a continuation of the fighting, the Qing court desperately sued for peace. America, which had been friendly to Japan throughout the latter's aggression against China, acted as a mediator.

As a newcomer to the imperialist club, the Japanese made up for their belated entry by showing a voracious appetite for devouring their prey. Japan had exposed how weak Qing China's military forces, both army and navy, had become despite China's modernization projects in the 'Self-strengthening Movement' since 1861. Now, Japan was to lead the other imperialist powers in starting a new era of more intense penetration of China for economic exploitation and political control - the era of 'scramble' for partitioning China into foreign 'spheres of influence'. The defeat by Japan was a great catastrophe for China, which was soon to be reduced to a quasi-colony of the Western powers and Japan, with the Qing government sinking into the position of an internal peacekeeper and tax-collector for its oppressors.

The Treaty of Shimonoseki that brought the war to an end in April 1895 obliged Qing China to cede Taiwan, the Pescadores (Penghu) and the Liaodong Peninsula to Japan, to pay Japan an enormous indemnity of 200,000,000 taels of silver, and to open seven cities including Shanxi, Chongqing, Suzhou, Hangzhou, and Wuzhou to Japanese trade, in addition to allowing Japan to trade in all the existing treaty ports. This treaty ended China's suzerainty over Korea, whose 'independence' China was to recognize. An important new concession Japan extracted from China involved the right to establish industrial and manufacturing facilities in China's opened ports. The other treaty powers had Japan to thank, as the most-favoured-nation clause enabled them also to enjoy the same right to build factories in all the treaty ports, and to trade in the additional opened ports in China. Soon, not only the right to build factories to take advantage of the cheap Chinese labour, but also the rights to operate mines, construct railways, and to set up banks, were to be conceded to all the treaty powers by China. These concessions signified a new phase of heightened foreign economic exploitation of China. This type of new development enabled the rich industrialized or industrializing countries to extract large profits from investing their surplus capital in China, whereas previously the focus was solely on trade, which continued as before.

Since Russia also had territorial ambitions in China's *Donghai* (the Northeast region of China), she was not happy with Japan's occupation of the Liaodong Peninsula. (The terms *Dongbei*, and *Dong San Sheng* – the Three Northern Provinces - were used by the Chinese in reference to what the Japanese later called Manchuria. The Japanese invented the term Manchuria to justify their detaching this whole region from China.) After being pressured by the 'Triple Intervention' of Russia allied with Germany and France in April 1895, Japan was obliged to give up Liaodong in exchange for a compensation of 30,000,000 taels from China. But China was not allowed to keep Liaodong for very long. A total of 230,000,000 taels, amounting to 3 years of the total income of the Qing, had to be paid to Japan within 3 years.

Because the Qing was financially exhausted by the war, between 1895 and 1898 it raised three loans of 16,000,000 GBP each, at punitive terms from foreign banks, one from a Russo-French syndicate of six banks, and two from an Anglo-German syndicate, composed of the Hong Kong and Shanghai Banking Corporation (the present-day HSBC) and the Deutsch-Asiatische Bank. These loans were secured on the maritime customs service (MCS) revenue. Owing to the insufficiency of the customs revenue from foreign trade at this point, the income of seven *Lijin* stations was to be dedicated to the repayment of these loans. These stations were to be placed under the control of the Inspector General of the MCS. The contracts of both Anglo-German loans contained an article stating that the status quo of the MCS was to be preserved during the duration of the loan. This meant that the MCS was to be managed and controlled by a British I.G. until 1943.

Modernization in nineteenth century China and Japan

The Sino-Japanese War brought out the stark contrast between China's failure to modernize and Japan's success. Although both were East Asian countries with considerable similarities in culture, there were important differences, in addition to their obvious disparity in size. One should be cautious when making comparisons between them regarding modernization, and attributing reasons for the success of one and the failure of the other. Nevertheless, we shall suggest some possibilities. One important reason certainly lay in leadership. Although the centralization of the Qing might have appeared to be an advantage, unfortunately there was decay at the top. Japan was fortunate in that when the foreign threat appeared, she was ruled by the decentralized regime of the Tokugawa Shogunate, which though too corrupt and incompetent to provide resolute leadership against the foreign menace, left room for some of the outer domains to experiment with different strategies for meeting the foreign challenge. When the winning strategy emerged, the modernizers from the outer domains had the good fortune to awaken a dormant imperial authority, which could be used as a rallying point to overthrow the decaying Shoguns and the feudal lords. With the dead wood at the top removed, Japan was able to start afresh to modernize Japan, with a strongly centralized imperial authority and with the modernizers at the helm backed by the authority of the Meiji emperor. Alerted by the example of China's defeat in the Opium Wars, but without being so badly battered by the foreign invaders and being also relatively free from China's cultural pride and deep attachment to old traditions, the Japanese leaders were able to pursue modernization single-mindedly, without having to compromise on account of criticism from colleagues or adverse public opinion.

Leaving quality of leadership aside, the Qing government, since the 1840s, had been continuously troubled by domestic insurrections and foreign pressures that left it with neither any breathing-space of prolonged peace, nor financial resources to focus on systematic modernization, even if it had had the will to do so. Apart from a short period of civil war, Japan had been free from serious and prolonged domestic rebellions since its opening. Considered much less of a target for economic exploitation, Japan had not been under such continuous and relentless pressure as China from the imperial powers. The Japanese did not have the bitter experiences of the Chinese and could be persuaded more easily by their leaders of the advantages of modernization, and to change, even in revolutionary ways, by adopting whatever seemed to be needed from the West for the sake of making their nation strong and wealthy.

With China's rural economy largely ruined by wars, cheap imports, and the outflow of silver, the government had to exercise restraint in collecting taxes from the impoverished and restless peasants to meet its increasing financial needs. To make up for the shortfall, the Chinese authorities resorted to foreign loans with high interest rates, which had to be repaid, and the income from the *Lijin* transit tax on Chinese goods, which rendered the domestic products less competitive against similar imports. Japan, on the other hand, could rely on taxing her peasants to support her early modernization projects, and her fiscal policy encouraged and protected her young modern industries, which could be expected to provide government revenue from taxes when they matured. The privatized Japanese industrial enterprises provided a much more successful model for modern industrial growth than the Chinese type of industrial operations supervised by government officials, which were not reliable as a regular source of tax revenue, though they lined the pockets of those in charge of them. Although the Japanese under the Shoguns had to pay reparations to certain foreign authorities for killing their nationals, these limited sums were nothing in comparison with those the Chinese had to pay.

The example of Europe seems to suggest that successful modernization requires the unifying force of nationalism or of national identity. The emergence of modern Chinese nationalism was a result of imperialism, but the process was relatively slow when compared with Japan. Most of the people under Qing rule, including those who wished to restore the Ming and destroy the Qing, such as the members of the Triad society, and even the Taiping rebels, were not able to make the leap in identifying themselves fully as members of a Chinese nation, and recognizing what nationhood stood for, until after China's transformation from the Qing empire into a nation-state.

In fact, the name *Zhongguo Ren* (literally a person or people of the central or middle country or state) as applied to a Chinese person or people became current only during the twentieth century. Earlier, it was common for the Chinese in the West to describe themselves as *Tang Ren*, *Han Ren*, or *Hua Ren* (a person or people of the ancient dynasty of Tang or Han, or the even older Huaxia cultural area). From the start of the imperialist encroachments in the 1840s to 1911, there were various kinds and degrees of a consciousness that grew and developed into Chinese nationalism of the twentieth century, but the maturity of this nationalism in China appeared more slowly than that in Japan. When Sun Yat-sen strove to unite and restore China as a nation starting from the late nineteenth to the early decades of the twentieth century, he described the Chinese people as a 'sheet of loose sand', out of his frustration. Japan's reaction to the Western threat was intensely nationalistic soon after Western intrusion began. It was easier, it seemed, for a compact island nation like Japan, which had a relatively homogeneous people sharing the same language, culture, and historical experiences to develop nationalism under aggressive foreign impact, than for a vast multi-ethnic country like China, with striking regional differences and greater diversity among her peoples.

The 'scramble' for concessions

After China's defeat in the Sino-Japanese War in 1894-5, it was obvious that China's efforts at modernization had borne little fruit. Since this was a time when the technological changes in the capitalist countries of the West were gathering momentum, the gap between China and the industrializing nations in terms of military power and economic development became even wider. As a result, China was bound to be on the receiving end of a new phase of heightened imperialist drive to carve China up into 'spheres of influence', where the powers commandeered leased territories to extract inordinate returns through exploiting China's natural resources and cheap labour, through developing railways and steamship transportation, and establishing banks and other modern enterprises in these territories. The rivalry among the powers prompted them to aid and abet their allies, or to exercise checks against the advancement of a competitor. They closely watched each other's moves, jostling and competing in a chain of frenzied one-sided negotiations with the defenceless Qing, with results that resembled a vulgar scramble for concessions. Within a short period of four years, the most economically desirable parts of China had become the 'sphere of influence' of one European power or another and Japan, as we shall shortly see. This development further impinged on China's sovereignty and administrative integrity, as the Qing were forced to give to the power concerned the right to station troops and to administer the leased territory in its sphere of influence. China sank more deeply into the position of a semi-colony of all these powers, the competition between which, however, prevented China from becoming the colony of any single one.

Soon after the Sino-Japanese War ended, France, a participant in the 'Triple Intervention' in April 1985 which forced Japan to relinquish Jiaozhou, asked the Qing, as did Russia and Germany later, for further concessions. Having control of Vietnam, the French were interested in extending their power and influence into Chinese territories adjacent to Vietnam in China's south and southwest. In 1895, the French began to press the Qing for the right to build a railway from Tonkin to southwest China, and to open mines there. In 1897, France requested the Qing to provide a guarantee not to cede or lease to another power the provinces of Yunnan, Guangxi, and the island of Hainan. At the same time, France also asked the Qing for a 99-year lease for Guangzhou Bay in Guangdong province. France got what she desired: in 1899, the Qing signed a treaty with France, whereby Guangzhou Bay was leased to France together with the right to build certain railway lines to southwest China. These three provinces in China's south and southwest thus became the sphere of influence of the French.

Russia, a French ally, was greedier. In 1896, the Russians requested Li Hongzhang to represent the Qing at the coronation of Czar Nicholas II in Moscow, with the intention of getting this powerful official to agree to a premeditated Russian scheme. Since Russia was one of the powers that had forced Japan to return Liaodong, it did not take much persuasion, in addition to a substantial bribe, for Li to sign in Moscow a secret mutual defence pact between Russia and China against Japan. This pact allowed the Russian navy to frequent all Chinese ports and gave Russia the right to build a 950-mile-long Chinese Eastern Railway across Heilongjiang and Jilin in China's northeast, to connect with the Trans-Siberian Railway, which was in the process of being built, and would extend to Vladivostok. In 1897, Russian naval forces in China flexed their muscles in support of the Russian demand for leasing Dalian and Lushun (which had been renamed by the Westerners as Port Arthur to make it sound less Chinese). Yielding to the Russian threat, Li Hongzhang signed a new protocol, this time with the Russian representative at Beijing, which leased these two port cities for 25 years to the Russians, as well as the right to build a 650-mile north-south railroad line, the South Manchurian Railway, which would connect the Chinese Eastern Railway to these two port cities. On the land adjacent to all these railway lines, the Russians were given the right to log, to build factories, to open mines, to enjoy either reduction or exemption from customs and transit duties, to station troops and police forces, and to have local jurisdiction during the leased period. These protocols allowed Russia to make China's northeast into her sphere of influence. The Russians designated this region as their province of Guangdong (east of Shanhai Pass). Since Japan was desperate to get hold of this region also, the seeds for a Russo-Japanese conflict were sown.

Germany, a latecomer on the imperial scene like Japan, was also in a hurry to make up for her tardiness. In 1897, Germany used an unfortunate incident involving a German mission in China as a pretext to send troops to occupy the Jiaozhou Bay in the southeast of Shandong Province. Then in 1898, with Russian support, Germany was able to force the Qing to sign a treaty to lease Jiaozhou Bay including Qingdao for 99 years, during which time this region would be under German jurisdiction. Germany also obtained the right to build two railways and to open mines within 15 kilometres along these lines. As a result, Shandong became a German sphere of influence.

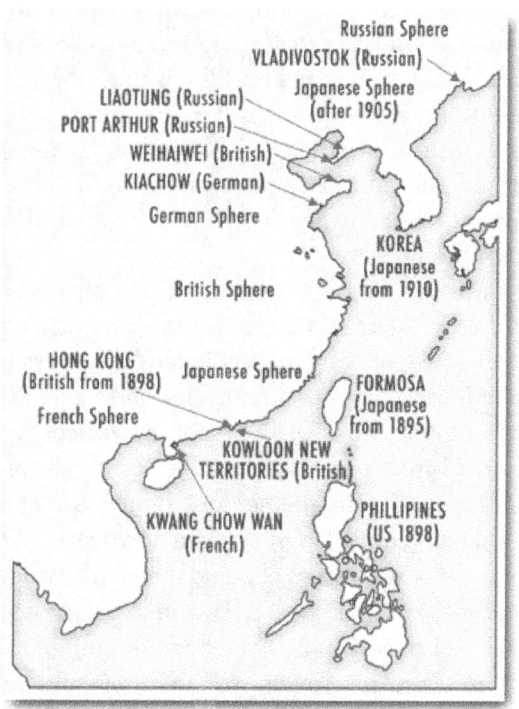

Spheres of influence of the imperialist powers (*MIT*: retrieved on 30 November 2023 from https://visualizingcultures.mit.edu/throwing_off_asia_03/toa_essay01.html)

Britain, the most senior of the imperialist powers, still dominated China's foreign trade. Although remaining deeply interested in maintaining the treaty system it had introduced, Britain was not going to be left behind in the scramble to divide up the spoils in China. Having a strong navy and the control of the land frontiers from Burma and India to China, the British were well placed to develop spheres of influence in the different regions of China. To balance the French influence in south and southwest China, Britain obtained the right to build a railway in 1897 from Burma to southwest China, and to trade along the Xi (West) River to Guangzhou. Britain considered the region along the Yangtze River as her primary sphere of influence and decided formally to stake her claim by forcing the Qing to guarantee, in February 1898, not to alienate the entire Yangtze Valley and Delta to a third party. A few months later, the British forced the Qing to lease an area around Kowloon, a peninsula near Hong Kong, for 99 years. This could be viewed as another balancing act against the French, this time in southern China. Soon afterwards, Britain leased Weihaiwei, an important north China port city in Shandong, opposite Lushun that had been leased to Russia, to check the southward advance of Russia. In western China, Britain's designs on Tibet and her rivalry with Russia led to her using persistent military and diplomatic pressure on the Tibetans and the Qing, especially from the late nineteenth to the early twentieth century, to exclude Russian influence from this region and to pry Tibet away from Qing China.

Watching how other powers were rapidly dividing up China, Japan became dissatisfied with possessing only Taiwan. In 1889, she forced the Qing to agree not to cede or lease Fujian, the Chinese province opposite Taiwan, to any other country. Thereafter, Fujian effectively became a Japanese sphere of influence.

America did not participate in the 'scramble' in China, because she was preoccupied in 1898 with a war against Spain over Cuba, though the main military contest took place in the Philippines, which was taken over as a colonial possession by America from Spain, which lost the war. In 1899, the United State was free to turn her attention to China, but the desirable regions had all been taken. In order not to be handicapped by the spheres of influence of the other imperialist powers, America proposed the 'Open Door Policy', the acceptance of which by all the powers would ensure equal and impartial trade in all parts of China, and protect the rights guaranteed by treaty to them all. When most of the powers except Russia agreed with the American proposal, America proclaimed it as an operative principle, even though there was no provision to back it up by force, should it be violated. For it to operate, China needed to exist as an integral unit to collect the duties and enforce the customs provisions, as well as to guarantee the rights and privileges she had given away. The Open Door Policy was therefore partly intended to help Qing China to continue to exist, rather than to be broken up into colonies of the imperialist powers. But it is more likely that what saved the Qing at this point was the result of the rivalry of the powers, and their realization that there was more to be gained by letting the Qing remain viable.

Imperialism in China towards the end of the Qing (*Pinterest*: retrieved on
30 November 2023 from https://www.pinterest.com/pin/561261172290490415/)

The 'Hundred Days' reforms

When the news of the Sino-Japanese Treaty of Shimonoseki with its harsh terms reached Beijing, where the candidates were gathered to take the metropolitan exam for the highest *Jinshi* degree, these promising young Confucian scholars and potential government officeholders became deeply alarmed. With two outstanding patriotic activists Kang Youwei (1858-1927) and his pupil Liang Qichao (1873-1929) as prime movers, in May 1894 over 1,300 of these scholars put their names to a long petition to Emperor Guangxu (r. 1875-1908) urging him to reject the peace terms, move the capital to a less vulnerable region, strengthen the military for determined resistance against aggression, and implement a programme of wide-ranging and radical reforms to make China strong and prosperous. Although the petition was blocked by conservatives in the office responsible for its transmission and never reached the emperor, it had an impact on society because it became widely known to the educated public through its printing and circulation.

Soon afterwards, Kang passed the exam and was given an official post at the Ministry of Works. He continued to write impassioned memorials to Emperor Guangxu, making a cogent case for radical reforms using Meiji Japan as a model. In contrast to the earlier 'Self-

Portraits of Kang Youwei and Liang Qichao (*The China Project*: retrieved on 30 November 2023 from https://thechinaproject.com/2018/10/15/kuora-kang-you-wei-or-liang-qichao-for-president/)

strengthening Movement', this generation of reformers not only wanted to acquire Western gunboats, guns, and other technology of material production; they also espoused institutional reforms and changes at a much deeper level. Although some of Kang's memorials did reach the emperor, others were intercepted by the anti-reform conservative officials.

Without any power to influence the actions of the government, Kang Youwei, Liang Qichao, and other patriotic reformers, such as Tan Sitong (1865-1898), endeavoured to inform the public and to gather support for their drive to change and save China by organizing study groups and meetings, and by publishing journals and newspapers in Beijing, Shanghai, Changsha, Tianjin, and other big cities. Also notable among these was Yan Fu (1854-1921), who had been to England and devoted much effort to publishing his translation of Western works to promote radical ideas, such as peoples' rights and constitutional monarchy. His translation of Thomas Henry Huxley's 'Evolution and Ethics' (1893) was to serve as a warning that unless the Chinese made themselves strong, they would not be fit to survive. This was an age when social Darwinism went hand in hand with imperialism. Yan's works were influential among the educated, particularly the reformers. Although there were enthusiastic public responses all over China to the reformers' call, with a mushrooming of patriotic study groups and journals, the political impact of the public support was not immediately felt, because China was not a democracy. And, unlike their counterparts in Japan, the Chinese gentry reformers lacked the power of the modernizing samurais. Indeed, they had powerful enemies among the recalcitrant conservative officials. The latter opposed them strenuously and attacked them vehemently with the support of Empress Dowager Cixi.

In 1897, through the good offices of Weng Tonghe, the personal tutor of Emperor Guangxu and a Grand Minister of the Privy Council, Kang's reforming ideas, with which the emperor had some previous acquaintance, were made known and elucidated more fully to him. Kang wanted Guangxu to emulate Peter the Great, who introduced Western advancement to Russia. Kang was not aware that, unlike the Russian Czar, Guangxu had little real power, even though Weng Tonghe tried to make Kang realize how manipulative the empress dowager was, and how ubiquitous were her informers in the palace.

By 1897 Emperor Guangxu had been on the throne since the age of four for twenty-two years after the death of Emperor Tongzhi, the son of the Dowager Empress Cixi, but political and military power still resided largely in the hands of his aunt, the dowager empress. Cixi had chosen him and put him on the throne as a minor so that she could continue the tradition of presiding at court, while sitting behind a curtain (*Chui Lian Ting Zheng*), and running the country as she had done for many years during Tongzhi's minority. Taught by his aunt since the age of four to fear and obey her as his father, mother, and sovereign all rolled into one, Guangxu had difficulty escaping the fate of being Cixi's puppet, even though by 1887 Cixi had to keep her promise of letting the sixteen-year-old Guangxu start managing the affairs of state himself, as an adult at the court (*Qin Zheng*).

To retain the reins of power, she placed her own trusted officials in key posts, made her own niece Guangxu's empress, and required the young emperor to see her daily and report to her all important matters that came up at the court before acting on them. This situation still prevailed in 1897, notwithstanding that Guangxu had already ruled as an adult for ten years and had managed to appoint a few men who were loyal to him to important posts. During this period, Cixi kept herself busy pulling strings at court and monitoring Guangxu's activities, while living outside the palace in Yiheyuan (the Summer Palace), ostensibly in retirement. Today this beautiful scenic spot with its famous marble, built with money diverted from funds for China's modern Beiyang Fleet, has become a popular tourist attraction.

Portrait of the Dowager Empress Cixi (*popmatters*: retrieved on 30 November 2023 from https://www.popmatters.com/180025-empress-dowager-cixi-by-jung-chang-2495676757.html)

During the Sino-Japanese War, the emperor supported the war party, but he was outmanoeuvred by the peace party led by Li Hongzhang and supported by Cixi. He was deeply unhappy about having to put his seal on the Treaty of Shimonoseki, and the subsequent 'scramble for concessions' compounded his unhappiness. Kang Youwei's ideas on reinvigorating China through reform, transmitted through Weng Tonghe, were received by Emperor Guangxu like rain falling on a parched desert. When Guangxu wished to see Kang himself, he was thwarted by prince Gong, who reminded him of the rule that only officials of Fourth Grade or above were allowed to have an audience with the emperor; Kang, being only Second Grade, was too junior. At the beginning of 1898, Guangxu decided to invite Kang to come to an office of the *Zongli Yamen* where, using Weng Tonghe as an intermediary, he and Kang were able to have a conversational session without coming face to face. Then he ordered the officials concerned to transmit all Kang's memorials to him without delay. Soon after, Kang presented more memorials exhorting Guangxu to promulgate edicts on reform, emulating the modernization of Meiji Japan, and using his royal prerogative, like Peter the Great of Russia, to force through a slate of reform measures. Kang used Poland, which had suffered the fate of being partitioned (by France, Russia, and Austria), as an example of what might befall China, unless Guangxu acted quickly.

Feeling an urgent need to advance the reform measures, Emperor Guangxu had asked a royal relative to transmit to Cixi the message that 'if the Empress Dowager would not give him the authority to act, he would prefer to give up his throne than to be the monarch who lost China'. In view of the grave situation in China, Guangxu made up his mind to strike out on his own, even without Cixi's prior blessings, and he embraced reform with an edict on 11 June 1898. A few days later, he arranged to meet Kang, who was promoted to work in the *Zongli Yamen* to focus on matters concerning reforms. Several of Kang's fellow reformers, with Tang Sitong among them, were given official posts with ranks above Fourth Grade to work with him and the emperor. During the three months between 11 June and 21 September, Emperor Guangxu, with the help of the reformers, flooded the country with around 180 edicts, promulgating a wide range of reforms covering educational, economic, and military fields, in addition to political and cultural institutions.

The reforms on education included changing the contents of the state-sponsored examination, setting up a modern school system and a university in Beijing, sending students to study abroad, and establishing translation bureaus. On the economy, the state was to set up bureaus to protect and encourage agriculture, commerce, and industry, and to develop railways and mines. There were to be rewards for innovations. The old government postal relay stations were to be replaced by a state-wide post office. Changes were to be introduced in government administration, and a budget office was to be established in connection with financial reform. The old military organizations were to be replaced by a new-style army and navy, with the forces trained and drilled along modern Western lines. On political matters, the people were to have the right to publish and to form study societies, and to send memorials to the government to express their opinions. For understandable reasons, Guangxu's decrees did not include the reformers' proposals for a parliament and a constitutional government.

These decrees electrified the country and galvanized the diehard conservative officials to rally around the empress dowager for support. There were even suggestions of her returning to take over the reins of state again. They insisted on adhering to the ancestral ways, and feared the harm these radical changes might do to China. Many of them ignored or resisted the reform decrees. Soon after the appearance of the first reform edict, Cixi demonstrated her power and displeasure by forcing Guangxu to dismiss Weng Tonghe and to appoint Ronglu, a staunch supporter of hers, as the governor general of Zhili and the supreme commander of the Beiyang Army. Since Beijing was situated inside Zhili, she was sure of military support if her power were challenged. Despite this setback and warning, Emperor Guangxu went ahead with his plan, and he even fought back, dismissing Li Hongzhang, Cixi's protégé, and some other high officials who obstructed the reforms. Since Cixi repeatedly sent emissaries to Tianjin to have secret meetings with Ronglu, who made certain alarming troop movements, rumours began to spread, both in Beijing and Tianjin, that the empress dowager and Ronglu were conspiring to force the emperor to abdicate during the time when she and the emperor were due to review the new troops in Tianjin.

For many years previously, the empress dowager had balanced her support for both the self-strengthening type of modernizers and the recalcitrant conservatives in her government, and she played one side against the other to bend both to her will; but this time she came down strongly against the reformers. In addition to her own conservative sympathies, the empress dowager must have felt threatened by Guangxu's new assertion of independence, and his attempt to control his own and the country's destiny, instead of remaining an instrument of her will. At that point they were opposing each other on the most critically important issue of the day. It became a struggle not just of whose policy was going to prevail, but of who had the power to rule. It was an unequal power struggle, because most of the top military and civil officials owed Cixi their loyalty. Guangxu did not have many powerful supporters among the high officials, and the reformers were inexperienced neophytes in government.

As the day for the review of the troops drew near, the deeply worried Guangxu sent, on 13 September, a secret message to the reformers, alerting them to the fact that his own position had become insecure. He wrote that unless the reforms were carried out, China could not be saved. To go through with the reforms, the conservatives with the contrary outlook had to be removed and the open-minded, courageous, and outstandingly able officials must be put in charge. He informed them that the empress dowager did not see things this way, and that his repeated appeals to her only angered her more. Revealing his fear and anxiety, he urged them to find a way to save the situation quickly. At first, they were at a loss as to what to do. As a last resort, they staked their hope on a military man, Yuan Shikai, who had attended a study society they had organized in the past. They approached him on the assumption that he was sympathetic to their aims. They also went to the Legation Quarters in Beijing to enlist the support of foreign ambassadors, who expressed sympathy but declined to interfere. They then worked out a plan in which Yuan, who commanded a modern army of over 7,000 soldiers stationed near Tianjin, was expected to play the key role. According to this plan Yuan was to kill Ronglu during the review of the troops, and then use his troops to surround the Summer Palace. Being an opportunist, Yuan agreed enthusiastically to support the emperor, who promptly promoted him to a high rank.

Unfortunately for Emperor Guangxu and his supporters for reform, Yuan was not worthy of their trust. Having been a subordinate of Ronglu, and a calculating politician by nature, he placed his bet on the side the empress dowager. Yuan promptly revealed the reformers' secret plan to Ronglu. The latter lost no time in warning the empress dowager, who hastened to return to the Forbidden City on 18 September to keep Guangxu in check. On 21 September 1897, Cixi staged a coup: she imprisoned Emperor Guangxu in the palace, and then declared in an edict that she was returning to the court to manage the affairs of the state as she had done before Emperor Guangxu began to rule officially. Discovering that they were betrayed, Kang Youwei and Liang Qichao escaped abroad. Tan Sitong, refusing to flee, was willing to face martyrdom in the name of reform. He and five other leading reformers were soon arrested and executed, and other officials, who supported the reform, were dismissed. Thus, the *Wuxu Bianfa* (the ` Hundred Days' Reform) came to an abrupt end.

Despite the political setback, the seeds of reform had been sown. The efforts and sacrifices of the reformers marked another halting step on China's long road towards modernization. Although Tan Sitong's life was tragically cut short, he is still remembered by many, particularly in his province of Hunan, as a hero and martyr. His best-known work, *Ren Xue* (On Benevolence), that denounced autocratic monarchs and advocated peoples' rights, contributed to the revolutionary current that was soon to engulf China. The failure of this movement politically did not prevent it from having a profound impact on Chinese culture, rendering it more open to modern influences.

With Cixi's return to power, Guangxu's reform edicts were shunted aside for the time being, apart from the one creating a modern university in Beijing. However, during the next few years, the court found it necessary to enact many measures contained in Emperor Guangxu's reform edicts, because of the pressure of public opinion. It was China's great misfortune that someone like Cixi dominated China during the long period of forty-eight years, from 1860 to 1908, when China was seriously menaced by imperialism. This was a crucial time, when strong central leadership was desperately needed to steer China onto a course of modernization much like Japan, and to join the West in earnest in the deployment of capital and in industrial development. Because Cixi's central concerns were focused on her own personal pleasures and her desire to hold on to the reins of power, rather than the fate of her country and the distress of her people, a government controlled by her did not and could not provide such leadership. When her nephew, the nominal emperor, and the young, innovative gentry reformers had ventured, in a desperate bid, to put China on the path towards modernization, she had promptly put an end to it. Japan, on the contrary, had the good fortune that, during the reign of Emperor Meiji, the old regime under the Togugawa Shoguns, who might have undermined efforts at reform, were out of the way when the new regime, led by the dynamic young samurais under the banner of the reinvigorated imperial authority, was ready to go ahead with implementing their policy on the modernization of Japan.

The Boxer Rebellion (1899-1901)

After her coup, the empress dowager wanted to force Guangxu to abdicate, but Britain, Japan, and America were against it. She then declared that the royal physician had found Guangxu seriously ill, whereupon the British Ambassador warned the *Zongli Yamen* that the Western powers might act in way detrimental to China should the emperor die at this juncture. When the British sent a well-known physician to check up on Guangxu's state of health, he was found not to be ill. Cixi's next abdication ploy was to set up an Heir Apparent to replace Guangxu in due course. Although this was against ancestral rule, because Emperor Kangxi had abolished this institution, Cixi managed nevertheless to select a fifteen-year-old royal prince and instal him as the Heir Apparent. Again, the imperialist powers expressed their disapproval and refused to attend the installation ceremony. The powers favoured Guangxu, not because he wished to make China strong, but because of his expressed intention to open China more to the West. They wanted to avoid China returning to the closed-door era, under the leadership of the diehard conservatives. Although Cixi was incensed by the imperialist interference, she dared not force Guangxu to abdicate. She saw her chance for revenge in the militant anti-foreign peasant uprisings - the *Yihe Quan* or *Tuan* (the Righteous and Harmonious Fists or Society) - that began to draw the authorities' attention in 1898 in Shandong Province. The foreigners called them the Boxers because they practised Chinese boxing to improve themselves physically and morally. Their adherents superstitiously believed that they could render themselves invulnerable to bullets through magical powers.

The Boxers were groups of peasants attached to various secret societies such as *Gelao Hui* (Brothers and Elders Society), *Dadao Hui* (the Big Sabre Society) or even some branches of the ancient White Lotus Society, that perennially lurked under the surface in rural and sometimes even urban China. The resurgence of these militant self-help and grievance-filled groups was often a sign of rural economic distress and a precursor to insurrections. Sometimes social or political issues or injustices also spurred the growth of these societies. During the closing years of the nineteenth century, the Chinese economy was indeed in dire straits, as we have seen.

Groups of Boxers first broke into open rebellion in Shandong, attacking foreign churches and properties and driving away missionaries, with the slogan of 'support the Qing, destroy the foreign'. Parts of Shandong had already been laid waste by the Sino-Japanese War, invaded by the Germans and the British, and devastated by floods and famine. The Boxers' slogan and attack on all things foreign demonstrated Chinese patriotism or even nationalism, though not of a fully developed and conscious kind.

Christianity and the missionaries

Why did the Boxers target the Christians and Christian churches as objects of their hatred? It was likely the result of the countless conflicts and disputes that sometimes erupted into violent incidents, which had occurred over the years between the missionaries and Chinese people of various localities.

Had China being mistress of her own house, Chrisitan missionaries in China would not have had the privilege of extraterritoriality and the protection of foreign gunboats; they would have had to exercise far greater circumspection operating in the Chinese environment, where the culture and traditions were very different from their own. In the context of the unequal treaties, the Westerners were placed in a privileged position without being bound by Chinese law, and the Chinese were often at a disadvantage should disputes arise between them and the Westerners. In the treaty ports, the Westerners kept themselves to their own communities, while enjoying the services of Chinese inside the international settlements, and the cooperation of the local officials and merchants outside. Friction between the foreign and Chinese communities seldom occurred in the treaty ports. But after the French wrested the right to buy land and establish mission stations not just at the treaty ports, but also in the interior of China in the 1840s, the spread of Christian missions, especially the Catholic ones, into the interior of China led to countless conflicts and disputes between local Chinese and missionaries and their Chinese converts, who became effectively extra-territorialized under the protection of the foreign missions. If the missionaries and the Chinese Christians rode roughshod over the local Chinese from their privileged positions, Chinese officials were often reluctant to protect the interest or to redress the wrong of the Chinese parties, for fear of provoking foreign military intervention, or the threat of it. Many incidents involving missionaries did result in the intervention of foreign governments, leading to the Qing having to indemnify, apologize, or give more privileges to the foreigners. Furthermore, some Chinese found it difficult to understand and accept that the foreigners who came to reside in their midst not only rejected the culture, tradition, and usage of the Chinese, but made their Chinese converts do the same. Over the years, grievances and resentment built up among the Chinese, with the literate resorting to anti-foreign propaganda while the illiterate took to rioting and violence. Later, by the 1920s, when the tide of modern Chinese nationalism reached a high point, the foreign missionary movement came under attack as a form of cultural imperialism.

To be fair to those who came to China primarily to spread the Christian Gospel and save souls, it was not their purpose to stir up social unrest in China. When considering the overall missionary efforts and activities in China during the treaty century (1842-1943), one should not forget the missionaries' pioneering work in bringing to China modern education, medicine, and knowledge of the West, as well as their charitable activities, such as famine relief and caring for the sick and the poor. In addition to the Chinese who believed that their souls were saved, all those who benefited from the missionary efforts in doing good works in the secular society were likely to look upon the missionary movement more favourably.

While the Catholic missionaries, mostly French, concentrated their efforts on conversion and on doing pastoral and charitable work among their flocks, many of the Protestant evangelists established educational and social institutions in addition to churches, because they valued improving the prospects of their living communicants as well as the salvation of their souls. There was a strong belief among some of the Protestant missionaries, as exemplified by Timothy Richards, that humanity could be brought closer to the Kingdom of God through improving earthly institutions. For this reason, some of the British and American missionaries established many modern schools, some of which later became colleges or universities, set up hospitals and dispensaries of medicine, and campaigned against Chinese institutions of which they disapproved. They also published journals, notably the *Wanguo Gongbao*, translated as the *Globe Magazine* or the *Review of the Times,* which provided news of Western countries and spread ideas, information, and knowledge from the modern West to the interested Chinese. This journal was a source of Western knowledge to the Chinese reformers of 1898. Many of the modern institutions pioneered by the missionaries of this period endured and contributed to China's modern transformation.

As regards making Christian converts, it was a slow and uphill struggle, especially for the Protestant missionaries. Though their number doubled every decade, from a tiny trickle in the 1840s to over 1,300 in 1890, the number of Chinese communicants reached only 37,000 during half a century. Although the number of Catholic missionaries was half as many as that of the Protestant ones at that time, there were half a million Chinese Catholics in China. Considering this rather small number of Christians scattered among China's population of well over 400 million in the late nineteenth century, the friction and hostility between local Chinese communities and the foreign missionary communities, which included Chinese Christians, led surprisingly often to serious ill consequences for China. The Boxers' rampage against Christian churches was an example of such a phenomenon. Since their hostility was directed not only against the Christians and the foreign armies of occupation, but to all things foreign, their patriotism was mixed with xenophobia.

The Boxer rebellion erupts, and the powers intervene: the defeat of the Boxers

As the violent disturbances of the Boxers spread rapidly in Shandong in the late 1890s, some of the officials like Yuan Shikai were for suppressing the movement. With his modern army of about 7,000 and the support of the local forces, he moved against the Boxers energetically, and succeeded in restoring order in Shandong province. Others, like Yuxian, the governor of Shandong, preferred appeasing them and organizing the more cooperative ones into militia, although he also fought against the recalcitrant ones. Officials at the court in Beijing were similarly divided. The British and Americans, whose interests in China remained largely commercial, pressed the Qing to suppress the Boxers and restore a peaceful and stable environment favourable to trade. The Qing Court's vacillation between suppression and appeasement only helped the movement to grow.

Early in 1900, some of the Boxer insurgents, driven from Shandong by Yuan Shikai, moved to Zhili, where they joined forces with local Boxers. With the support of some of the gentry and officials there, they spread like wildfire, threatening both Beijing and Tianjin, where foreigners were concentrated. The foreign communities became alarmed. The British, American, French, and German ambassadors all warned the Qing court in April 1900 that their governments were considering military intervention, unless the Qing put an end to the Boxer menace within two months.

In the spring of 1900, with the Boxer Rebellion gathering enormous momentum, some conservative royal princes and other high officials at the court counselled appeasement, or even making use of the Boxers against the foreigners. The insurgents' rallying cry of 'support the Qing, exterminate the foreigners' aroused a sympathetic chord in them, for they desired nothing less than to drive out the foreigners and regain control over China. If they thought they could rely on large mobs of ignorant and superstitious peasants without military training to accomplish what their army and navy could not, as some indeed did, they must have allowed despair and despondency to overrule their better judgement. The empress dowager had her own grudge against the imperialists because they had thwarted her attempts to dethrone Emperor Guangxu, and given shelter to the escaped reformers, Kang Youwei and Liang Qichao, enabling them to continue to promote Guangxu's cause in Japan. She decided to listen to the voice of the appeasement party and to channel the energy and power of the insurgents against their common enemy, the imperialists. With the collusion of the court, the Boxers, no longer treated as outlaws, streamed into Beijing and Tianjin, where they harassed foreigners and destroyed their properties. The phenomenal growth of the Boxers inspired disaffected peasants in other provinces in the north, and in parts of the south, to rise up under the banner of 'support the Qing; exterminate the foreigners'.

Towards the end of May until early June 1900, as their deadline to the Qing ap-

proached and the situation further deteriorated, the representatives of the foreign legations in Beijing moved several hundred soldiers from the more than 2,000 stationed in
Tianjin to Beijing, to protect themselves and their headquarters. Meanwhile, two dozen
warships from various imperialist nations assembled at Dagu, the port near Tianjin, ready
for action. After having received the go-ahead from their home countries, on 10 June
1900 over 2,000 troops from eight different nations - Japan, Russia, Britain, America,
Germany, France, Italy, and Austria - formed the Eight Nation Alliance and landed at
Dagu, under the leadership of a British officer, in the name of 'rescuing embassy officials'
in China's capital. Even with their primitive weapons, the Boxers supported by Qing soldiers forced the Eight Nation Army to find shelter in the international settlement in Tianjin,
instead of proceeding to Beijing. Around that time, the foreign fleet at Dagu demolished
the Qing shore batteries and landed more troops, including 2,000 Russians, to invade Tianjin. Despite having cannons, these foreign forces also sustained heavy casualties at the
hands of the Boxers, the Qing army, and the Red Lanterns, a young women's brigade.
The news of foreign forces coming to Beijing emboldened the foreign soldiers and staff
at the Legation Quarters, an area of about three-quarters of a square mile, to attack the
Boxers. The German minister, Clemens von Ketteler, was particularly provocative in firing
on Chinese soldiers and militias. On 20 June, he was killed when they returned fire, and
from that date angry Boxers and Qing soldiers began to surround the Legation Quarters,
which accommodated, apart from the foreign embassy officials, their families, their Chinese employees, and several hundred foreign soldiers, in addition to many foreign missionaries and some 3,500 Chinese Christians who were sheltering there.

On 16 June, about a week after the landing of foreign of forces in Dagu, and the start
of armed combat between the Boxers and Qing soldiers on one side and the Eight Nation
Army on the other in an undeclared war, the empress dowager began to hold daily meetings on the question of war or peace, and how to deal with the Boxers. On the one side
were the revenge-seeking conservative officials, including two royal princes, who made a
case for appeasing the Boxers and using them to fight the foreigners with their 'magical
prowess'. Opposing them were the advocates for suppressing the Boxers to achieve peace
with the powers, and to stop their forces from advancing to Beijing. Permitted to attend
these meetings, Emperor Guangxu spoke strongly for peace. Pointing out that China had
lost a war fighting Japan alone, he questioned how China could possibly oppose the military strength of the combined forces of the imperialists. He was also sceptical of the magical power of the Boxers. As regards sending them out to battle, he asked: 'Why play
games with peoples' lives?' The empress dowager hesitated between the two options and
temporized. She did not move to suppress the Boxers on the one hand, but on the other
hand she sent soldiers to protect the Legation Quarters. She was politely rebuffed when
her officials tried to persuade the foreign ambassadors to stop the advance of the Eight
Nation Army.

The Boxer Rebellion and the Eight Nation Alliance (*Wikipedia*: retrieved on
27 December 2023 from https://medium.com/the-dock-on-the-bay/the-boxer-rebel-
lion-db217283f0b2)

Her inclination towards war increased considerably after she received a notice, allegedly
from the imperialist powers, which demanded her retirement and the restoration of Emperor Guangxu to power. Even though she later discovered that some members of the war

party had forged the notice, the trick achieved its purpose. On 17 June, at an audience at court she rehearsed a drama in which she took a warlike stance. On 21 June, after the news of the foreign destruction of Dagu reached her, and war could no longer be stopped, she decided to declare war with an edict in Emperor Guangxu's name. As soon as war was mooted, the *Zongli Yamen* asked the foreign officials, their families, their staff, and their guards at the Legation Quarters to leave for Tianjin within twenty-four hours. This was not a demand that they could practically obey, and on 20 June the Legation Quarters once more came under attack. She then ordered the 'righteous' - meaning obedient - Boxers in Beijing to be registered and organized into official units; those who resisted orders were to be treated as criminal or bandits. After war was declared, the Boxers in some northern provinces carried out attacks on foreign missions and Christians, both foreign and Chinese, without official restraint. In Shanxi Province, the pro-Boxer governor Yuxian treacherously initiated the Taiyuan massacre in July 1900, which killed forty-four missionaries and members of their families to whom he had promised protection.

The court's declaration for war was strongly opposed by most of the heads of provinces south of the Yangtze River, and along the eastern seaboard. These included Li Hongzhang, Zhang Zhidong, and Yuan Shikai, and many wired their objections to the court. With the British anxious to keep the commerce of the Yangtze Valley from being damaged by the war spreading south, the foreign consuls in Shanghai and local Qing officials produced an agreement that the Chinese authorities were to protect southern and eastern China from anti-foreign violence, while the powers were to keep the Shanghai international settlements secure. This kept the provinces south of the Yangtze and along the eastern seaboard out of the war, and the authorities there strenuously suppressed the Boxers and similar movements. The regional leaders felt sufficiently strong to defy the central government, because after the Taiping Rebellion the balance of power between the centre and the regions had shifted in favour of the latter. The senior regional officials' staunch anti-war and anti-Boxer stance weakened the Empress Dowager's resolve and swayed her to their side. Instead of reprimanding these officials for objecting to her declaration for war, she praised them for their prudence, and asked them to prepare for war, nevertheless. She also pointed out to them that China did not start the hostilities. Four days after she declared war, she started a peace overture to the ambassadors in the Legation Quarters, promising them protection and stating that she was looking for opportunities to punish the Boxers. However, in the absence of a peace accord, the attacks on the legations were resumed.

Meanwhile the war proceeded inexorably from the imperialist side. By early July, the number of foreign troops had increased to 18,000, and they started to besiege Tianjin, where the Boxers and Qing defenders put up a stout resistance. At this point, the court ordered a strongly anti-Boxer military commander to fight, not against the foreign invaders, but to annihilate the Boxers. Attacked from both sides, the Boxers lost their ability to defend Tianjin, which was captured by the Eight Nation Army on 14 July. After Tianjin fell, the empress dowager made fruitless appeals to the German Kaiser and the Presidents of America and France to stop the fighting. She also ordered Ronglu to stop the attack on the Legation Quarters and instead sent fruits, vegetables, and other foodstuffs to each of the eleven legations. The off-again and on-again attacks on the Legation Quarters did result in some foreign fatalities, but the unit with modern weapons under Ronglu did not coordinate with the Boxers to press the attack home, sparing the lives of most of the residents until the end of this calamitous episode.

Despite the empress dowager's appeals and friendly gestures, the war did not stop. International rivalry slightly delayed the march of the multi-nation expeditionary force that had been built up to around 20,000 (about half of which were from Japan) to Beijing until 4 August. Because a single German, Clemens von Ketteler, had lost his life, the Kaiser won the right to put a German, Alfred von Waldersee, in overall command of this force. Neither the Boxers nor the Qing army were able to withstand this mixed modern foreign army, competing to enter Beijing. On 14 August, the British-led Indian troops, who entered Beijing through the Water Gate under the city wall, were the first to relieve the siege of the Legation Quarters. Early next morning, the empress dowager fled hurriedly westward in disguise, with Emperor Guangxu and several other royals in tow, accompanied by some 2,000 guards.

After the foreign expeditionary force overran Beijing, there was a mad rush by the invaders and other foreigners there to kill the Boxers and plunder the city. They emptied the Forbidden City and the Summer Palace of their treasures and took away priceless books and historical and cultural relics accumulated there since the Ming. The Japanese robbed the Ministry of Finance of more than 3,000,000 taels of silver. A total of approximately 60,000,000 taels of silver were taken from other offices of the government.

From the Forbidden City, then doubling as the foreign command centre, the commanders of the imperialist powers continued sending their armies out, all the way to the Shanhai Pass in the northeast of China. The Boxer episode gave the Germans an opportunity to demonstrate their military prowess, and they continued military action for another six months. Under Alfred von Waldersee as commander-in-chief, the Germans continued to increase the number of their troops and conducted punitive expeditions against some two dozen cities in north China. They also attempted to occupy the city of Yantai and strengthen German control of Shandong Province. In the name of protecting their railways, the Russians also took advantage of the Boxer episode to send 150,000 troops to occupy almost the entire Northeast of China. As Japan also aspired to expand into this region, the Russian action sowed the seeds of future military conflict between these two imperialist powers.

Since the landing of the soldiers of the Eight Nation Army[17] in Dagu, there had been

---

[17] Actually, it became an army of eleven nations after Spain, Italy, and Belgian, each of which had an endangered legation in China, also joined the fray.

many atrocities: burning, pillaging, and indiscriminate and unrestrained killing of civilians in the cities and countryside, where the imperialists conducted their campaigns. Since the Russians sent 150,000 troops spreading all over Heilongjiang, Jilin, and Shengjing (present-day Liaoning Province), the inhabitants of this region suffered severe depredations, countless villages were burned to the ground, and people there were massacred en masse. Far from driving out the foreign aggressors, the anti-foreign Boxer movement, and the folly of the Qing Court in using this rabble against modern well-drilled armies, equipped with artillery and guns, merely invited further foreign aggression. The insurrection of the Boxers, and the foreign invasion in connection with it, was yet another calamity for China, which had fought five wars against foreign invaders and four prolonged domestic rebellions during the sixty years since the 'opening of China' in the early 1840s.

Soon after the imperialists took over China's capital, the empress dowager, still on the move, issued an edict blaming the Boxers for the disastrous events and ordering their eradication. Before she left Beijing, she had already appointed Li Hongzhang and a Manchu prince to start peace negotiations with the eleven powers involved. The negotiations were somewhat prolonged, not because the empress dowager could not accept the harsh terms, but because of lack of agreement among the powers, each of which wanted to get the maximum benefit out of this invasion for its own country. On condition of the Qing agreeing to Russia's sole control of China's northeast, Russia was willing to support Cixi's return to rule the country and end the war with troop withdrawals. The British favoured restoring Emperor Guangxu to power under their tutelage and without interference from Cixi. The Germans wanted to punish her, in addition to a list of high officials, whom the powers collectively found culpable for their support of the Boxers. The Germans would not settle for peace until they had taught the Chinese a lesson on anti-foreign violence by spilling more blood on Chinese soil. The French supported the Russians because of their rivalry with the British in southern China. After a year of contentious negotiations among themselves, the powers settled once more for America's 'Open Door' proposal of preserving China's nominal territorial and administrative integrity. To avoid open hostility with each other over what each of the imperialist nations wanted out of China, they agreed to let the Qing continue to exist so as to serve their collective interests. It was in their common interest to let the Qing maintain the treaty systems, collect the taxes that were channelled into paying indemnities to them, and strike down Chinese rebels, so that they did not have to bear the cost of stationing many soldiers in China to keep peace and order, without which commerce and industry could not thrive. They agreed to allow the empress dowager to continue to rule, because she accepted their onerous demands without demur.

Peace was formally achieved by the Boxer Protocol concluded in September 1901 between Qing China and the eleven countries that participated in the invasion of China in 1900. Among its provisions were apologies to the foreign governments, the erection of monuments in memory of the over two hundred deceased Westerners, the execution of the leading Qing official supporters of the Boxers, and the prohibition of Chinese anti-foreign movements in perpetuity, with the death penalty for those who violated the ban. Defensive armaments and foreign guards were to be placed permanently to protect the foreign Legation Quarter, where Chinese were not allowed to reside. The *Zongli Yamen* was to be replaced by a new Foreign Ministry, which was to take precedence over all the other ministries in the Qing government. The defensive artillery emplacements in Dagu were to be removed. The powers were allowed to station troops on strategic spots along the railways from Tianjin and Beijing to the Shanhai Pass in the Northeast. The powers extracted a crushing indemnity of 450,000,000 taels of silver, which was to be paid in annual instalments over a thirty-nine-year period in gold, with an interest of 4% until the debt was extinguished on 31 December 1940. At the end of this period the total amount paid by China would have amounted to 982,238,150 taels. This was a colossal sum, considering that the total Qing annual tax collection around that time was estimated at 250,000,000 taels.

How was China to pay this enormous debt? The powers saw to it that all available maritime customs revenue, which had grown into a major source of Qing revenue on account of the increasing Sino-foreign trade, was to be earmarked entirely for the payment of the Boxer indemnity. They knew that they could rely on the security of payment from this source, because the Qing MCS in 1901 was a foreign-managed organization and was likely so to continue in the foreseeable future. But more money was needed than the maritime customs collection. The revenue collected from several local regular customs and salt gabelles was also committed to pay the Boxer indemnity. These tax offices were transferred from the normal Qing system, to be placed under the oversight of the foreign MCS's Inspector General who, in 1901, was still Robert Hart.

The Boxer Protocol imposed additional infringements on Qing China's already seriously compromised sovereignty and administrative integrity. China sank further into the quagmire as a quasi-colony of the imperialist powers. The massive indemnity meant greater hardship on an already impoverished people and obliged the financially straitened Qing government to levy miscellaneous fees and taxes. When these highly damaging terms of the Boxer Protocol were presented to the empress dowager, she was only relieved that she did not find herself on the list of the guilty Qing officials, against whom the powers demanded punishment for their crime of supporting the Boxers. She was grateful that the victors did not force her to hand over power to her nephew Guangxu, who was still nominally the emperor. She therefore accepted the foreign-imposed peace terms willingly, stating that she was ready 'to win the good graces of the powers to the limit of China's material resources.' As regards any of the Boxers who might have survived and continued their agitations, she ordered their destruction without any equivocation. As long her own position was intact, she seemed to accept her role willingly as an instrument and tool of the foreign imperialists. After concluding the peace protocol in January 1902, the empress dowager returned with Emperor Guangxu to the Forbidden City, where she presided over two unprecedented receptions, one for the members of the foreign diplomatic corps, and another for their ladies, as gestures of reconciliation.

Russo-Japanese Hostilities

While all the other powers were withdrawing their invading armies, the Russians, pursuing their ambition to annex the whole of China's Northeast, refused to do so. They even managed to force the Chinese governor general there to sign a draft agreement that implied the Russian annexation of this region. When its terms became known, Britain, Japan, and America protested strongly against it. As a result, the Qing found the strength to resist its ratification. In April 1902, a Sino-Russian Agreement obliged the Russians to withdraw their troops within sixth months. When the time arrived, instead of withdrawing their forces, they put forward further demands, which the Qing regarded as unreasonable and with which they refused to comply. The Russians then decided to disregard China and negotiated with Japan. As an imperialist power straddling both Europe and Asia, Russia could make a deal with Japan, the rising East Asian empire, on sharing out some of the spoils in East Asia.

Japanese power had been growing steadily after the Sino-Japanese War in 1894. Her military expenditure in that war was more than paid for by the hefty indemnity of 230,000,000 taels of silver, the payment for which the impecunious Qing government had to borrow from European banks at a high rate of interest secured, as already noted, on the maritime customs revenue. The injection of this fund brought Japanese economic prosperity and allowed the country to go on the gold standard in 1897. To support her imperialist ambition, Japan had been rapidly building up her army and navy with huge increases in military expenditure. With so many other ambitious imperialist powers in East Asia competing for economic or territorial advantages, or both, to achieve her expansionist goal Japan had to play the game not only militarily, but also diplomatically, building alliances or making bilateral agreements so as to strengthen her hand against an opponent, or to neutralize a third party.

A veteran Japanese statesman, Ito Hirobumi, favoured a Russo-Japanese agreement, whereby Japan would recognize Russia's special position in China's Northeast, which the Japanese named Manchuria, in exchange for Russian recognition of Japan's special position in Korea. Other prominent Japanese politicians believed that Russia had to be stopped by military means, so they proceeded to strengthen Japan's military. With the memory still fresh of having to give up Liaodong on account of pressure from Russia, France, and Germany acting in concert, the Japanese would need an ally if they were to tackle Russia.

Britain appeared the most promising candidate because of her rivalry with Russia in Tibet and other parts of the world, and her objection to Russia's attempt to annex China's Northeast. If Japan needed Britain as an ally, would an alliance with Japan suit the British? With a global empire to defend, the British found their military resources stretched too thin if simultaneous military actions were required in different parts of the world. For example, between 1899 and 1902, with 250,000 troops tied down by the Boer War in South Africa, the British found themselves not in a position to take strong action against Russian aggression in East Asia, if they had so wished. Furthermore, Britain was concerned about the rapid rise of an aggressive Germany as a rival in global imperialism. Although Japan was also a rapidly rising and imperialist nation, she was not competing for empire with the British globally. Consequently, Britain ended her 'splendid isolation' to sign, in January 1902, the Anglo-Japanese Alliance with Japan to counter Russian expansion in East Asia, to pre-empt a possible settlement between Russia and Japan along the lines proposed by Ito Hirobumi, to secure Japan's support for the treaty system in China, and to make up for any British military shortfall in Asia. For Japan, the Anglo-Japanese Alliance had the advantage of isolating Russia, should she go to war against the latter. According to the terms of the alliance, Britain would be obliged to come to Japan's aid if another party joined the war on Russia's side. Another benefit of the alliance was British recognition of Japan's special position in Korea.

With Britain as an ally, in August 1903 the Japanese were able to negotiate with Russia from a position of strength. Although Russia would accept Japanese domination of Korea in exchange for Japanese recognition of Russian domination of Manchuria, Japan, using the preservation of China's integrity as a justification, would only accept Russia having rights along the railways developed by the Russians. As the negotiations stalled, the movement of 7,000 troops per month by the Russians into this region using the Trans-Siberian Railway prompted the suspicious Japanese to terminate the talks and torpedo the Russian fleet in Lushun on 8 February. On 10 February, Japan declared war against Russia.

The Qing declared neutrality. The weak court let its own territory, Liaodong, become the battlefield, where many innocent people suffered death and other disastrous consequences of a year-long war between the two foreign powers. Constantly outflanked by the Japanese on land, the Russians evacuated Shenyang (Mukden) to the north. Hoping to gain victory at sea, the Russians had despatched their Baltic fleet of a motley collection of 45 vessels in October 1904. They had to take the long route of rounding the Cape in Africa because the British would not let them through the Suez Canal. Finally, in the Spring of 1905, the fleet reached a safe haven in French Indochina before proceeding to Vladivostok. En route, it was waylaid by a Japanese fleet ready for battle at the Straits of Tsushima, where the Japanese sank 32 out of the 35 ships that got there. This naval battle effectively brought the Russo-Japanese War to an end. In the prevailing climate of racial consciousness, Japan's defeat of Russia, of a white power by an Asian one, was considered a remarkable feat. This striking victory made Japan a fully-fledged member of the imperialist club. Britain renewed the Anglo-Japanese Alliance for another five years, and this time the two powers agreed to join together to fight any third party, with India included in the area covered.

Through America's diplomatic efforts under President Theodore Roosevelt, Japan and Russia signed the Treaty of Portsmouth on 5 September 1905 that restored peace between them. This treaty gave the Russians a sphere of influence on the Liaodong peninsula, which included Lushun and Dalian, and the South Manchurian Railway built by Russia to Japan. It also recognized Japan's 'paramount interest' in Korea. It awarded the southern half of Sakhalin to Japan, which was not able to extract an indemnity. In 1907, Japan and Russia secretly divided China's Northeast between them, with Russia taking the north and Japan the south, while they continued to declare themselves publicly as supporters of China's integrity, and America's 'Open Door' policy.

Late Qing Reforms, and Moves Towards a Constitution: The End of the Qing

After the dust of these wars settled, China was in an even deeper grip of imperialism. Although the country had survived outright partition, the powers intensified their encroachment, especially in connection with their spheres of influence. They coerced the Qing for railway rights inside their spheres of influence and vied with each other to build railways elsewhere in China. Within a certain distance from these railway lines the foreign power or powers concerned would normally obtain the right to exploit the natural resources, such as mining and logging. They also wrung from the Qing the right to transport and station troops. Foreign establishments controlled the production of over 90% of the coal from mechanized mines, and 100% of iron. In an age when railways became the new arteries of popular transportation and communication, it was easy to see that the power that controlled the railways of a given area effectively dominated that area.

To the educated Chinese, the ringing of the alarm bells that had alerted the Hundred Days of Reform in 1898 continued to ring even more loudly during the first decade of the twentieth century. Amid growing pressure for reform from the educated and local elites, the court introduced, from 1901 onwards, a limited number of new measures borrowed from Kang Youwei's programme, insisting that the changes it was making were orderly, while Kang's were disorderly.

These measures included abolishing the government examinations for official selection, setting up modern schools, sending students abroad, reorganizing the military, setting up a police force for maintaining public order, creating new government offices, promoting new Chinese industries, and preparing for a government constitution. To win its subjects' support, the Qing was willing to adjust some of its institutions, but not the essentially auto-cratic character of the regime. To ensure the powers' support, the Qing pointed out to them that the changes introduced should enhance friendly relations with them and help them to enjoy boundless benefits from China in perpetuity. The court also responded positively to foreign demands to lay down regulations to protect foreign investments in railways, mines, and other sectors in China. While the purpose of Kang's reforms was to make China strong and prosperous to free her from foreign domination, those of the late Qing were aimed at keeping the Manchus in power.

Instead of strengthening the embattled dynasty, many of these measures produced the opposite results. Modernizing schools and sending students abroad bred revolutionaries. In military modernization, the Qing established local war boards in the provinces to train and equip with modern weapons a 'New Army' with 36 divisions of 12,500 men each. When it tried to bring this New Army under central and Manchu control, through estab-lishing a new Ministry of War in 1906 with a Manchu official, Yinchang, at its head, the provincial ties, personal loyalty, and revolutionary ideology of the officers and men ren-dered central control difficult to achieve. This army did succeed in restoring Qing control of Tibet, but it would play a crucial part in toppling the dynasty in 1911.

In September 1906, the court proclaimed its willingness to prepare for a constitution, after the high officials it sent to Japan, Europe, and America to investigate the subject, in 1905, declared on their return that such a move would help the Qing to perpetuate the monarchy, and lessen internal disorder. The provincial elites, and some Chinese abroad, among whom were the famous reformers in exile, Kang Youwei and Liang Qichao, re-ceived the court's announcement with enormous excitement, and promptly proceeded to organize committees to prepare themselves for political participation. They became known as the constitutionalists, as they networked with one another inside and outside their provinces to pursue this goal actively. Since the abolition of the official examination in 1905 removed the traditional path for the educated to enter officialdom, a constitutional monarchy would open up a new route for them to become members of the ruling elites, through participating in the provincial assemblies, or as representatives of their provinces at the capital. Pointing to the ignorance of the people, and its own need to work out the regulations and institutions in connection with the introduction of a constitution, the court enjoined the public to accept some inevitable delay.

Nearly two years passed, owing to the lack of action on the part of the Qing on this matter, and in August 1908 the constitutionalists sent a joint petition to Beijing, urging the court to convene a National Assembly. In response, the court proclaimed its 'Outline of the Constitution', stating that the rule of the Qing emperor was sacred and supreme, and all powers of the government were to be concentrated in his hands. He controlled the legislative, executive, and judicial branches of the government, and the appointment of civil and military officials, together with the institutions and laws to govern them. He was the commander-in-chief of the armed forces with power to declare war, make peace, and sign treaties with foreign countries. He had the authority to convene, to close, and to dismiss the National Assembly, which had no authority to interfere in matters concerning the military, appointments, and foreign relations. Provincial Advisory Bureaus were to be set up to take part in the preparation for the Constitution. The preparatory phase was to take nine years, at the end of which a National Assembly was to convene.

Not long after the court's pronouncement, on 13 November 1908 Emperor Guangxu died, ending his thirty-four years' reign as a figurehead. The day after, Empress Dowager Cixi, who had already celebrated her seventy-fourth birthday, also passed away. She had been the actual ruler of China for 44 years, during the reigns first of her son and then of her nephew. Before their deaths, she had already chosen, as Guangxu's successor, his three-year old stepbrother, Puyi, who was to rule as Emperor Xuantong (r. 1909-1911) upon Guangxu's death. Since Xuantong was a minor, his father, prince Chun, assumed power as the regent.

Wishing to win public support, prince Chun encouraged the speedy formation of Advisory Bureaus in the provinces and at the capital to continue the preparation for the constitution. Although the Qing 'Outline on the Constitution' said nothing about limiting the emperor's power, many of the provincial constitutionalists threw themselves into setting up advisory bureaus. They joined together to petition the Qing on three occasions, pressing the court to shorten the period for the preparation of the constitution, and to convene the National Assembly in 1911, when they expected the formation of a cabinet. The court agreed to convene the National Assembly in 1913, rather than the original plan of 1917. In May 1911, it announced the establishment of the Cabinet. This new office was composed of 13 members, 9 of whom were Manchu aristocrats, including 5 who were members of the imperial clan. It was dubbed the 'Imperial Cabinet'. Instead of limiting the power of the monarchy, and establishing a more broadly based government, the court used the constitutional movement to affirm its autocratic control and consolidate the power of the Manchus. The constitutionalists and other local powerholders felt cheated. They considered the Qing approach a violation of the principle of constitutional monarchy and demanded the court to form another cabinet. Upon the court's refusal, the Provincial Advisory Bureaus joined together to publish a 'Declaration to the Entire Country', in which they painfully admitted their 'utter despair of the Qing'.

The Qing dynasty was finally brought to an end in 1912 by Yuan Shikai, who forced Emperor Xuantong to abdicate, and his regent to resign. Yuan held the essential lever of power – the control of the entire Beiyang Army. He became president of a reunited Republican China but would soon reveal his preference for an imperial system.

References (for chapters 5, 6, and 7)

General sources:
A History of Chinese Civilization by Jacques Gernet (English Edition, Cambridge University Press, Cambridge, second edition 1996), chapters 22-29.

The Search for a Modern China by Jonathan D. Spence (W. W. Norton & Company, New York and London, 1990), chapters 2-11.

East Asia: The Modern Transformation by Edwin O. Reischauer, John K. Fairbank, and Albert M. Craig (George Allen & Unwin Ltd, 1965).

China: A History Volume 1 From Neolithic Cultures through the Great Qing Empire 10,000 BCE – 1799 CE by Harold M. Tanner (Hackett Publishing Company, Inc., Indianapolis/Cambridge, 2010), chapter 11.

The Taiping:
The Taiping Heavenly Kingdom: Rebellion and the Blasphemy of Empire by Thomas H. Reilly (University of Washington Press, Seattle, 2014).

The Taiping Revolutionary Movement by Jen Yu-Wen (Yale University Press, New Haven, 1973).

The Chinese Maritime Customs Service:
The Chinese Maritime Customs Service in the Transition from the Ch'ing to the Nationalist Era: An Examination of the Relationship between a Western-style Fiscal Institution and Chinese Government in the Period Before the Manchurian Incident by Jean Aitchison (Thesis, University of London, School of Oriental and African Studies, 1983).

Aspects of the British Empire in Asia:
Empire: How Britain Made the Modern World by Niall Ferguson (Penguin group, London, 2004).

INDEX